CHILDREN OF THE WATERS OF MERIBAH

CHILDREN OF THE WATERS OF MERIBAH

Black Liberation Theology, the Miriamic Tradition, and the Challenges of Twenty-First-Century Empire

ALLAN AUBREY BOESAK

CASCADE *Books* • Eugene, Oregon

CHILDREN OF THE WATERS OF MERIBAH
Black Liberation Theology, the Miriamic Tradition, and the Challenges of Twenty-First-Century Empire

Copyright © 2019 Allan Aubrey Boesak. All rights reserved. Except for brief quotations in critical publications or reviews, no part of this book may be reproduced in any manner without prior written permission from the publisher. Write: Permissions, Wipf and Stock Publishers, 199 W. 8th Ave., Suite 3, Eugene, OR 97401.

Cascade Books
An Imprint of Wipf and Stock Publishers
199 W. 8th Ave., Suite 3
Eugene, OR 97401

www.wipfandstock.com

PAPERBACK ISBN: 978-1-5326-5671-2
HARDCOVER ISBN: 978-1-5326-5672-9
EBOOK ISBN: 978-1-5326-5673-6

Cataloguing-in-Publication data:

Names: Boesak, Allan Aubrey, 1946–, author.

Title: Children of the waters of Meribah : black liberation theology, the Miriamic tradition, and the challenges of twenty-first-century empire / Allan Aubrey Boesak.

Description: Eugene, OR : Cascade Books, 2019 | Includes bibliographical references.

Identifiers: ISBN 978-1-5326-5671-2 (paperback) | ISBN 978-1-5326-5672-9 (hardcover) | ISBN 978-1-5326-5673-6 (ebook)

Subjects: LCSH: Black theology. | Social justice—Religious aspects—Christianity. | Bible.—Old Testament—Feminist criticism. | Bible.—New Testament—Feminist criticism. | Bible—Africa—History.

Classification: BT82.7 .B634 2019 (paperback) | BT82.7 .B634 (ebook)

Manufactured in the U.S.A.   09/10/19

In remembrance of James Hal Cone and Katie Geneva Cannon, the trees under whose shade we all sat and learned; the wells from which we all drank and lived; the shoulders upon which we all stand to see, believe in, and shape a different future. How blessed we were to know them and call them teacher, friend, brother, and sister.

CONTENTS

Acknowledgments | ix
Introduction: One More River to Cross | xiii

Chapter One
Poisoned Well or Waters of Life? Black Theology, Black Preaching, Scripture, and the Challenges of Empire | 1

Chapter Two
The Birthing Stool, the Burning Bush, and the Throne of Pharaoh: Black Theology, the Women of Exodus, and the Righteousness of Resistance | 31

Chapter Three
Standing Her Ground: the Riverbank and the Seashore: Black Theology, the Miriamic Tradition, and the Cry for Freedom | 58

Chapter Four
Drinking from the Waters of Meribah: Black Theology, Liberation, and the Integrity of Radical Engagement | 89

Chapter Five
Jesus, a Woman, and Biko's Ghost: Black Theology, Empire, and the Liberation of the Colonized Mind | 122

Chapter Six
The Secret of the Human Child: Black Theology, the Canaanite Woman, and the Walls of Internalized, Imperialist Patriarchy | 159

Chapter Seven
A Bucket, a Well, and the Gendered Politics of Water: Black Theology, Jesus, and the Sister from Sychar | 184

Bibliography | 221
Index | 235

ACKNOWLEDGMENTS

As one works on a project like this, the debts pile up along the way. Mine are great to many folks, friends, colleagues, students, and family who have all become conversation partners as my thoughts for this book have developed. I am deeply grateful for the great honor bestowed on me by Yale Divinity School for having invited me as the 2017 Lyman Beecher lecturer. It was a wonderful experience, starting it all, and I thank Dean Greg Sterling, the faculty, and the students at Yale for their warm hospitality, their critical and friendly engagement with my offerings, as well as for the encouragement to have these lectures published. The Beecher lectures comprised chapters 1, 2, and 3, and would form the foundations of this work. Different versions of chapters 2 and 3 were published also as articles and I thank HTS *Hervormde Teologiese Studies/Theological Studies* for permission to publish them here albeit in radically edited and rewritten form. I was honored to be invited as keynote speaker at the Council on World Mission's DARE conference in May 2017 held in Bangkok, Thailand, and that address formed the basis of chapter 1. SunMedia in Stellenbosch graciously gave permission to use my reading of the woman at the well (John 4:1–42), as well as Jesus and the Canaanite woman (Matt 15:21–28), written for *Die Vlug van Gods Verbeelding* for what, respectively, have become chapters 5, 6, and 7 in this book. These are perhaps the most prominent examples of how my thinking has been impacted by what I have learned from women over the last few years, and of the difference a counter-imperial reading makes to understanding and interpreting the biblical texts. I also especially thank South African Spoken Word poet Lelethu Mahambehlala (PoeticSoul) for permission for the use of her poem BLACK.

Much of what is written began as thoughts shared with students at several institutions as well as with colleagues in different contexts. I am intensely grateful to those who took time to read some of the chapters and provided me with valuable advice, especially Diana Hayes, Christina

Landman, and Isabel Phiri, friends and respected colleagues all. My friend and brother, J. Alfred Smith, pastor emeritus of Allen Temple Baptist Church in Oakland, California, was, as usual, sterling in his steadfast encouragement. Walter Brueggemann, peerless scholar and mentor, and Hebrew Bible scholar Gerald West at University of KwaZulu-Natal also read first drafts of some chapters and were very helpful in their feedback. Throughout this project my dear friend Andries van Aarde at the University of Pretoria has been a rock of support and encouragement, reading and offering critique on some chapters. All of them in their own ways have deeply inspired me and hopefully have helped to keep me from going off the rails completely, but I remain responsible for what is written here. I thank them all sincerely.

Completion of this work would not have been possible without the invitations from Dean Chad Berry at Berea College in Kentucky and Vice Provost Reitumetse Obakeng Mabokela at Illinois University at Champaign/Urbana to spend the Spring semester at these institutions. Sister Addie Lorraine Walker and Dean Scott Woodward at Oblate School of Theology in San Antonio Texas offered a chance to teach a summer class, and their wonderful library became a place of both intense reading and much-needed, quiet meditation. During the last period of writing we were back at Berea College where our friend Chad Berry made sure of the necessary peace and quiet the finishing of this book needed. I am overwhelmed at their unstinting hospitality and generosity of heart.

When I wrote *Die Vlug van Gods Verbeelding* (*The Flight of God's Imagination*) back in 2005, I wrote it in Afrikaans, my mother tongue. It was important for me to do this then, since reading the Bible through the lens of liberation theology, from "the underside of history"—a phrase now more important than ever, it seems—and positioning women at the center of biblical stories, was not widespread in Afrikaans. My wife Elna was persistent in reminding me that the work was important, and deserved a wider reading public. She pleaded for an English translation of that work. It never came to that. I did use some material from that book in other works in English in partial fulfillment of her request,[1] but she made it clear that that was not enough. I am glad I waited though, and I am even more glad she insisted. The work of African and other feminist theologians has become indispensable for my personal process of learning and un-learning, and I am deeply grateful to all of them, including Elna and her important work in her PhD dissertation on televangelism, communication, and gender justice issues. As always, Elna and our daughters Sarah and Andrea, older now and

---

1. See for instance my treatment of the story of Rizpah (2 Sam 21:1–14) in *Radical Reconciliation*.

more ready than I have a right to expect to talk about their father's work, have been amazing throughout this process.

This is my second book at Cascade and I am grateful for the patient, professional assistance of my editorial team, Charlie Collier, Sallie Vandagrift, and Ian Creeger.

This book is dedicated to the memories of James Cone and Katie Cannon. I first met James Cone in 1973 at Union Theological Seminary as a Visiting Scholar and since then he has become a mentor, a friend, and a brother. My meeting and collaboration with him and Gayraud Wilmore has changed not only the direction of my doctoral study, but my life as well. Katie Cannon has become a wonderful friend and engagement with her and her work has enriched my life. We still have no idea of the enormity of the loss their deaths have caused, but I know, thank God, that the shadow of their astounding legacies will only become longer, stronger, deeper.

Allan Aubrey Boesak,
Berea College, Kentucky,
Summer 2018

INTRODUCTION
One More River to Cross

"One more river to cross" is a line from a well-loved black spiritual firmly rooted in the faith traditions of African Americans in their struggles for freedom. It was the formidable Vincent Harding, in his groundbreaking work[1] who, with the exodus story and the history of the struggles of African-American people as intertwined frameworks for understanding of these issues, first explored these in terms of a river as metaphor.

Harding's work and thoughts have universal application. It cannot be otherwise since Harding, involved completely in the plights, struggles, and hopes of his people "in the wilderness of North America" as Malcolm X would put it, knew also his deep rootedness in Africa. As such, he speaks for all of us, still yearning for a freedom defined by ourselves and knowing that there is still a river, perhaps many, to cross before we are done.

In this ongoing metaphoric depiction of black history, black faith, and black struggle toward freedom there are, like ancient Israel's crossing of the Jordan, rivers black people have to cross,[2] and as one struggle ends a new struggle begins. Hence chapter 16, becoming the title of the book, is aptly called, "There Is a River." It is this last particularly that appeals to me, at a time where oppressed people across the globe are facing situations where one struggle has come to an end and another begins. In South Africa and in the United States, the so-called "post-apartheid" and "post-racial" eras present us with just such a moment. That is precisely a point I tried to make in my very first work on Black theology more than forty years ago, in my most recent book, and here.[3] I endeavor to engage in a global conversation.

    1. Harding, *There Is a River*.
    2. See chapter 10, "On Jordan's Stormy Banks."
    3. See A. Boesak, *Coming in Out of the Wilderness* (1974) followed by my doctoral dissertation, *Farewell to Innocence* (1976). It is heartening to see how global prophetic reflection leading to global prophetic engagement continues to expand. Since my

"We are the river," Harding writes, "and the river is more than us ... It is driving us into the future ... We are moving like a river toward our best possible evolution."[4] We are "moving like the river," because if we resolutely claim agency of our own historic destiny, we can determine its course. But the river is also "more than us," because it will still flow after our generation is gone; it represents more than who we are, personally and collectively, at this particular point in time. It was there long before us, and carries within its bosom our ancient selves, the dreams, hopes, failures, and amazing achievements of our ancestors, and the lessons we have to learn from them, lest we lose sight of who we are meant to be and perish. It is more than us, and its waters will nourish the hopes and visions of new generations. The struggles for justice and dignity, for possession of our own aspirations, will become new because they will have discovered other neglected causes. But rivers can sometimes be formidable barriers—think of Harding's discussion of "Jordan's stormy banks"—we reach their banks and we can see the land beyond, that land of our own new becoming. But this time the river is those realities we have refused to see, or lacked the wisdom to understand, and the lack of wisdom has crippled our being. We are limping on this side of the river while on the other side our wholeness beckons. In this book I argue that, not hearing and following the wisdom of the women, Black theology has missed what should have been at the heart of it all for us from the very beginning. We have failed to cross the river and we have not yet fulfilled the promise of wholeness that awaits on the other side.

The women have tried to teach us, but we have not always listened well enough. As a result, more than forty years later a new generation is asking the question, "What lessons has Black liberation theology not learned in these years?" The young poet, wrestling with the realities for women, the young, and the poor in post-1994 South Africa, is taunting us with her devastating honesty, "What does the Black gospel have to say?" This river

---

last publication (*Pharaohs on Both Sides of the Blood-red Waters*, 2017), which I subtitled a "transatlantic conversation" focusing on South Africa, the United States, and Palestine, I have begun to extend this conversation through my engagement with the Dalit Christian community in India, whose struggles for justice, freedom, and human dignity mirror those of other oppressed communities across the world. Recently the World Communion of Reformed Churches held a consultation in Bangalore, India, and Bangkok, Thailand, with the express purpose of examining the relationship between the Dalit community and African Americans in their common struggles against oppression, racism, nationalism, and imperialism. I contributed to that process with a paper entitled "'Full Humanity Requires Freedom'—Being Reformed: Yearning for Justice, Fighting for Freedom, Standing in Dignity." See also especially the very instructive volume on Dalit theology that served as background material for this consultation, Kolkata Symposium, *Dalit Theology in the Twenty-first Century*.

4. Harding, *There is a River*, xxv.

is teeming and roiling with hard questions, and in order to reach that next possible best place of our continuing evolution, Vincent Harding advises, we need to cross that river. We are the river, the river is us, and even more, Harding says, the river is *more* than us. It is time we yield to its flow, even as we become its flow.

When liberation theology first burst onto the scene and forced Eurocentric theology off center-stage for oppressed Christian communities across the world, it helped us look at Christianity and the Bible with new, more critical eyes, and the women joined our excited explorations. Together with us, they discovered the joy of knowing God's preferential option for the poor and the oppressed. Through the eyes of the poor, Elsa Tamez writes, "the Bible took on new meaning. In a context of hunger, unemployment, repression, and war, this was a joyful, liberating experience." This joy was not only in discovering God as the God of justice for the oppressed, but also in discovering just how dangerous a book the Bible can be "for those in power." That is indeed liberating. "However," she continues,

> it is not that [women] don't feel included in the main liberating experiences of the Bible, the exodus and the historical role of Jesus. It is that women find clear, explicit cases of marginalization or segregation of women in several passages of both the Old and New Testaments. There are, then, differences between reading the Bible from the point of view of the poor and reading it from a woman's perspective.[5]

Tamez then issues a challenge: the Bible has to be reread and reinterpreted. But "it is here, then, that the collaboration of women experts in the Bible or of male exegetes with feminist perspectives is needed to reinterpret the texts, using a new hermeneutical approach."[6] Since then, of course many male theologians have tried to do just that, but those efforts have remained scarce. Much has changed since then and I remain challenged by Tamez's reference to that heartbeat of liberation theology—the exodus and the story of Jesus of Nazareth and how these have come to form the heartbeat of Black liberation theology, and here I try to speak to those issues as directly as I can. I am continuing that effort in this specific call to Black liberation theology and the specific issues that confront us in these first, already unbelievably distressing years of the twenty-first century.

---

5. See Elsa Tamez's "Women's Rereading of the Bible," in Fabella and Oduyoye, *With Passion and Compassion*, 173–80. The quote is on 174.

6. Fabella and Oduyoye, *With Passion and Compassion*, 176.

It is not the first time I have dared to write on the subject of women, the Bible, our preaching, and our theology.[7] But the intervening years have taught me much—and I have learned much from the women whose words, writings, and actions have caused me to think again and again about the ongoing struggle for justice, dignity, and the agency of women. So the reader who knows my previous work will easily see how much I have learned and where my mind has been changed. These have become years of learning and un-learning, of rereading, reinterpreting, and exploring new possibilities for understanding, and it will hopefully become clear just how much I have learned in this process, even though it can still be argued that there remains much yet to learn and understand. This time this work wrestles especially with Black theology, biblical interpretation, and African feminist interpretations of the Bible. As in all my previous work, and as liberation theology as a people's theology demands, I persistently ask how our reading, understanding, and interpretation of the Bible can be applied to the real life situations of oppressed, marginalized, and exploited people who want to live as followers of Jesus of Nazareth, and how these understandings can be helpful in the people's continuing struggles against domination and oppression, and for freedom, justice, peace, and dignity.

In South Africa, in the euphoric period after 1994, there was a somewhat triumphant haste in certain quarters to declare Black liberation theology passé, now that "freedom" has come and "apartheid was over." Themes of "liberation" should now be replaced by themes of "democracy" and "reconstruction." But as we are discovering (black people, the poor, women, and LGBTQI+ persons, for example), the struggle for true liberation is far from over. The naïveté of our rainbow-nation fixation has cost the vast majority of South Africans dearly. More than 50 percent of South Africans (the vast majority of them black) live in desperate poverty, and it is an undeserved, generational impoverishment that is the flip-side of the undeserved, generational white enrichment. The wealth gap is now wider than it was under apartheid. Because we attempted reconciliation devoid of justice, that process is under savage strain, social cohesion remains elusive, and racism, never conquered, is resurgent. The need for liberation theology is great and most of these issues have caught us unprepared. These have been constant themes in my work over the last fifteen years or so.[8]

One of the younger generation of African theologians, Rothney Tshaka, has returned to an important issue my generation has battled with, namely

---

7. See A. Boesak, *Die Vlug van Gods Verbeelding*.

8. See, e.g., *Tenderness of Conscience* (2005), with Curtiss Paul DeYoung, *Radical Reconciliation* (2012), *Dare We Speak of Hope?* (2014), and *Pharaohs on Both Sides*, (2017).

the relationship between Black liberation theology and African theology. I write as a Black liberation theologian, one who has begun to do theology outside of the academy (and still mostly does) and as a result has never been bothered much by the fact that Black theology has not been taken seriously, indeed has been actively resisted, in the South African academy so completely captured by Eurocentric thinking. For me, it was reward enough that Black theology take root among ordinary Christians and that the fruits of its labors are seen in the embrace of the radical gospel in the struggles for freedom and dignity on our streets. My generation engaged in what we sometimes called "guerrilla theology": not only outside the walls of the academy but also outside the stringencies of our ecclesial institutions. Ours was a theology developed for the pulpits of proclamation and for the streets of struggle. We discovered the meaning of combatant, revolutionary love, and the indispensability of a spirituality of struggle. And the products of our reflection and praxis were meant for the inspirational use and revolutionary practice of the people as they engaged in struggles for freedom, justice, and dignity: the ABRECSA Charter (1981), the Belhar Confession (1982), the Theological Rationale for the Prayer for the Downfall of Apartheid (1985), the *Kairos Document* (1985).

Our struggles have borne some fruit, and the transformation of South Africa demands the fundamental transformation of the academy, as it demands the transformation of society. It is time that we claim our legitimate space in the academy, and for that reason I am wholly supportive of the fight for what is called Africanization, decolonization, and Africanity. In these new contestations Black liberation theology has its place. But I am an African, and therefore gratified that, like we did forty years ago, the new generation sees what has been called the "tension" between African theology and Black theology as largely artificial. Tshaka agrees with Desmond Tutu—in a statement from over forty years ago—that African theology and Black liberation theology are "two sides of the same coin." There must be, he writes, "a unity between liberation and inculturization—it is in this unity where inculturization and liberation thrive."[9]

But the voices of reproach and challenge do not only come from theologians. Reading on my wife's Facebook page, she pointed out a posting from a South African organization working for gender justice and the equality of women in society. There appeared a young woman poet, a sensational new voice on the South African cultural scene, Lelethu Mahambehlala. She recited from her poem "BLACK." Her voice, filled with power and righteous indignation, filled my ears as she spoke words full of anger, truth, and power.

9. See Tshaka, "How Can a Conquered People Sing," 91–106.

Beginning with the iconic freedom song intimately associated with the Women's March on the Union Buildings in August 1956, the same one I had used in a previous publication to celebrate the strength of South African women in our struggle for freedom, she proceeded to destroy any romantic glorification of that song. She does not deny the truth of the song—that it was the women who, arising in empowered protest, posed an unprecedented challenge to the apartheid regime. But as she makes plain, it is not the only truth about women in South Africa. It is a shocking opening line. It shatters the expectation that in a society filled with devastation for women through systemic, protected, and sacralized patriarchal violence in all its forms, women are always able to endure. It strips men of their ideal version of women and their unshakable strength, cultivated by a beloved, but nonetheless complex freedom song.

Wa' thint' abafazi! she begins, recalling the opening lines of the song that praise the women who in their historic 1956 march against apartheid "Pass" laws tell the apartheid Prime Minister Strijdom that he "has touched a woman; he has struck a rock!"

> This is a false statement!
> This is a statement that suggests
> That all women are strong and hard as a rock
> A statement that has women covered
> In a multi-colored blanket of heroism,
> Like *all* women have something to live for . . .
> But not all women die heroically
> Some women die begging, some burned, bleeding
> Hoping to awaken from some kind of nightmare.
> But in the BLACK of the night
> women's lives are in the hands of men's rage
> For the markets, for the magic
> For whatever reason
> All we know is that at the crack of dawn
> women's bodies are found
> Flowering the dumping pits of cities

And then came the lines that stunned me:

> What does the gospel have to say
> When BLACK women are not on their knees
> Rubbing the feet of a self-proclaimed man of God?
> What do BLACK politicians have to say
> What do they do about the BLACK situation
> When they're not imprinting their fat fingers on the faces of
> young defenceless BLACK girls

> Who must speak and say what for this pandemic to end?
> What fancy hashtag will be conducive
> To the healing of our nation?
> And before you scream confidently #Menaretrash
> Watch that your own five-year-old son is not in a room nearby
> Lest he heeds your prophecy
> And aims to achieve what your words predestined for him.

Black politicians must of course speak for themselves, but the preachers and practitioners of "the Black gospel" certainly have a lot to answer for. And this is what, in the context of this work, remains as the ultimate challenge: what does the Black gospel, in other words, the gospel as understood by Black theology and the preaching of the Black church, have to say? What fancy theological phrases will be conducive to the healing of the nation? This is "Slam Poetry" or also called "Spoken Word." What does it mean for us that the "spoken word" from the angry mouths of the youth has more truth, more power, more authenticity than the Word spoken from the pulpit? These are the questions this book tries to ponder. My hope is that this effort will spur us on to answer these questions with a redeemed sense of purpose.

The issues I am raising in this book (and the list is by no means complete) all represent a river that Black theology must still cross, one by one, to reach that next possible better place Vincent Harding, now having taken his place with the ancestors, has pointed us to. This book grapples with the question: if Black liberation theology had taken the issues mentioned here much more seriously, struggled with them much more intensely, thoroughly, and honestly, would it have been in a better position to help oppressed black people in South Africa and the United States, in fact in Africa as a whole, and oppressed communities everywhere face the challenges of the last twenty-five years? I think we would have. South African Black theologian Vuyani Vellem raised the question: "What lessons has Black theology not learned?"[10] Vellem is speaking of the challenges of empire globally and within the South African context, the role of Scripture, and the burning questions a new generation is now facing.

My tentative answer to these questions is, no, we have not taken these challenges as seriously as we should have, and no, we did not help oppressed communities respond better, and yes, our teaching and preaching, our reflection and praxis had suffered because of this serious lack in understanding the dynamics of our world and the imperial realities that shape our lives. Somehow every answer involves the women.

10. Vellem, "Hermeneutical Embers," 2.

In chapter 1, we consider the question of our reading, interpretation, and preaching of Scripture, Black theology and the overwhelming and pervasive presence of empire, and how Black theology has dealt with the challenges of empire. The role of Scripture in Black theology is well-established. Black theology is unthinkable without its rootedness in Scripture. There was heated debate about this central place of Scripture in the 1980s and in my view Black theology has engaged the matter very well indeed. Quite prominent in this debate was South Africa's Itumeleng Mosala who castigated us quite severely because, as Africans, he argued, we too uncritically used Western tools and the Western embrace of the Bible; questioning, in the language of the time, "the use of the master's tools to destroy the master's house." In particular, Mosala has done me the honor of critical engagement.

In part, my argument then was that just as Mosala reserved for himself the right, somewhat contradictory some might say, to use a materialist reading of the Bible with Eurocentric Marxist hermeneutical tools, so have I reserved the right to read the Bible as a counter-imperial force in what I regarded as my right to engage the Reformed tradition on its own terms to derive from it my "radical Calvinism," as my friend and colleague Dirkie Smit called it, to fight the white Dutch Reformed Church's apartheid perversion of that tradition. In the contentious, contemporary discussions in South Africa around the questions of decolonization (in politics, the economy, education, social relationships, the life of the church), the debate on the centrality of Scripture in Black liberation theology is receiving renewed impetus through the work of a younger generation of African theologians. Once again intensified attention is called to the old African saying about Africans, the Bible, the land, and the white colonizer.[11]

But even in the quite vigorous defense of Black theology's embrace of Scripture and its role in our thinking and our faith convictions, we black theologians did not, I believe, sufficiently engage the Bible as *counter-force to imperial abuse,* and do not yet understand, as completely as we should, our struggle as a struggle in partnership with other oppressed peoples across the world against global empire. It is true that the 1985 South African *Kairos Document* and even more the *Road to Damascus* (1989), a global Kairos Document produced by Global South theologians from nine countries opened that possibility in its language and its theological, socio-economic, and political challenge, but with a few exceptions we did not, *as black theologians,* take that on as a serious and necessary theological task. Consequently, chapter 1 engages the issues of Scripture as once again a site

---

11. This is a reference to the saying attributed to Kenya;s liberation icon Jomo Kenyatta, see p9, n22.

of fierce contestation for Black liberation theology and Black theology's response to empire as an overwhelming global reality impacting the lives of the poor and defenceless in immeasurable ways. My reading of the Bible is a counter-imperialist one.

When women theologians critically challenged Black theology on its exclusivity, not sufficiently taking into account the situation, struggles, and worth of black women, we responded. Belatedly, I admit, but we did. We felt ourselves thoroughly, and justly, chastised by the likes of African feminist theologians such as Musa Dube, Roxanne Jordaan, Mercy Amba Oduyoye, Rose Zoe Obiada; from Asia, Aruna Gnanadason and Virginia Fabella; and from the United States, Jackie Grant, Katie Cannon, Francis Beale, and Theresa Hoover, to name just a few. Led by James Cone, we repented of our sexism and tried to do better, though it must be said that while that happened by and large in Black theological thinking it has not at all made such breakthroughs in the preaching and practice of the Black church in South Africa and in the US. In general, our language remained painfully sexist and exclusive, and our reference, and allegiance, remained to a male, patriarchal God. Even though we opened the ministry to women, there are still precious little signs of real equality in ministry. We still wallow in the sinfulness of male domination. Moreover, the age of Trump has brought renewed and quite serious pushback on the gains we have made in the matters of gender justice and equality.

But more seriously, we have not engaged the women as equal partners in our *theological* work on what can be considered the *foundational assumption* of Black liberation theology, namely that our struggles for liberation, our reach for dignity, and our hopes for justice are all rooted in the exodus story. African Americans, writes Allen Dwight Callahan, but most assuredly also South Africans, heard, read, and retold the story of the exodus more than any other biblical narrative.

> In it they saw their own aspirations for liberation from bondage in the story of the ancient Hebrew slaves. The Exodus was the Bible's narrative argument that God was opposed to American slavery and would return a catastrophic judgment against the nation as he had against ancient Egypt. The Exodus signified God's will that African Americans too would no longer be sold as bondspeople, that they too would go free.[12]

That is true. I will contend here that Black theology's uncritical embrace of the "burning bush" narrative as exodus narrative leads inexorably to a patriarchal, violent, conquest narrative. The critical questions directed to

12. See Callahan, *Talking Book*, 83.

us from indigenous and colonized communities are completely justified. In other words, we have not allowed ourselves to be engaged, questioned, persuaded by the women on the issues of our understanding of the exodus; that the exodus story is not the story of the burning bush, but of the birthing stool, the riverbank, and the seashore. In chapter 2, I grapple with the assertion of feminist theologians that "the exodus story begins and ends with the women."[13] We concentrate on the exodus story as it finds its origin and lasting meaning in the defiance of the pharaoh by the midwives and ask what that point of departure would have meant for Black theology's embrace, understanding, and interpretation of the exodus as paradigmatic for our struggles for liberation and justice.

We will follow Miriam's story from the riverbank to her prophetic leadership on the seashore in what is known as the "Song of Miriam" and the "Song of Moses." What do we learn from the tone and language of this song? What does it say about Miriam, Moses, the nature of Israel's deliverance, and the God of liberation? The point we make is that already here Miriam exhibits an ideal kind of leadership and as prophet establishes what J. Cheryl Exum calls a "Miriamic" prophetic tradition.

After the deliverance and exultation at the sea, Miriam disappears from the story. In chapter 4, we move to the wilderness as this experience is depicted in the Book of Numbers, where Miriam reappears. By looking at Miriam and her radical engagement of Moses' leadership in her challenge to him, I raise the issue of our understanding the quality and integrity of leadership. The question here is whether a Black theology rooted in the prophetic tradition of Miriam would have been better prepared for the serious issues around political leadership black people are experiencing today. All these have important consequences for our reflection and preaching, and for the equipping of oppressed people in their response to political realities today.

There are still other rivers to cross, and in the final chapters we reflect on the critical and deeply enlightening and challenging African feminist readings of two stories in the New Testament: Musa Dube's exploration of the Canaanite woman in Matt 15:21–28 and Jesus's encounter with the Samaritan woman in John 4:1–41. Along the way, we grapple with gender justice and gender-based violence, justice for and the dignity of LGBTQI+ persons, and the decolonization of our minds, a challenge raised by Black Consciousness decades ago but now emerging as a matter of urgency in our times, to name some of the most urgent. Not paying proper attention to these matters has left Black theology, Black preaching, and black Christians

---

13. See J. Cheryl Exum, "You Shall Let Every Daughter Live," 37–61.

in general extraordinarily vulnerable to the assaults of what I consider to be a new imperialism that our people find hard to withstand. These remain matters for further exploration and serious engagement.

The past few years have seen important issues raised in South Africa, for the academy, for the church, and for society as a whole. The debates about the decolonization of our education systems and curricula, about Africanization and Africanity are in full flood. And they should remain so. I sincerely hope that all those who claim true Africanness will not budge one single inch in their efforts to make this debate the center of what we so often call matters of national importance, the "national question." What I say in these pages on these matters is only an initial response. One does not know yet where they might lead. One thing is for certain though: these debates should not be entered into without full awareness of the realities of twenty-first-century empire, its power, and its devastating impact on communities of the Global South. Neither should we forget the lessons we have learned from Black Consciousness: that the fight for Black dignity, freedom, and indeed for humanity, for the "human face" of the world Steve Biko pleaded and worked for, begins with the decolonization of the mind.

When my generation raised the issues of Black theology and African culture, we raised it vigorously. In fact the very last words of my 1976 dissertation were devoted to a plea that Black theology take African culture seriously, even if this may sound "utopian": making its values such as humanity, dignity, and wholeness the heart of our Black theology.[14] The point I will keep on making in these pages is that my generation did not think long and hard enough about how much we excluded women when we made these lofty claims, and how detrimental that would be not just for the women, but for ourselves, our struggles, our ecclesial practices, and the integrity of our theology. The new struggles around the politics of Africanization, Africanity, and decolonization, dare not make these same mistakes again. The women are either full, equal partners in these endeavors, or we shall not be at all. We will either cross these rivers together, or we shall not cross them at all, and like Moses, we may see the promised land, but we may not ever get there.

Back in 1984, James Cone, writing "for my people," reflected on Black theology, the Black church, and the world we faced then. With brutal honesty, wonderful foresight, and prophetic boldness, he wrote about how far we have come and how far we had yet to go.

> Neither the civil rights organizations, nor black churches and their theology, *in their present form*, will be enough to take us

---

14. See A. Boesak, *Farewell to Innocence*, 151–52.

into the twenty-first century with sufficient political power and spiritual health to cope with the problems, injustice, and poverty that are rampant in the black community. The ideals of integration and nationalism are insufficient for the problems we now face and for the issues with which we will have to deal in the future... *We need a vision of freedom that includes the whole of the inhabited earth and not just North America, a vision enabling us to analyze the causes of world poverty and sickness, monopoly capitalism and anti-democratic socialism, opium in Christianity and other religions among the oppressed, racism and sexism, and the resolute will to eliminate these evils.*[15]

On the threshold of the third decade of the twenty-first century, all of these prophetic challenges and more are undeniably before us right now; they are global, and they burn with flaming urgency. So we need to think not just about the present form of these challenges, but about the present state of Black theology and the Black church.

This work seeks to honor Jim Cone's and Katie Cannon's prophetic presence still in our midst in an attempt to respond to the challenges they have left for us. James Cone also taught us something I have never forgotten, and which I have endeavored to honor in all my writings since the beginning, and this work is no different. It was also something that resonated strongly with my Reformed theology roots: the theologian, Cone said, is *before all else,* an exegete of Scripture and of existence:

> To be an exegete of existence means that Scripture is not an abstract word, not merely a rational idea. It is God's Word to those who are oppressed and humiliated in this world. The task of the theologian is to probe the depths of Scripture exegetically for the purpose of relating that message to human existence.[16]

This book is titled *Children of the Waters of Meribah.* Chapter 20 of the Book of Numbers offers an intriguing scene. The tensions between Moses and the people he is trying to lead come to a climax, Miriam dies, and the water at the wells of Meribah dry up. It is a place of mourning, but it is also a place of final confrontations and final decisions. It is also a place of re-evaluating Miriam, her words, her life, and her role as prophetic leader

---

15. See Cone, *For My People,* 193–94, my emphasis. Cone's critique of both "monopoly capitalism" and "anti-democratic socialism" must not mislead us to think that he takes some neutral stance in order to distance himself from both. In fact, his "vision for a new social order" includes not only "a global vision that includes the struggles of the poor in the Third World" but also quite emphatically one that "should be democratic and socialist, including a Marxist critique of monopoly capitalism" (see 204).

16. Cone, *God of the Oppressed,* 8.

and as paradigm for our theological reflection. For us, reading this story today in our own contexts, it offers life-changing choices. This book is hoping that we will rethink older decisions, make the right choices that reshape our vision of the future, seek new paths—in other words, drink deeply from the waters of Meribah. For the sake of the character of our liberation, the integrity of our theology, and the authenticity of our praxis in the world, we should be, I am saying, not children of Moses and the burning bush, but children of Miriam and the waters of Meribah.

Chapter One

POISONED WELL OR WATERS OF LIFE?

Black Theology, Black Preaching, Scripture, and the Challenges of Empire

AN IMPERIAL ERA NOT YET ENDED*

THE YEAR 2017 MARKED the 500th year of the Reformation, and Martin Luther's bold act of October 31, when he published his "Disputation" that included the Ninety-Five Theses, an act that changed the history of the church and the world.[1] Helmut Gollwitzer, respected German theologian and pastor of the Confessing Church in the struggle against Nazism, wrote words we would do well to ponder as we consider these historic events:

> The Reformation did not change a thing in the fate white people prepared for the colored peoples of the world. Whether Rome, or Wittenberg, or Geneva prevailed; whether it was to be justification through good works or by faith; whether the Decrees of Dordt or the Statements of the Remonstrants were to become the official church doctrine; whether Cromwell or Charles I would be the victor—for the red, yellow, and black people of the

---

1. Whether Martin Luther in fact "nailed" the Ninety-Five Theses "to the door" of Wittenberg church seems to be open to dispute. What is not in doubt is the enormous impact the theses have had on the history of the church and the world since.

world this was all irrelevant. This had no bearing whatsoever on their situation. . . Nothing of all this would stop the capitalistic revolution as the revolution of the white, Christian, Protestant peoples that would spread all over the world to open the era of slavery which even today (albeit not in the same form), is not yet ended.[2]

I found this citation from Gollwitzer in 1974 and used it in my doctoral dissertation in 1976,[3] and James Cone and Gayraud Wilmore included it in their *Black Theology* compendium in 1979.[4] In that compendium, Gollwitzer drove the point home: "For the white confessors of the faith, regardless of their particular Christian hue, the people of color were all destined for bondage; 'oneness in Christ' might pertain to heaven, but certainly not on this earth."[5] Gollwitzer's use of the words "prepared for" means that there is nothing accidental about empire, its intentions and its workings. The era of globalized wealth creation built on invasion, oppression, slavery, and exploitation was an era that Europe and later the United States had indeed well prepared for the nations they overran and colonized to make this enrichment and world domination possible. However, for some reason these truths did not seem to have real impact on our thinking since then. Early on in his writings, James Cone offered this observation:

> While not diminishing the importance of Luther's theological concern, I am sure that if he had been born a black slave, his first question would not have been whether Jesus was present at the Lord's Table but whether he was really present at the slave's cabin, whether slaves could expect Jesus to be with them as they tried to survive the cotton field, the whip, and the pistol.[6]

This insight was both brilliant and correct and an important step toward the continued decolonization of our theological thinking and endeavors, although we did not name it so at the time. On the whole, however, Black theology did not find a way to let the implications of these words—however much they could have helped us plumb the depths of the challenges Black theology is presently facing—steer us into the deeper waters of serious discussion beyond the immediate racial reading of our situation.

2. Gollwitzer, *Die Kapitalistische Revolution*, 45.
3. See Boesak, *Farewell to Innocence*, 31–33.
4. See Wilmore and Cone, *Black Theology*. Gollwitzer's contribution with this quote is on 152–73.
5. See Gollwitzer, "Why Black Theology?" in Wilmore and Cone, *Black Theology*, 155.
6. Cone, *God of the Oppressed*, 13.

But Cone's utterances on Luther and the Lord's presence followed an earlier comment on the ancient creeds:

> I respect what happened at Nicea and Chalcedon and the theological input of the Church Fathers on Christology, but that source alone is inadequate. . . the *homoousia* question is not a black question.[7]

I did return to Cone and these insights in a 2009 work:

> The Jesus of Nicea, Chalcedon and the ancient creeds—Light from light, begotten, not made, of one substance with the Father—was beautiful, but so painfully remote, untouched and unmoved by human misery caused by injustice and inhumanity. Indeed, in the rendition of the European Renaissance, this Jesus was *too* beautiful, too aloof, too aristocratic for the pain, filth and ugliness of slavery and degradation, too light for the darkness of our misery as black people. The Jesus of Constantinian Christianity, without the crown of thorns, but with the crown of laurels, with his wounded hands holding the sword and the standard of the empire, in whose holy name we were caught and chained, disrobed and shamed, flayed and slaughtered, disowned, unnamed and unmade and finally baptized—*that* Jesus bore no resemblance at all to the Human Son.[8]

Still, though I did understand that the Christ of the creeds was too far removed from the "messiness of human life" as Jeorg Rieger puts it,[9] I did not take it any further than as reflection upon the understanding of the Human Child within the situation of oppression, occupation, and humiliation as the black Messiah of the black situation of racial oppression and humiliation. The scope of these understandings, in their capacity to unmask the realities of empire, did not dawn on me. I did not make and develop the proper connections between church and empire, and how much the deliberations of ecumenical councils called on the insistence and authority of an emperor were done within the imperial context, to the imperial pleasure, and to what extent the theology of the creeds reflected imperial ideology.[10]

So in one sense, Cone was correct: the *homoousia* question, of the coequality of Jesus with God—coequal with God in terms of his divinity and

---

7. Cone, *God of the Oppressed*, 13.
8. Boesak, *Running With Horses*, 39.
9. Rieger, *Christ & Empire*, 70.
10. For the development of these insights, see the brilliant analysis of Jeorg Rieger; see Rieger, *Christ & Empire*, especially ch. 2.

coequal with us in terms of his humanity—was not a black question, because these were not debates that even remotely took into account the black situation of slavery, genocide, racism, and dehumanization. The *homoousia* humanity was not a black humanity. In another sense, Cone, and those of us who agreed with him, did not nearly go far enough. We did not discern how much that question, framed within an imperial context and imperial theological mindset, would have theological, social, and political consequences for the people "of the lower strata," the slaves, the poor, the women, the disenfranchised at the time, and, in turn, would have for us, the black, the poor, the women, the disenfranchised, the newly enslaved, living in an imperial situation that even today "has not yet ended." The consequences for us, in our response to this present imperial reality, are facing us still.

Although in South Africa we did take Gollwitzer seriously in our engagement with the perversion of the Reformed tradition exposited in the theology of apartheid, we did not grasp the vast ramifications of the argument as it pertains not just to white racism and its onslaught on black humanity but to white supremacy as an essential function of white, global Christian imperialism. We did not fully grasp or engage the reality of empire, its all-encompassing reach, its power to capture, enslave, and exploit not just the entire cultural, political and socio-economic workings of our colonized societies, but its deadly attempt to nullify all that made us human and worthy.[11]

What Gollwitzer was talking about was the overwhelming reality of empire which, even though it has in the last five centuries or so changed hands from the Europeans and Ottomans to the British, and presently to the Americans, is still not yet ended. So it would indeed not matter whether in the various colonization conquests the colonized were overrun by Catholics or Lutherans, Calvinists or Anglicans, Baptists or Methodists. They would all be representatives of the nations of the rich North, empires that had as their goal the theft of land and people, oppression, slavery, and genocide, all with the express intent of exploitation, deprivation, and enrichment. Invasion and colonization went hand in hand with domination and subjugation, and the Christianization of subject peoples was unthinkable without the demonization of their culture and beliefs, that wide-open door to the

11. This does not nullify the theological and biblical truths uncovered by the Reformation, the notions of justice, liberty, and human dignity especially the Calvinist Reformation brought to the light, as we have discovered in our struggles in South Africa. It does, however, help us understand the ways in which these truths have been appropriated solely for the benefit of the empire, the privileged in Western societies and the "white, Christian peoples" over against the "savages" of the worlds they overran, conquered and subjected. It also opens our eyes to the work that remains to be done in all these respects.

eradication of their history and their physical annihilation. Inasmuch as it had to do with doctrine it was purely incidental.

Particularly crucial was the Christianizing of the process, for the purposes of self-righteous rationalization and indemnification at the heart of which was the pulsating darkness of exceptionalism. Central to it all was the Bible, the source of an all-encompassing justification of acts unspeakable in their cruelty, and the sanctifier of bigotry, hatred, and greed so deep it could only exist and endure through the most obstinate denial. It became the preserver of the vilest forms of pseudo-innocence with the deadliest consequences.

At the same time, from the earliest days, the Bible was, and had remained, central in the lives, faith, and struggles of black people suffering under Western Christian imperial rule, and consequently remained just as central in black theological thinking.[12] "Even beyond the confines of African-American religion," writes Cain Hope Felder, "Black people are fundamentally people of the Book."[13] Black theology's concentration on racism and race matters was not misplaced at all. However, it came at the cost of our understanding just how deeply white supremacy and privilege, as these were reflected in our localized colonialist structures, were inalienably embedded in global imperialist realities. We searched the Bible for the black presence and the biblical narratives for inspiration for our struggles against racist intentions,[14] but we failed to read the Bible to discover the prophetic nodes critical of empire and the ways of empire among subjected peoples. As a result, we were not fully equipped, in our theologizing and in our preaching, to engage the challenges of empire in our own times.

In saying this I am not denying the ongoing, terrifying realities of racism in the United States, South Africa, or elsewhere, or its horrific boldness in the age of Trump. I agree with Wendell Griffin when he writes that there is a call to pay proper attention to the deepest problem with white racism,

---

12. See for instance, Cone, *God of the Oppressed*, 28–35: "Thus the black experience *requires* that Scripture be a source for Black Theology. For it was Scripture that enabled slaves to affirm a view of God that differed radically from that of the slave masters" (my emphasis). Note that Cone emphasizes the agency of the slaves in their affirmation of God as a God of freedom and justice, and de-emphasizes the appropriation of Scripture by the slave masters. This is, in my view, another way in which the oppressed embraced the "self-interpretation" of the Scriptures Tinyiko Maluleke seems to reject, see below. And again: "Scripture established limits to white people's use of Jesus Christ as a confirmation of black oppression." Quotations are on 29. See also Wilmore, *Black Religion*, ch. 3.

13. Felder, *Troubling Biblical Waters*, 6.

14. See for example Felder, *Troubling Biblical Waters*, especially Part I. Also Felder, *Race, Racism, and the Biblical Narratives*.

white supremacy, and white privilege, namely that they have not only been systematized, they have been sacralized:

> Racial injustice continues and has persisted across the entire history of this society—legally, economically, politically, socially, and culturally—because white supremacy and racism is now—and has always been—*sacralized.*
>
> By *sacralized* I mean that white supremacy has always been considered sacred. Whiteness has always been the standard of "rightness." It is, therefore, a fundamental mistake to view and treat white supremacy as merely an attitude or a set of practices and policies. White supremacy is something approaching a theology in this society, if not the world! The historical evils I've already mentioned and contemporary evils (such as mass incarceration, state sanctioned abuse and homicide of black and brown people by police agencies, racist immigration policies that target persons from South and Central America, South Asia, Africa, and Muslims, dislocation and other economic oppression of communities of color through gentrification and other commercial schemes, and the refusal to engage in the long overdue work of reparations) are based on the conviction that white norms are superior, that white culture is superior, that whiteness entitles one to a presumption of superior morality, dignity, intellect, and privilege, and that the only legitimate remedies for racial injustice are those fashioned and/or accepted by white persons based on white norms and objectives. In this sense, race is not only a social construct. White supremacy is a theological construct in which white norms, goals, and aims define what is right, good, true, healthy, fair, and otherwise worthwhile.[15]

Black South African Christians have begun to do some of this work when we declared South Africa's racial apartheid as not only politically nonsensical, socio-economically misguided, and morally reprehensible, but theologically a sin, a heresy, and a blasphemy, because we understood that apartheid was not just a racist construct, but also because in its assault on the humanity of black people, it was also an assault upon the dignity and worthiness of God. And in South Africa the theologizing of apartheid in the theology of apartheid became not only a theological discipline but an article of faith.

But Griffen is correct: the work is far from complete. In the aftermath of our Truth and Reconciliation Commission we are beginning to realize

---

15. See Griffen, "Racial Justice, Public Theologians," 5, 6.

that perhaps the fundamental reason why—barring a small number of notable exceptions—it is well-nigh impossible for white South Africans, from F. W. De Klerk down to ordinary young white persons, to acknowledge the evil of apartheid, show genuine remorse and repentance, and bring themselves to ask forgiveness of black South Africans for the untold harm done to them for over nearly four hundred years—imperialism's undeserved black impoverishment and undeserved white enrichment over generations—is precisely because racism deifies white existence, or as Griffen puts it, has become sacralized in white minds. It is, after all, in the nature of a god to do anything to anyone without ever feeling the need for acknowledgment, remorse, or repentance. Not being able to ask for forgiveness is not a sign of white people's fragile human nature, nor is it merely the arrogance of power or a supreme sense of entitlement—it is at heart a feeling of assumed godlikeness. So indeed, our work has hardly begun.

It is important also to keep in mind that Gollwitzer's "not yet ended" means not only that enslavement is continuing in all its modernized forms today,[16] in the enslavement of global, neoliberal, capitalist structures, and financial institutions, like the World Bank and the International Monetary Fund holding poorer countries to ransom, for example. It also means that the propagation of a new, imperial, slave religion, a new Christian fundamentalism with its devastating consequences for the peoples of the Global South, is no longer the sole province of the "white, Christian peoples." Gollwitzer's "white, Christian Protestant peoples" have found for themselves black (and Latinx) neoliberal capitalist junior partners, the new prosperity gospellers who cross the borders of our lands in their private jets and the boundaries of our existence in their supreme imperial power to bring our people a poisoned gospel of Christian, capitalist, neo-colonialist, consumerist enslavement.[17] In the Global South, they are more and more the face of

---

16. Human trafficking and child labor are particularly vicious forms of the consequences of globalism, endless war, and the unfettered reign of neoliberal capitalism. A new example of modern-day slavery is the African migrants "traded in Libya's slave markets." The head of the International Organization for Migration reported that "migrants are being sold in the market as a commodity. Selling human beings [at between $200 and $500 per person] is becoming a trend among smugglers as the smuggling networks in Libya are becoming stronger and stronger." See Al Jazeera's report, "African Migrants Traded in Libya's 'Slave Markets.'" This also means the continued enslavement caused by obsessive consumerism, the devastation of what Naomi Klein calls "disaster capitalism," the ravages of "structural adjustment" and the general predatory polices of the World Bank, the International Monetary Fund and the working of the financial institutions controlled by the rich North.

17. For an enlightening discussion on these matters, see, e.g., McGee, *Brand® New Theology*; Walton, *Watch This!* For an even more explicit study of the impact of North American televangelism on questions of justice in the South African constitutional

the fundamentalist so-called "third Reformation," the black, lavishly paid and ostentatiously rich high priests and priestesses of the empire. In poor, desperate, and vulnerable communities, they are the religious frontrunners and shock troops of empire's relentless reach.

In South Africa, our introduction to the white imperial Christ was facilitated by the representatives of first the Dutch Empire and then the British. Throughout the centuries of colonization and slavery and the five decades of apartheid, the toxic legacy of the colonization of Scripture, as perfect instrument of domination and subjugation used by Christianized Empire, continued to endure. And so we hear Rev. Dr. Koot Vorster, leading figure in the white Dutch Reformed Church, as vigorous a proponent of the theology of apartheid as he was a staunch defender of apartheid as policy of both church and state in South Africa, speaking in 1970:

> Our only guide is the Bible. Our policy and outlook on life are based on the Bible. We firmly believe the way we interpret it is right. We will not budge one inch from our interpretation [in order] to satisfy anyone in South Africa or abroad. . . . We are right and will continue to follow the way the Bible teaches.[18]

In South Africa, we dealt decisively with the theology of apartheid. We reclaimed the Reformed tradition not simply as an adversary to be challenged or a burden to be resignedly carried; a lethal tool in the hands of Afrikaner Calvinists.[19] We understood, and claimed, that tradition as genuine inspiration for our struggle for liberation, justice, and dignity. Like the African slaves in America, as Gayraud Wilmore writes of Nat Turner, we rediscovered "the God of the Bible who demanded justice," and once again came to understand that "to know God's son, Jesus Christ, was to be set free from every power that dehumanizes and oppresses."[20]

SCRIPTURE, CENTRALITY, AND EMPIRE

Nonetheless, it is this scandalous abuse of the Scriptures evident in the theologies of white-supremacist Christianity that led to the serious questioning of the Bible by non-Western, colonized Christians as instrument

---

democracy and raising compelling arguments around religious fundamentalism, biblical interpretation, patriarchy, and gender-based violence, see the unpublished PhD dissertation of Elna Boesak, *Channeling Justice?*

18. Koot Vorster, *The Sunday Times*, November 8, 1970, cited in Villa-Vicencio, "An All-Pervading Heresy," 59.

19. See A. Boesak, *Black and Reformed*, especially ch. 9.

20. Wilmore, *Black Religion*, 89.

of imperialist, colonialist oppression, quite aptly called a project of "God, gold, and glory" by African scholars.[21] In the 1980s it was especially Itumeleng Mosala who critically, even severely, engaged us in the struggle for the meaning, efficacy, and appropriateness of the Bible for African Christians. It is telling that the well known saying about Africa, the Bible, and the white colonialist has resurfaced with such emphasis.[22] A younger generation—mostly women, among them African feminist theologian Musa Dube and black theologian Vuyani Vellem—have reopened the debate and are reemphasizing the question: What lessons has Black theology not learned for the challenging times oppressed communities in the Global South are facing now?[23]

In a critical and important piece, Vuyani Vellem addresses the issue of the "displacement" of the Bible from the "centrality" in black life apparently taken for granted by some. He especially engages Reformed theology here, "Sola Scriptura" and "Sola Fide" as used "by the Reformed faith," but more importantly, and broadening the question, speaks to the "relationship of the Bible and racism." Vellem then asks, "What lessons have we not learned in Black Theology of liberation that racism continues to elude us in the context of Empire?"[24] Vellem is talking about lessons "not learnt" about the Bible, its uses and abuses in efforts to alienate Africans from themselves, their land, their identities, and their destiny? That is the crucial question within the framework of the issues under discussion here for the Bible has indeed been "seriously and vehemently problematized in Black Theology" (2).

For Vellem, the problem is not only historical. Already in the nineteenth century with the rejection of "the white man's religion" in the frontier wars of resistance, the Bible has "lost its pristine innocence" in the tensions within the nineteenth-century Xhosa community surrounding the work of Rev. Tiyo Soga.[25] It is also contemporary. At issue for him is "the black

---

21. See Mazrui, *Cultural Forces in World Politics*, 1, 14. This term is also appropriated with great effect by Dube, *Postcolonial Feminist Biblical Interpretation*, 11. See also the early views of Mosala, *Biblical Hermeneutics and Black Theology in South Africa*.

22. Ascribed to Kenyan liberation icon Jomo Kenyatta and first president of independent Kenya, the story tells of how, when the white man came to Africa, Africans had the land and they had the Bible. They told us to pray. When we opened our eyes, we had the Bible and they had the land.

23. Mosala, *Biblical Hermeneutics and Black Theology in South Africa*; Dube, *Postcolonial Feminist Biblical Interpretation*, 8.

24. Vellem, "Hermeneutical Embers," 2.

25. Vellem explains how Xhosa leaders, in their anger at the Christian invaders and at Soga's embrace of Christianity, called the Bible "Soga's book," rejecting both Soga's Westernized Christianized ways, and the ideology that held him captive in their view. "Hermeneutical Embers," 4–7.

person in whose hands the Bible is post-1994," ostensibly for the reclamation of the land that was taken away (3). Presumably, having had the Bible for so long has not helped in reclaiming the land. Now he writes, "Young people ask, 'Why did the 1976 generation of the struggle leaders fail the young? How did the exponent of Black Consciousness or Black Theology become such a disappointment?'" (4). Because of this, the Bible no longer holds "a central, innocent place," it is in fact "displaced from every aspect of the lives of the black person." One has to assume that Vellem means that the disappointment of the young has to do with the absence of justice and restitution despite the "centrality" of the Bible in the lives and thinking of the "1976 generation." Whether this question is deemed completely fair or not, one cannot avoid it.

But secondly, Vellem is deeply concerned that in contemporary African fundamentalist Christianity, deeply impacted and controlled by empire (i.e., American fundamentalist Christianity in its zeal to spread its brand of Christianity across the world), the Bible—unquestioningly accepted as the inerrant "Word of God"—is once again doing great harm to African people. Predatory prosperity-gospel pastors prey upon the needs of the poor to better their socioeconomic conditions and ruthless clerics "with the gift of healing" make congregants eat grass and swallow poisonous substances, with the promise that no harm will come to them, as if these pastors have control over the power of God. This is "the Bible in the hands of the post-1994 black person." But this is a person completely captured by and under control of empire. In the process black persons are not just harmed physically. They are spiritually disabled, robbed of their personhood and their faith, and their agency is all but destroyed. They have been dispossessed of their critical, intuitive capacities to read the Bible differently and discern in the Bible the Word of God.[26] This reflects a point I have made elsewhere: the post-1994 black South African is not by any means necessarily a postcolonial, or more precisely, a decolonized person. And even if some have succeeded in that transition, it does not necessarily mean that they have

---

26. In a personal conversation with the author, Vellem also expressed the concern that in our contemporary situation the supremacy of imperial powers and imperial Christianity have "restored" the power to misuse the Bible for evil ends, thereby reviving the relationship between the Bible and racism offering new fertile ground for the old, discredited Christianized apartheid ideology. Indeed Donald Trump's election as president of the US with the electoral support of 82 percent of white evangelicals does seem to have created fertile ground and provided new safe havens for the flourishing of patriarchy and heteronormativity, homophobia, an even more belligerent militarism, more aggressive and predatory neoliberal capitalism, and narrow Christian nationalisms with fascist tendencies across the world.

become *anti-imperial* persons. And for Christians, our reading and interpretation of the Bible has everything to do with it.

Agreeing with Tinyiko Maluleke, Vellem holds that the Bible "does not constitute the only subject matter of theology" (4), and seems to quote Maluleke with approval when he writes that "the equation of colonialism with Christianity and where it has occurred has done far less harm to Black and African theologies than the equation of the Bible with the Word of God."[27] The only way "Sola Scriptura" could now be claimed is in the "epistemological commitment to the preferential option for the poor, the black, everywhere in their social conditions. . ." (7).

My response to these arguments will become clear as our own argument unfolds but I should here react to what Vellem, speaking for that younger, disappointed generation, has to say. We must first state that it is gratifying that Vellem, in this discussion, and following in the footsteps of African feminist theologians, takes the issues of imperialism and colonialism head-on. That is indeed the proper framework for our ongoing work. It is equally important that he articulates the anger and disappointment of the younger generation without whose conversation and insights Black theology will not prosper or deepen. In itself that takes the debate forward considerably. My own work for the last forty years should be an adequate indication of the Black theological response to the perverted Reformed theology of white apartheid South Africa, an issue that Vellem also raises. It is not necessary to repeat that here.

There is no dispute when he states that the Bible "has lost its pristine innocence." It will become clear in this and subsequent chapters that it is my view that the Bible has never been "innocent," since it has always been a site of contestation, and that there has always been a struggle not just *about* the Bible, but *within* the Bible. I hope my argument below will also be an adequate response to Maluleke's assertion that it is no longer possible for African theologians "to pretend that the Bible, the gospel, the Christian faith interprets itself and things only go wrong when people misinterpret a faith."[28] That "Scripture" (not "the Christian faith") interprets itself is a particularly Reformed point of view and in my understanding of it does not in the least undermine "the agency of Africans." My argument is much to the contrary.

However, I have to take issue with the statement that the Bible has been "displaced from every aspect of the lives of [the African masses]." In my view that statement cannot hold against the facts. Although Islam is

27. Vellem refers to Maluleke, "Black and African Theologies," 3–29.
28. See Maluleke, "Rediscovery of the Agency of Africans," 31.

the fastest growing religion globally, Christianity is Africa's fastest growing religion, and by 2050, it is forecast, 50 percent of Christians in the world will live in Africa.[29] And although conservative writer John J. Allen sees "persecution" by Muslims as the greatest threat to Christianity in Africa, I tend to think that the unbridled fundamentalism, with its disastrous reading and interpretation of the Bible, its rabid homophobia and untrammeled patriarchy all driven by the unparalleled global media monopoly of "Christian networks," among other things, is the greatest threat to a genuine, vibrant, inclusive, relevant, and life-giving Christian faith. And despite Vellem's claim, in fundamentalist Christianity the Bible's centrality is without doubt, and the way it is being read and interpreted has a devastating impact not only on ecumenical relations, but on the African church and society as a whole.

On this point, influential Nigerian Anglican primate Peter Akinola expresses the essential view of "Bible believing Christians." Instead of the "relativism of liberal views of the Bible" that tend to "hop from one ethic paradigm to another," he argues, "the primary supposition is a high view of Scripture as inerrant and a sufficient guide in all matters of faith and conduct, such that its ethics and injunctions are of timeless relevance."[30] The archbishop is speaking of his and the majority of African Christianity's views on LGBTQI+ matters. "I didn't write the Bible. It's part of our Christian heritage. It tells us what to do. If the word of God says homosexuality is an abomination, then so be it."[31]

It is this view of holy writ, Christian or Islamic, that has influenced over forty African countries in their deadly criminalization of same-sex relationships. As far as Christians are concerned, this is of course not "part of our Christian heritage" as Akinola claims. It is not even what the Bible claims. At most, it is part of a particular fundamentalist reading tradition that Africa has appropriated from neo-colonialist Western theological impulses. But the archbishop's confidence is telling. As it is, according to the most recent studies, some 60 percent of Christians in Southern Africa believe that "the Bible ought to be the law of the land."[32] That is a far greater threat to Christianity than Islam.

29. Allen, "Africa."
30. Quoted in Jenkins, *New Faces of Christianity*, 3.
31. See Jenkins, *New Faces of Christianity*, 3.
32. See Pew Foundation, "Tolerance and Tension," 11. For Muslims across sub-Saharan Africa, 62 percent believe the Qur'an should be the Constitution. It should not be necessary to remind us of the Apartheid State's "Christian" constitution with its pre-eminent claim on the biblical God, or the lethally waxing influence of white Christian evangelicals, "Bible believing Christians" all, to begin to understand the destructive dangers inherent in such views.

Not only is the Bible "the basis of African Christianity [in the twenty-first century]," writes David Tuesday Adamo, it is also the indisputable guide for daily life. The world is full of gods and sacred works, "But in the vast confusion the one source which can be relied upon for the truth is the Bible."[33] Adamo goes even further:

> The Bible contains a unique perspective on ethics, law, sociology, economics, and politics that is difficult to comprehend without first understanding the message of the Bible.[34]

With these reminders of the African realities in mind, I should hope that instead of arguing that the Bible "has lost its place" in the hearts of the black masses in Africa, Black theology should be in the frontlines fighting this neo-colonialist, imperialist scourge. Here, as well, and not only in the fight for the poor, God's preferential choice for the poor, the wronged, and the vulnerable should be proclaimed. If the God of Jesus of Nazareth is the God of liberation and freedom, of peaceability and justice and dignity, Black theology must remain clear that whatever in the Bible does not reflect this truth, is not of God, and cannot be uncritically accepted as "the Word of God."

African feminist theologians saw this early and sounded the alarm: There is high demand for the Bible in many African languages, writes Nyambura J. Njoroge, and raising the question we have to be insistent upon, she asks, "But what kind of Christianity are we talking about?" Are we speaking of a Christianity that appears "impotent before the bush fires of poverty, violence, ignorance, disease, corruption, and greed that are sweeping the continent"? Then she narrows it down and asks the hard questions:

> What does this Bible . . . have to offer in the midst of bloodshed among the youth of Africa, of the prime ages of fifteen to forty? What can a book offer that is used to exploit its illiterate and ignorant listeners, the elderly women and men, who watch helplessly when their children and grandchildren die, leaving no name behind to carry on life? What can a book offer that is interpreted to enrich the greedy preachers, the vultures, the crusaders who take advantage of the poor, deaf, cripples, and

---

33. See Adamo, "Bible in Twenty-first Century Africa," 25–32. "The stories in the Bible are everyone's stories," he writes, and quoting Mary Getui, he continues, "There is no position in life, no phase in human experience, for which the Bible does not contain valuable instruction. Ruler and subject, master and servant, buyer and seller, borrower and lenders, parent and child, teacher and student—all may find here lessons of priceless worth" (see 26).

34. Adamo, "Bible in Twenty-first Century Africa," 26.

the dumb? What can a book offer that is used by the so-called messengers of the good news to stigmatize and ostracize those dying from HIV/AIDS? What can a book offer that has been used to keep Africans, women, and slaves, "in their place"? No doubt, this same book has also brought hope and life to people's lives and communities. So is this book a curse or a blessing, to the weary and lamenting people of Africa?[35]

South African Hebrew Bible scholar Madipoane Masenya underscores this point as she recalls the South African struggle song, sang as a song of mourning:

Senzeni na (What have we done?)
Isono sethu ubumnyama (Our sin is our blackness)

She adds, "Our sin is not only our skin color, but also our female sex: we are Black women, daughters of Africa." Remembering how the Bible was systematically used to sanction racial apartheid in South Africa, she asserts that Africa's daughters "have been, and still are, at the receiving end" in those local and global life-denying struggles in which the Bible still occupies a central role. "As African women we experience patriarchy from those of our own kind even as we, together with them, at times on account of the abuse of the Bible, remain subjected to American and European imperialism through globalization and neocolonialism."[36]

It is these questions Africa's Christians and oppressed Christians across the globe have to engage, and do so seriously, and it is proper that the women of Africa take the initiative in this endeavor.

A CRITICAL, SUBVERSIVE INTUITION

My issue with these friends and colleagues has never been about the abuse of the Bible by racist, colonialist structures and the subjugation of the Bible to these racist, colonialist, and exclusivist ideologies. That could never be disputed, and I remain grateful for the way in which they have kept these critical issues front and center. Neither do I want to take issue here with those who have lost any hope that the Bible could ever be rescued from the hands of its powerful abusers. I do need to say, however, that precisely because the Bible remains so crucial in the life of oppressed communities and for reflection in Black liberation theology, I am not at all prepared to give up the Bible as a source of life and a powerful resource for empowerment,

---

35. Njoroge, "Bible and African Christianity," 214.
36. Masenya, "Women, Africana Reality, and the Bible," 33, 35.

inspiration, and witness in that struggle against ruthless, powerful, and conscienceless forces who clearly understand the place of Scripture in the life of oppressed Christian communities very well, perhaps better than some who seek to contest their power in these same communities.

My argument has been fourfold:[37] First, that the central, and most enduring message of the Bible itself stands in opposition to and in rejection of, indeed is subversive of and stands in resistance to such manipulation—which is both a manipulation of the message of the Bible and of the God of the Bible. Second, that rather than treat the Bible as a wholly compromised sacred text irredeemably contaminated by Western imperialist readings, we should approach the Bible as sacred Scriptures *appropriated* by imperialist powers for the sake of domination, the subjugation of peoples, justification of the theft and exploitation of their lands and resources, and for the purposes of ideological control.

Third, for those who hold that the enduring message of the Bible is liberation, freedom, justice, dignity, peace, and inclusivity, the Bible has always been seen as what South Africans used to call "a site of struggle." That is, there is a struggle (not just *about* the Bible but *within* the Bible itself) between two voices, two traditions, two understandings of specific contexts within the biblical stories, and two alternative futures for the people of God. That means that the questions, "Which God?," "Which Bible?," "Which Jesus?" and the questions, "How do you read?," "Do you understand what you read?," and "What is written?" would always be central and critical in our approach to the Scriptures and those readings seeking to make the Bible submissive to empire.

Scholars have now come to identify what is called the "Great Tradition," the tradition that seeks legitimacy for the way in which the dominant forces in ancient Israelite society—the wealthy, powerful, and privileged—have laid claim upon the Torah. In opposition to this stands the "Little Tradition," the tradition that calls upon the liberation tradition of the exodus, which knows and confesses God as the God of the exodus—that is, the God of liberation, freedom, and justice, the God who sides not with the powerful but with the powerless and the wronged, the God who is the God of justice for the poor, the meek, and the exploited.[38] That is the tradition rooted in the

---

37. See Boesak, *Farewell to Innocence*, ch. 1. In continuous conversation with others it has of course been deepened over the years.

38. The usage of the terms "great tradition" and "little tradition" was sparked by the groundbreaking work of sociologist Robert Redfield. See his *The Little Community and Peasant Society and Culture*. These terms have been appropriated by theologians and biblical scholars as well; see for example van Aarde, "Jesus and the Son of Man," 423–38. I do not, however, agree with van Aarde that the early Christian church, in

acts of prophetic defiance by the midwives of Exodus 1 and Miriam on the riverbank, the seashore, and in the wilderness, and embraced by the eighth-century prophets of social justice, Jesus of Nazareth, and the *am ha'aretz*, the little people, the voiceless and powerless ones in Israel. We are beginning to recognize that Galileans such as Jesus and his followers would not have known the same Torah/Law in the same way as the "scribes and Pharisees" in Jerusalem, writes Richard Horsley. "The 'little' or popular tradition(s) in Galilee would have formed and guided the distinctive patterns of belief and behavior valued by the peasantry."[39] This is the tradition of resistance against empire we find in the Gospels and in Paul, and in the early Christian church before the Constantinian captivity of the Christian church and faith.

Fourth, I believe that from the earliest times communities of the Book—from the Africans in slavery to subjugated communities in our own colonial and neo-colonialist times—have always, at some deep level, understood this tension. Evidence suggests strongly that oppressed black communities, in reading the Bible, have approached it with a conscious awareness of this internal biblical struggle, from the theology of slave insurrectionists to the famous story of Howard Thurman's grandmother and her reluctance to let him read to her from the Apostle Paul because of the misuse of his writings to justify slavery,[40] to my own mother's theological insights in our nightly prayers at the family table.

Despite the decades-long teachings of white missionaries, this too-early-widowed woman who did not get beyond primary school education somehow held fast to her firm belief that the most consistent, enduring, and trustworthy understanding of God was of a God who is the "Father of the fatherless, the protector of the widow and orphan, and the defender of the defenseless." She learned this from the Bible, clung to it throughout her

---

claiming honorific titles for Jesus (e.g., Lord, Son of God, Prince of Peace) was simply "giving him the position of founder of the cult" and in doing so "the 'little tradition' was reconceptualized in terms of the 'great tradition'" (429). I agree instead with scholars such as Crossan and Horsley that these titles were instead signs of resistance against imperial power and the imperial religion and especially aimed against the emperor who was at the very center of imperial worship. See, e.g., Crossan, "Roman Imperial Theology," 59–71.

39. Horsley, *Jesus and Empire*, 61–62. "The multiple movements in Galilee, Samaria, and particularly Judea that took the forms of popular messianic movements and popular prophetic movements were all informed by the Israelite 'little tradition'" (62). And again, in reference to John Dominic Crossan, Horsley states, "Once we recognize the difference between the 'great tradition' and the 'little tradition' it seems highly questionable procedure to draw upon documents of the literate elite, such as the *Psalms of Solomon* as direct sources for what Galilean peasants and artisans such as Jesus and his followers were thinking." See Horsley, *Jesus and Empire*, 164 n. 4.

40. Thurman, *Jesus and the Disinherited*, 30–31.

life and the onslaughts of apartheid during her lifetime, and taught it to her children. This was, I suppose one could say, my earliest and most foundational introduction to a theology of liberation.

US historian Eugene Genovese's observation drawn from his study of the religion of the African slaves in America makes an excellent point:

> For while much went into the making of the heroic black struggle for survival under extreme adversity, nothing loomed so large as the religious faith of the slaves. The very religion that their masters sought to impose in the interests of social control carried an extraordinarily powerful message of liberation for this world as well as the next.[41]

Genovese expresses his surprise at this finding, but it was inescapable. "The empirical investigations disturbed a historian with the biases of an atheist and a historical materialist who had always assumed, however mindlessly, that religion should be understood as no more than a corrosive ideology at the service of the ruling classes."[42] That conclusion is correct, not because of the slave masters' generosity of spirit, but precisely because of the irresistible, inalienable message of liberation and justice permeating the biblical story, and what I call below the intuitive theological ingenuity of the slaves who had heard in *that* message, rather than in the ideologized preaching of the slave masters, the "Word of God."

Emerson B. Powery and Rodney S. Sadler Jr. observe, "The authority of Scripture for African Americans, at its root has the authority granted to these texts [the texts carrying the message of God's love for justice, freedom and human dignity] by their ancestors. . ." And even though often their introduction to the Scriptures was not "a neutral experience but a hostile activity whereby Holy Writ was used to pacify them (Exod 20, 21; Eph 6:4–9) and justify their subjugation," in these texts they found not just an otherworldly God offering spiritual blessings. In fact, they found "a here-and-now God who cared principally for the oppressed, acting historically and eschatalogically to deliver the downtrodden from their abusers."[43]

As Powery and Sadler intimate, it was not a disembodied intuitivity; white colonialists and slave masters had not completely succeeded in cutting off their powers of remembering, as Allen Dwight Callahan makes clear:

---

41. See Genovese, "Marxism, Christianity and Bias," 88–89. Genovese's original study, *Roll, Jordan, Roll: The World the Slaves Made*, remains a seminal and still hugely relevant work.

42. Genovese, "Marxism, Christianity and Bias," 88.

43. See Powery and Sadler, *Genesis of Liberation*, 6.

> American slaves did not read the Bible through, or even over against, the traditions they brought with them from West Africa: they read the Bible as a text into which these traditions were woven. The characters and events of the Bible became the functional equivalent of the ancestors and heroes long celebrated in West Africa. The many ancestral and natural spirits were subsumed in the Holy Spirit, and the mighty acts of God supplanted tales of martial valor. Biblical patriarchs now sat on the stools of the esteemed ancestors of ages past.[44]

At the same time, though, enslaved African people discerned something in the Bible that was neither at the center of the ancestral cultures or in evidence in their hostile American home: a warrant for justice in this world. "They found woven into the texts of the Bible a crimson thread of divine justice antithetical to the injustice they had come to know so well."[45]

Vincent L. Wimbush saw it clearly, and what he writes is also true for Africans and other colonized peoples:

> Almost from the beginning of their engagement with it, African Americans interpreted the Bible differently from those who introduced them to it, ironically and audaciously seeing in it—the most powerful of the ideological weapons used to legitimize their enslavement and disenfranchisement—a mirroring of themselves and their experiences, seeing in it the privileging of all those who, like themselves, are the humiliated, the outcasts, and powerless. It was seen as a sort of rhetorical paint brushing of their existence and a virtual manifesto for their redemption and triumph.[46]

This is a key element that African women, members of the LGBTQI+ community, and other marginalized persons would come to insist on, as we shall see as the argument in this work is developed.

For Christians from the Reformed tradition, this should be less surprising. The Scriptures, the Reformed tradition claims, "interpret themselves." Contra Maluleke, I take that to mean that the Scriptures resist interpretations, meanings, and applications that distort the heart of the biblical message, which is the tradition of liberation initiated by God in the earliest memory of ancient Israel and embedded in the truths articulated by Miriam and continued by the prophets. Koot Vorster's misplaced confidence and

---

44. See Callahan, *Talking Book*, xii. The same argument largely holds for African slaves brought to the Cape colony at the start of the South African colonization project.

45. Callahan, *Talking Book*, xiv.

46. Wimbush, *African Americans and the Bible*, 17.

apartheid's thoroughly discredited biblical interpretations are as excellent an example of this subversive self-interpretation as one can find.

This self-interpretation finds its most enduring forms in the resistance to empire, from the liberation from slavery in Egypt to the popular resistance against the idea of a monarchy; against kings and ruling elites in Israel in the preaching, teaching, and actions of the prophets; from the midwives Shifrah and Puah to Miriam and Hannah, to Mary in the Magnificat and Martha in her confession; from Elijah to Isaiah and Jeremiah, to Amos, John the Baptist, and Jesus of Nazareth.

Oppressed people have understood this and taken it seriously in their encounter with the Bible, its interpretation by oppressors of all kinds and all times, and in their encounter with God in their situations of oppression, and in their hope for freedom. Liberation theology has named this "a hermeneutic of suspicion." I agree, of course, but perhaps we should be more precise. It is not just suspicion of the Bible in its complexity and an even stronger suspicion of the way the Bible has been and is being interpreted and presented by those who think they own not just the Scriptures but have also laid claim upon God, appropriating God for the side of oppression, power, and dominion. It is a suspicion that is informed by something far more sophisticated. Oppressed people had, and exercised, an intuitive, critical, subversive theological ingenuity. They intuited that what they heard from slave masters, white missionaries, and the spokespersons of the empire was wrong, not just because it did not respond to their lived reality and their needs in situations of unspeakable suffering, but because they could not square it with what they, from the beginning, understood to be the heart of the biblical message. They were, as James Cone would demand from all Black theologians, "before all else, exegetes of Scripture and of life."[47]

It was *critical* because it questioned a reading that decontextualizes the biblical message as well as the reading of it in its appropriation of that message for the purposes of oppression and control. It was a *subversive* theological intuition and it made it impossible for them to hear the exodus story as a story of and for the white, oppressive, slave-holding classes identifying themselves with ancient Israel as "chosen" of God with a divine manifest destiny to subject them to such cruel, despotic, murderous rule in a "Promised Land" that stank of blood and oppression. They knew only too well who in that situation was the pharaoh and who were the slaves.[48] Similarly, they looked at the crucified Jesus and understood, intuitively, the relationship between the suffering of Jesus and the suffering of oppressed

---

47. Cone, *God of the Oppressed*, 8.
48. See Wilmore, *Black Religion and Black Radicalism*.

people, as James Cone has recently brilliantly pointed out, between the cross and the lynching tree, despite the claims laid upon him by the slave master's religion.[49] And what they could not articulate in theological argument, they put into song.[50] In the words of African-American scholar Dwight Hopkins, for the arduous journey toward freedom, "on the rough side of the mountain," they made "shoes that fit their feet."[51] Hopkins speaks of the "interpretive cunning of the poor," those who "developed [their] theological critique from the Bible's powerless voices."[52]

For Black preachers, Black people's "enslaved leaders" from the earliest times of slavery in America, it meant that even without the power of literacy and formal education, "they preached what they knew about the progression from patriarch to priest to prophet to Jesus to Paul and testified to what they have seen, exalting the Word of God above all other [human, enslaving, dehumanizing] authorities," writes womanist theologian Katie Cannon. They preached, in Cannon's elegant phrasing, "with one ear on the ground hearing the cries and longings of the people and the other ear at the mouth of God."[53]

Simply put, they understood intuitively that one could not say "God" and abide with oppression, and one could not say "Jesus" and abide with injustice. The Scriptures had interpreted themselves to them and they knew that what responded most truthfully to faith was fundamentally different to what was presented to them as a religion that pampered the wickedness of the powerful. That interaction between the oppressed and the Bible, between hearing and believing, between the self-interpretation of Scripture in its resistance against manipulation and appropriation and the understanding of the oppressed in faithful response to both God and their own situation of oppression, I would call not merely a hermeneutical suspicion, but an intuitive, critical, subversive theological ingenuity.

It is this critical ingenuity that opened up an understanding of Scripture and of the well known and utterly crucial distinction between ideologized

---

49. See James Cone's inspiring work, *The Cross and the Lynching Tree*.

50. See Cone, *Cross and the Lynching Tree*; Cone, *Spirituals and the Blues*.

51. See Hopkins, *Shoes That Fit Our Feet*. For Hopkins there was never any doubt that the religion of the Africans in America was a religion of freedom; they "lived a faith of freedom" (1). "Enslaved African Americans creatively forged their own understanding of God, Jesus Christ, and the purpose of humanity. Through scriptural insights, theological imagination, and direct contact with God, black bondsmen and bondswomen combined faith instincts from their African traditional religions with the justice message of the Christian gospel and planted the seeds for a black theology expressed through politics and culture" (13).

52. Hopkins, *Shoes That Fit Our Feet*, 14.

53. See Cannon, *Katie's Canon*, 115, 116.

religiosity and faith by the African slave turned abolitionist Frederick Douglass. And few articulated it so well:

> I love the religion of our blessed Savior ... which comes from above, in the wisdom of God which is first pure, then peaceable, gentle ... without partiality and without hypocrisy ... which makes it the duty of its disciples to visit the fatherless and the widow in their affliction. I love that religion ... It is because I love this religion that I hate the slave-holding, the woman-whipping, the mind-darkening, the soul-destroying religion that exists in America ... loving the one I must hate the other; holding to one I must reject the other.[54]

The literary eloquence and soaring rhetorical brilliance quite aside, one would be hard-pressed to find a statement more steeped in theological wisdom and scriptural discernment than these words by a non-theologian. And whether it is the now legendary wisdom of Howard Thurman's grandmother in her intuitive hermeneutical discernment; the daily prayers of my own mother Sarah to the God she, against the grain of white missionary indoctrination, worshiped as a God of justice; or the deep insights of Frederick Douglass, they are all drawing from the deep well of the biblical prophetic tradition which they understood without much formal book learning, and against all odds and the wishes and laws of the ruling classes, much as the crowds of poor, oppressed, colonized peasants in first-century occupied Palestine heard, understood, and believed Jesus. They knew, intuitively, but with that great certainty brought on by faith and not by sight, that the certitude of the oppressor, built on power, privilege, status, and might but not on wisdom or faith, was the antithesis of what they heard the Bible say to them.

Black theology understood this very well. What Black theology did not fully appreciate, it seems to me, is that this was a reading not just in resistance to a white, racist, pro-slavery hermeneutic, but to an imperial interpretation that sought not only domination and subjugation, but total dispossession of their intuitive knowledge and embrace of the enduring message of the Bible, above all depicted by the exodus story and the life and ministry of Jesus of Nazareth.

---

54. See Douglass, "My Bondage and My Freedom."

A RELIGION WEAPONIZED FOR DESTRUCTION

South Africa's Steve Biko has made an observation that is both profoundly true and profoundly pertinent, and it calls for closer attention to the workings of empire. It turns the spotlight on empire *and* its collaborators within the oppressed communities, and raises the question of our complacent embeddedness in empire, our desires for the rewards of empire, our surrendering to the temptations of empire, and our complicity in empire.

> Thus if Christianity in its *introduction* was corrupted by the inclusion of aspects which made it the ideal religion for the *colonisation* of people, nowadays in its *interpretation* it is the ideal religion for the maintenance of the *subjugation* of the same people.[55]

I understand Biko to say at least three things: First, it is true that Christianity, as "corrupted" and appropriated by the empire and brought to us as a colonizing religion weaponized for our oppression, was and is indeed the ideal religion for the subjugation and domination of people. In the first instance, in other words, Biko lays the blame squarely at the door of Western, imperialist Christianity and its white missionaries. Secondly, it seems that it is not the Bible per se that presents us with the problem. The problem in the struggle against empire is not the Bible. "No people can fight a struggle without faith," Biko says elsewhere.[56] "Nowadays," he states, it is the *interpretation* of the Christian faith that continues to make Christianity an instrument of the subjugation of our people.

That means, third, that the problem is no longer just the erstwhile and contemporary white missionary or the twenty-first-century imperial spokespersons in their use of global media for instance—the problem is the church in the communities of the oppressed, who should by now know better. Note that "nowadays" Biko uses. Modern-day Western Christian fundamentalism, with its vicious exclusivism, predatory capitalist consumerism, sacralized bigotry, baptized homophobia, and sanctified patriarchalism, is trumpeted to people of the Global South—on forty-three television

---

55. Biko, *I Write What I Like*, 56, original emphasis.

56. Biko, *I Write What I Like*, 60. In this context, Biko was speaking of the Christian faith, but it is obviously true of people of other faiths, as they perceive their faith to be an inspiration for struggles for justice and freedom. See, e.g., the statement of Ayatollah Khomeini: "Islam is the religion of militant people who are committed to faith and justice. It is the religion of those who desire freedom and independence. It is the school of those who struggle against imperialism." Sajeed Ruhollah Khomeini, *Islam and Revolution; Writings and Declarations of Imam Khomeini*, translated by Hamid Algar (Berkeley: Mizan, 1981), 28, cited in Horsley, *Religion and Empire*, 60.

channels in South Africa alone—not just by whites, but by Africans and African Americans as the favored faces of imperial religion in the Global South. They have swallowed whole that peculiar Christianized militarism of American "patriot pastors" and emulate "spiritual warfare" wholly based on a peculiar, American, imperial, violent jihadism across the globe. And, in the end, it is all about power and greed. We are not forced, coerced, or blackmailed into this: we are "conniving" as Biko rightly says.[57] We have made the Bible a "poisoned well."

Frederick Douglass's persistent and fine distinction between "the two religions" and by the same token the two different readings of the Bible holds true still:

> I assert most unhesitatingly, that the religion of the south is a mere covering for the most horrid crimes,—a justifier of the most appalling barbarity,—a sanctifier of the most hateful frauds,—and a dark shelter under which the darkest, foulest, grossest, and most infernal deeds of slaveholders find the strongest protection.[58]

Yet it is not the Christian faith or the Bible Douglass rejects. He had enough discernment to understand what Powery and Sadler call "a bastardized version of American religion."

> What I have said respecting and against religion, I mean strictly to apply to the *slave-holding religion* of this land, and with no possible reference to Christianity proper; for, between the Christianity of this land, and the Christianity of Christ, I recognize the widest possible difference . . . I can see no reason, but for the most deceitful one, for calling the religion of this land Christianity.[59]

That is a crucial distinction, and just as valid today as we try to discern the working of empire in its claims upon the Christian faith and the Bible. We can no longer simply regard, and sometimes reject, the Bible as a "Western book," now that we know this and now that we can know and read, and in reading *reclaim*, the Bible as "a history of *faithful* resistance to Empire."[60] As a collection of books, the Bible was written and compiled under continuous imperial rule. Those books reflect the struggle against empire as well as

57. Biko, *I Write What I Like*, 58.
58. See Douglas, *Narrative of the Life of Frederick Douglass*, 77.
59. Douglass, *Narrative of the Life of Frederick Douglass*, 118; Powery and Sadler, *Genesis of Liberation*, 6.
60. See Horsley, *In the Shadow of Empire*.

empire's appropriation of Scripture for its own ends.[61] It seems to me that it is not so much the Bible that is holding us captive and subservient. It is us holding the Bible captive to the evil impulses of the empire, to our own paucity of prophetic courage and to our own abundance of self-pampering self-interest.[62]

Black theology was not prepared for this fundamentalist onslaught, not just on liberation theology but on the Bible's message of liberation as understood by Black liberation theology, turning it into a message of neo-capitalist consumerist enslavement, not seeking liberation for the oppressed masses but pacification through a gospel of consumerism and instant material gratification. Black theology was not well prepared for this disturbing turn of events and seems to have very little defense against the "Walmartization" of the Black church and the message of the Bible,[63] where God is no longer the God of the oppressed but the CEO of a heavenly corporation imitating Wall Street, with rich, earthly rewards as "blessings."

"God is a business man," says Bishop T. D. Jakes. "He is not going to do business with someone who shows no sign of potential return. . ." In the same vein, "No woman wants to be in submission to a man who is not in submission to God." The message is differently tailored, but it is the same form of enslavement.[64] The issue, for Jakes, is clearly not whether women should be subjugated to men at all—that is presented as self-evident truth. The issue is only that she should be submitted to a man who in turn submits to God. How *that* is realized is no concern of women. They simply have to accept it. The sacralized hierarchy is unquestioned.

It is now much better understood that "issues of imperial rule and response to it run deep and wide through most books of the Bible."[65] Biblical texts are not unanimously or unambiguously anti-imperial or pro-imperial. The Bible has been used to justify both imperialism and to inspire struggles against imperial domination. Reading the Bible as a history of faithful struggle against empire will include our understanding of that struggle

---

61. See Horsley, *In the Shadow of Empire*, Introduction and *passim*. See also Crossan, *God and Empire*.

62. What Mosala et al. missed perhaps is the fact that both the faith of ancient Israel and Christianity are the result of the interaction between imperialism and the peoples it subjugated. See Horsley, *Religion and Empire*, 45. Obery Hendricks is clear: "Christianity began as the faith of the oppressed." *Politics of Jesus*, 85.

63. See McGee, *Brand® New Theology*. See also McMickle, *Where Have All the Prophets Gone?*

64. See T. D. Jakes Quotes: https://www.goodreads.co./author/quotes/72902-T_D_Jakes.

65. Horsley, *In the Shadow of Empire*, 7.

within the texts themselves, exposing the struggle between power and powerlessness, privilege and exclusion, centering and marginalization, domination, oppression, and resistance, through it all understanding the meaning of prophetic faithfulness.

The problem, I suggest, in agreement with Biko, is not with the Bible. The problem is very much us. Our own disciplined struggle should be to approach the Bible as sacred Scripture, aware of its appropriation and misuse by the powerful.

DISCERNING AN IMPERIAL WORLD

The imperial world in which we do theology and preach liberation today is a world in great and terrible upheaval. It is not the world created by God. It is a world of the *tohu wa-bohu*, the chaos before the Spirit of God made her creative presence felt; a reminder of a world so flooded by iniquities correctly described as "violence" that God "regretted" the creation of human beings (Gen 6). It is a world recreated and ruled by tyrants and warmongers, plunderers and profiteers, homophobes and misogynists, traffickers of women and the killers of children, enslavers of the defenseless and stealers of human souls. It is a world where might is right, where mendacity is hailed as deft political footwork, incivility as boldness, loudmouthed arrogance as forceful leadership, aggressive, predatory patriarchy as entitlement; where stupendous stupidity and the politics of deceit and fear are the normalized path to power.

In a world such as this, Walter Brueggemann reminds us, "the task of prophetic ministry [and theology] is to nurture, nourish, and evoke a consciousness and perception of the dominant culture around us," and then to work towards *dismantling* that dominant culture.[66] It is to join God in God's work of reconciling *that* world unto Godself in Jesus Christ, and by embracing God's call to us to become ambassadors of reconciliation—reconciliation that is real, radical, and revolutionary, and dedicated to the fundamental transformation of that world into a world of radical justice, radical inclusivity, radical equality—in other words, a world of peace, love, and joy.[67] Black liberation theology has not completely engaged in this work of disruption, resistance, dismantling, and reconciling as prophetic work *against empire*.

---

66. See Brueggemann, *Prophetic Imagination*, 3.
67. See Boesak and DeYoung, *Radical Reconciliation*.

In Africa we have seen the beginnings of this realization in the work of Musa Dube, for example.[68] It continued, in more concentrated fashion, in a project in a partnership between the Uniting Reformed Church in Southern Africa and the Evangelical Reformed Church in Germany ("The Globalisation Project"), intended to help the church to respond to our globalized imperial reality and the impact of empire on the people of our world, especially in the Global South.[69] In summarizing that argument: we defined our world of imperial domination as a calculated coalescing of global forces pooling their economic, political, military, and cultural resources together in unprecedented and frightening ways.[70]

They are, as the Bible describes them, powers and principalities, representing crushing realities of domination, oppression, and control. They are murderous powers, but not by accident—euphemisms such as "collateral damage," "humanitarian intervention," or "enhanced interrogation" are the arrogantly transparent veils with which they seek to mask their calculated homicidal, ecocidal, and cosmocidal intent. For this reason, we call these powers "lordless," not meaning an egalitarianism with no "lords" or "underlings," for that is precisely what they create and maintain, and they demand absolute submission. But these lords are not the Lord Jesus Christ. Indeed, they set themselves up as God in the place of God, and therein lies the idolatry the prophetic church has identified.

But we should remember that the empire we face is the work of human hands and minds—it is not divinely sanctioned, God-given or historically determined, nor irreversible, unchangeable or unchallengeable as it purports. Its claims of benevolence mask the persistent violence—ideological, systemic, psychological, structural, and physical—inherent in that imperial reach and the destruction it wreaks upon whole communities for the sake of

---

68. See the wonderful way she tells the story of "Mama Africa" and her "fifty years of bleeding" in which she describes the stages Africa had to go through, from colonization to the struggle for independence, independence itself, followed by neo-colonialism and globalism. See Dube, "Fifty Years of Bleeding," 50–60. The story ends on a note of hopeful defiance: "Mama Africa is standing up. She is not talking. She is not asking. She is not offering any more money—for none is left. Mama Africa is coming behind Jesus. She is pushing through a strong human barricade. *Weak and still bleeding but determined, she is stretching out her hand. If only she can touch the garments of Jesus Christ*" (59–60), emphasis original.

69. See A. Boesak, "Theological Reflections on Empire," and other essays in Boesak and Hansen, *Globalisation*, 59–72. The project produced two volumes of research material and a final report, Boesak, Weusmann, and Amjad-Ali, eds. *Dreaming a Different World, Globalisation and Justice for Humanity and the Earth, The Challenge of the Accra Confession for the Churches.*

70. For a full discussion of this matter, see A. Boesak, *Dare We Speak of Hope?*, 55–56.

profits for the few. There is nothing God-like about it. We are called instead to discern, challenge, and dismantle the idolatrous, blasphemous nature of empire.

We called empire an "all-encompassing reality"; it lays claim upon every facet of life. It serves, protects, and relentlessly defends the interests of the powerful: corporations, nations, national elites, privileged groups—the beneficiaries of empire, to the detriment of those who are its perpetual prey. The imperial arrogance we are speaking of is not simply a misguided attitude, stumbled upon by some inexplicable turn of history. It is a deliberate, continuous act of violent intent.

Empire manifests itself everywhere, presents itself as the right, necessary, and natural way to think, be, and exist. To think, exist, and act differently would be unnatural, an aberration. So in the logic of empire, which captures and colonizes our logic and our imagination, it is justice, freedom and dignity that become the ultimate myths, the unattainable reach, the unsustainable and foolish hope, so easily crushed by the ruthlessness of imperial *Realpolitik*.

Empires cannot survive without myths: the myth of exceptionalism; the myth of benevolent domination, of mutual beneficiation as long as the hierarchical structures—racial, social, gender, economic—remain intact; and the myth of redemptive violence, absolutely necessary for social and political control. Closely related to that is the myth of invincibility and irreversibility—Margaret Thatcher's famous "There Is No Alternative!" comes to mind—which by itself produces the myth of the futility of resistance. Fundamental to all these are the myths of religious sanction without which none of the above is possible to sustain because they provide moral justification and ideological control. So central was this role in the Roman Empire that John Dominic Crossan deliberately speaks not of "emperor worship" nor of the "emperor cult" but of "Roman imperial theology," because it was the "ideological glue that held Roman civilization together."[71] Unlike the God of liberation, the empire cannot hear the cry of the oppressed, it refuses to see the destruction its own rapaciousness and violence are causing, and it cannot respond with compassion and justice. It is a world the same Gollwitzer we have quoted earlier, speaking of his times in Nazi Germany, described as "shaken by deadly convulsions."[72] It was indeed a world intentionally prepared for those who are empire's constant prey.

---

71. Crossan, "Roman Imperial Theology," 59.
72. Gollwitzer, *Way to Life*, xii.

A HOLY RAGE

To do theology and preach liberation today means engaging—with discernment, judgement, and action—the forces of empire and the havoc it is wreaking upon the earth and God's people across the globe. In South Africa, in 1984, just as we entered the last phases of our struggle, I quoted Danish pastor and resister against the Nazis, Kaj Munk, who, in the darkest hour of his day, understood exactly what the prophetic church needed:

> What is therefore our task today? Shall I answer: "Faith, hope, and love?" That sounds beautiful. But I would say courage. No, even that is not challenging enough to be the whole truth. Our task today is recklessness. For what we Christians lack is not psychology or literature... we lack a holy rage—the recklessness which comes from the knowledge of God and humanity.[73]

What I wrote then for South Africa is, I think, as applicable to our imperial reality today. What we need is this holy rage: the ability to rage when justice lies prostrate on the streets, and when with every tweet the lie rages across the face of the earth; a holy anger about the things that are wrong in this world. To rage at the blasphemy when a US president places his hand on the Bible to claim authority for whatever he deems necessary for the preservation of American exceptionalism, supremacism, and domination. To rage at the sight of Barack Obama's hand on Martin Luther King Jr.'s Bible while Commander-in-Chief of the country who, in Martin King's own words, "is the greatest purveyor of violence in the world today." To rage when Donald Trump, his Bible still warm from the imprint of his hand, orders (on the same day!) an attack against defenseless Yemen, leaving at least 25 civilians dead, nine of them children, the oldest 12 years, the youngest three months old.[74] Prophetic preaching in the tradition of the Black church in this world today must mean a holy rage against all injustice, every murderous intent, every false claim on God's name. It means knowing the names of the innocents we obliterate from 10,000 miles away, in acts of terror in a war against terror we continue to create.

We need a holy rage every time a South African politician, from Thabo Mbeki to Trevor Manuel, from Cyril Ramaphosa to Jacob Zuma, uses the Bible to justify unjust and oppressive policies, their abuse of power, and

---

73. See A. Boesak, *If This Is Treason*, 54.

74. Villagers reported the victims as three-month-old Asma Fahad Ali al Ameri, Aisha Mohammed Abdallah al Ameri, 4; Halima Hussein al Aifa al Ameri, Hussein Mohammend Abdallah Mabkoudt al Ameri, both 5; Mursil Abedraboh Masad al Ameri, 6; Khajija Abdallah Mabkout al Ameri, 7; Nawar Anwar al Awlaqi, 8; Ahmed Abdelilah Ahmed al Dahab, 11; Nasser Abdallah Ahmed al Dahab, 12. See Moore, "Full Details."

their abuse of and disdain for the people's faith, as South African Hebrew Bible scholar Gerald West shows in his most recent study with the very apt title *The Stolen Bible*.[75] To rage at all political kleptocracy because we know it is not only money and resources, but the very future of our children and the hope of our people they are stealing.

We need a holy rage against what seems to have become a uniquely South African phenomenon, called "corrective rape." This occurs when gangs of young men, in many cases Christian young men, driven by the distorted teachings from the Bible in the myriad fundamentalist churches across the country, target, hunt down, and rape young lesbians, in the belief that being raped by a "real man" will "cure" them of their "disease." So in their view this is not a despicable crime, it is "corrective" action. All in the name of a terrifyingly homophobic Jesus. I am not being cynical when I say that this horror is the not-so-surprising outcome of that innocent-sounding but nonetheless perverted doctrine they call "hating the sin but loving the sinner."

The urgent task of Black liberation theology is to have the courage to make that crucial distinction we have learned from Frederick Douglass, between the religion of the empire and the religion of Jesus of Nazareth. And like him, we must be willing to make the choice: we cannot serve God and Mammon; we cannot worship at the altar of justice and peace and at the altar of empire; we cannot preach Jesus and practice baptized bigotry. Loving the one we must hate the other, embracing the one, we must reject the other. Bringing that clarity to our preaching and teaching, our reflection, and our action is what is needed.

We must let those "powerless voices of the Bible," as Dwight Hopkins calls them, and the voices of the oppressed and powerless speak to us, rather than be beguiled by the threats or seductions of the empire. We must not only break the silence. We must turn away from the poisoned well, and turn instead to the One who offers the waters of life, and speak a different language. Our language must be a prophetic, liberating, transformative, healing, inclusive language, the counter language to the language of distortion and perversion, of hate and violence, discrimination and demonization; of subjugation and domination, of exclusion and extremism. It must be a language counter to the imperial language of pre-determined mendacity, preemptive legitimation and ex post facto justification.

Let me turn again to Danish pastor Kaj Munk, who, like Bonhoeffer in Germany, was prominent in the resistance against Hitler on the streets

---

75. See West, *Stolen Bible*.

as well as in the pulpit. Speaking of the testimony of the church and its prophetic testimony in his own dangerous times, Munk said:

> When fire and murder are unleashed upon the people of the earth, it is our task to denounce in the name of the God of love, everything which we know to be the work of the devil. When the deck is loaded, when cowardice heaps praises upon that which before was recognized as despicable, then it is the task of the church to realize that the signs of the church have always been the dove, the lamb, the lion and the fish, but never the chameleon.[76]

Remembering this, I believe, is the promise and presence of prophetic faithfulness in Black liberation theology, in preaching, teaching, and living.

---

76. Quoted in Boesak, *If This is Treason*, 47.

Chapter Two

THE BIRTHING STOOL, THE BURNING BUSH, AND THE THRONE OF PHARAOH

Black Theology, the Women of Exodus, and the Righteousness of Resistance

THE WOMEN OF EXODUS

IN THIS CHAPTER WE are narrowing our focus to a specific issue that needs more detailed discussion. Let us begin with perhaps an altogether trite observation. As a theology of liberation, nothing is more central to Black theology than the exodus story and the story of Jesus of Nazareth. These two biblical realities anchor liberation theology as nothing else. But it begins with the exodus with its powerful message of slavery, liberation from bondage, the contestation between the gods of Egypt and the God of Israel; the devastating power of the pharaoh, the liberating power of Yahweh, and the resilient power of the resistance of the suffering, hopeful people. Every expression of Black theology testifies to this.[1] African-American historian Albert Raboteau was not wrong when he wrote,

---

1. This has been so since the earliest forms of Black theology in the prophetic preaching of enslaved African preachers. See Wilmore, *Black Religion and Black Radicalism*, and Howard Divinity School's professor of preaching Kenyatta R. Gilbert's most recent book of sermons on justice and hope (2018) titled, *Exodus Preaching: Crafting*

[s]laves prayed for the future day of deliverance to come, and they kept hope alive by incorporating as part of *their* mythic past the Old Testament exodus of Israel out of slavery. The appropriation of the Exodus story was for the slaves a way of articulating their sense of historical identity as a people. That identity was also based, of course, upon their common heritage of enslavement. The Christian slaves applied the Exodus story, whose end they knew, to their own experience of slavery, which had not ended. In identifying with the Exodus story, they created meaning out of the chaotic and senseless experience of slavery. Exodus functioned as an archetypical event for the slaves.[2]

Clinging to the exodus story was as essential for survival as it was for resistance. However, the exodus paradigm has been seriously challenged. Black theology, having more or less taken this paradigm for granted, has not responded very adequately to the targeted and justified critique of Native Americans, Palestinians, and Africans who raised serious questions about our understanding and use of the exodus story in the Bible and its consequences for invaded, conquered, colonized, and decimated peoples. But the exodus is a foundational paradigm, not a fundamentalist doctrine.

Even if, for most African Americans, the "Promised Land" was not to be taken literally, but more in the sense of Martin Luther King Jr.'s "Promised Land of racial justice," rooted in the "American dream," that too was being seriously critiqued. Black theologian Charles Shelby Rooks was one of the first in the post-King era to question the exodus/promised land paradigm as not altogether workable for African Americans. It was, he argued, "difficult to apply":

> The biblical image which had been at the heart of the Black man's [sic] faith in the eventual appropriation of the American myth must be replaced because it is no longer believable—the idea that America is the Promised Land is compromised almost beyond repair. Injustice, war, ecological devastation, runaway technology, etc., have served to tarnish the dream, perhaps forever.[3]

Rooks was not wrong. But African Americans' close identification of the "promised land" with the "American dream" would perhaps make

---

Sermons About Justice and Hope. See also Callahan's informative chapter 5 in *The Talking Book*.

2. See Albert J. Raboteau's classic text, *Slave Religion*, 311, quoted by Powery and Sadler, *Genesis of Liberation*, 9.

3. Rooks, "Towards the Promised Land," 8.

The Birthing Stool, the Burning Bush, and the Throne of Pharaoh   33

that a perennial problem. However, that is a different approach from that of colonized and occupied peoples who wrestle with the exodus as liberation paradigm. For them, that "Promised Land" never was a mere metaphor, but had become a genocidal, soul-destroying reality. And that is more the issue we are engaging here.

Accordingly, Native American scholar Robert Warrior has taken Black theology to task, and he seems to speak for all colonized peoples in his critical reflections on this issue. The exodus story, he writes, is no doubt inspiring: "The Exodus with its picture of a god who takes the side of the oppressed and powerless, has been a beacon of hope for many in despair."[4] But the dream of freedom is not complete when the Red Sea is crossed. The liberated oppressed "seek a place of safety, away from their oppressors," a promised land, in other words. In the exodus story, "Yahweh the deliverer becomes Yahweh the conqueror." Native Americans [Africans, Palestinians, and indigenes everywhere invaded by Christian colonizers], by the same token, become the Canaanites, their land the promised land. They are the ones who literally are the victims of "Yahweh's command to mercilessly annihilate." However one interprets the exodus story, in his view, "historical knowledge does not change the status of the indigenes in the narrative and the theology that grows out of it."[5] This constitutes the most serious critique of the exodus paradigm I think. Black theology has had no adequate response to this because there just isn't one.

This goes beyond the argument whether the "Promised Land" ought to be regarded as a physical, geographical space, despite the raging debates in African-American circles since the days of Martin R. Delany, Marcus Garvey, and Henry McNeal Turner. Martin Luther King Jr. had argued persistently that for African Americans the "Promised Land" is "the promised land of racial justice." Whether that "Promised Land," as we have seen Shelby Rooks argue, can actually be realized in America has in turn become a matter of serious dispute, theologically and politically, and quite rightly so. The question I am raising here, though, is about the exodus as foundational paradigm for Black liberation theology.

Womanist theologian Cheryl A. Kirk-Duggan has responded directly to Warrior's critical remarks.[6] What about the plight of the Egyptians who

---

4. See Warrior, "Canaanites, Cowboys, and Indians," 261–65. This critique was closely followed by Naim Ateek's rejection of the exodus paradigm in his *Justice, and Only Justice*, raising the same questions with regard to Palestinians and the occupation and theft of the land by the State of Israel since 1948, using the same biblical justification of exodus and conquest.

5. Warrior, "Canaanites, Cowboys, and Indians," 261–62.

6. Kirk-Duggan, "How Liberating Is the Exodus." The first to do so to my knowledge, Kirk-Duggan engages Warrior directly on this matter.

were subject to Pharaoh? she asks. What about the violence that does not spare the firstborn children of the Egyptians, an issue raised quite sharply by Jacqueline Lapsley.[7] She points to an "oft-overlooked facet" of the exodus liberation story which she finds in 3:21. The verse relates how "each woman shall ask her neighbor and every sojourner living in the neighbor's house for jewelry of silver or gold, and clothing" so that the liberated slaves should not leave Egypt empty-handed. Not only is this something that specifically women are to do, the assumption is that the women of Egypt, out of compassion, or perhaps out of solidarity in being just as much oppressed as the enslaved women of the Hebrews, are complicit in the "plundering of Egypt." Lapsley concludes, rightly I think, "the boundaries of ethnicity and class are again breached in the service of liberation."[8] But despite the fact that this was Yahweh's plan, Yahweh nonetheless kills the firstborn of these same women. This is an insoluble situation and the contradictions cannot be explained away. But this is the impossible paradox a violent, capricious, God presents us with. An exodus story that begins like this cannot but end up as a tale of conquest, wanton destruction, and genocide.

Finally, Kirk-Duggan asks, "Who is the God of the Exodus?"[9] and this last question is precisely the question I consider most unavoidable, and propose to engage in the chapters that follow, since it is at the heart of the question about the quality and integrity of the liberation Black theology proclaims. In terms of that integrity we should consider ourselves seriously challenged by the women. Kirk-Duggan is right when she discerns right from the start that the exodus does tell of liberation but "it is framed as a patriarchal, genealogical narrative."[10] She quotes Cheryl Townsend Gilkes with approval, "if it wasn't for the women Moses would not have made it."[11] "Women, who are normally powerless in this culture, ultimately salvage Moses' life, and help to stymie Pharaoh's power."[12] I will argue that these observations, critical as they are, still focus essentially on Moses as the central figure. These women were "stifling Pharaoh's power" on their own, long before they were replaced by Moses. But Kirk-Duggan is right as she cautions us "to keep the Exodus from becoming a narrative of conquest."[13]

---

7. Lapsley, *Whispering the Word*, 83–84.

8. Lapsley, *Whispering the Word*, 84.

9. Kirk-Duggan continues to raise this question within another context, see "Divine Puppeteer: Yahweh of Exodus" in Brenner, *A Feminist Companion*, 75–102.

10. Kirk-Duggan, "How Liberating is the Exodus," 6.

11. Kirk-Duggan, "How Liberating is the Exodus," 6.

12. Kirk-Duggan, "How Liberating is the Exodus," 8.

13. Kirk-Duggan, "How Liberating is the Exodus," 17.

The Birthing Stool, the Burning Bush, and the Throne of Pharaoh   35

Dolores Williams as well warns of the necessity of telling "the entire" exodus story, "which involves reparations from the Egyptians, God's acts of violence against the Egyptians, genocide against the Canaanites, and the theft of Canaanite land." Williams chooses the wilderness experience because it is more inclusive—and in her powerful reading has the slave woman Hagar as the center of the narrative—"and indicates leadership roles of Black mothers and women."[14]

But I will argue that what Williams discovers in the wilderness, in terms of the leadership roles of Black mothers and women, is true from the start, from the birthing chamber and the resistance of the midwives, to the house of Jochebed, to the riverbank and the seashore, and especially in the wilderness where Miriam is central. I will also argue that in order to keep the exodus narrative from becoming a narrative of conquest and annihilation, Black theology must rethink this paradigm. We must discover the exodus narrative as a story of women's revolutionary agency, rather than a narrative of patriarchal dominance. We must, in other words, return the story to Miriam, rather than cling to it as a story with Moses in the center.[15] *How* to do that becomes the question we have to grapple with.

It is doubtless true that Black theology, my own included, has without question or self-critique accepted, embraced, and retold the male-centered exodus as *the* paradigmatic reference. Moses and the burning bush, the fiery inspiration of Yahweh's words to Moses, "I have seen the misery of my people, I have heard their cry. . . . I know their sufferings, and I have come down to rescue them . . ." (Exod 3:7–8); these are the lifeblood of Black theology. Moses before the throne of Pharaoh demanding, "Let my people go!" sounds as clear as a bell throughout the history of black struggles for liberation. From song to slogan to sermon—it is at the core of our belief and our yearning for freedom. And at the heart of it all is the towering figure of Moses. And that has been the problem all along.

To be sure, we did listen to the women when they told us that our sexism excluded them, and was an inadequate partner, no, an *obstacle* in their struggle for equality in the church and society.[16] James Cone wrote then,

> Among professional theologians and preachers as well as seminary and university students, few black men seem to care about

14. See Williams, *Sisters in the Wilderness*, 147–52; 160–61.

15. Once one begins to notice, it is remarkable at how many levels the exodus story has been turned into an exclusive and overwhelmingly masculine story. See, for an excellent analysis, Rashkow, "Oedipus Wrecks," 59–74.

16. See Wilmore and Cone, *Black Theology*, Part V, 363–442, where womanist theologians like Jackie Grant are prominent. Volume Two devotes even more space to womanist theology.

the pain our Black sisters claim that we inflict on them with our sexist behavior. If we expect to be taken seriously about our claim to love them, must not our love express itself in our capacity to hear their cry of pain and to experience with them their mental and physical suffering?"[17]

Reading this some forty years later Jim Cone would probably have been the first to admit that this is far too little, perhaps even evasive of the real issues. Are the pain and suffering of women really only a "claim"? And is the call to males only to "hear" their cry? And is "our love" all women need in their seemingly unending struggles for equality, justice, freedom, and dignity? Clearly not. Women today will also be insistent that we speak not only of their suffering but also of their empowerment and agency, not only of our compassion but also of their rights. I am speaking with the hindsight of forty years of course, and women have taught us much in these years. So it behooves us to reflect on this point with a sense of deep humility.

But even if we may find Cone's words inadequate today he *was* the first among Black theologians to even acknowledge the problem. It took the rest of us some time to catch up, and most of us are still not there. Cone raised the question, "If Black women's liberation is a serious issue in the society at large, what then is the role of the Black church in this struggle?" That is indeed the question. "Because the Black church has a long history of struggle against racism," Cone continues, "it should be the vanguard of the struggle against Black women's oppression."[18] It should be, but as we have discovered in the struggles of LGBTQI+ communities for example, the Black church, despite its "struggle credentials" on the racial justice issue, is not a partner, let alone the "vanguard" in other struggles for liberation. It is, rather, a bastion of patriarchal hostility and exclusivity. Women, Black Christian women, and Black queer persons must find sanctuary, support and empowerment elsewhere, where their dignity and agency will not constantly be under siege.

That struggle is the struggle men must join, with all women, under their leadership and not just on their behalf. It is a struggle for full equality and against specious dogmas in church and theology about the "headship" of men, designed for the submission of women. It is a struggle for justice and against the blatant or subtle macro- and micro aggressions males seem either to revel in or tolerate too easily. It is for the freedom of women in decision-making and the freedom over their bodies and their health. Even though some victories have been won in the past, these victories are being

---

17. Wilmore and Cone, *Black Theology*, Part V, 365.
18. Wilmore and Cone, *Black Theology*, Part V, 365.

rolled back or stifled in language and public discourse, in politics and policies, in church, society, in the courts of law, and in theology, with an aggression that does not so much smack of "backlash" as indeed of revenge and a dark determination to regain control.

It is reflected in Black preaching. Katie Cannon writes, and this seems universally true,

> A critical study of Black sermons shows that African American church traditions and redactional processes follow certain androcentric interests and perspectives that do not reflect the historical contributions of African American women's leadership and participation in the life of the church.[19]

But even more to the point:

> What happens to female children when Black preachers use the Bible to attribute marvellous happenings and unusual circumstances to an all-male cast of characters? The privilege, power, and prerogative in developing such sermons are in themselves significant. The marginalization of women from the cast of characters constitutes a significant choice within these larger patterns of decision.[20]

As imperial greed for dominion and lust for blood rage across the earth, and the people's revolutions are captured by imperial forces and their minions in desperate and vicious counter-revolutions to keep or regain control over people and resources, or to turn back the gains the people have made with their sacrifices, one of the persistent features of these inhumanities is the way in which women's bodies have become occupied territory. From the Cape to the Congo to the killing fields of Yemen, Somalia, Syria, and Iraq; from Cairo's tyranny restored to Palestine's conquest and occupation reenacted; from Nigeria and the Central African Republic to India and the far-off regions of Pakistan and Afghanistan, to Saudi-Arabia despite its holy places and Jerusalem despite its holy temple. From the unsafe borders of Christian-Nationalist Europe to the delusive sanctuaries of civilized Europe. From the violent streets of New York to the glittering studios of Hollywood to the campuses of elite colleges, and from the beauty competition stages of Latin America to the desecrated Native American lands—it is the women, next to the children, who are not just the perpetual victims, but the deliberate targets.

---

19. Cannon, *Katie's Canon*, 114.

20. Cannon, *Katie's Canon*, 120. Notice Cannon's choice of words here though: nothing is accidental; these are larger *patterns* of *decision*.

Unless Black theology responds much more vigorously to these realities, we are still not hearing or understanding the women, nor heeding Jim Cone, and we remain on the wrong, dark side of history, despite our struggle credentials. We have attempted to respond to the women with regard to our individualized sexism, but we have not found an adequate remedy for our systemic, structurally entrenched patriarchy.

But our belated conversion on this point still did not mean that we have taken women seriously in our engagement with the bedrock of our theology, namely liberation and the exodus paradigm. Our continued uncritical embrace of the patriarchal version of the exodus is a sign not of liberation but of enslavement to what one would call an Egypt mindset, a serious question mark hanging over our reading and interpretation of the Bible, and the character and integrity of our liberation.[21] It is also a major reason why Black liberation theology has offered such feeble resistance to the patriarchal fundamentalist religion now flooding our churches and countries.

Taking the women seriously means recognizing the legitimacy of the firm assertion by J. Cheryl Exum that the exodus story begins and ends with the women.

> Like the beginning, the ending of the Exodus story belongs to the women. They are the *alpha* and *omega*, the *aleph* and *taw* of deliverance.[22]

This is a statement with significant consequences for Black liberation theology and one we will have to engage as seriously if we are concerned with the character of liberation. Like bookends, women open and close Exodus 1–15 "as major players."[23] What Dolores Williams did with the story of Hagar, J. Cheryl Exum, Phyllis Trible, Cheryl Kirk-Duggan, and others[24] did with the

---

21. This despite the sterling work of Dolores Williams, who has given us a totally new perspective on the meaning of the wilderness and how Hagar the slave woman becomes a person of revelatory significance in those foundational stories from the book of Genesis. See Williams, *Sisters in the Wilderness*.

22. See Exum, "You Shall Let Every Daughter Live," 37–61. Also Nechama Rubenstein in "The Untold Story of the Hebrew Midwives and the Exodus": "The redemption of the Jewish nation from the bondage of Egypt, and indeed the bondage of exile throughout time, is a direct result of the actions of the Jewish women of their time."

23. Cone has remained persistent in this matter. See his "vision of the future," in Cone, *For My People*, 203–4, where he writes, "The vision of the new social order must be non-sexist . . . There can be no compromise on the idea that justice means true equality of all, with mutual sharing of responsibility in all areas of the decision-making process. A truly liberated social order cannot have men dominating women."

24. See Brenner, *A Feminist Companion*. As we develop our argument throughout this work, our engagement with these authors continues.

women of Exodus. It is a challenge that male black theologians have largely left unanswered.

The critical work of Donna Nolan Fewell and David M. Gunn offers a succinct summary of the essence of the argument we would want to engage here.[25] We should perhaps start there.

The women emerge against the backdrop as "vague cardboard collections" of a kind of simplicity that "coaxes the reader to read over the ethical and theological ambiguities that arise when one tries to imagine real people in these roles." Even so, the women do emerge "as some of the few independent personalities in the story of the exodus and wandering."[26] But despite this,

> As characters, they are perhaps no match for Moses. They are hardly singled out by God personally for confrontation and leadership. For them there is no burning bush, there are no signs and wonders. They are not called upon to leave their mundane lives and do something extraordinary. God gives them no instructions, offers them no assurances. Yet they, like their predecessors in Genesis, are unknowing but indispensable caretakers of God's promise.[27]

"Through their 'mothering', the role so firmly assigned to women in Genesis 3, they continue to salvage the promise long after the seed has been multiplied. . . It is their mothering that distinguishes these women as characters and makes way for the nation's leadership. Without them, there would have been no Moses."[28]

In the exodus story, writes feminist Bible scholar Drorah O'Donnel Setel, the women "are of interest only in their relationship to the male protagonist."[29] But, it seems to me, all this might be an unnecessarily easy bow to patriarchal, imperialist readings of the story, which these analyses are vowed to resist. The women are doing much more than preparing the (listener) reader for the coming of the "true" liberator. Here I shall argue that far from being mere conduits for Moses, the women are at the very heart of the liberation of ancient Israel from slavery. They represent the first testimony of faithful resistance to empire the Bible offers us. In order to grasp the great import of what is happening here, we need to understand what the women were up against.

25. See Fewell and Gunn, *Gender, Power and Promise*, 90ff.
26. Fewell and Gunn, *Gender, Power and Promise*, 90, 91.
27. Fewell and Gunn, *Gender, Power and Promise*, 91.
28. Fewell and Gunn, *Gender, Power and Promise*, 91.
29. Newsom and Ringe, *Women's Bible Commentary*, 34.

It was the king of Egypt, John Calvin observes, whose "perverse strivings" drove the pharaoh and his people to a "blind impetuosity"; their "folly" and "obstinate lust" hurrying them forwards so that they "compound their opposition to God." The twice repeated "inhumanity" of the treatment of the slaves, what Calvin calls "this dreadful barbarity," is now more than mere power. It is power driven mad by fear.[30]

If the exodus is the *locus originalis* for liberation theology and paradigmatic for our resistance against empire, then it is not Moses who is the first prophet of liberation as Black theology has held all along, but rather the women: the midwives, Moses's mother, whom tradition identifies as Jochebed, and Miriam his sister. It is they, rather than Moses, who represent the powerlessness of Israel against the brutal power of empire. It is they who encapsulate the meaning of "the power of the powerless," and it is they who provide the impetus for the songs of liberation in the Bible: the song of Miriam, the song of Hannah, and the Magnificat of Mary; and as a subsequence the sorrow songs and freedom songs of black liberation struggles across the centuries. Then the exodus and the story of liberation have their focus not on the burning bush and the throne of Pharaoh but on the birthing stool, the riverbank, and the seashore.

J. Cheryl Exum was one of the first to pay detailed attention to the story from a feminist theological point of view in her "You Shall Let Every Daughter Live" from 1983. But her slight dissatisfaction with the way she had treated it in her first attempt required her to revisit Exodus and the women in "Second Thoughts about Secondary Characters."[31] In her "You Shall Let Every Daughter Live," Exum has done important and impressive work on the women in Exodus 1 and 2. Her approach then was that of "a close reading of the text or rhetorical criticism, which investigates the narrative in its present form on the premise that an understanding of its literary contours will aid us in perceiving its meaning."[32] Such an approach she found useful, for "The women in Exodus 1 and 2 are portrayed positively . . . they are active and enterprising, and their actions are important for the future of the Israelite people." The text offers much that is a "striking affirmation of the role of women in the opening chapters of Exodus."[33]

---

30. John Calvin, *Commentaries*, Exod 1:13.

31. Both these articles appear as separate chapters in Athalya Brenner (ed.), *A Feminist Companion to Exodus to Deuteronomy*, 37–61 and 75–87 respectively.

32. Exum, "Second Thoughts About Secondary Characters," 77.

33. Exum, "Second Thoughts About Secondary Characters," 77.

The Birthing Stool, the Burning Bush, and the Throne of Pharaoh

Now, however, in "Second Thoughts" she considers the fact that that very same approach places "logocentric constraints on feminist criticism."[34] One now has to see how the positive portrayal of women in Exodus 1 and 2 nevertheless serves male interests. "What androcentric interests does this positive presentation of the role of women serve here?"[35] (E.g., God behind the scenes using the weak and lowly to overcome the strong and powerful; the inferior but clever women successfully defy the powerful pharaoh.) The point is made through the portrayal of the "exceedingly foolish" pharaoh, "so foolish that even women can outwit him!"[36] In the story's intense focusing on infants, the women affirm traditional roles, that of mothering and nurturing for instance, which appeals to women's subordinate position, as does the fact that their acts are confined to the domestic, and not the public sphere where patriarchal power remains unchallenged.[37]

RESISTANCE TO TYRANNY

While respectfully keeping these observations in mind, I am not sure this is the full picture that emerges from the story. The tyranny of the pharaoh we meet in Exodus 1, and the challenges this poses for the midwives, leave no room for misunderstanding. The Egyptian taskmasters aimed to "bend," "to wear out anyone's strength," "to break them down physically," to "crush" the Israelite slaves. Their goal was not only physical. It was also to "crush their spirit so as to banish the very wish for liberty," so confirm German scholars Keil and Delitzsch.[38] "This Pharaoh," writes Benno Jacob, "suggested three means of oppression: the first was forced labour, the second infanticide, [and] . . . the third was mass infanticide." This despotism, as all despotism, "knows only two paths—enslavement and murder."[39]

Shifrah and Puah, the Hebrew midwives, defy the command of Pharaoh to kill the baby boys even as the Israelite women are on the birthing stool. They become the symbol of resistance, standing in for the whole people of Israel. It is not just the people under imperial rule who cannot stand tyranny, however, John Calvin writes, reflecting not only the political situation in his own time, but building a framework for resistance against such conditions generally. Human intolerance of tyranny becomes divine

---

34. Exum, "Second Thoughts About Secondary Characters," 78.
35. Exum, "Second Thoughts About Secondary Characters," 78.
36. Exum, "Second Thoughts About Secondary Characters," 79.
37. Exum, "Second Thoughts About Secondary Characters," 80.
38. Keil and Delitzsch, *Biblical Commentary on the Old Testament*, Vol. 1, 422.
39. See Jacob, *Second Book*, 22.

intolerance. God "cannot endure tyrants and [God] listens in empathy to the secret groans of those who live under them."[40]

Elsewhere Calvin will radicalize this thought considerably. Not only does he tell us that the longing for freedom and justice is "implanted in us" by God, and not only that the cries against oppression are heard *by* God, but "it is as if God hears [God]self in the cries of the oppressed."[41] Now the cries against oppression are no longer "secret groans"—the oppressed "cry out." And God no longer just "listens in empathy." God *becomes* the poor and oppressed and their cry "How long?" becomes God's cry. Their impatience with tyranny becomes God's impatience. Their struggles are now God's struggles.

In a sentence that underscores the endurance and revolutionary patience that ancient Israel will come to need so much in the wilderness as this story unfolds, Calvin writes that resistance to oppression does indeed bring risks and unforeseen changes, but "only a degraded people could prefer the yoke of tyranny to the inconveniences of change."[42] Calvin's judgment on those who for some reason or another are afraid to resist tyranny is quite harsh. "There is no doubt that God has struck with a spirit of cowardice those who, like asses, willingly offer their shoulders for burdens."[43] Since tyrants do not "rest their injuries until the wretched people have altogether given up," resistance is inevitable and Calvin finds inspiration for such resistance in the example of the Hebrew midwives who stood up against the pharaoh.[44] All this is in stark relief as we read the story of Shifrah and Puah.

Drawing lessons from the pharaoh's ever harsher oppression of the people of Israel, Calvin makes sure that there is no misunderstanding about the intentions of oppressors. First, he teaches us, tyrants want the people to become inured to their own oppression, to meekly accept that there is no alternative to slavery. Tyranny invariably loses "all regard for justice." There are "no bounds" to its harshness because it knows "that this is the best recipe for governing them, so to oppress them that they dare not open their mouths . . . till they grow hardened, and, as it were, callous to their own bondage."[45] "The best ally of the oppressor," writes South Africa's Steve Biko

---

40. Calvin, *Commentaries*, Isa 14:7–8.

41. Calvin, *Commentaries*, Hab 2:11. See for a more detailed discussion of this, Boesak, *Kairos, Crisis, and Global Apartheid*, chapter 2. I repeat these arguments here because they are so crucial in our understanding of the acts of courage and liberation the women perform, and they become essential framework for the way we read this story.

42. Calvin, *Commentaries*, Matt 2:9.

43. Calvin, *Commentaries*, Isa 3:12.

44. Calvin, *Commentaries*, Exod 1.

45. Calvin, *Commentaries*, Exod 5:9.

as if he had read Calvin, "is the mind of the oppressed." But this, Calvin says, is nothing but "tyrannical insolence."

Thus tyranny must be resisted because—and this is Calvin's second lesson to oppressed people in resistance against empire and in search of freedom—it serves the purpose of all tyrants, designed "in order that they [the people] may. . . renounce the hope presented to them from on high." In other words, to not just helplessly give up under pressure of the tyrant, but willfully *renounce* all hope for freedom and all faith in God and in God's justice. This is the worst thing oppressed people could do. To renounce hope is not only to be resigned to one's oppression, it is to invite death. Whereas elsewhere for Calvin it is the tyrant who denies God by injustice and oppression, here it is the people who deny God by renouncing all hope in God's liberating power. Renouncing all hope in God is the same as depriving God of God's right to do justice in love and freedom.

Calvin goes on. The tyrant will not stop until he has "destroyed in them all recollection of God," that is, erased from their memory all the promises of God, and all God's deeds of liberation through which Israel came to know God. It means to erase all recollection of the truth that God is a God who loves and desires justice; that God's own freedom to be a God of shalom and compassionate justice is the guarantee for the freedom of God's people; all remembrance of the life-saving truth that against that love for justice and freedom no tyrant, however mighty and powerful, shall prevail. Within this context we dare not diminish the agency of the women in their resistance to Pharaoh or their place in ancient Israel's, and subsequently our, liberation story. They are no mere "cardboard figures."

In the critical reading of Exum, Fewell, and Gunn above, the role of the women is inextricably linked to "mothering," a patriarchal ploy to make sure the women—and we, the readers—know their place. This is as far as their participation in this drama goes. But it seems to me that the story is not so much about "mothering" as about emphasizing defiance of illegitimate authority and resistance to abusive power.

This is a story of the overturning of patriarchal power in Egypt *and within* Israel. In their defiant actions, the women challenge the pharaoh even as they are challenging the patriarchal framework of their lives. The image conjured up here is not one of passive mothering, cuddling babies to their breast. It is far more an image of the women, against enormous odds and facing the threat of death, standing up and standing their ground, actively blocking the path of the ungodly. The narrative will eventually tip the scales toward Moses, but at this point the women cannot be deprived of the role they have claimed for themselves as empowered and powerful agents of defiance and liberation here at the very origins of Israel's deliverance.

If we read the story as a story of faithful resistance to empire, the emphasis does not fall on "mothering" but on defiance, not on weakness as a typical feminine trait, but on how weakness as result of oppression is overturned and emerges as courageous defiance of an unimaginably powerful enemy. That is how powerlessness, through the agency of the powerless themselves, in the words of Hannah's song "gird on strength." The male deity stays "behind the scenes" and the Israelite patriarchal male is nowhere in sight. God retreats to the shadows, so all the focus is on the women. The patriarchy the midwives are facing is not simply domestic as Exum asserts;[46] it is instead thoroughly imperialistic. The birth of Hebrew babies is no longer a family affair. Slavery, and now the pharaoh's death command, has turned it into a deeply political issue for the empire. In Pharaoh's view, and in his policy, the empire's geopolitical standing, its present stability, and its future prosperity, as well as its historic importance, are at stake here. The implications are not simply domestic. For Egypt, it is thoroughly public and global.

Furthermore, the women do much more than just set the stage for Moses, as is asserted. "God's plan for the future of the children of Israel," writes Terence Fretheim, "rests squarely on the shoulders of one of its helpless sons, a baby in a fragile basket."[47] But is it not more correct to say that, as the story is told and its priorities are set before us, God's plan for the future of the children of Israel rests squarely on the shoulders of these two powerless women in the political pressure cooker the birthing chamber has become? And it is the way in which this powerlessness is turned into acts of power, challenging and finally nullifying the power of the empire, that is the most striking feature of the exodus story. It seems the narrator could not help himself or deny what stands out as undeniable truth: the story of Israel's liberation *does* begin with the women. It is not so much that without them there would have been no Moses. It is that without them there would have been no liberation to begin with. Already here are the Black women leaders Dolores Williams yearns for Black theology to discover, acknowledge, and honor.

GOD IN THE SHADOWS?

It is true that Shifrah and Puah did not experience a special call from God such as Moses did. It is also true that they saw no burning bush, heard no voice, had no engagement with the Divine as Nolan Fewell and Gunn point out. But does that de-legitimize their calling and their place in the

46. Exum, "Second Thoughts About Secondary Characters," 80.
47. Fretheim, *Exodus*, 37.

The Birthing Stool, the Burning Bush, and the Throne of Pharaoh

act of liberation from slavery? "God is not the subject of a single verb in their various undertakings," writes Fretheim.[48] True, but that need not be a disqualification, in my view. Can it not also mean that these women, unlike Moses, required no divine prompting in order to do what needed to be done? That they had that intuitive ingenuity, that critical consciousness for the *kairos* moment, knowing that if they did not seize that moment, it would pass Israel by, and freedom would never come? Can it not mean that, unlike Moses, they did not need God to remind them of what is right, what serves justice, and how the righteous should respond to injustice and oppression? No, their lives were not "mundane" at all; their's were lives filled with the purposes of freedom: obedience to God, resistance to Pharaoh, liberation for their people.

They had no direct encounter with God. Also true. But then there was no need on Yahweh's part to cajole, prod, and push them to hear and understand their calling and the need for liberation. As we will see again in chapter 7, that prodding, pushing, and overcoming of resistance seems to be a predominantly male thing in the Bible. Here it is Moses. In the New Testament on resurrection Sunday, it is the male disciples. Moses clearly needed signs and wonders in order for him to be convinced. No wonder his first instinct before the pharaoh was to resort to signs and wonders. In the first chapters of Exodus, however much it is called the "Book of Moses," it is not the hesitancy of Moses, but the courageous spontaneity of the women, not the reflexive reluctance of Moses, but the intuitive ingenuity of the women, not the apparent disinclination of Moses, but the openness toward defiance and liberation of the women, that prove to be decisive and set the stage, not for Moses, but for God's work of liberation in the life of Israel and in history. Unlike Moses, the midwives come to us with a liberation-minded consciousness. Properly understood: waiting for the miracle of a voice from a burning bush, or boldly redefining freedom in unhesitating judgment on evil and decisive action against evil—which is real, radical, and revolutionary?

Read thus, "the signs and wonders" are not in the first instance signs of God's preference for Moses, and certainly not signs of the "power" of Moses and Aaron before the throne of Pharaoh. They are perhaps more signs of God's tested patience with and exasperated accommodation of Moses (3:14a). If this reading is right, Shifrah and Puah can hardly be described as "being no match for Moses." That may be what the male narrator intended in his retelling of the story, and what the male audience expected, but it is also what the male narrator could not hide, suppress, or ignore. The

---

48. Fretheim, *Exodus*, 37.

Spirit will have her way. That is what a reading against the ways of empire will discover. They are only "no match for Moses" because the patriarchal mindset *requires* the women to be set aside for a male deliverer, chosen, and blessed by God. Looked at from a liberationist point of view (with Moses and his inopportune, violent impetuousness, his misplaced judgment of his own position as well as of the mind-set of the oppressed Hebrews, followed by his unproductive, self-imposed exile in the desert), it is Moses who is no match for the women.

Terence E. Fretheim remarks,

> God uses the weak, what is low in the world, to shame the strong. Rather than using power as it is usually exercised in the world, God works through persons who have no obvious power; indeed, they are unlikely candidates for the exercise of power.[49]

Exum seems ambivalent about this description. But what power do the women unleash upon the pharaoh here! The women are not weak because they are women; they are weak because they are being oppressed, first by the empire as members of a subjugated people, then as women in a patriarchal society, then as women whose role in the liberation story needs to be suppressed, faded, and submerged in order to allow the male deliverer to take center stage. The midwives raise the question, not only about gender and the struggle, but also, and perhaps primarily, about one's readiness for full, intelligent, and courageous participation in the struggle, male or female.

BETWEEN THE LISTING OF THE NAMES OF THE MEN

A small detail like the mentioning of the names of the women helps us to better understand what is happening here. Exodus is also called the "Book of Names." In a book that begins with naming all, and only, the sons of Jacob, the naming of two women is remarkable indeed.

Nechama Rubenstein makes the point that "Between the listing of the names of the sons of Jacob in the first five lines of Shemot, and the naming of Moses in chapter 2 v. 10, the only other people to merit a name at all are the midwives Shifrah and Puah. That leaves 28 lines of anonymity. So, why do the midwives have this honor?"[50]

They have this honor, I would suggest, not because they "facilitated" the birth of Moses, and not because they displayed such excellent "motherly" instincts, but because in the midst of an unnamable oppression they

---

49. Fretheim, *Exodus*, 37.
50. Rubenstein, "Untold Story."

The Birthing Stool, the Burning Bush, and the Throne of Pharaoh

seized the moment to become the primary agents in the act of liberation in their resistance to the might of Pharaoh. By the naming of their names, the ones who usually do not merit naming or recognition, the marginalized ones not counted, are placed in the center of the most foundational story of ancient Israel's life and faith. Naming turns the story inside-out, calls attention to something completely out of the ordinary. Naming the women endows them with the power to influence, shape, and claim the narrative.

This story has no beginning without them. The great deeds of God have no holding center without them. The history of ancient Israel's coming into being makes no sense without them, and not as mothers and nurturers but as resisters to empire and shapers of ancient Israel's destiny. Two women change and end 28 lines of anonymity; they transform history. They are named because the breaking of the chains, the liberation from slavery, the exodus, begin with them. The fact that the midwives are faded out of the story by the close of chapter 1 with its abrupt ending, and that chapter 2 begins with the birth of Moses without reference to the women, marks a return to the "anonymity" of the 28 lines in Exod 1:1—2:8. It is not simply an omission; it is a conquest. This conquest will reassert itself in the "Song of Moses." It will be complete when the military "conquest of Canaan" becomes the dominant narrative.

The women are named, but the pharaoh is not. It is not because he is unimportant or to be dismissed as inconsequential. The consequences of his power are terrifying and the story knows it. It is, rather, because he represents what the oppressed already know: the raw, untamed, arrogant power of empire. He is known by what he does, which is what empires always do: dealing in death and destruction, oppressing the innocent and annihilating the vulnerable. But this is the point I want to make here: to the victims of empire in Exodus, it makes no difference what his name is. He does what every other king of Egypt has done before him and every king after him will. Oppressed peoples have learned at great cost not to fall prey to "new expectations" as a result of power shifts within ruling classes. That is a luxury reserved for the privileged and the pseudo-innocent.

It made no difference to oppressed South Africans whether the name of our tyrant was Hans Strijdom, or Hendrik Verwoerd, John Vorster or P. W. Botha, Andries Treurnicht or F. W. De Klerk. Every single one of them represented the might of apartheid and white hegemony, and the aim, overtly or covertly but always unwaveringly, remained our continued oppression and their uninterrupted domination. And to our shock and deep dismay, so it remained after 1994. It did not matter that we had "freedom," with the African National Congress in power and with Nelson Mandela, Thabo Mbeki, Jacob Zuma, and now Cyril Ramaphosa in the presidential chair—they all turned out to be minions of the empire, not true servants of the people.[51] So long as the framework of domination and subjugation holds, internal tensions or subtle shifts of power among the dominant classes should never be mistaken as beneficial to struggles for freedom.[52]

When the civil rights struggle came to Birmingham, Martin Luther King Jr. recalls, one of the points of discussion was whether it would make a difference to the strategies of the struggle if the "liberal" Albert Boutwell, rather than the rabid segregationist Bull Connor, would be elected mayor of that city. When Boutwell was indeed elected, the white press exclaimed "New Day Dawns for Birmingham." Amidst the celebrations in the white media, Rev. Fred Shuttllesworth kept his mind on the business of the struggle: Boutwell, he stated, "was just a dignified Bull Connor."[53] King concurred: "[Boutwell's] statement that 'we citizens of Birmingham respect and understand one another' showed that he understood nothing about two-fifths of Birmingham's citizens, to whom even polite segregation was no respect."[54]

Likewise for those living in the shadow of empire: it does not change reality whether we are faced with Ronald Reagan or Bill Clinton, George Bush the elder or the younger, Barack Obama, or Donald Trump. It is the *systems* of ongoing oppression they represent that count. The details of their destructive rule may vary. The one may prefer bombs and hit squads, the other bombs and invasions as the realization of a "New World Order"; yet another may prefer bombs and life-crushing sanctions visited upon children. Another may choose bombs, "extraordinary rendition," and torture in fulfillment of a new Christian "crusade." Yet another, besides the bombs, may have his own personal Tuesday morning "kill list" and prefer assassination by drone; and yet another may have glowing praise for the "beautiful chocolate cake" he was eating while bombing Syria, or announce his "great" next war from a golf course. Their lust for power remains the same. In Yemen, for the tens of thousands being killed throughout the war, and for the millions dying of hunger and illness through the naval blockade, does it really matter whether the limitless political ambitions, untrammeled greed, and boundless arrogance that caused their annihilation are concocted,

---

51. See, e.g., Terreblanche, *Lost in Transformation*; Calland, *Anatomy of South Africa*; Bond, *Elite Transition*; and A. Boesak, *Pharaohs*.

52. See the discussion of the tensions about "reforms" to the apartheid system within the ruling National Party of the time in my address to the Transvaal Indian Congress issuing the call for the formation of the United Democratic Front on January 23, 1983, "Truth Crushed to Earth Will Rise Again," in A. Boesak, *Running with Horses*, 128–30.

53. See King, *Why We Can't Wait*, 55.

54. King, *Why We Can't Wait*, 55–56.

The Birthing Stool, the Burning Bush, and the Throne of Pharaoh 49

harbored, and acted upon by Mohammed Bin Salman of Saudi Arabia and Barack Obama, or Mohammed Bin Salman and Donald Trump?

For the world now living under renewed threats of nuclear annihilation, it does not really matter whether Mr. Obama, having advocated a "nuclear-free world" during his campaign, only "reluctantly" bent under the pressure to enhance the US nuclear weapons capacity in a $1.7 trillion program,[55] or whether Mr. Trump is continuing it because "the power, the devastation is very important to me."[56] The philosophical "reluctance" or the childish bombast does not matter. What matters is that the unimaginable danger, the continued suffering of the poor and defenseless, and the ongoing devastation to the world is the same.

The *targets* of their arrogance remain the same, the *aims* of world domination remain the same; the misery of the innocent across the world remains the same, because all of them represent empire. For the people who suffer and are in resistance it is enough to know that they are facing *Pharaoh*, and the pharaoh, in whatever shape or form, of whatever color, gender, or creed, must be resisted. *Because they are Pharaoh*. What remains also unchanging it seems, is that the world looks on, uncaring, or seemingly helpless to do anything. Once we said, Black people need to know that they are on their own. Now we must embrace the fact that oppressed people across the world are on their own. This does not mean that we cannot have allies. But it does mean that without our own firmly embraced agency and determination, no ally is able to help.

"THE MIDWIVES FEARED GOD"

Not at all surprisingly, "fear" plays a significant role in this passage. We see this at three contrasting but not contradictory levels. First, the creation of a climate of fear in the Egyptian population goes hand in hand with the scapegoating of the Israelite slaves (1:9). The politics of fear always creates room for the demonization that in turn creates room and provides justification for the politics of oppression and annihilation. Second, the politics of fear create the necessary space for the *collective condition* of the politics of deceit, preemptive destruction, and disproportionate, collective punishment. Exod 1:8 reads, "Let us deal shrewdly with them." Again, Calvin proves instructive.

This, says Calvin, is the politics of preemptive war. Calvin notices that the word used in verse 8, *chakam*, is often taken in the sense of "to overreach with cunning." The empire lies and deceives and pretends that the

---

55. See Broad and Sanger, "As U.S. Modernizes Nuclear Weapons."
56. See Rosen, "Trump on Nuclear Weapons."

preemptive murderous intent is necessary for the security and the good of the nation. Calvin calls it "a specious, yet fallacious pretext"; he speaks of "that detestable sentiment . . . that we should be beforehand [pro-active] in crime" used by "wicked and desperate characters" even though they know that it is "unjust and absurd." Yet it is commonly considered "the best mode of precaution, so that only those are accounted provident [prudent] who consult for their own security by injuring others, if occasion requires it."[57]

To me, Calvin seems to be describing the preemptive war policy, feeding on deliberately calculated fear, so calamitously normalized by the Bush administration in cahoots with Britain's Tony Blair in their pretexts for the so-called war on terror, and since then, however disastrously, still mindlessly called upon in subsequent undeclared wars the US is waging in seven Muslim countries in the world as we write. With deep insight Calvin writes,

> From this source almost all wars proceed; because while every prince fears his neighbor, this fear so fills him with apprehension, that he does not hesitate to cover the earth with human blood. Hence, too, amongst private individuals, arises the licence for deceit, murder, rapine, and lying, because they think that injuries would be repelled too late, unless they respectively anticipated them. *But this is a wicked kind of cunning (however it may be varnished over with the specious name of foresight) unjustly to molest others for our own security.*[58]

Third, the fear the pharaoh needs to instill in all the people reflects the fear in his own mind. And it is this fear that spawns the irrationality of the strategies he employs. The instruction to kill all the Hebrew boys goes to the midwives at first but then also to the Egyptian people as a whole. It is meant to strike even greater fear into the hearts of the slaves, but it is the fear of Pharaoh himself that drives him to the "madness," the "foolishness" of his decisions. Quite deliberately he turns his personal fear into a national phobia as he transfers it to all Egyptians. It now becomes the collective responsibility, and as a result the collective guilt of all Egyptians. The genocide of the Hebrews' boys is now the shared guilt of the nation. Their fear of the Other is turned into a desire to annihilate the Other. It is a shared national blindness, a macabre bonding; the fear that leads to destruction of the Other is what is holding the nation together. No one can plead neutrality. What up to now has been done "in their name" would now be done with their own hands.

US historian Norman Pollack explains this further:

57. Calvin, *Commentaries*, Exod 1:8.
58. Calvin, *Commentaries*, Exod 1:9, my emphasis.

> The cold war never ended, not even, for that matter, gone underground; rather, its permanence was set in stone... Penetration, ideology, militarism, all, when tightly integrated, bespeak strength interlaced, however, with fear—else why the constant emphasis on force, the muscularity of response (overkill), being ever vigilant? To the systemic/structural characteristics this displays must be added the psychological composite of ethnocentrism and xenophobia, in which fear of the stranger, the Other, the Enemy at the Gates... falls naturally into place with the erection of defensive walls to reinforce the all-important dichotomy of We and They in international politics...[59]

We saw this in Nazi Germany. The never-ending American "war on terror," the Rwandan genocide, and the ethnic cleansing effected by Israel *vis-à-vis* the Palestinians and in Myanmar *vis-à-vis* the Rohingya people are the everyday frightening examples of what we mean here.

The Bible does not deny the overwhelming reality of the politics of fear in the rule of empires. The context of chapters 1 and 2 makes that crystal clear. In this context of fear, obedience to the empire, which can inflict punishment on, or offers "protection" from, the Other we are taught to fear, becomes a crucial way of survival, an essential way of life. Rising up against this fear and recognizing the politics of fear as a device for control and subjugation is one of the first lessons the story of the midwives teaches us. "But the midwives feared God." That means, they consciously—and consistently—countered the fear for the pharaoh with their distrust in the pharaoh and their trust in God. As the midwives are summoned before Pharaoh (twice!) he was the visible, tangible, embodied, and manifested presence of fear. Yahweh was the intangible and invisible but nonetheless real presence of courage, faith, and defiance.

"PHARAOH SUMMONED THE MIDWIVES"

Pharaoh summoned the midwives not once but twice. It is crucial that we remember that here, as always, in order to maintain domination and the status quo of oppression and exploitation, the empire needs the collaboration of the subjugated. That is the primary reason for calling the Hebrew midwives to account here. Pharaoh's plan cannot work without them. When he resorts to his "Plan B" he descends into the abyss of a desperation that not only defies reason; more importantly it also loses whatever legitimacy

---

59. See Pollack, "Price Tag for International Villainy" cited in Giroux, *America at War with Itself,* 14–15.

the cooperation of the oppressed may have given those plans. By the same token he also loses the advantage of confusion created by the cooperation of the oppressed in their own oppression. As long as the women stood firm in their refusal, all excuses within captive Israel for neutrality, resignation, or collaboration are voided.

"In this story the king of Egypt is under the impression that these two Hebrew women will comply with his wishes," writes Hebrew Bible scholar Martin Noth.[60] That is not surprising since power always expects unquestioning obedience from the powerless. But resistance to empire, and setting the limits to tyranny, begins with understanding and refuting the *expectations* of empire.

It is not just civil disobedience we are seeing here, as both Durham and Fretheim have it. Shifrah and Puah are not passively disobeying; they are actively working against the command of the pharaoh. Passive disobedience would have been protest, but in the words of South African philosopher Adam Small, protest as "a kind of begging."[61] But protest within the context of refusal, defiance, and sacrificial commitment to fundamental upending of the ways of empire is entirely different. In risking their own lives they were no longer begging, but issuing a demand: that the pharaoh take the responsibility for the death of the Hebrew children upon himself. They are willing to die for the sake of the life of the Hebrew children. They are, however, not willing to accept co-responsibility for the hideous actions of the pharaoh. They will not allow their state of oppression to become an excuse for the moral responsibility the pharaoh and his people should rightly bear. That they are oppressed is one thing, but that they should willingly shoulder guilt for that oppression would be inexcusable. Unlike the prescription of the secret deals made between the African National Congress's elite leadership and the white apartheid elites to concoct a "reconciliation" process that did exactly that, the midwives resisted that temptation. They are setting down the limits of their endurance, and the limits of their endurance prescribe the limits of their oppressor's power. No wonder the pharaoh is "outraged."

The midwives "responded." It was a "wonderfully resourceful" response.[62] That is right. There is, as far as I can see, no sign of timidity, false modesty, or what the privileged classes call "peasant cunning." Wise to the thinking of empire, they count on the delusionary superiority complex oppressors always have. That the slaves behave like animals, and have the

---

60. Noth, *Exodus*, 23.

61. See Boesak, *Pharaohs*, 205 n. 25, originally in a volume on Black theology edited by Basil Moore. In the Dutch translation *Zwarte Theologie in Zuid Afrika*, Small's contribution is on 33–39. The quote is on 37.

62. Fewell and Gunn, *Gender, Power and Promise*, 92.

appetites of animals, is a "natural" way for them to think of "the savages" under their control. Subjugated peoples know it only too well. It is a blinding stupidity, but oppressors seem to have a deep need of it nonetheless.

But does this, as Exum expresses her suspicions of the patriarchal motives of the male narrator of the story, make the pharaoh so "exceedingly foolish" that he is "even" outwitted by "mere women"? There is indeed an exceeding foolishness about oppression and oppressors. They always believe that their power is unassailable, that the ones they have conquered will always remain helpless victims; that their brutality is an unbreakable shield, that their violence is a redemptive force, that they are innocent because they are entitled, and that their exceptionalism makes them untouchable and hence god-like. That is indeed the height of foolishness. But that does not make them less lethal, less prone to destruction, or less averse to acts of extreme cruelty and death.

The women are facing a formidable foe, a powerful monarch, a death-dealing tyrant. The foolishness of oppression does not nullify the reality of it. This pharaoh might have been extremely foolish, but there are reasons why his back-breaking policies of oppression continued: "*After a long time, the king of Egypt died.*" We cannot even begin to imagine what that "long time" translated into. And clearly, whoever succeeded him understood why it was important for Egypt that these policies should continue: "The Israelites groaned under their slavery, and cried out" (2:23). Western scholarly critique, diminishing the character of the resistance against empire by emphasizing the "foolishness" of the oppressor, is perhaps not entirely surprising. Subjugated peoples, however, under the vicious oppression of imperial forces, would be careful not to undermine the agency and belittle the courage of resisters by de-emphasizing the power and murderous intent of oppressors. Only those who have not experienced oppression dare do so.

From one point of view, Adolf Hitler was exceedingly foolish in holding up his dream of a thousand-year, racially pure *Reich* as an ideal for which millions of lives of "lesser human beings" should be sacrificed. But that foolishness did not make him less lethal for the victims of his evil madness. Madeleine Albright, in making her infamous statement on national television that the death of 500,000 Iraqi children as a result of the crippling sanctions regime exercised by the US was "a price worth paying," seemingly without caring that neither she nor her country would be paying any price at all, was exceedingly foolish, but she remained nonetheless extremely deadly for those helpless children. George W. Bush and Tony Blair, in resorting to lies and deceit to justify their lust for war and profit in their disastrous invasion of Iraq, were exceedingly foolish, but that did not nullify the appalling destruction they represented to those lands they invaded, nor the crime against humanity and the moral and political consequences for America and Britain themselves.

Empires always have genocidal intent, and the twenty-first-century American Empire is no different. It does not only have the intent, it has, in the famous but ominous words of George H. W. Bush, "the means to back it up." The US and Britain do this directly and blatantly in collusion with their Saudi Arabian allies in Yemen and in Palestine in collaboration with the state of Israel. But there is also the more subtle, but no less shocking, drift toward genocide in the United States itself in what President Obama allowed to happen through his stance on the Standing Rock resistance.[63]

In the midst of the daily, horrifying, and growing confrontations between the water protectors and police, private security forces and soldiers of the National Guard at Standing Rock in service of the corporation building the pipeline through sacred Indian land, an undertaking that would simultaneously violate sacred sites, enhance immensely the chances of pollution of the water and the environment, and run roughshod over a treaty with the Lakota people dating from 1853, President Obama had an interview on the *Now This News* website. This is a key passage:

> We're monitoring this closely. And, you know, I think, as a general rule, my view is that there is a way for us to accommodate sacred lands of Native Americans. And I think that right now the Army Corps is examining whether there are ways to reroute this pipeline in a way... So—so, we're going to let that play out for several more weeks and determine whether or not this can be resolved in a way that I think is properly attentive to the traditions of the first Americans...[64]

Journalist William Boardman gets right to the heart of the matter: the president, while paying lip service to the "traditions of the first Americans," did not mention the broken treaties made with a sovereign nation, because "he is not about to break with the traditions of the second Americans: that such treaties are only a means to a genocidal end and aren't to be taken seriously by the United States of exceptional, manifestly destined Americans whenever such treaties interfere with what the U.S. wants."

The president is willing to "let this play out for several more weeks." But that means that since sacred lands have been and are being destroyed, nonviolent protectors have been and are being savaged, and the situation in North Dakota has already taken on the hallmarks of a police state, Mr. Obama is perfectly willing to allow this to continue. Meanwhile, peaceful

---

63. See Boardman, "Obama is Pathetic on Human Rights in North Dakota."
64. Boardman, "Obama is Pathetic on Human Rights in North Dakota."

protesters are being pepper-sprayed, they and their horses terrorized by low-flying helicopters; some are shot in the back and front with rubber bullets. Journalists (from progressive alternative media) are being arrested for trying to report these brutalities; protesters detained are being held in dog cages and in conditions that violate international law. The police actions in Standing Rock were as brutal as anything I have seen during the worst years of apartheid.

The Army Corps is "examining ways of rerouting the pipeline" the president said. But the truth is that the pipeline has already been rerouted, away from the (mostly white) state capital city of Bismarck, after the residents expressed fear that the pipeline threatened their water supply. Now that same pipeline threatens the water supply of the Native population and that would be a death sentence for thousands, and Mr. Obama knows this. "But that is more acceptable to the American power structure," writes Boardman. It is acceptable because the Native people, unlike the rich corporation who owns the pipeline, and the privileged white residents of Bismarck who understand the dangers the pipeline poses, are the powerless ones. The only power they have is the power of righteous resistance.

Why, Boardman asks, does the president, as Commander-in-Chief, not simply order the Army to stop the pipeline? Why doesn't he order the police to stop their terrorizing of peaceful protest for the right to clean water? Instead he chastises the peaceful protesters, admonishing them to be peaceful, acting as if their peaceful protest is the same as the vicious, violent, reckless response from the militarized police from seven states, equating their passion for the environment, their compassion for powerless communities, their commitment to justice and humanity, with the barbaric onslaught from state-backed law-enforcement. "And you know, I want to make sure that everybody is exercising their constitutional right to be heard, that both sides are refraining from situations that might result in people being hurt." All the while peaceful protesters are being savaged, sacred land is being raped and the people's rights are trampled upon.

So we have a president who gravely ponders the situation, "letting things play out" while nonviolent, peaceful, praying protectors of the environment and the deepest scared heart of a powerless people are set upon by dogs, assaulted by rubber bullets, sound cannons, and chemical weapons. "That is strange beyond comprehension," writes Boardman. That is the dark heart of empire. It is foolishness, but it is the foolishness of Psalm 42: "The fool says in his heart, 'There is no God.'" We are reminded of the wise and gentle admonition from William H. Willimon as he spoke to the Obama presidency of the "prophetic truth" the president would do well to remember, "that God, not nations, rules the world and that all of us, even at our best, stand under the judgments of a righteous God whose ways are higher than our ways."[65]

THE INTELLECTUAL BARRENNESS OF DESPOTISM

Hebrew Bible scholar Benno Jacob comments on what he calls "the intellectual barrenness" of all despotism. "This Pharaoh suggested three means of oppression: the first was forced labor, the second infanticide, [and] with that, his 'wisdom' was exhausted, for the third was mass infanticide." Jacob continues, "Despotism is intellectually barren; it is capable of only two paths—enslavement and murder."[66]

Endless deceit through numerous "intelligence agencies"; endless threats and intimidation through limitless powers of surveillance; endless exploitation through boundless and unregulated capitalist greed; endless war for the sake of endless profits, announcing death decrees from the opulence of a golf course or in the mindlessness of a tweet—none of these are signs of the intellectual maturity necessary for the complexities of our world. None of these are signs of the wisdom that sees worth in peace, dignity, justice, respect for life, and reverence for the preciousness of the Earth. Like the pharaoh, the empire does not see that its exercise of blind power is a stupidity beyond belief.

The intellectual creativity of the women, on the other hand, not only contrasts that of the pharaoh's despotism, it also contrasts the lack of imagination in the almost mechanical engagement of the pharaoh by Moses and Aaron. Just as Moses's unthinking act of violence did not bear any fruit, the use of "tricks" and "magic" as "signs" of authority does not work either. The magicians of Pharaoh can do the same. That is not demanding justice and liberation; it is negotiating freedom. A far cry from the creative resistance of Shifrah and Puah, it is mere imitation. They do not rise above the level of the empire's competencies and therefore fail to accomplish their mission. In the employment of "signs" Moses and Aaron get caught in a senseless cycle of the reproduction of signs of death (a snake, a leprous hand, and water turning into blood). The men, in their desire to match Pharaoh's power with the same kind of power, are caught in the syndrome of recycled fear. The creative, intelligent resistance of the women breaks that cycle and produces life-giving acts. What was intended to be a death-dealing instrument, the birthing stool, and what was a place fraught with danger and stalked by

---

65. See Willimon, "Preacher-Prophet Obama," 86.
66. Benno, *Exodus*, 22.

death, the riverbank, are both turned into life-giving, life-affirming spaces by the courageous, life-giving defiance of the women.

The women are the representatives of that wisdom that exposes, mocks, challenges, overturns the "wisdom" of the pharaoh of which we read in 1:9, the political cunning that can only lead to disaster, as we have heard from Calvin. The women are a reminder that brute force is brute force—it is not creative power. That creative power is in the hands of the powerless: courage, faith, hope, the fear of Yahweh that is the trust in the trustworthiness of Yahweh. It is not mere wit but wisdom that determines the women's response to Pharaoh's questions in 1:17. Not only do the women lay the foundation of Israel's faith, "The fear of the LORD is the beginning of wisdom" (Prov 1:7 and 9:10; Ps 111:10), they also lay the foundation of the truth and conviction as expressed by Hannah, the mother of Samuel, "Not by might shall one prevail" (1 Sam 2).

A Black theology rooted in the courage and the wisdom of the women would perhaps have had a better grasp of the barrenness of our current global politics; it would have discerned better the moral and political bankruptcy of the African National Congress that produced Jacob Zuma and America's equally corrupt oligarchy that produced Donald Trump. We would have been wise to the rhetorical charm but political emptiness of Obama's "post-racialism" and Mandela's "rainbow-nationalism." We would have been better prepared for the incomprehensible violence visited upon our people in the Marikana massacre by their own liberation movement, and would have had better understanding of the reasons behind #BlackLivesMatter and #FeesMustFall, and the rightful anger of a disillusioned younger generation who claim that we have so bitterly betrayed them. With the wisdom of the women of the Exodus, we would not feel the need to debate the merits of #MeToo and the South African women's #ThisMustEnd.

With the wisdom of the women, we could have been a better bulwark in the continued struggles for a freedom defined by ourselves; a better partner in the fight for the preservation of the character of our liberation, the sanity of our politics, and the sanctity of our humanity.

In this, one's fervent hope must be that we have the wisdom to know that it is not yet too late.

Chapter Three

STANDING HER GROUND: THE RIVERBANK AND THE SEASHORE

Black Theology, the Miriamic Tradition, and the Cry for Freedom

THE MIRIAMIC PRESENCE

WE FIRST MEET MIRIAM as guardian and protector on the riverbank, then as prophet and leader after the deliverance at the Red Sea, and finally as prophetic challenge to patriarchal power in the wilderness. The young woman who keeps watch on the riverbank is not named, but tradition has it, and scholarly consensus—which I shall follow—seems to be that this "sister" of Moses is the same person who takes the lead at the seashore in Exod 15:20-21 and who speaks on behalf of others in the wilderness, recorded in Numbers 12.

What Hebrew Bible scholar Phyllis Trible calls the "Miriamic presence"[1] begins here on the riverbank and becomes the Miriamic tradition, which I understand as the prophetic tradition of faithful resistance against empire, against the early temptation in ancient Israel to imitate the ways of empire, as well as against patriarchal power and privilege. It is the tradition that in the face of ruthless power insists, prophetically, publicly, and unflinchingly upon God's preferential option for the poor, the weak, and the downtrodden.

1. Trible, "Bringing Miriam Out of the Shadows," 166–86.

As our previous discussion makes clear, Miriam emerges against the darkness of unimaginable oppression; a darkness pierced only by the light of the fierce, audacious hope held by three women. She will be the fourth.[2]

CRY FREEDOM!

Moses is born under the menacing clouds of the genocidal cruelty of the king of Egypt. The narrative calls for the mother to take an extraordinarily risky and courageous initiative. It is proper, therefore, to devote some attention to her. We must resist the temptation to read this as solely the "motherly instinct" to protect her own child, or the divine plan to "set the stage for Moses." The framework of the exodus story, set with the midwives in chapter 1, does not allow for such an individualized, personalized reduction. This is, as was the case with the midwives, to be interpreted as a bold act, or better still, a series of acts of defiance of great political significance. She is a woman who, in the face of the devastation surrounding her and her people, decided upon resistance, and her deeds would echo in the lives of other women, enabling liberation and, true to her name ("Yahweh is [her] glory!"), would glorify the name of Israel's liberator-God. The name sounds like a cry, and perhaps it is. But then it is not a cry of desperation or despair, but a cry for freedom.

Her husband enters the story simply as "a man from the house of Levi," unnamed here, mentioned only once, and uncommented upon in this remarkable story beyond Exod 2:1. In this text, she is not named either, though biblical tradition identifies her as Jochebed, her husband as Amram, and calls her the mother of Moses, Aaron, and Miriam (Exod 6:20, Num 26:59). Remarkably, the male presence simply fades away.

Jochebed's act, like that of the midwives, has vast political implications, not because of her son's role-in-waiting, but because of her decisive agency. She engages the pharaoh not simply as a mother but as a member of a subjugated, enslaved people, as one not at all ready or willing to subject herself to the dictates of the empire. While the Israelite masses, the men included, contented themselves with "crying out" and "groaning" of which we hear only in 2:23, and which the Lord "heard," already in chapters 1 and

---

2. In her 1987 dissertation, Rita J. Burns does not take into consideration Exod 2:1–10 since she argues that in this story the Miriam here is not mentioned as Moses's sister. The woman named Miriam who appears at the seashore and in the wilderness is instead a leader of a wilderness cultic community. See Burns, *Has the Lord Indeed Spoken Only Through Moses?*

2:1–10, it becomes clear that the women are done with groaning. Their "crying out" is already a cry turned into acts of resistance.

The story throbs with tensed-up energy, the verbs tumbling over each other as if in a race to keep up with the actions of the women. Cognizant of the danger and weighing the risks, Jochebed, having *conceived* and *given birth*, *decides* to *hide* her child, stretching it for three months. Then she *decides* to *weave* the basket, taking time and using bitumen to make it waterproof and as safe as possible, her technical know-how and skills mentioned as a matter of course. She *hides* the basket in one of the unsafest places in an unsafe Egypt, *placing* it among the reeds on the riverbank. Miriam *stood* guard. For how long we are not told. Like the mothers in the South African struggle who turned their homes into sanctuaries, hiding activists and offering shelter to children not their own fleeing from persecution and sometimes certain death at the hands of the security police, Jochebed, taking those same deadly risks, turned her home into a house of resistance.

Perhaps one should take a moment to reflect here. There is a reason why, I think, in just about every struggle for liberation, women are so prominent *in its origins*. Such was indeed the role played by women in the twentieth-century South African freedom struggle's first phase of active, nonviolent militancy in the anti-pass laws and the racist "residence permits" movements in the 1910s and the Defiance Campaign and the Women's March of the 1950s, as it is true of the Palestinian struggle for freedom.[3] It is true also of the role of the women in the origins of the black freedom struggle in the United States: Sojourner Truth against the enslavement of Africans; Ida B. Wells against the brutalization and lynching of blacks in the nineteenth century;[4] and in the 1950s and the civil rights struggle, Mamie

---

3. South African historian Tom Lodge (even though he does this reluctantly, as an aside almost) cannot but note the role of *Manganos* (members of women's church organizations) in the Defiance Campaign; see Lodge, *Black Politics in South Africa*, viii. See my response to Lodge in A. Boesak, *Tenderness of Conscience*, 108–9; also my reflections on the significance of the women's march in 1956 in A. Boesak, *Pharaohs*, 20–22. The same principle holds in general for the Palestinian struggle for freedom, justice, and self-determination, and the Arab Spring Uprisings since 2010. For Palestinian struggles, see the story of how women in 1893 demonstrated against the building of a Jewish settlement on Palestinian land, and how, in 1936, the women with their children, of the village of Baqa-al-Gharbiyeh, descended upon the military base at night, armed with rocks, to demand the release of the men of the village held there; see Alsaafin, "Role of Palestinian Women." For the Arab Spring, see, e.g., UN Chronicles, "Women and the Arab Spring." In the now famous Standing Rock confrontation with international oil companies, "women are the foundation of the fight against the Dakota Access pipeline." See "Women Are 'Backbone' of the Native Actions Against Dakota Pipeline."

4. See Painter, *Sojourner Truth*, and Wells, *Southern Horrors and Other Writings*. It

Till-Mobley and Ella Baker, Claudette Colvin, and Rosa Parks.[5] They and all the unmentioned but unforgettable women were, each in their own way, upholding the prophetic, Miriamic tradition.

There is a reason why we discover traces of Jochebed in Mamie Till-Mobley, the mother of Emmett Till who, after Emmett's brutal torture and murder in 1954, left his casket open, with the hideously ravaged face uncovered so that the evidence of the manner of his death by two white men would not be hidden, denied, or forgotten. This, too, is a story of defiance of the forces of empire. First she had to fight the authorities in Mississippi and challenge authorities in Illinois to have the body returned to Chicago. She overcame. Then, defying orders from Sherriff Clarence H. Strider that the coffin containing her son's body would remain shut, she threatened to take a hammer to smash open the padlock herself, in the process smashing the power of racist patriarchy. She overcame.

"She saw Emmett as being crucified on the cross of racial injustice,"[6] and she was determined that the world would recognize it as such. People were not to focus on her pain as a mother, but on the injustices done to her people, and that on a global scale: "The murder of my son has shown me that what happens to any of us *anywhere in the world*, had better be the business of us all."[7] She left the coffin of her son open for the world to see, to be

---

also seems that the first African American to refuse to get up from a seat in a train car apparently reserved for "white ladies" only was Ida Wells. On a Saturday in 1883, she not only refused to get up from her seat but pursued legal action against the railroad company. Her resistance included not only polite refusal. When the white conductor tried to manhandle her, she clung to her chair and "[sank] her teeth into the conductor's hand." See Bay, *To Tell the Truth Freely*, 45–58.

5. Fifteen-year-old Claudette Colvin was the first to refuse to stand up from her seat on the bus in Montgomery, a full nine months before Rosa Parks did so. Claudette Colvin suffered for this brave act of resistance. She was imprisoned, and after her release was shunned by parts of her community. She was not politically unaware and knew what she was doing in defying white power on the bus that evening. But because she was a pregnant teenager, she was not considered by the NAACP and the churches to be the right kind of person to be held up as the face of black resistance in the South: "Civil Rights leaders felt she was an inappropriate symbol for a test case." See Adler, "Before Rosa Parks." See also Phil Hoose's *Claudette Colvin, Twice Toward Justice*. Like Mary the mother of Jesus was shunned and became an embarrassment to Joseph, Claudette was too much of an embarrassment to be the model for the struggle. Mrs. Rosa Parks did become this model. It still fills me with a certain sense of wonder to think that in this process it is almost as if God had given the freedom movement in the US a second chance, despite the middle-class, judgmental reluctance that made it shun Claudette Colvin nine months before. My sense of awe is deepened when I reflect that, even in giving the movement a second chance, God's insistence on a woman as the channel of agency is undeterred.

6. See Nodjimbadem, "Emmett Till's Open Casket Funeral."

7. See http://www.azquotes.com/author/31909-Mamie_Till, my emphasis. It is this

confronted, not so much as testimony of her suffering as a mother, but with the truth of white racism's apocalyptic violence as the deed was planned and done, white supremacy's evil and guilt as it was covered up, and white privilege's calculated complicity as the murderers were found "not guilty" by an all-white, all-male jury in Mississippi.[8] Indeed, it was not so much Emmett's death—the horrific nature of which was common enough in "the Southern Way of Life"—as it was his mother's defiant actions, challenging both the perpetrators of injustice and the fighters for justice, that "reignited the civil rights movement."

Jochebed had to hide her son, Mamie had to expose her son, but both did it as fierce resistance against the might of evil principalities immeasurably more powerful than themselves, though not stronger. Both acts by these women, of hiding and exposing, covering and unmasking, concealing and revealing, set a bold standard of resistance for all generations.

I see Jochebed and the Miriamic tradition in Nomonde Calata. She is the widow of Fort Calata from Cradock in the Eastern Cape, one of the leaders of the United Democratic Front, the last great people's movement in the freedom struggle in South Africa. He was one of four young men, now known as "The Cradock Four," ambushed, detained, tortured, and murdered by the South African secret police in 1985. I preached at their funeral in July of that year.[9] I met her again just recently, in the home of her son in Cape Town.

In 1998 Mrs. Calata testified before the Truth and Reconciliation Commission's Amnesty Committee. She had just started to speak when she suddenly broke down, threw her body backwards and opened her mouth in a primeval scream of pain, suffering, and grief. Archbishop Tutu, the TRC, and the people in the hall listened in stunned, awed silence. This is how South African journalist Antjie Krog describes the moment:

---

global understanding of the struggle, which Mamie Till understood already then, and which Martin Luther King Jr. came only to understand fully much later, around 1964 after his Nobel Peace Prize, that I am pleading for. It is also an understanding well grasped by the youth of the #BlackLivesMatter movement. See A. Boesak, *Pharaohs*, xvii, 52–53.

8. In *Look Magazine*, Emmett Till's murderers bragged publicly about their deed and their victory in court only weeks after their acquittal. See Huie, "Shocking Story of Approved Killing in Mississippi."

9. For the text of that eulogy, "Raise a Sign of Hope," see A. Boesak, *Running with Horses*, 207–15.

> The starting point of the hearings was the indefinable wail that burst from Nomonde Calata's lips, the signature tune, the defining moment, the ultimate sound of what the process is about . . .[10]

Today, more than twenty years after the Truth and Reconciliation Commission, Nomonde Calata's cry is still not heard by the rich and powerful, the privileged and forgetful, the pampered and the self-sufficient. They hide in a political fog of ritualistic, self-protective, sadistic deafness. It does not matter though, for it does not change or lessen the power of her appeal to God, to the conscience of the nation, or to the open ears and hearts of the young now flooding the streets with their resistance to the injustices that continue long after her husband's sacrificial death.

Nomonde Calata did not cry in an appeal to an apartheid regime no longer in place, who did not hear her those twenty-one years ago, could not hear her now, and like all oppressors who live off the pain of their victims, never intended to hear her. If they could hear her, they would hear her in the way all oppressors, all torturers, all lovers of violence of yesterday and today always do: as the cry that merely confirms their power, their control over others, their ability to inflict and end pain. And they always gain from all of it.

She did not cry to elicit the sympathy of the Commissioners. Eleven years after the death of her husband that sympathy would be of little help. The cry was beyond the TRC, for she understood that they could not give her justice—not justice as revenge and punishment, wishing the violence visited upon her husband, upon her and her children, upon a community and a whole people whose only desire was freedom and justice, to be inflicted upon the torturers of her husband sitting in front of her. The justice of violent retribution, of blood-filled self-gratification is not the justice Nomonde Calata craved. She cried for justice, not for the dead, which could only be retribution, but for the living, which is the justice that breaks down systems of oppression, transforms societies, works toward the restoration of rights, dignity, and equity, and seeks the healing of persons and communities. The justice that is able to create a future. But the grand design of the TRC did not include that form of justice.[11] She did not cry to white South Africa either, the majority of whom did not want to hear such a cry despite the piercing urgency described by Antjie Krog; who recoiled from it because the hardness of their unrepentant hearts could only fearfully conceive of revenge, of desperate excuses for the inexcusable, or of a feverish desire to

---

10. See Krog, "Facing the Second Day of the TRC Hearings."

11. See, e.g., Mamdani, "Amnesty or Impunity?," 33–59. See also A. Boesak, *Pharaohs*, ch. 4.

"just move on." Their wish was not for her to find peace, for her community to build on the solid rock of justice, but rather for the whole country to seek refuge in the draughty caves of collective amnesia.

She did not cry to the black community who, if they were not consumed by such rage that revenge was indeed their only thought, would be in too much unhealed pain themselves, in mourning still for their own disappeared—who would in any case only later discover the true nature of our reconciliation process—and for children, parents, and siblings who died sudden, or slow, but always painful, too-early deaths. Neither did she cry for the African National Congress to hear her. On that day, she already intuited what she would later experience and articulate: a "pervading sense of abandonment and betrayal by the Commission, the African National Congress and President Mandela," all of whom were warming themselves cozily by the fires of negotiated complacency, "and no longer felt the cold."[12]

No, the cry was for something deeper, for the truth of bleeding memories: the man you are talking about was a fighter for justice, true; he was a leader, true; he was admired by those who knew his courage, revered by so many because his love for justice made them strong, also true. But the man who died that day in your torture chamber was also my husband, my friend, my lover, the father of my children. No refusal of amnesty, and no amount in reparation would even begin to touch that reality. What she cried for was the justice informed and sustained by the love of the wounded God.

Nomonde's cry was for even more than the collective grief apartheid wrought, or the collected outrage against the horrors of that system. It is a cry that, amidst the political theatre, human drama, and political maneuverings at the TRC, wanted to carve out sacred space for true reconciliation, true justice, true dignity, true freedom. Nomonde's cry was saying: none of this is possible, unless you first hear the cry. Hearing the cry, opening your ears and your hearts to the cry, letting your soul be touched, no, scorched by that cry, is the first step. Hear with your ears and see with eyes truly open, understand with your opened mind, and stretch out your open hand to undo the damage your close-fisted violence has inflicted upon others. A life of fulfillment is not possible unless the cry is heard.

Nomonde Calata's cry that day was a cry to God. Not the racist, genocidal god of apartheid who blessed our oppression and made white people exceptional; that exceptionalism that does what all exceptionalism always does—make for themselves a god whose chosen people they become, with the right to steal, destroy, enslave, and dehumanize. She did not cry out to the god of pacification black people were told to believe in (and too many

---

12. Nomonde Calata in Oliver, "For Nomonde Calata, the Truth Is Not Enough."

Standing Her Ground: The Riverbank and the Seashore 65

times did): the god who has children whose lives are precious, and stepchildren whose lives do not matter; the god who takes no issue with injustice, the god who blesses violence, the god whose prophets cry "Peace! Peace!" where there is no peace. She cried out to the God of justice and peace, of love and compassion; the God of the birthing chamber, the riverbank, and the seashore.

But why did she choose the TRC, this most public of public platforms, in front of the nation and an international television audience, to utter that keening from the heart, that wail from the very core of that peculiar mix of misery, anger, pain, and defiance?

I think it was first because the moment chose *her*. She did not practice it in front of a mirror; neither did she plan for it. In a sense, she was overcome by the moment. But also: that moment was her first encounter with the torturers of her husband, their arrogance, their unrepentant braggadocio, and their offensive certitude that there was really nothing she could do to them. In that moment a woman who was in her own right a "mother of the struggle" would discover what helplessness was. It was a moment she could not face without her God. So that was her moment before *God*. To confront God with her unreleased grief, her unrelieved pain, her unspeakable suffering, and her unanswered questions. For her, that was the moment when the words from the Bible become mockingly, inescapably real: "Vengeance is mine, says the Lord. . . Beloved, do not be overcome by evil, but overcome evil with good" (Rom 12). That was why the cry was beyond the understanding of those present and those who heard it.

But because it was a cry to God, it was a cry of resistance. Not just against apartheid, but against the temptation to accept a shallow forgiveness without the genuine remorse and repentance she had been waiting for for so long. She did not hate the men in front of her. She did not insist on someone, anyone, to inflict upon them the pain they made her husband endure, the pain that would never leave her, or her children. But she would not bow to the pressure of a politically inspired apology and a politically acceptable forgiveness. She could not accept a confession of convenience even though by that time "apology" and "forgiving" had almost become an inescapable ritual at the TRC.[13] That day she came to see justice and peace embrace. That

---

13. TRC observer Philip Wilson was disturbed by the fact that "the hearings were structured in such a way that any expression of a desire for revenge would seem out of place. The virtues of forgiveness and reconciliation were so loudly applauded that emotions of revenge, hatred and bitterness were rendered unacceptable, an ugly intrusion on a peaceful, healing process." See Graybill, *Truth and Reconciliation*, 50. Wilhelm Verwoerd, also an observer at the hearings, quotes a young woman as saying, "I don't know if I will ever be able to forgive. I carry this ball of anger within me and I don't know where to begin dealing with it. The oppression was bad, but what is much worse,

did not happen. Not then, and not later. She wailed because perhaps more than anyone else in that room, she understood the loss and what that meant for her and for her country.

It was a cry to God because she knew that in that hearing, on that world stage, in that politically created moment where so much was predetermined and so much was at stake, so much beyond her will or reach, she was powerless. She needed a power that was beyond earthly power. She knew that on her own she would not be able to make it through this moment. From God she needed the strength she would never be able to muster on her own. From God she needed the love—even for these men—to overcome a hatred that would have been completely understandable, but by the same token completely self-destructive. From God she needed the power to offer, if at all possible, a forgiveness that would bring healing but not a forgetfulness that cannot stop the bleeding. From God she needed the grace to find a peace anchored in something deeper than the false peace of quietism, resignation, or managed desperation. Every moment in that hearing was a terrifying, violent onslaught upon her unhealed soul. That cry was not the cry of an emotionally distraught, unstable woman. It was the cry of an unshakeable peace secured by her faith.

In front of her sat the violent men of the apartheid regime's killing machine. In their eyes she could see, if she had wanted to, the simmering violence that tortured her husband with a blow torch. Was it the calm, detached violence of a person only doing his job? Was it the functional, bureaucratized violence only intent on getting information; his well-trained mind always ready to call it something else—some useful, politically prepackaged, cynical but palatable euphemism, like "enhanced interrogation techniques"? Was it a gleeful violence such as of one drenched in hatred of black people, or the fanatic, sacralized violence of one doing this for God and country? It did not matter.

Like Hannah in the First Book of Samuel, she cried out against the violence surrounding her, "pouring out her soul before the LORD" from whom she expected mercy, and peace, and grace. And like Hannah, Nomonde knew that "there is no Rock like our God"; like Hannah she knew that in the face of violence the bows of the mighty are broken. It is from this God she draws the strength to endure and to resist.

In South Africa then and now, with our longing for cheap reconciliation and our careless forgetfulness; with our resurgent racism and bubbling

---

what makes me even angrier, is that they [the Amnesty Committee] are trying to dictate my forgiveness." See A. Boesak, *Tenderness of Conscience*, 195–96. See also my argument for giving respectful space for righteous anger in the process of forgiveness in A. Boesak, *Tenderness of Conscience*, 196–200.

tribalism; with our rapacious greed and disdain for the poor; with our easy hatreds and our reluctance to love, we did not begin to know how "defining" that moment was—of the fraud of secret talks and of trust betrayed; of the loss of truth and the desecration of innocence; of political pietism and the manipulation of faith; of the fragility of hope and the resilience of combatant love.

In Nomonde's cry they all come together. All the women in resistance, crying defiance and freedom against the terror of might and power; against the violence of muscular mendacity, breaking the tyranny of wordlessness. There is a reason why we discover the ongoing call for resistance and liberation, justice and freedom, humanity and dignity in Jochebed and Miriam, in Mamie Till and Claudette Colvin, in Winnie Mandela and Nomonde Calata, and why that call resonates, empowers, and frees.

Their disregard for the decrees of Pharaoh, for the dictates of white supremacy, and for the decorum of negotiated politeness mirrors their disregard for the consequences of the risks they are all taking. Their disregard for Pharaoh then, and in all his modern reincarnations now, is their disregard for the logic of empire. The logic of empire dictates that they be silent, resigned to whatever fate empire has decided for them; that the sheer might of empire should leave them no alternative but to submit; that as women, they should know their place. The logic of resistance, which is their logic, dictates that they claim their humanity, their dignity, and their agency. Hence they act, despite the brutality of empire. Might, power, and the threat of death do not impress or intimidate Jochebed, or Mamie, or Nomonde. Their disregard is not the foolishness of hysterical women who, overrun by their emotions, cannot see "the bigger picture." It is the disregard of humanity rising. As Jochebed decided she could hide her child no longer, and Mamie decided she would reveal her child so all the world would hide their guilt no longer, so Nomonde decided she would hide her outrage no longer and reveal South Africa's truth for all the world to see.

"WHEN SHE COULD HIDE HIM NO LONGER..."

Jochebed wove a basket, put the baby boy in it, placed it among the reeds close to the riverbank, and tasked the young Miriam to stand guard. But that was a measure she took only after she could "hide him no longer." For three months she had hidden him in her house, and took the risk of discovery, of being betrayed for favors from the powerful, or sold out because of fear, or pressures of circumstance she had no control over. Would the pharaoh, not finding cooperation from the midwives, not at least have taken measures such as raids on the homes of Hebrew slaves? A baby is not a secret one can keep for long; a forbidden baby even less.

How many Hebrew slaves, having lost their sons, thinking themselves and what they had left endangered by one daring to flout the powers, would not be willing to tell on her? The sheer pressure alone should have been unbearable. We will never know what ultimate truth lies behind the words, "when she could hide him no longer." Is it practical necessity, betrayal from within the enslaved community? Is it internal tensions with Amram, her husband? Has something happened that triggered the risk of discovery? Whatever it was, it was not enough to make her abandon her intentions to protect the life of her child.

Yet she kept it up for three whole months. And when she took the next step, it was not to make it easier for herself or her family, and it is telling that the one she calls upon is the daughter. There seems to be a deliberateness to all these actions, a stubborn determination to not take a single step back. But also as deliberate is the passing on of the tradition of resistance. So the basket becomes more than a safe place for the baby—in fact it is not at all safe—it becomes rather a symbol of the continuation of resistance.

In these initiatives there seems to be no real expectation that God would directly intervene, and there is no sign of such a promise. And tellingly, once again, there is no Hebrew male even close. It is almost as if the baby in the basket has no father, which, for a narrative within a patriarchal framework, is extraordinary. For all intents and purposes, as the story is told, Jochebed is a single mother. The decision to risk all in the attempt to secure his life is made by the women. The power of decision, in its making and in its execution, lies in the hands of the mother and her daughter. And as in chapter 1, all this does not happen to merely "set the stage for Moses." It is rather to create space for the active agency of the women in God's acts of liberation, and these acts will be acts of radical inclusion. It is an inclusivity that has no bounds and reaches even into the heart of empire in the role ascribed to Pharaoh's daughter. She not only decides to keep the baby when he is discovered; she adopts him, names him, and takes him to her father's house.

What binds these women is not so much an overwhelming, motherly instinct, or their destiny to be mere pawns, "setting the stage for Moses." What binds them is the power of a fundamental decision to defy the stated and implied intentions of empire. In these decisions, boundaries of animosity necessitated by empire's desire for domination and subjugation are crossed because in joining the oppressed in their acts of liberation, Pharaoh's daughter too defies the logic of empire, breaks with empire, and refuses submission to empire. There is an important difference though. Pharaoh's daughter has decided, like the midwives, Jochebed, and Miriam, *but against her own self-interest*, to choose for the life of the Hebrew child and against the death-dealing decrees of the empire. The rules she is breaking are the rules—so she has been told all her life—designed to keep her safe and privileged; to secure her future. She joins the Hebrew women in the risks they are taking.

In doing so, she creates a possibility oppressors do not deserve but because of her are now offered: she opens the door to all oppressors of all times to choose for the solidarity of struggle, which for them is the precondition of freedom, the end of the enslavement of ignorance and of the tyranny of pseudo-innocence. It is the denouncement of the hold of the lesser loyalties to kinship, power, and class privilege in embrace of the greater loyalty to the openness to a common humanity and a shared future. For the children of oppressors, it is an act of salvific power. Nonetheless it is a fragile power, fraught with risk and threatened by malevolent forces, and unless embraced by both the oppressed and the oppressor, as fragile as that baby in the basket among the reeds.

In chapter 1, as we have seen some scholars point out, God is "in the background," remaining "behind the scenes." And again here it is the case. The women's agency is the point of focus. But although God is not mentioned here, this is the exodus story, the story of God and the liberation of the people of Israel, and this God is a God who rises up in resistance against the gods of Egypt, the One who stands with the enslaved, the oppressed, and the threatened. That God, not directly spoken of, is nonetheless wondrously present. The women here, as in chapter 1, need not be reminded. They act in faith, and it is a faith anchored in trust, not in sight; in strength, not in might.

STANDING HER GROUND ON THE RIVER BANK . . .

On the riverbank Miriam is standing "at a distance" (NRSV). At first glance, the impression is of physical space. However, Dutch Hebrew Bible scholar Jopie Siebert-Hommes reminds us that the same verb has an additional meaning: "unattainable," "far away."[14] She cites Hebraic scholar Rochus Zuurmond who writes that the word used here denotes a *qualitative* rather than a *quantitative* separation, and it applies not to Miriam's physical distance as much as to the utter vulnerability of the baby in the basket. "Lying in the bulrushes, the child is delivered up to death." In other words, he is as far from help as one could imagine. The risks here are as obvious as they

---

14. See Siebert-Hommes, "But if She Be a Daughter," 69–70.

are chilling. The life-threatening circumstances of a river in Africa aside, the easy discovery of the child in the basket by Pharaoh's daughter proves it.

Zuurmond writes, "The delicate connotations of qualitative unattainability [of help] are not captured by the phrase 'at a distance.'" If there is a sense of "distance" here, the "distance" is more the distance from help and safety in light of the lurking imminence of death.[15] Siebert-Hommes concludes that the translation "afar off" captures that concept better. It is important to keep this valuable distinction in mind as the story continues, for two reasons. First, it is not just the baby in the basket that is "far from" help. Miriam herself, and on her own, is that too. The risk she takes is as immediate as the risk taken by her mother. Second, even while drawing attention to the vulnerability of the baby, it emphasizes the attentive, courageous presence of Miriam.

But Siebert-Hommes takes this still further and opens up a whole new, and in my view, crucial, understanding of the verb used in this verse. The Hebrew word used here has two meanings, she argues: 1), "to take one's stand," and 2), "to stand one's ground." As in the "striking example" of the use of the same word in Exod 14:13 where Moses urges the people to "stand firm" as they were pushed against the Red Sea by Pharaoh's armies, Miriam is standing and waiting in anticipation of Yahweh's wondrous deeds. In this sense, "it seems legitimate to suggest that Miriam stood there in order to see how God would deal with the matter." But Miriam is also "standing her ground."[16] So "standing firm" here means resisting fear and panic, determined to remain and face whatever may come. The riverbank, like the birthing chamber and Jochebed's home, becomes a place of risk and resistance, of standing her ground, of refusing to give one inch because young as she is, she knows what is at stake.

In weighing the significance of this argument we should keep two facts in mind. First, it shifts the emphasis from the question of "distance" from the baby Moses to Miriam herself, from a mere physical placing and passive observance to the expectation of and readiness for active agency. Second, in this passage, unbearably crowded with risks and uncertainties, it offers perspective on Miriam's frame of mind, *on who this young woman really is*. To begin with, she is more than just "the sister of Moses." In the first meaning, I suggest, Miriam can be understood to wait in faith upon Yahweh's intervention, clearly aware of her own limitations under the circumstances, as well as the possibilities of danger. What if it were not Pharaoh's daughter, but

---

15. See Zuurmond, *Het Bijbelse Verhaal*, 2511; Siebert-Hommes, "But if She Be a Daughter," 69.

16. Siebert-Hommes, "But if She Be a Daughter," 69–70.

Standing Her Ground: The Riverbank and the Seashore

instead a search party of the palace guard, or for that matter any Egyptian acting in blind obedience to the pharaoh's killing instructions, who came to the river in the course of executing the pharaoh's command and discovered the child? After all, the killing of Hebrew boys was now a national obligation. And what if the pharaoh's daughter were of one mind with her father, sharing his fear and the whipped-up national paranoia about the Israelite numbers as a threat to the security of the Egyptian state, and thought it her duty to call the guards?

Moreover, even when Miriam saw that it was Pharaoh's daughter, there could have been no rational expectation in Miriam's mind of a "motherly" response from one who, at that crucial moment on the riverbank, was first and foremost a representative of the Egyptian empire and everything that frightening reality represented. She was, after all, *Pharaoh's daughter*, as the text keeps reminding us. Miriam could not have foreseen the unfolding of events as verses 5–10 describe them. Thus understood, waiting upon the LORD, but still waiting not in passive timidity but *with vigilant alertness* becomes an attitude of faith and trust only affirming Miriam's strength of character. It means waiting upon Yahweh's intervention to create the opportunity in order for her to act as decisively as she was ready for. When she does act, her quick-witted response to the presence of Pharaoh's daughter suggests not only spiritual maturity, but considerable political savvy as well. Even here, the text cannot help but tell us, it is all about extraordinary abilities. She takes her stand, and despite the risks when discovered, she stands her ground.

In Exod 14:14, when Moses tells the people that Yahweh will fight their battles for them, inviting what one could call a spirituality of passivity, there comes a surprising response. It is a spirituality Yahweh is not prepared to condone. The reader is "not prepared for it" writes Fretheim, and many scholars believe it rightly belongs after verse 12.[17] But with Fretheim, I would suggest that it belongs perfectly well here, and is in tune with the emphasis on an activist waiting the verb wants to convey. It is quite possible that Moses himself was not prepared for God's impatient response either. The sentence is emphatic, and it is as if God does not want any misunderstandings here: Yahweh will work, but the people must be ready to actively embrace it. "Why do you cry out to me? Tell the Israelites to go forward!" (v. 15) Where to, though? Into where there is nowhere else to go: the sea!

In this text, waiting upon the LORD to intervene is not despondently sitting down, limply waiting for something to happen. Yahweh acts as the people are ready to move forward in faith and in the firm expectation that

---

17. Fretheim, *Exodus*, 157–58.

deliverance is unfolding. In these mighty acts of liberation, it seems, Yahweh is not willing to act alone. The people *must* embrace it, claim it, own it, and run with it. The women in chapter 1 already understood this completely, but it seems a lesson that must continually be learned. Accordingly, if Miriam is waiting in anticipation, it is a tense anticipation, a coiled readiness to act the moment God creates the opportunity. She knows, unerringly, that this God, the God of the birthing chamber and her mother's house, will not stop until the forces of oppression and enslavement are defeated.

In any event, and no matter how we read this, the NRSV's translation of Miriam "standing at a distance" gives an impression not completely reflective of the text. If the situation should develop into something dangerous and threatening to the baby in the basket in the sense that Zuurmond's reading suggests, Miriam's "standing her ground" means exactly that. It depicts a readiness to act, a commitment that whatever happens, she would not run away, leaving Moses on his own. She was determined, come what may, to find a way to intervene, to defend the baby's life, and that is precisely what she does. It also means, quite obviously, that she was not going to hide, or remain "at a distance" even if that would be safest and a quite defensible action, seeing the odds. She is ready to reveal herself as the one associated with the child (which is, again, exactly what she does), and who knows what the consequences then might have been?

It is the firmness of her resolve in the face of the uncertainty from all sides that makes this young woman so remarkable. With or without divine intervention, Miriam was by no means sure what would happen to her. What stands out here is her readiness to take her stand, and once taken, to stand her ground and face whatever danger may befall her. If something happened to the child, it would not be for lack of courage or action on her part. Under these stressful circumstances, the way she sums up the situation, presents herself and a ready-made plan to the pharaoh's daughter, make for a convincing picture of intellectual dexterity, moral courage, and extraordinary commitment. It is prophetic engagement of empire, no less courageous and faithful than the actions of the midwives and Jochebed. So Miriam, in standing her ground, stands firm, and firmly in the prophetic tradition begun by Shifrah, Puah, and Jochebed.

. . . AND LEADING AT THE SEASHORE

Miriam is disappeared from the exodus story after the events on the riverbank to emerge again only on the seashore, after the miraculous deliverance from the pharaoh's pursuing armies and the people's march "on dry land"

Standing Her Ground: The Riverbank and the Seashore

through the sea. But she emerges emphatically as prophetic leader. "Then *the prophet* Miriam . . .," Exod 15:20 tells us.

Something else becomes clear as well. Here we see for the first time how dramatically different Miriam's leadership is from that of Moses. It is inclusive, not the exclusivist patriarchal leadership of Moses. On Moses's tongue, the Song of the Sea becomes a bellicose, military song, with a tone of muscular triumphalism that is completely absent in the song Miriam sings. Miriam, with her tambourine in hand, singing and dancing out the people's praises to Yahweh, sends out an invitation to joyful worship of a God who has "triumphed gloriously." Moses's song is a warlike claim upon Yahweh as a grim, vengeful, "Man of War." The two songs sing of one event, but portray two completely versions of it, sing of two very different deities, leave two different and opposing traditions for the generations to follow and make choices. That is yet another great gift Miriam bestows on us: the gift of having choices.

When the people of Israel walked through the sea "on dry land," leaving the Egyptian armies "dead on the seashore" and the mighty empire for all intents and purposes defeated (14:30), Miriam *the prophet* took a tambourine in her hand, opened her mouth in song, and led the people in a dance of praise (Exod 15:20–21). This song represents the oldest extant writing concerning the exodus, and is the oldest poem in the Hebrew Bible. There is of course considerable difference of opinion among the scholars. Benno Jacob, speaking of the poem (vv. 1–19) as "the song of Moses," maintains: "The poem reflected the mood of a recent experience" (the exodus) and [as a whole] it is "older than the song of Deborah or the Psalms."[18]

Traditionally, male commentators, John Calvin, Benno Jacob, and a host of modern exegetes such as Millard C. Lind[19] among them, accept the song as originally from Moses. Whereas the poem proper is the Song of Moses, Jacob thinks, verses 20 and 21, where Miriam sings, "dealt with the musical rendition of the song . . . Miriam with timbrel in hand, leading the women," but *only* the women.[20] Calvin, too, cannot imagine "women taking the lead over men."[21] Here Miriam is decidedly secondary, reduced from prophet to choir leader. Miriam may have been so "enthusiastic" about what she had heard [Moses say] writes Jacob, that she led the women in *repetition* and for that she changed Moses's "I will sing" to "We will sing."[22] But why

---

18. See Jacob, *Exodus*, 434.
19. See Lind, *Yahweh is a Warrior*, 46ff.
20. Jacob, *Exodus*, 423.
21. Calvin, *Commentary*, Exod 15:20.
22. Jacob, *Exodus*, 423.

allow Miriam the power to change Moses's words to fit the occasion she has devised, instead of acknowledging her the power of original authorship? As many have pointed out, it is more reasonable to accept that the shorter version is original and the longer version an embellishment of that original.

However, Drorah O'Donnel Setel, articulating a growing consensus[23] amongst many others, calls it the "Song of Miriam." Miriam's version (vv. 20–21) is the shorter and *older than* the longer version (vv. 1–19),[24] John Durham, admitting that this is disputed, argues that ultimately "it does not matter."[25] But it clearly does matter a great deal since it raises quite pertinently the question of how the story of the exodus rooted in the faith and actions of women becomes a story of patriarchal power, with only the males having privileged access to a patriarchal God whose appointed agents they become.

> The fact that this citation has been preserved despite later perspectives that augment the significance of Moses while diminishing that of his sister has led scholars to believe that the work was indeed originally preserved as her creation.[26]

Richard Elliot Friedman, like Setel, suffers no uncertainty on both questions, that of the authorship of Miriam and the age of the hymn: "This poem, known as the Song of the Sea (or the Song of Miriam) is an independent, possibly the oldest composition in the Hebrew Bible."[27]

A SONG OF WAR?

It seems reasonable to conclude that the original song is in verses 20–21, whose words are taken up again verses 1 and 2, and are now laid in the mouth of Moses. Does it matter that as from verse 3 the song becomes an unabashedly military song? It matters a great deal, I think. Millard C. Lind considers that it is an "adjustment" such as is made in the song of Deborah: "It is an adjustment also made by Moses after the exodus by his acceptance

---

23. See Setel, "Exodus," 35ff.; Trible, "Bringing Miriam," 169–73; Jansen, "Song of Moses," 187–99. Jansen claims the whole song (15:1–18) for Miriam, although he does not seem to think the nuances in tone make any difference: "Thus by an analysis—diachronic or synchronic—the Song at the Sea is the Song of Miriam, and its performance as narrated in 15:1–18 comes as Moses and his fellow Israelites 'second' her hymnic initiative" (194). See also Fretheim, *Exodus*, 161.

24. Setel, "Exodus," 35.

25. See Durham, *Exodus*, 205–10.

26. Setel, "Exodus," 35.

27. Friedman, *Bible*, 144.

Standing Her Ground: The Riverbank and the Seashore

of the military role of Joshua."[28] Lind sees this adjustment occurring in Exod 17:8–16, but in reality it happens already in Exod 15:3. The argument holds here correctly, however, for Lind is right: essentially "[such an adjustment] is a threat against the Yahwist tradition, the entrenchment of a secular power that would use religion to achieve its own ends."[29] The "ends" here, in my view, are the imitation within Israel of the ways of empire, claiming Yahweh's consent to, and approval of military engagements where the glory is no longer Yahweh's alone, but now shared by Yahweh and the military leader, the king. It is an inevitable result of the patriarchal appropriation of the exodus tradition.

For the first time, Yahweh is praised as military leader, quite specifically a male warrior, a "man of war." The tone changes dramatically, as it equally dramatically changes the framework in which this song is now sung and meant to be read. With the praise of Yahweh as a "warrior," the language becomes warlike and more belligerent; war as war is glorified and Yahweh becomes the mere instrument through whose power the war is waged. Yahweh may be praised as the supreme "Man of war" but the implication is clear: Yahweh cannot win this war without Israel's "men of war."

The masculine bombast, the nationalistic belligerence, and the stringent muscularity of the theology in the poem is striking, and strikingly different from the Song of Miriam. Emphatically too, this warlike language changes the reality of the exodus story, from a story of God's glorious intervention to a glorification of war and conquest. And it is this moment, in the conflation of the miraculous delivery from Egypt with the myth of the blitzkrieg in and conquest and occupation of Canaan and the glories of a Jerusalem not yet reality, but here foreseen (15:14–17) that completely changes the character of the exodus story as it is taken from the women and placed in the hands of the men. In fact, it seems to me that here the exodus story ends, with the women, and the story of conquest begins, with the men.

Millard Lind seems to take no cognizance of the fact that the "military" character of the poem starts with verse 3, after the appropriation of the Song of Miriam and at the "take-over" of the patriarchal narrative with Moses at its center. He is emphatic: "There is no question but that the exercise of military power is the theme of this poem"[30] even though Lind, seeing his pacifist reading of these narratives, insists that "it is described as a battle, but not in the conventional [i.e., military] sense."[31] Setel also sees the song

---

28. Lind, *Yahweh Is a Warrior*, 76.
29. Lind, *Yahweh Is a Warrior*, 76.
30. Lind, *Yahweh Is a Warrior*, 49.
31. Lind, *Yahweh Is a Warrior*, 49.

as a warrior song. There is, she argues, a familiarity in the Hebrew Bible with the image of female warriors. "Beside the fact that there is no evidence of women's participation in battle, modern cultural prejudices should not prevent us from considering that possibility."[32]

But our "modern cultural prejudices" hardly come into play here, I should think. Setel seems to make the American situation a universal one. In liberation wars in the quests for freedom in the Global South, women have long played significant roles in violent struggle. The armed forces of the American Empire have accepted women for some years now and recently made that inclusion more comprehensive. Women are now fully recognized as soldiers and combatants at the same level as men, facing the same risks and dangers, even though one would be hard-pressed to describe that situation as one of equality.

Whether, as well, that is a strong argument for the equality of women in general in modern society, I would doubt sincerely. South Africans have words for such misguided desires for "equality" with men that do not take into account that it is patriarchy that is the ultimate determinant and beneficiary of this stance, not women. It is what a young man from the black townships, in a series of conversations on South Africa's reconciliation process I had led in 2011, tellingly called "bureaucratized feminism." Psychologist Cheryl Potgieter and theologian Sarojini Nadar, also both South African, in an even better formulation, called this phenomenon "for*men*ism."

> For*men*ism, like masculinism, subscribes to the belief in the inherent superiority of men over women, but unlike masculinism it is not an ideology developed and sustained by men, but an ideology designed, constructed, and sustained by women. Like its phonetics suggests, this is a concept for men—that is to say, men are the chief beneficiaries of the hierarchical social positioning that it advocates.[33]

This describes women placed or allowed in positions of influence and sometimes considerable power but only after they have completely embraced the kind of masculinity that in turn embraces aggression, violence, and hunger for power for power's sake, but shuns compassion as "weak." In fact, their politics display the same kind of intellectual and political barrenness inherent in imperial rule that Shifrah and Puah have so decisively dealt with in the first chapter of Exodus.

Potgieter and Nadar, and—taking further their analysis—Elna Boesak, discuss this phenomenon mainly as a religious one and make the point that

32. Lind, *Yahweh is a Warrior*, 35.
33. Potgieter and Nadar, "Living it Out," 143.

discourses that support and justify it are "particularly authoritative because they are 'sacred'. . ."[34] But the truth of their findings also holds for politics. We have seen this in the politics of women such as Indira Gandhi and her suppression of dissent in India in the late 1970s; in Madeleine Albright, Secretary of State in the Clinton White House, and more recently with Condaleezza Rice in the George W. Bush administration, Hilary Clinton as US Secretary of State under Barack Obama and as presidential candidate, and Samantha Power, Obama's ambassador to the United Nations. The same is true of Nicky Haley, current US representative at the UN as I write this. The fact that both Condoleeza Rice and Nicky Haley are women of color strengthens our argument against the politics of sentiment: it is completely irrelevant. What matters is that both of them are committed to the politics of the American Empire, not to the politics of justice and peace and life.

The police commissioner who ordered the South African police to fire live ammunition at striking workers, killing 34 on the spot in a horrific event now known as the Marikana Massacre in 2012, is a woman, Riah Phiyega. She, like the rest of the African National Congress leadership, has shown little remorse even as they have not been able to show any compassion with justice consequences for the victims or the families.

In former President Zuma's cabinet of 37 full ministers there were 15 women, making up 40 percent of the total. Even though the ANC's ideal number (50 percent) has not been reached yet, the South African Gender Equality Commission have declared themselves "pleased" with female representation in these positions of power. Yet organizations that fight gender inequality, gender-based violence, and rape have been continually underfunded for years, because government clearly does not care enough to see rape as the crisis it is.

Rape Crisis Cape Town Trust, an admirable (and actually indispensable) organization doing the hard work amidst the most alarming and rising statistics of rape in South Africa, does not receive enough political or financial support from the Western Cape Provincial government with Helen Zille, a woman, as provincial premier, or from Cape Town city, with yet another woman, Patricia De Lille, and both from the Democratic Alliance, because there is "no political will." The "lack of political will" seems a nonpartisan malady, spread across the political landscape. Rape Crisis Director

---

34. Potgieter and Nadar, "Living it Out," 143. See also E. Boesak, *Channelling Justice*, 126. Boesak, through thorough discourse analysis of the sermons and publications of two televangelists, Bishop T. D. Jakes and Prophetess Juanita Bynum, presents in her study evidence that these televangelists "build their authority and power over those who listen to them by claiming that they speak on behalf of God." E. Boesak, *Channelling Justice*, 128.

Kathleen Dey sums it up: "We've never had a leader in government who feels strong enough to take this matter forward and to champion the issues and ensure the correct legislation is formed to protect and empower the victims of rape."[35]

In the deliberately created crises devastating the Rohingya people in Myanmar, which the United Nations have called "a textbook example of ethnic cleansing" and Amnesty International has named "a crime against humanity similar to apartheid," Nobel Laureate Aung Sun Suu Kyi, once the very embodiment of the gentle, compassionate democrat the world was yearning for, is perhaps the most disturbing example of all.[36]

They are women, and they claim to represent the interests of women, even feminism, but their politics leave patriarchal hierarchical normativity completely intact. They exercise power for the benefit of empire, serving the patriarchal agenda and strengthening patriarchal power instead of challenging and subverting it. They are *for* men, not feminist or for women; theirs is not feminism but for*men*ism.[37]

In the course of this writing, Donald Trump has appointed Gina Haspel to head the Central Intelligence Agency, and she has been easily confirmed by the US Senate. Haspel was responsible for running at least one "black site" in Thailand, during a period in the George Bush years when the CIA's torture program was at full throttle. She was in charge when Abd al-Rahim al Nashin was waterboarded at least three times and interrogated using the CIA's "enhanced interrogation techniques." Haspel was also part of the chain of command that ordered the destruction of video tapes of the torture of Abu Zubaydah—waterboarded a staggering 83 times. "She earns a promotion," writes journalist Rebecca Gordon. "There are times when women might want to celebrate the shattering of the glass ceiling, but this shouldn't be one of them."[38]

The equally large question, though, is whether male Black liberation theologians have been bold enough to take the matter of gender-based violence seriously as one of the central issues for our theological reflection, of our theology and theologizing, knowing that our theological integrity is

---

35. See Dey, "'Rape Victims' Care Centres."

36. For the UN, see Cumming-Bruce, "Rohingya Crisis in Myanmar"; for Amnesty International see "Amnesty International calls on Myanmar." Even the US has belatedly stepped forward and recognized the actions of the Myanmar government as "ethnic cleansing;" see Al Jazeera News, "US: Myanmar Attacks on Rohingya 'Ethnic Cleansing.'"

37. I thank Elna Boesak who alerted me to this argument, used to such great effect in her own work. See her unpublished PhD dissertation, *Channeling Justice*.

38. See Gordon, "Trump's Recycling Program."

Standing Her Ground: The Riverbank and the Seashore 79

dependent on it, helping the Black church in its teaching and preaching. In 2013 when news of the horrific rapes in India spread shock, nausea, and anger across the world, in the same time span South African women had been brutalized by men in the same horrific crime: *9,000 rapes in seven weeks* including the horrifying rape, torture, and murder of 17-year-old Anene Booysen. As Black theologians we should ponder and respond to the question put by a secular newspaper in Cape Town: "If we [men] are not shamed into action by that statistic, what on earth will it take?"[39]

It is not enough, nor proper, nor right to assume that these are matters that should be addressed by women. It comes down to the issue we raised in chapter 1, namely that we have been alerted to our sexism, but we have hardly scratched the surface when it comes to combatting systemic, generational patriarchy in society in general and the black communities and church in particular, not its denial in society in general and the total neglect in addressing it in the Black church in particular.

SONG OF DEBORAH OR SONG OF HANNAH?

The challenges here are on multiple levels. Setel likens the Song of Miriam to the Song of Deborah (Judges 5) and as such it "challenges sexual stereotypes about women in ancient Israel," because "it [favorably] conveys an image of women as singers of war songs."[40] Again, it is strongly doubtful that this kind of equality with men—in belligerence, the despicable politics of war and the inevitable crimes of war, the mindless annihilation of the vulnerable of the world, the thousands upon thousands of women and children, and the utterly senseless destruction of the earth in every place America has been waging its endless imperial wars—is the kind of equality women, and the world, are in need of.

These arguments aside, however, the Song of Miriam is not a battle song as Setel insists. As Exodus 14 makes clear, this was no military battle; it was divine intervention on behalf of Israel. The point the Song of Miriam makes is exactly this: the vast military power of the empire is not able to withstand the power of God exercised on behalf of God's powerless people. The assurance that "Yahweh will fight your battles" means that Israel does not take up arms.

Miriam is not a comrade in the fight for the dubious right of women to be the equal of men in war, in violence and killing, the spilling of blood and the destruction of life, and in the case of the American Empire, in the

---

39. See *Cape Times*, "Editorial: Our Rape Crisis."
40. Setel, "Exodus," 35.

expansion of neoliberal capitalism and US militarism, all under the sanctifying power of American exceptionalism. Miriam is not a warrior reveling in the glorification of the might of empire, but a prophet in resistance to empire. The text explicitly calls Miriam a prophet, and that is what she is.[41] She is the first to contrast the power of Israel's prophetic faithfulness with the empire's violent power, a conviction firmly embraced in Israel's prophetic tradition as we hear from the lips of Elisha as Eljiah is taken up in the chariot of fire (2 Kgs 2:12).

In biblical Israel, the mark of greatness was not superiority in war and domination in imitation of empire. It was instead the imitation of the power of Yahweh: liberation from slavery, steadfast mercy and love, justice done to the vulnerable, the widow, the stranger, and the orphan. Indeed, Israel's very greatness was in preserving the presence of faithful prophetic witness, proclaiming *this* God over and against the gods of "the nations." As Elisha watches Elijah ascending on the "chariot of fire and the horses of fire," Elisha cries out, "Father! Father! The chariots of Israel and its horsemen!" (2 Kgs 2:12). Other ancient texts read "Woe! Woe!", appropriate to the deep sense of mourning at the loss of the heart of Israel's life: the prophetic presence. Israel's "weapons" were not chariots and horses and horsemen with their bows and swords and spears, is what Elisha means to say, but rather the faithful, courageous prophetic presence personified by Elijah. Not military strength, but prophetic power. Not the threat of intimidation and the destruction of violence, but prophetic faithfulness.

The solemn warnings in Deut 17 against royal abuse have as one of the very first: "[The king] shall not take the people back to Egypt." "Taking the people back to Egypt" can only mean taking them back to the deadly imitation of the super power, to the state of mindless enslavement, to before the liberation, away from the prophetic presence, to the other side of those "blood-red waters."[42] The deliberate focus on "Egypt" (the empire) and "horses" (military might) is a persistent protest against violence, the myth of the redemptive power of violence, and the empire's need for endless war. It is, in my view, a protest in the tradition of the women and the exodus, begun in the birth chamber, continued on the riverbank, and ending at the

---

41. See also Renate Jost's "The Daughters of Your People Prophesy" in Brenner, *A Feminist Companion*, 74, who makes the point that it would be incorrect to call Miriam simply "a singer." She is also emphatically one who intervened in political affairs. Jost quotes Hermann Speckermann: "True prophecy in Israel and Judah always attended something other than the good will of the king and for that reason it was well armed against any attempt to force it into line."

42. I have made this point before, and it seems worthwhile repeating here; see A. Boesak, *Dare We Speak of Hope?*, 9–10.

seashore; and against the tradition of the conquest begun with the "Song of Moses" in Exod 15:1–19.

Here, at the very dawn of Israel's birth as a free nation, comes the first and foundational confession about who Israel's God is. This God is not only in opposition to the gods of Egypt who the divine pharaoh represents and symbolizes, Yahweh is indeed the *total opposite* of the gods of the empire. Where Egypt depended upon military strength and weapons, Israel trusted in the prophetic presence, the prophetic word, and the *hesed* of God.[43]

"This is Israel's first song which celebrated [Yahweh] and [Yahweh's] wondrous deeds exclusively," argues Jacob. This is not a song praising the glory of war, Jacob goes on to say.

> This song sprang from the experience of Yahweh as judge and helper; therefore, it has been elevated to the crown of all poetry. It awakened only lofty feelings, not bitterness; as divine rather than human victory was celebrated. It did not combine praise of God and a treacherous murder in the same breath, as in the song of Deborah. *Israel had not yet reached that stage of nationalism which could have celebrated murder as heroism.* It believed that 'Mine is vengeance.' [Yahweh] is a God of vengeance, a God from whom revenge emanates.[44]

Ironically, Jacob can only say this of the original song sung by Miriam. The very first words out of the mouth of Moses nullify this otherwise accurate description. The Moses of 15:3ff. seems to be a far cry from the Moses of 14:13 who knew that if Israel would only "stand firm . . . Yahweh will fight for you."

Read thus, the Song of Miriam, in contrast with the Song of Moses, celebrates what Martin Luther King Jr. understood so well in reading this text as "a great moment" in Israel's history, "a joyous daybreak that had come to end the long night of their captivity." But here is King's important insight:

> The meaning of this story is not found in the drowning of Egyptian soldiers, for no one should rejoice at the death or defeat of a human being. Rather, this story symbolizes the death of evil and of inhuman oppression and unjust exploitation.[45]

And for King, "evil" is not something esoteric, the result of primitive thinking or the stuff of overwrought imaginations:

---

43. See also Jacob, *Exodus*, 411.
44. Jacob, *Exodus*, 414, my emphasis.
45. King, *Strength to Love*, 79.

> Within the wide arena of everyday life, we see evil in all of its ugly dimensions. We see it expressed in tragic lust and inordinate selfishness. We see it in high places where men [sic] are willing to sacrifice truth on the altars of their self-interest. We see it in imperialistic nations crushing other people with the battering rams of social injustice. We see it clothed in the garments of calamitous wars which leave men [sic] and nations morally and physically bankrupt.[46]

For Black liberation theology, this issue raises at least two questions. First, would the long and intense debates about violence and nonviolence in Black liberation theology have been different if we had understood that in proclaiming the exodus tradition we are not calling upon Moses's God as "a man of war" who blesses our violence, military might, and acts of vengeance, but on Miriam's God as the One who parts the waters and lets us see the death of evil upon the seashore? The One, as Hannah sings, who "breaks the bow of the mighty" and "cuts off the wicked in darkness, for not by might shall one prevail" (1 Sam 2:9), and who, in Mary's Song, will "throw down the powerful from their thrones" (Luke 1:52)?

In the history of ancient Israel, this is the moment when the first "freedom song" is turned into the first "song of war" with all of the dire consequences that a culture of violence always brings. A Miriamic Black liberation theology might have enabled South Africans to better discern the moments when the freedom songs of the students—*Akanamandla*, "the power of Satan is broken!"—that we sang during the states of emergency during the 1980s[47] were turned into Mkhonto we Sizwe's *Kill the Boer!* and Jacob Zuma's triumphalist war chant, *Umshini wam*, "Bring me my machine gun!" with all of the disastrous consequences *that* has brought us, and that will continue to confront South Africans for the foreseeable future.

Would we have been stronger in countering the romanticized, glorified violence seemingly so essential to struggles for freedom? Would we have a stronger ability, as had Albert Luthuli and Martin Luther King Jr., to insist upon the greater wisdom of militant nonviolence while not only understanding but intensifying the fight against the *causes* of counter violence in our struggles? Second, and perhaps even more crucially, would the image of God in Black liberation theology have been entirely different—not only less violent, but also less patriarchal, more feminine, with less lust for dominance and more desire for servanthood; less exclusivist and more inclusive, and all this more unhesitatingly proclaimed? How much does it

---

46. King, *Strength to Love*, 78.
47. See Boesak, *Pharaohs*, 87–88.

matter when we encourage the church to embrace the God of Shifra and Puah, of Jochebed and Miriam, of Mamie and Nomonde, rather than the God of Moses, the "Man of War," inseparable from Joshua, the man of total conquest and total annihilation, or Samson, the man of wanton destruction? And how much more emphatic would our resistance against the lust for power, possession, and control have been, against which the Confession of Belhar so pointedly agitates?[48]

A church in denial of the God of Miriam and Hannah, of Mary the revolutionary mother of Jesus and Mary Magdalene, will continue the tyrannical teaching of male dominance and "headship" in our churches, falsely ascribed to the Apostle Paul, and so devastatingly harmful to women in too many ways to adequately describe.

Benno Jacob reads the song as a celebration of contrasts. This song is not about Israel's military strength, military tactics, or courage in battle. These events were the works of God's hands. Not arms and horses and chariots, but the elements of nature were God's tools: "But there was a difference. God was not *in* the water [roiling in and with it] but *above* it [in control of it]." The divine breath had parted the waters, consumed the foe like stubble. "This presented a contrast to Pharaoh's boast which emphasized, 'I will pursue'; 'my sword'; 'my hand'. The enemy's destruction was paralleled by God's gentle leadership of Israel."[49]

Miriam's song also contrasted the disdain and hatred of the pharaoh for his slaves with the love God has for God's enslaved people expressed in God's judgment of the slaveholder, "for [God] favored the oppressed and was their redeemer."[50] This thought, argues Jacob, is the focal point of the entire poem and it is also its "ultimate lesson": first, that Israel's God is a God who sides with the oppressed; and second, that Pharaoh's might was

---

48. See the Belhar Confession, https://www.pcusa.org/site_media/media/uploads/theologyandworship/pdfs/belhar.pdf. See 10.7, "[We believe] that the church as the possession of God must stand where the Lord stands, namely against injustice and with the wronged; that in following Christ the church must witness against all the powerful and privileged who selfishly seek their own interests and thus [seek to] control and harm others." *Belhar* is more relevant now than when it was written. The current raging factional battles within the African National Congress, the far-too-often deadly internecine violence in the province of KwaZulu-Natal, and the relationships within the top leadership strained to breaking point, are all, in my view, the tragic consequences of the lust for power, position, control over others, and monetary reward that has gripped the organization since its return from exile. These are at the root of what ails the organization, and they cannot be "self-corrected." It is a deeper spiritual cleansing that is needed. Is the Black church, as "possession of God" and not as the political captive of the ANC, able to speak truth to power in these matters?

49. Jacob, *Exodus*, 418, emphasis in original.

50. Jacob, *Exodus*, 418.

established upon chariots and riders, for he was a *human king* who ruled by military force. Israel's kings felt no need for such displays of power until Solomon who imitated the Egyptians, Jacob argues. "God's might was presented in contrast, so they were immediately destroyed by [God] who ruled only through the power of [God's] name. [God] is the One who has no pleasure in the strength of horses" (Ps 147:10).[51]

The song is not only a song of celebration and contrast. It is also a song of protest. It protested the teaching of the powerful, who claimed that God was always on the side of the strongest armies. "There were mightier forces [than the power of empires] and God is showing that here."[52]

Miriam's is a theology that explicitly praises God *not* as a warrior. Hers is not a muscular, masculine God whose power seeks to match the power of Egypt's empire. Her God has a power that through radical love for a slave people and taking sides with the enslaved, overcomes the power of the slaveholder. In doing this, Miriam recalls the God of the exodus, who begins the acts of liberation with the women, to whose faithfulness, courage, and defiant obedience the freedom of the people is entrusted.

PROPHET OF THE PEOPLE

Jacob makes the point that Miriam, in verses 20 and 21, "turns the song into a congregational hymn," meaning that whereas Moses had done this as an individual, on Miriam's lips it is a song of praise and celebration for the whole people. Jacob makes it sound as if this were a negative development, presumably because of the inclusion of all the people, not just the men, and the implied leadership position it gives Miriam, also over the men. But in doing this Miriam proves herself to be a prophet of God *from among the people*, insisting on the inclusion of men and women in the glorification and hence the ownership of the mighty acts of God, thereby owning their agency in their liberation, as did Shifrah and Puah.

Phyllis Trible points out that the text reads that Miriam, with tambourine in hand, sang responsively to "them." "Yet, the Hebrew pronoun 'them' is masculine, not feminine, gender, yielding an ambiguous referent." Her conclusion is not far-fetched: that under the leadership of Miriam, the ritual includes *all* the people, "though the major participants were women."[53] Already here Miriam's prophetic leadership is qualitatively different than that of Moses. It is radically inclusive.

---

51. Jacob, *Exodus*, 418.
52. Jacob, *Exodus*, 419.
53. Trible, "Bringing Miriam Out of the Shadows," 171.

What happens here is quite radical, in my view. And even here Miriam is setting the precedent, seemingly too dangerous for men to consider, most importantly for women's prophetic leadership, but also for women's equal participation in ritual and worship, in claiming the wondrous delivery from Egypt for the people as a whole. Moses claims individual ownership; Miriam opens ownership of the praise for Yahweh to the whole people. Moses's song is the praise of an individual standing in for the whole. Miriam's song is a celebration of the collective thanksgiving, praise, and worship of the God who is the Savior of all the people. Miriam's theology is one that does not abide mediators and "middle men": she stands and brings the people with her, directly before the One who hears, knows, sees, and rescues. There is a radical inclusivity of worship at work here, and a radical overturning of the patriarchal paradigm as there was radical inclusivity in the acts of liberation in the birthing chamber and on the riverbank. Miriam holds up the God who does not need to take refuge in violence in order to be worshiped, a God not in need of muscled, exclusivist, harmful masculinity in order to be God. It is also a radical, collective embracing of the responsibilities that come with freedom. Miriam is the people's prophet.

Miriam's leadership of radical inclusivity goes one step further, I believe. As we shall see in the next chapter, traditional interpretation holds that the series of rebellions in the wilderness that would engulf Moses and put his leadership in crisis, started with the "rabble," the non-Israelites who fled out of Egypt with the Hebrew slaves (Exod 12:38; Lev 24:10). In that interpretation they are the troublemakers who contaminate the people, enticing them away from Moses and the Lord. But there are other, more important reasons to mention here.

First, this means that in the original struggle for freedom and flight toward freedom, the "oppressed" were not just the Hebrew oppressed. Other slaves, not Hebrews, were also seen as part of the "oppressed masses" yearning for freedom. They were part of the struggle, part of the flight, and part of the rejoicing masses on the other side of the Red Sea, led by Miriam in those acts of rejoicing. In South Africa's struggle for freedom, the notion of "the solidarity of the oppressed" gained from the philosophy of Black Consciousness would prove indispensable, even redemptive. It overcame the divide-and-rule chaos caused by apartheid's racial and ethnic hierarchies and seriously subverted apartheid's tyrannical pigmentocracy. It provided political discernment, overcame centuries of internalized powerlessness, social destructiveness, and religious divisiveness, helped to focus our revolution in ways seldom seen before. It also provided sound grounding for one of the struggle's most precious, and most fragile ideals, namely non-racialism.

Second, it is only later, in the wilderness, under the patriarchal and exclusivist leadership of Moses, that they become the "Other," that despised "mixed crowd" of Exod 12:38, mentioned in one breath with the "livestock, flocks, and herds." This is the beginning of a growing ideology of supremacist disdain, the introduction of a fateful "othering." Miriam's radical inclusivity would succumb to political and ethnic expediency. Eurocentric commentators would not even notice: "It is the refusal to be satisfied with the gifts God has given that leads the rabble to stir up a mood of disgruntled dissatisfaction among the Israelites" writes Olsen.[54] Of Miriam's notion of the solidarity of the oppressed there would remain no sign.

Third, it is also the beginnings of a much disturbing trend. In his detailed and still brilliant scholarly study, Joachim Jeremias, in the course of a quite different argument, quotes from a letter from Sextus Julius Africanus, third-century Libyan philosopher who referred to the people who "came out of Egypt with the Israelites" as "that mixed race."[55] The prejudice some have—wrongly, in my view—perceived in Miriam regarding Moses's Cushite wife, was not the first sign of what today would be called racial animosity in ancient Israel. It seems to have come with the choice for the Mosaic, patriarchal tradition.

Fourth, it is here, in the actual disdain for and distancing from "the mixed crowd," that we find the firm establishment of the idea of Israelite superiority, of "chosenness" over against "the other nations," a belief that has become the focus of such insistent critique from scholars in the Global South, as we shall see. It is a belief of uniqueness above all others clearly and unambiguously articulated by Moses, "In this way, we shall be distinct, I and your people, from every people on the face of the earth" (Exod 33:15–16). It is the notion of exceptionalism essentially based on racial superiority disguised as "religious uniqueness" that has informed and sustained the ideologies of superiority and supremacy at the heart of all historic acts of conquest and colonization from the conquest of ancient Palestine to the occupation of Palestine, and so eagerly embraced by white imperialists and colonizers from Gollwitzer's "white Christian peoples" to white Christian invaders of America, white colonizers of Africa and modern Israelis in their occupation

---

54. Olsen, *Numbers*, 65.

55. See Joachim Jeremias's reference to "Letter to Aristedes," *Jerusalem in the Time of Jesus*, 281. Jeremias references Walther Reichardt, *Die Briefe des Sextus Africanus*, 61. According to Richard Gottheil and Samuel Kraus, Sextus Julius Africanus was, as predecessor of Eusebius, the "founder of Church history" who in this letter "also shows that he is well versed in Jewish history." See Jewish Encyclopedia, http://www.jewishencyclopedia.com/articles/13459-sextus-julius-africanus.

of Palestine.⁵⁶ It has produced land theft, genocide, and dispossession on a scale that will never be equaled, and slavery that "even today has not yet ended." It has also produced the supposed Calvinist "predestination" theologies that drove white American and white South African exceptionalism, white supremacy, and white superiority. And the devastating consequences for colonized and neo-colonized people are equally as far from over.

Miriam the prophet of the people—women and men following her in praising the glory of Yahweh, sings a song that will be picked up by Hannah: this God is the one who empowers her to chastise the "arrogant" not to "talk so proudly, and to remind all that God is a "God of knowledge" who is not impressed by loudmouthed verbosity, but who "weighs" our actions. While the "bows of the mighty are broken" it is "the feeble" who "gird on strength." So let no one be fooled, for "not by might shall one prevail" (1 Sam 2:1–10). It is a song that praises the One overcoming not only the violence of the powerful and the wicked who "shall be cut off in darkness," but also the desire for violence on the part of those whose trust is in God.

The God of Miriam who "triumphed gloriously" in the liberation from Egypt, in the birthing chamber, on the riverbank, and at the parting of the waters is the One Mary's Magnificat magnifies, the One who "scatters the proud in the thoughts of their hearts," and who, in every generation, does "great things." This is the God of the poor who "fills the hungry with good things," sending the rich away empty-handed. What would that insight have to say about the neoliberal capitalist theologies now prevalent in what Paula McGee calls "the new Black church," that bless the overflowing hands of the rich and exploit the empty hands of the poor; about our tolerance of the

---

56. The immutable problem at the heart of this matter that is only now being seriously addressed is succinctly formulated by Rosemary Ruether: "For the ancient Hebrews, as well as the Jewish people through the ages, the chosen people are Israel, a particular people created by a religiously defined ethnicity. Israel is those who covenant with God to be his people, yet Jewishness is also an inherited ethnicity. This national God gave his people the law as a way of life through whose observance obedience to God is fulfilled. This God also promised his people a land and a flourishing future in relation to all the other nations in the Middle East." See Ruether, *America, Amerikkka*, 7. She then offers a devastating and convincing analysis of how this notion and its inherent contradiction has determined the belief, and its consequences "that America is uniquely innocent and good, chosen by God to defend freedom and democracy around the world" as she sums it up on 1 and 2. The issue here of course is not so much that the unique and special status ancient Israel claimed for itself was "in relation" to other peoples of the Middle East, but precisely at the cost of the ancient inhabitants of those lands. This is what indigenous peoples from Palestine to Africa to South America and the United States are no longer willing to accept, and that is precisely the challenge Black liberation theology must now come to terms with. White, powerful, and privileged beneficiaries of empire apparently live comfortably with the "contradictions" inherent in these views as Reuther points out on practically every page. Oppressed people cannot.

disastrous and growing chasm between rich and poor everywhere? How would Mary's song help us fight the fatuous but nonetheless blasphemous claims of the prosperity gospel that has now overtaken our churches and our people with such emphatic triumphalism?[57]

What difference would it have made if Black liberation theology not only had Jesus's sermon from Luke 4 as anchor text, but also, and with as much acclaim, honor, embrace, and attention, the Magnificat of Mary? What if our revolutions were more inspired by Mary's belief that the "powerful" have already been "brought down from their thrones" and less by Moses's fruitless negotiations with empire before the throne of Pharaoh—the staff turning into a snake; the water turning into blood; a hand turning leprous, all seemingly good political theater but getting the people nowhere? What if we paid less homage to Moses but embraced more fully the "lowly servant" of the Mighty One, the young, poor, but stunningly strong Afro-Asian woman who caught all this in a revolutionary song, long before her son said it in a revolutionary manifesto in a synagogue in Nazareth?

---

57. See the strong argument of McGee, *Brand* New Theology*; also McMickle, *Where Have All the Prophets Gone?*, who speaks of the "obstructions" in the way of prophetic preaching such as "a narrow definition of justice that does not extend beyond abortion and same-sex marriages," the focus on praise and worship that "does not result in any duty and discipleship," and the "vile messages of prosperity that seem to have overtaken the pulpits and the airwaves. . ." (vii).

Chapter Four

DRINKING FROM THE WATERS OF MERIBAH

Black Theology, Liberation, and the Integrity of Radical Engagement

IN THE WILDERNESS

THE WILDERNESS BECOMES THE place of the final revelation of the power of Miriam's prophetic calling. Trible vividly speaks of the "wilds of the wilderness."[1] It is more than just a place of wandering. The uncertainties, complaints, confusions, and conflict make this a "wild" place. Everything, including the deity, becomes ambivalent. The people rebel and this causes great shifts in the narrative, but there is more at hand:

> Entangled in the wilderness multiple layers of tradition defy source analysis and internal coherence to become much like the chaos they report. The task of the interpreter is to discern Miriam's story amid the muddle.[2]

So we are put on notice. The contention is not just between siblings, or representatives of different views in the camp, or even (male) rivalry for leadership. Fundamentally, it is between "layers of tradition." That in this

---

1. See Trible, "Bringing Miriam Out of the Shadows," 173.
2. Trible, "Bringing Miriam Out of the Shadows," 173.

contentious moment Miriam is central, and crucial, will become clear. And we shall continue to try and discern "amid the muddle" Miriam's story from a Black liberation theology point of view, keeping in mind that what is at issue here is not just a different side of the story, but two distinct traditions, the one dominant, the other suppressed, inviting us to make a choice.

Most commentaries read the series of rebellions as a lack of faith in the promises of Yahweh that lays a heavy burden on the leadership of Moses. The blame is on the recalcitrant people. The ecumenical Dutch *International Commentary on the Bible* sums it up well in the "first orientation" to the reading of Numbers. The headline to the second subsection reads, "The Faithfulness of God to His Promises Despite the Faithlessness of the People." The authors write, bringing God, Moses and Aaron neatly together,

> The people, however, begin to doubt God's word: the agreements made are put under suspicion and the authority of Moses and Aaron are resisted. The Israelites refuse to follow [God's] way to conquer the land of Canaan... Despite revolt and rebellion God keeps his promises. Of course the guilty ones are punished, but Israel remains heir to the Promised Land.[3]

Note how this commentary conflates "God's way" with the conquest of Canaan. In this reading the impression is that the people may have reservations, hence the stern responses from God and Moses.[4] It is a pro-imperial, pro-exceptionalist reading.

Naomi Graetz, appropriately, urges us to read Miriam's role in the wilderness within the context of recurring rebellion against Moses; a "people's rebellion" she calls it.[5] It begins in Numbers 11. Ominously, the chapter opens with the reference to "Taberah," which means "burning." The fire that destroys only the periphery of the camp is Yahweh's inflamed response to the people's first complaints. That fire is only the beginning though. The growing, rebellious restlessness reveals as much about the people as it does about Moses and the God Moses calls upon.

---

3. Eynikel et al., *Internationaal Commentaar op de Bijbel*, Band I, 548. My translation.

4. The Book of Judges, chapter 1, tells us that this was no blitzkrieg and no total conquest, rather the impression is of a gradual settlement amongst the original inhabitants of Palestine. The total conquest of Palestine as described in the book of Joshua with its God-ordained wholesale slaughters is more and more exposed as an ideological rendition of history rather than as historical fact. But the power of this ideology, coupled as it is with the religious myth of "election," "chosenness," exceptionalism, and divine right, is devastatingly clear in the continued illegal occupation of Palestine by the state of Israel today.

5. Graetz, "Did Miriam Talk Too Much?," 231–42.

But what Graetz calls a "peoples' rebellion," B. Maarsingh sees as the rebelliousness of disgruntled groups he identifies as "rabble" (or "riff-raff"), a "mixed company" of people (not Israelites) who came along with the Israelites when they left Egypt.[6] Philip J. Budd thinks that the "degree of contempt" that may be in the word "riff-raff" indicates those among the Israelites "governed not by powers of discrimination and insight, but by sensual appetite."[7] At the seashore these people, under Miriam's prophetic leadership, all participated in the joyful celebration of God's acts of deliverance. That seems to have changed drastically. The disdain for these alleged troublemakers is not hidden. At this point the "anger" of the LORD does not yet claim human lives although comes perilously close, and the people are now put on alert that complaining against Moses carries a great cost.

It is only later that the text discloses that the complaints are about food, to be precise, the lack of meat, and for Maarsingh, it is among the "rabble" that the demand for food begins and spreads to the Israelites.[8] So too surmises Dennis T. Olsen, who states that the "discontent" seems to be "spreading from the margins [the "mixed crowd"] to the center of the camp."[9] This "mixed group" may be the rabble here, but by the time the rebellion reaches its peak *all* the people will be rebellious rabble in Moses's angry eyes (Num 20:10). At this point, the pretext is the boring menu of manna every day that makes them long for the plenty of Egypt. Earlier, they were somewhat vaguely longing for "the flesh pots of Egypt" (Exod 16:3). Now, in their heightened agitation, the abundance and variety of Egypt's menu is detailed (Num 11:4–6). Food might be the matter they raise, but the deeper issue is that enduring longing for "Egypt." It is this "Egypt mind set" that really characterizes this rebellion.

Moses's response is intense and deeply personalized as he takes his plight to God. He uses words like "onrush," "pressure," and "attack." The Vulgate repeats his "Why?" three times.[10] There are immediate consequences: a) Moses's realization of the difficulties of sole, highly personalized leadership; b) God's solution: the sharing of responsibility for governance by the appointment of seventy elders. So perhaps even though the complaint is only about food, Moses's political instincts tell him that there might be more just below the surface. He recognizes the dangers of the slippery slope that starts with ignoring ostensibly small matters. The institution of the elders

---

6. Maarsingh, *Numbers*, 38.
7. Budd, *Numbers*, 127.
8. Maarsingh, *Numbers*, 38, 39.
9. See Olsen, *Numbers*, 64.
10. Maarsingh, *Numbers*, 39.

is a device for the sharing of responsibility for governance. However, it soon becomes clear that sharing of responsibility does not mean sharing of power. The power seems to remain wholly in Moses's hands. What Moses and God propose and implement is not transformation of leadership; it is piecemeal reform. It is not fundamental change; it looks more like a grudging, tactical concession.

Almost immediately the limitations of Moses's reforms in the style of leadership are exposed. It essentially remains what one could call benevolent dictatorship: the elders did not really "share" power with Moses; Moses's authority remained unchallenged. They were given *some* of the spirit "that was upon Moses" (11:25). In reality, however, that was a top-down arrangement, not an unreserved gifting, seemingly in Moses's control, a spiritual "trickle-down" act of limited power and hence limited effect: the elders began to prophesy, and then they stopped. "They did not do so again" (11:25).

However, two "rogue" prophets who "remained in the camp" emerge, Eldad and Medad. Is it in rebellion against the severe limitation of the "democratization" of leadership—only the seventy and a still unchallengeable Moses? Or is it in support of Moses? When the elders "stopped" prophesying (we are not told why), these two prophesy. They did so because "the spirit rested on them" (v. 26). The contents and target audience of their prophecies the text does not disclose. Enough people hear them though and news of this extraordinary event spreads quickly. Not surprisingly, Moses's young protégé from the circle of "chosen men,"[11] Joshua, "ran" to complain to Moses—possibly seeing his chances of taking over the leadership threatened by this bold act. He took with him another unidentified "young man," possibly already part of Joshua's "transition team."

Moses, however, sees their concern for what it is: "Are you jealous for my sake?" (11:29). Instead of admonishing Eldad and Medad, Moses utters the surprising, and still inspiring words, "Would that all the LORD's people were prophets, and that the LORD would put his spirit on them!" One cannot really imagine this to be a corrective on Yahweh's decision that Moses should choose only seventy elders on whom "some" of his prophetic and leadership spirit would rest, while Moses himself would have wanted what we today would call "full, participatory democracy."

Clearly Moses saw no danger in these men also having received the gift of prophecy. Perhaps Moses thought that their concerns were about personal ambition, not reflecting the will of the people. Or was the deciding factor that they were male? For them, there is no rebuke and no punishment. Not for the act of prophecy, nor for the fact that they apparently

---

11. Maarsingh, *Numbers*, 42.

ignored the command for "all" the men to gather at the tent: they "remained in the camp"—with the women. Perhaps Moses did not think that a prophecy, whatever its content, could have significant impact on the situation because the hearers were only women who had no meaningful say in matters of governance anyway.

Perhaps their prophecy was in Moses's favor, upholding his leadership as a gift from God to Israel. As such their gift would only help Moses, already struggling to manage a whole people now showing signs of restlessness, and would help secure some much-needed support and legitimation from the governed. It could also constitute a threat only to Joshua's hopes of leadership, because who knows whether the people, moved by the bold act of prophecy given wholly to Moses and only partially to the elders, would come to see not Joshua, but Eldad or Medad, as the natural successors to Moses.

The fact that out of the whole camp only two very self-interested men raised a complaint may perhaps also mean that the people were indeed ready for less authoritarian rule, a nascent yearning for the egalitarian community Israel would become, as Norman Gottwald has powerfully argued,[12] before the disastrous longing for a king in order to be "like the other nations" (1 Sam 8). If it is, it is a yearning that will return more forcefully in chapter 16.

"AND MIRIAM SPOKE."

"Has the LORD only spoken to Moses? Has he not spoken also through us?" (Num 12:2). Two sentences of seven words each are about to shake the patriarchal world of the trekkers through the wilderness. Miriam's speaking "against Moses," so we recall Graetz's reminder, occurs within the broader context of the people's rebellion, or better: the recurring and intensifying rebellions of which we are told in Numbers 11, 12, 14, 16, and 20, beginning with the grumblings about food. Then follow the independent prophecies of Eldad and Medad, the response of Moses, and Miriam's question (Num 11, 12). In chapter 14 it is the people's fearful response to the spies' report that becomes the issue. Not only do they want to return to Egypt, they want a new leader. "Let us" (not God), "choose a captain" (14:4). This displays a stronger tone of rebelliousness so disturbing that God wants "to strike the people with pestilence." Here Moses intervenes, and God forgives, though not totally (14:13–25).

Chapter 16 tells of a revolt with strong priestly undertones led by Korah, Dathan, and Abiram, and this is even more serious, representing

---

12. See Gottwald, *Tribes of Yahweh*.

a rebellion from different groups, some of them from the "elite" in Israel, "leaders of the congregation, chosen from the assembly, well-known men" (16:2). "You have gone too far!" the leaders tell Moses and Aaron. "All the congregation are holy, everyone of them, and the LORD is among them. So why then do you exalt yourselves above the assembly of the LORD?" In that "You are exalting yourselves"—behaving like the princes of Egypt—we may read a pointed critique of a perceived arrogance of power. This call for egalitarian inclusivity proves too much. Again God strikes on behalf of Moses, and this time Moses does not intervene. "The earth opened its mouth and swallowed them up, along with their households—everyone who belonged to Korah and all their goods" (v. 32). Here is an example of the terror of collective punishment, in our day all too often executed with such devastating effectiveness by the State of Israel against Palestinians—a whole family wiped out, a whole community obliterated, a whole village destroyed in revenge for one act of resistance against the occupation.[13]

But a rebellion on this scale had to be dealt with more thoroughly, and this God is nothing if not thorough. Not only Moses in his political supremacy, but this time Aaron too, would be secured in his priestly authority. "And fire came out from the LORD and consumed the two hundred fifty men offering the incense" (v. 35). This is on top of those who had already perished. As "the whole congregation," shocked by the severity of the punishment, join the rebellion, it goes beyond a quarrel over priestly functions and privileges: "You have killed the people of the LORD" (v. 41). What was a perception of the *arrogance* of power a few verses back, now becomes the recognition of the *abuse* of power. Through it all, Moses's control, albeit with God's aid—God strikes the people with a plague—holds up, although clearly shaken, until chapter 20. Trible's description of these events as "chaotic" is no hyperbole.

It is here, however, with Miriam's speaking in chapter 12, where everything changes.

Philip J. Budd suggests that "essentially, Miriam represents those who speak against the representatives of Mosaic authority.[14] This and nothing more is the point of the story." Miriam's "suitability as opponent" in the story lies "simply" in the fact that she is no more than

---

13. The outstanding example here is of course Israel's war against the citizens of Gaza; see *inter alia* Cohn, "Israel's Collective Punishment of Gaza." See also Wilson, "Israel's Collective Punishment Follows Jerusalem Attack," and Gostoli, "'Bad Palestinians' under Israel's Collective Punishment."

14. Budd, *Numbers*, 135, 136.

a leader figure from the past. Her "prophetic" connections were valuable because they showed that even those who claimed such inspiration had no right to speak against Moses. There is a uniqueness and supremacy about Mosaic revelation which must be recognized and acknowledged by all.[15]

Budd's comment on this matter should give us pause on two counts. First, he places Miriam's prophetic role in inverted commas, thereby placing the authenticity of her prophetic action at the seashore in doubt. Was Miriam a pretender, we now have to ask, an opportunist finally exposed and dealt with? Her prophetic acts on the seashore are now solidly in doubt. Second, even if granted a role at the seashore, she is a "leader figure *from the past*." Whatever she might have been at the seashore is over. The new leadership is male, and emphatically so. Miriam, groping for past glory, and those for whom she speaks have failed to "move on." But this proves the point so forcefully made by Cheryl Exum: that since biblical literature was produced by and for an androcentric community, women in the stories are "male constructs," they "serve androcentric interests." Where women are concerned, one must be suspicious of the motives of male narrators.[16] The duty of the interpreter is to ask why women are allowed to play important roles in the story.

While I do not think that particular suspicion applies to the role of the midwives in Exodus 1, as Exum also argues, I do think it is applicable here, not just in the story but in the commentary as well. As I read Budd, Miriam was "allowed" to play the "prophetic" role at the seashore, in order to later show the absolute "supremacy" of Mosaic leadership. The role, highlighted as it is, is important only insofar as it serves as a tool in the androcentric narrative, to be used as example of what will happen to those who dare to challenge that authority.

That Miriam was the example chosen means that the issue was not just about the "uniqueness and supremacy" of Mosaic leadership and authority as Budd argues. It was about the uniqueness and supremacy of *patriarchal* leadership and authority, here set in stone not just for Moses, but for the generations to come. The author is killing two birds with one stone, so to speak, making the matter of patriarchal supremacy and its untouchability not merely coincidental, but systemic. In dealing so emphatically with Miriam, however, the narrator also decisively deals with the image of God Miriam has held up at the seashore.

---

15. Budd, *Numbers*, 135.
16. Exum, "Second Thoughts About Secondary Characters," 79.

Again the narrative provides a pretext: the Cushite woman that Moses married. Mentioned only once, she disappears from the story. Within this broader context, the matter of the Cushite woman functions more as added confusion to the text than providing any real reason for what occurs. Since we know nothing specific, or more, about this woman, "we can only speculate."[17]

With accurate hermeneutical suspicion Trible,[18] and Graetz,[19] raise important questions around the issue: Is this a question of only ritual cleanliness, or perhaps of racism? Why does the narrator set woman against woman? Why does Moses remain silent when accused by Miriam and Aaron? Why did God [have to] defend Moses's honor in such a drastic way?

Womanist theologian Renita Weems also sees a racist motive here and goes further than both Graetz and Trible.[20] Moses's wife was a foreigner, a Cushite, an Ethiopian, and, therefore, an African.[21] Perhaps Miriam wanted to "protect Moses from some malicious gossip," Weems writes, making Miriam the articulator, even the representation of, the tribe's racism. Even if Moses's marriage "was a grave mistake, it was not the public crime Miriam made it out to be."[22] For Weems, Miriam presents a problem for both Moses and his wife, and in both cases Miriam's great temptation is deep, unsettling jealousy.[23]

In Weems's reading Miriam becomes the ultimate dangerous woman, caught in a deeply personalized, irrational anger: "Hurt, frustrated, insecure, envious and feeling displaced, Miriam set out to make life for her Ethiopian sister-in-law miserable."[24] Miriam becomes dangerous; not the danger of subversive combativeness, but the danger of self-indulgent pettiness: the

---

17. Trible, "Bringing Miriam Out of the Shadows," 175.

18. Trible, "Bringing Miriam Out of the Shadows," 175.

19. Graetz, "Did Miriam Talk Too Much?," 232-33.

20. Weems, *Just a Sister Away*, 75. Weems is not alone among women to follow this interpretation. Phyllis Silverman Kramer also accepts that Miriam's words of criticism are a token of "antagonism" and "jealousy" triggered by Moses's Cushite wife "and because of this bitter resentment she challenged God, expressing her bitterness verbally" (Kramer, "Miriam," 104-33).

21. Weems, *Just a Sister Away*, 75. One gets the impression that within this context, Miriam is presented as regarding herself, and the Hebrews, as "white."

22. Weems, *Just a Sister Away*, 75. Cain Hope Felder also strongly racializes this issue: "Numbers 12 attests all too well to the way individuals can quickly move from a sacred ethnic stance to racism of the worst sort." See *Troubling Biblical Waters*, 42.

23. Weems follows a "reconstruction of the tension between Miriam and her sister-in-law," one she admits is "hypothetical," but she nonetheless draws quite drastic conclusions from it (77ff.).

24. Weems, *Just a Sister Away*, 76.

new wife becomes a "threat" to Miriam, and Miriam's jealousy becomes a threat to Israel:

> Just think: If Miriam was daring enough to challenge her beloved brother's sacred leadership—Moses, appointed and acknowledged leaders of the Hebrews; Moses insulated from any attack Miriam (or anyone else for that matter) might have launched against him—there is no limit to what her conduct toward her sister-in-law might have been.[25]

As for Miriam's conduct toward Moses, the verdict is just as stern:

> How quickly the poet and prophetess of praise and thanksgiving became the instigator of discord and discontent! The same gifts Miriam had once employed to unite the people behind her brother's leadership, she now used to undermine his leadership.[26]

This drastic shift from public engagement to an intensely personalized family feud produces a strange circumstance. Weems sets woman against woman in a hypothetical battle and allows the decidedly non-hypothetical problem of patriarchal hegemony to go unaddressed. No less problematic is the (unintended?) contradiction: a domesticated, depoliticized Miriam reduced to petty jealousies but with nonetheless grave political consequences. In this reading, moreover, at the seashore Miriam provides no leadership uniquely her own. She merely "unites the people behind her brother's leadership"—a leadership that is sacred. This is quite the opposite of what my reading of the story discovers.

The text cannot pretend that the pretext cannot be sustained. It crumbles before the real question Miriam raises: that of prophetic authority. Miriam "speaks" and asks not only how *Moses* speaks but more importantly *whether* Yahweh speaks, if Yahweh speaks *only* through Moses. It is not petty jealousy at work here, it is radical engagement with the issues that really matter.

Graetz's question, "Why was Miriam punished and not Aaron?" and her response to it perhaps cover all those questions and exposes the heart of the matter here:

> I suggest that Miriam was punished with leprosy *because women in the biblical world were not supposed to be leaders of men, and that women with initiative were reproved when they asserted themselves with the only weapon they had, their power*

25. Weems, *Just a Sister Away*, 75.
26. Weems, *Just a Sister Away*, 74.

> *of language:* a power which could be used viciously and was, therefore, called *lason hara,* literally the evil tongue.[27]

Exum does not hesitate to define this situation as "gender politics at work."

> As a man, Aaron poses no threat to the symbolic order. On the contrary, his proper place is inside it; he remains within the camp. While leaving Aaron unblemished and unpunished, Numbers 12 efficiently humiliates and eliminates the woman.[28]

It is important that we remember when Miriam's intervention comes—at a time so politically critical she can no longer be ignored. Trible is correct—she steps "out of the shadows." The "rogue prophets" episode interrupts, but does not override, the story of the first rebellion, which is picked up again in verse 31. That episode ends in tragedy. But as I see it the point is not so much the punishment meted out to those who rebelled even though in itself it does stun the mind. The point here is the cool, calculated, deliberate premeditation of it, and the shock and awe with which it is executed. Between Num 11:16 and 11:23, Yahweh and Moses concoct not just the plan of the election of the seventy, but also a way to punish the rebellious. The plan is to invite the people to a ritual feast for which they must "consecrate" themselves (v. 18)—a "preparation for a solemn religious occasion," Maarsingh calls it. It was to be a "dinner" that would last "a full month and God himself [sic] would provide an abundance of meat."[29] Even though the story provides hints of something sinister afoot—they will eat meat until "it comes out of their nostrils"—the plan itself remains a secret between Moses and Yahweh.

There is a lengthy conversation about the availability of the meat the rebels craved and that should be ready for the feast, told in a way that leads up to Moses's having to be convinced of the power of God's ability to provide for the occasion. Moses pointedly reminds Yahweh of the numbers: "six hundred thousand on foot" (v. 21). It is a spirited discussion: "Look

---

27. It is not necessary here to indulge in the many ways the rabbis sought to denigrate Miriam because of her temerity to challenge Moses: slander, evil, malicious gossip, jealousy. Graetz does an excellent job of exposing and refuting this reasoning. She does not infer that to Miriam was indeed using the power of language "viciously," but shows that the rabbis linked the "evil tongue" to women's speech, and in this case specifically Miriam. Ironically, the attention paid to her shows the power of her presence and words. See Graetz, "Did Miriam Talk Too Much?," 232–33. Except for the transcription of the Hebrew phrase, emphasis is added.

28. Exum, "Bringing Miriam Out of the Shadows," 86.

29. Maarsingh, *Numbers*, 40.

around you!" Moses seems to say. He does not see enough flocks and herds to slaughter. Carried away by the heat of the moment, Moses asks, somewhat incongruously, "Is there even enough fish in the sea?"—an amazing question to ask in the desert (v. 22). "Is the LORD's power limited?" God retorts, putting an end to the argument (v. 23). One has to ask, though: Does Moses not suspect anything, or is he simply anxious that Yahweh might be underestimating the logistics involved?

As the story continues at verse 31, three things become very clear: one, the invitation to a feast turns out to be an act of premeditated deceit. There really is no other way to put it. The people seemed to have been lured with deceitful promises: they would have a feast lasting "a whole month." Instead, they have "consecrated" themselves for a feast of death. Two, the unlimited power of the LORD was after all not the power to mercifully *provide*; it was the power to mercilessly *destroy*. Three, the act is both ritual (a feast for which they must be consecrated), and political—this becomes a lesson, not only in the power and glory of God, but also in the untouchability of Moses's rule. As the narrative has it, the God who comes to Moses's defense is utterly ruthless. The terror inflicted upon those who challenged Moses will be a lesson to all.

It goes precisely as the divine plan intended. The people sat down to eat and would not stop. But if this were meant as divine punishment, *could* they even stop? They gorge themselves on the quails. In a horrific scene, through nausea, choking, and vomiting, they die "while the meat was still between their teeth" (v. 33). With the fresh mass graves behind them, the survivors journeyed from this place of destruction to Hazeroth. They leave the many dead bodies behind them, but they will carry the reality of the wrath of the God of Moses with them.

But are the terrorized now properly cowed into submission? While others might be, Miriam clearly is not, and it is at this point that her "evil tongue" interrupts, and disrupts, the flow of history. Again, as at the seashore, Miriam acts as prophet of the people. I read the words, "through us" as not simply referring to her and Aaron, but instead as a broader collective expression. By "us" she means the way Yahweh has spoken through the faith and determination of the people when they, squeezed between the horses, chariots, and armies of Egypt and the roiling sea, chose to trust Yahweh and go forward.

Naomi Graetz observes, "The rabbis wonder why the Hebrew word for 'spoke' *wattedabber* is in singular form rather than *wayyedabberu*, in plural form," since the text says that Miriam *and* Aaron spoke. Why does Miriam, they ask, a woman, precede Aaron since "ladies first was not a principle in ancient times?"[30] It is an issue because it is clear that it is Miriam who takes the initiative. She is providing leadership, challenging Moses, and it is a sin that will not be easily forgiven.

Miriam's act comes as a crucial intervention in the rebellion. In reality, it has the effect of a paradigm shift in the rebellion—from trivialities to matters of fundamental importance, from male leadership to female leadership, and from personalized, dictatorial leadership to prophetic leadership. Miriam introduces the real issues: of the people's participation in liberation, the quality and integrity of leadership, and the questions of power and authority. She raises matters she has given leadership in before, at the seashore: the legitimacy of the radical inclusion of all the people, male and female, in God's acts of liberation.

As at the seashore, through that crucial question here, she focuses attention on the question of violence: violence and the workings of God, violence and the character of liberation, and violence and the resilience of the people. Instead of speaking under the pretext of less important issues, Miriam's question goes to the root of the matter—Moses's increasingly autocratic, increasingly violent, and increasingly unpopular, rule. Miriam's critical question also exposes a basic fault line in the rebellion: the nostalgic yearning for Egypt and all that Egypt represents, the longing for the nonexistent kindness of the oppressor, the desire to return to the imagined safety of *Mitsra'im* instead of facing the hardships that come with struggles for freedom and the responsibilities that come with freedom itself.

And still it is about more. A world of meaning rests on the question, "Has the LORD spoken only to Moses?" Up till now the storyteller has taken great pains to ensure that we understand that Moses, and Moses alone, is God's chosen instrument. Also, it is never Moses on his own who makes decisions, but Moses *and* God, a God who boils in anger whenever Moses's authority is being challenged. And when God's anger flares up on behalf of Moses, the punishment is swift and severe as we have seen with the fire, the earthquake, and the "feast" of quails. Miriam's question is not only about the channel of God's voice. It is about the character of Israel's God.[31] Who is

---

30. Graetz, "Did Miriam Talk Too Much?," 231.

31. This means that the issue goes beyond the question of "God-language" and "authentic identification" Cone has identified in the fierce debates about the blackness of God as the essence of Black people's understanding of God. That God is a "God of liberation" is not in dispute (see Cone, *A Black Theology of Liberation*, 55–81). At issue rather, is the character of Black theology's God of liberation. Is it the God Moses claims for himself or is it the God Miriam yearns for? The question is whether Black theology can consistently embrace the consequences of the radical statement Cone makes about white theology's God, though Cone himself did not pursue it with regard to the exodus paradigm: "The God of black liberation will not be confused with a bloodthirsty idol." Cone, *A Black Theology of Liberation*, 62.

this God Moses claims to be on his side, who gives him sole authority, who punishes and strikes and kills at the slightest sign of challenge and protest?

In the acts of defiance of the midwives and on the riverbank, Miriam experienced a God who rises up in outrage against the violence and death-worshiping power of the empire. At the seashore Miriam, in contrast with Moses, rejoiced in a God not in need of violence, of horses, armies, and chariots. Now Miriam is saying that Moses's God is not the God she remembers from the tradition of the women. The God of Moses is a power-hungry, vengeful God, a frightening mirror image of the gods of Egypt who know only domination, submission, and death. Moses's God has taken on fearsome, terrifying proportions.

Self-described atheist Richard Dawkins offers a shocking description of what he calls "the God of the Old Testament."

> The God of the Old Testament is arguably the most unpleasant character in all fiction: jealous and proud of it; a petty, unjust, unforgiving control freak; a vindictive, bloodthirsty ethnic cleanser; a misogynistic, homophobic, racist, infanticidal, genocidal, filicidal, pestilential, megalomaniacal, sadomasochistic, capriciously malevolent bully.[32]

As far as it goes, Dawkins is not making this up. However, this is not "the God of the Old Testament." As we are discovering, the picture is much more complex than Dawkins might be willing to allow. It is, however, despite our feelings of discomfort, a not completely inaccurate description of the God in the narrative whom Moses claims as the God who has appointed him, and who is now leading Israel's people to the promised land—Moses's personal benefactor and the fierce protector of his rule. It is the God Miriam rejects. Her question is inescapable in its prophetic clarity. Is the God who "speaks only through Moses" indeed the God we have come to know? It is, emphatically, not the God of the birthing stool, the riverbank, or the seashore.

In truth, at heart Miriam's quarrel with Moses has to do with the fundamental question: Which God are we talking about and calling upon here? Within the context of a tradition and a dominant narrative forming around a male, violent, warmongering god, it is the most decisive question, essential for Israel and their God. It is the question persistently raised by the women who walk in Miriam's footsteps, determined to keep the prophetic tradition alive: Hannah in her song (1 Sam 2); Mary in the Magnificat (Luke 1: 46–56); the Canaanite woman in her persistence (Matt 15:21–28); and Martha in her bold confession (John 11:27). It is the question raised

---

32. Dawkins, *God Delusion*, 51.

by people oppressed by empires, invaders, and colonizers everywhere who seek justification for their imperial designs in the Bible.

"If one reads the Bible carefully," Graetz writes, "there are enough hints that Moses' distancing himself from the people may ultimately have been the cause of his downfall."[33] Despite Graetz's gentle phrasing—Moses's "distancing himself"—it is undeniable that Moses's style of governing was costing him serious support among the people, to the extent that it caused his "downfall" (Num 20). Miriam's speaking up, significantly, comes immediately after the incomprehensible punishment Yahweh metes out against those "who had the craving" for meat and hence complained bitterly to Moses, that is, against his leadership, and, so the passage lets us understand, in effect against God. Moses was "displeased" but it was the LORD who became "very angry" (11:10). The two of them worked in tandem and plotted a plan that has all the hallmarks of a setup. Num 11:31–35 is almost too painful to read.

But this is what happens when authoritarian rule, secure in the belief of its "manifest destiny," the certitude of its exceptionalism, and the blessing of God, is challenged. Miriam is therefore much more radical than the men who hid the anxiety about Moses's leadership behind complaints about food and yearnings for an easier road to freedom and for Egypt's "better life." For her, it is not the stomach and comfort that is at stake: at stake is the ultimate question: If Moses calls upon God, whose God, which God, is that? And if that is our God, what kind of liberation are we speaking of here, and what kind of people are we to be? That is radical engagement.

That is the question that haunts us with the steady rhythms of a desperately despondent drumbeat. Every time after a mass shooting in the United States in the five years we have lived there (and there has been one somewhere every second day) I heard President Obama say the words, "That is not who we are." With every horrific rape in South Africa there is some man who says, "Not all men rape." After every scandalous, deadly, inexcusable racial act, some white person tries to assure us, "Not all of us are like that."

Of course it is true: this is not who all Americans are; not all men rape; not all whites are "like that." But until and unless private forcefulness turns into public political will on gun control in America and the masses follow the lead of the young students "marching for their lives"; unless men in their thousands flood the streets in protest against gender-based violence and systemic patriarchy; unless and until whites cease their denialism and trivialization of racism and rise up in public indignation against all forms of racism; unless we all learn the worth of our common humanity and cherish

---

33. Graetz, "Did Miriam Talk Too Much?," 238.

the ties that bind us, and in our actions embrace the cry of the 2017 South African Campaign Against Gender-based Violence, "This Ends Now!," every time we say these things we create a new lie. And every time the lie is recreated, we offer preemptive justification for the next killing, the next rape, the next racist act. And every time the tide of empty indignation rises, until it drowns whatever hopes we carry to be what we should be. And it seems to me, for people of faith, until we ask Miriam's question, and until we know what kind of God we worship, we cannot begin to fathom what kind of people we should strive to be, let alone know who we are.

Moreover, Miriam is challenging an idea that has taken hold since the appropriation of the exodus story after the passage through the Red Sea and is now solidifying into a stringent, exclusivist, religious ideology: that Yahweh now only mediates, speaks, and guides through men. And it is a concentrated, jealously guarded transferral of power from a male god to the males in Israel, and the guarantee of an exclusive, male relationship between Yahweh and men in which women have no place, standing, or status except in the shadow of and subservient to the men. It is a distortion of the God who blessed the midwives when they turned their powerlessness into acts of liberatory courage without the permission or support of the men, and of the God who inspired Miriam to stand her ground at the riverbank and to prophesy at the seashore, showing what it means to be a leader of all the people. Now Miriam rises up against this ideology and this ideologized God. Of Weems's Miriam, "hurt, frustrated, insecure, envious and displaced" I see no sign.

This episode is bracketed by Moses's remarkable rejection of rebuke for the male prophets, his even more remarkable wish for "all the LORD's people" to become prophets, and Miriam's speaking. When Miriam, as a woman, reclaims her prophetic mantle for herself, however, it seems Moses has only the males in mind. Most commentaries see Miriam's speaking as a serious transgression. The rabbis call it "arrogance" and "slander," since she speaks against someone "greater than herself."[34] It is perhaps worthwhile to note that in this patriarchal view rape may be bad, but not nearly as objectionable as speaking up against a man. This is Miriam's grave and seemingly unpardonable sin, "worse than rape and equal to murder."[35]

And indeed these are dangerous, rebellious, and if read within the context of the ongoing conflict about leadership, subversive words: "Has the LORD spoken only through Moses? Has he not spoken through us also?" (11:2). If read within the context of the people's growing dissatisfaction with

34. Graetz, "Did Miriam Talk Too Much?," 237.
35. Graetz, "Did Miriam Talk Too Much?," 239.

authoritarian rule and cosmetic reform (the seventy), and most important of all, if we understand Miriam's question to be a prophetic, theological challenge, then Miriam's words are not petulant jealousy, slander, or arrogance, but prophetic truth spoken to power.

Indeed, she has already been called a prophet (Exod 15:20). Now she picks up that mantle again, reasserting herself in her calling by inserting herself into the rebellion, but correcting the rebellion from its flawed position (romanticizing Egypt and anger about bodily comforts) to fundamental revolutionary transformation of leadership and the theological integrity of the call upon God. But the circumstances have changed. The euphoria of the exodus, the wonders at the Red Sea, the drowning of the armies of Pharaoh, his horses, and his chariots are challenged by the hardships of freedom. Now it is not Pharaoh's armies the Israelites are seeing on the seashore, it is the bodies of their kin, slain by Yahweh in collusion with their leader, and left in the graves of craving at Kibroth-hattaavah. The revolution is eating its own children. That jubilation of freedom at the sea that could embrace the prophetic leadership of Miriam has perished in the Realpolitik of the wilderness, and the male-formulated demands of the transition. Miriam finds this unacceptable. She does not wait. It was "while they were [still] at Hazeroth" that she spoke up.

Miriam speaks prophetic truth to power, and it is so serious that not only Moses responds to this but Yahweh intervenes directly in defense of Moses. And this is perhaps the answer to Graetz's last question: "Did Miriam and Aaron pose a real threat to Moses?"[36] But in this pivotal moment, and for all intents and purposes, Aaron does not really count here. It is Miriam who speaks and refocuses the rebellion. Up till now, the people's rebellion was a rebellion about food. What Israel believed they needed was what they, in their desperation, imagined they had in Egypt: food "for nothing" (11:5). The longing for Egypt intensifies, and any excuse will do.

Forgotten are the chains, the crushing humiliations, and the severe hardships. Forgotten also is the truth that they paid for this for with their bodies, their hopes, their dignity, and the lives of their children. They cannot distinguish between food for free in slavery and freedom for life. They are like so many South Africans today. Daunted by the levels of corruption and lack of justice and equity, they are already giving up on democracy only twenty-five years after apartheid. Seemingly defeated by the challenges a new democracy faces, disappointed by the inadequacies of our politics and politicians, they are nostalgic for the days of apartheid. They speak as if, under a racist, corrupt, competent-for-whites-only regime, "we"—as if

---

36. Graetz, "Did Miriam Talk Too Much?," 232.

"we" were all white, privileged South Africans—had it better than now. This is the price we pay for not discerning the proper priorities of revolution, integrity in the face of political deceit, and the ongoing necessity of radical engagement.

Miriam's intervention not only corrects their priorities, it reshapes their imagination. A revolution is not won by recasting the past into an imagined and false generosity of the oppressor who gives you food because he needs your physical strength for slave labor. A revolution is not won by mistaking a basic right for a slave master's kindness. A revolution is won by imagining and shaping a different future, by understanding that hardship in the wilderness is hardship on the way to that alternative future. It is the difference between the delusionary imagination and what Walter Brueggemann calls "the prophetic imagination." This is an imagination that "embrace[s] the very imagination of God," and that means that it not only knows that things could be different, "but that the difference *could be enacted*."[37] And this is what Miriam's prophetic imagination does. She shows the difference and she enacts it. Miriam refocuses the rebellion on the questions of the character of the God of liberation, the quality of leadership, of power and powerlessness, and the difference between power and authority. Miriam's intervention exposes and corrects this fundamental flaw and redeems the rebellion.

In becoming more and more authoritarian, holding fiercely onto the power of prophecy for himself alone, more and more intolerant of criticism and correction, Moses, knowing he has no argument in himself (Yahweh has indeed not only spoken through him alone), more and more falls back on his own unique relationship with God, calling upon a despotic Higher Power who works only on his behalf. Miriam has spoken, not just against Moses, but against his claim that his way was God's way. That is not insolently challenging a younger brother who has done better. Rather, it is challenging a religious ideology bent on maintaining a male hierarchy, a revisionist, patriarchal version of the history of liberation, and a male god on the side of male dominance and the constant threat of deadly violence hanging over the smallest sign of dissent.

What Miriam represents is a yearning on the side of the people for that other history to be reclaimed: that history in which the women—the midwives, her mother, and Miriam herself—claimed legitimate and revered space in the story of liberation. What she represents is the longing for the God of liberation who takes the side of the oppressed and the weak, the marginalized and the excluded, the radically inclusive God who gave strength

---

37. Brueggemann, *Prophetic Imagination*, xxi, my emphasis.

to the women in their defiance of the power of Pharaoh when there was no male Israelite in sight: not in the birth chamber and not on the riverbank. This is taking the rebellion to a totally different level. It is no wonder the narrator cannot let Moses handle this alone. He calls in Yahweh—the same God who has just shown a fierce partiality for Moses and male leadership in Israel by brutal suppression of a rebellion merely about food. Miriam knew this. She must have known this. And yet, like her foremothers in Egypt, despite the risks, she acts.

"HEAR MY WORDS..."

The ominous words in 12:5, "and the LORD heard," now take shape in the form that appears in the doorway of the tent, summoning Moses, Aaron, and Miriam. But the words in verse 5 are preceded by a seemingly gratuitous sentence, out of the blue as it were, the words easily read and brushed over as some typical, cultural hyperbole: "Now the man Moses was very humble; more so than anyone else on the face of the earth" (v. 3). But it might, rather than some typical, childlike Afro-Asiatic exuberance Westerners find so condescendingly enchanting, be a superb piece of rhetoric serving a deeper purpose. It is a distraction. It focuses the reader's attention not on the power and extraordinariness of the woman Miriam's words, but on the macho vulnerability of the man Moses.

The aim, I think, is not only to draw attention to Moses's humility as yet another gift of this already supremely gifted man, but also, and more importantly, to emphasize with enviable subtlety the immeasurable impudence of Miriam. Moses's "humility" serves as the foil to highlight Miriam's shamelessness in daring to challenge him. It strips Miriam of all claims to protection or argument and it gives the patriarchal God in the tent's doorway all the excuse he needs. It is the genteel but barbed subtlety of phrasing that scores the points here. Moses is so humble he does not even defend himself. Confronted by an uncontrolled, obstreperous Miriam, we can virtually see him raising his eyebrows in shock at, and his hands in surrender to, this unjust, unreasonable onslaught. What otherwise, perhaps normally, would have been interpreted as arrogant male disdain has now become admirable humility in the face of undeserved attack. It is this humble retreat in the face of such unreasonableness that completes the "hell hath no fury" lesson of this scene. Moses does not speak until he "cries to God" on Miriam's behalf. He is the epitome of innocent humility, tested forbearance, and undaunted magnanimity. Moses, the man of quiet fortitude, keeps his peace. Miriam, impudent wretch full of baseless, senseless female fury, does not know how and when to stay silent. Within that tense cultural and political context, the gendered clash of power, authority, and authenticity, the contrast is no less than striking. And such is the intention. The narrator knows the power of words.

So after the subtle words of verse 3, and the ominous words of verse 5, the seemingly ordinary words of verse 6 take on the frightening hue of a death sentence. "Hear my words . . ." The narrator makes sure we understand it immediately. Miriam's words have been spoken, and they were found deeply offensive—on earth as in heaven. Now that the LORD has heard Miriam's words, God has words for Miriam directly now. These are not going to be life-affirming words. Miriam must learn how utterly offensive her desire for equality is in the eyes of this God. In order to deal with her God first creates uneven ground. It is to Yahweh, not to Moses, that the responsibility of response falls. If her inequality to her brother is debatable, her inequality to Yahweh is beyond argument, question, or reach. In verse 1, in the act of rebellion, Miriam was named first. Now in the act of retribution, she is already diminished. She is named last, set lower and set aside—for punishment. She is not spared humiliation and banishment, and this is compounded when her life is saved—by the two males in the story.

The proper order of things is restored. Aaron, chastened, unpunished, and his priesthood left intact, but clearly brought to heel, appeals to Moses—not to God, so great is his awe of Moses's power now—"Oh my lord! Do not punish us for a sin that we have so foolishly committed!" (12:11). Moses, restored to the status of prophet without peer and sole mediator of the people, appeals to God. Of an independent relationship between Yahweh and Miriam there is now no sign. The Spirit that had enveloped and inspired her on the riverbank and at the seashore is now crushed by the men and their God. She must either forget it ever happened or accept the lie that it never happened. It was all a figment of a petty, jealous, and ferociously ambitious female mind. Greater than the banishment is perhaps the diminishment of the truth about her life and worth.

She is put in her place not by Moses but by his God. In the two darkest and most revealing sentences of this pericope, God asks Miriam, "Why were you not then afraid to speak against my servant Moses?" (v. 5). We should absorb this: It is not love for or faith and trust in Yahweh that is required, it is *fear of Moses*—of men, in other words—that pleases this God. And as she is punished, God, still angry, responds to Moses's plea for her healing, "If her father had but spit in her face. . ." (v. 14). No longer a prophet or leader, she is no more than some father's daughter. The two males, God and Moses, oblivious of the lashes laid upon her soul, discuss the good fortune of the lightness of her bodily punishment. There are sobering lessons to be learned here. God heals, but sometimes only grudgingly. Of the God who is "merciful and gracious, slow to anger and abounding in steadfast love" (Ps 103:8), there is here no sign. At least not for this woman.

But second, almost as if to compensate for a weakness here, God's healing is followed by yet another blow on behalf of men to a woman's impertinence. So goes the sanctification of patriarchal violence. Every patriarchal father is justified in his anger at an impudent daughter, and every woman who does not know her place will know that being spat in the face is actually an act of mercy and generosity of spirit. She should be grateful—it could have been worse. A man can, and is allowed, to do so much more. She will have reason to be afraid. This is the spirit that has breathed its foul breath into our societies, our churches, and the highest levels of our politics; the same spirit the homophobic, heteronormative, patriarchal "Nashville Statement" of August 30, 2017 exudes.[38]

But even here the patriarchal tale cannot completely suppress the truth, and the attentive reader will not miss it. It is Aaron who begs for mercy for Miriam. *On her behalf.* Miriam herself keeps silent. From her there is no confession or remorse, no repentance or plea for forgiveness. Not because she has a hardened, unrepentant heart, or does not know how to put her case. Neither is it because those who accuse her of a sin "greater than rape" are proven right. It is because she knows she has done nothing wrong. She knows she has sinned not against the God of the birthing chamber, the riverbank, and the seashore, but against the patriarchal God of domination, violence, and vengeance. She knows that the God of the exodus had been captured by the God of conquest. The God who called her as a prophet, who sang and danced with her and all the people on the seashore, is not the God who was framed in the doorway of that tent of male supremacy, joyless arrogance, and punishment.

As Miriam is banished "outside the camp" until her leprosy is healed, (it appears God did not heal her completely after all), the people refuse to journey on without her. Such was her stature and their trust in her. Again Trible eloquently captures the situation:

---

38. The Nashville Statement, issued by the Council on Biblical Manhood and Womanhood, written by prominent members of the Southern Baptist Convention and signed by hundreds, is a vigorous reaffirmation of "traditional" views on marriage and human sexuality. It offers extreme condemnation of the LGBTQI community and is relentless in its insistence of women's submission to men in all things and all walks of life. It is also insistent that these views are the only correct ones, because they are "biblical." For the text of the "Nashville Statement," see https:/cbmw.org/wp-content/uploads/2017/08/The-nashville-statement.pdf.

> Those whom she has served do not forsake her in the time of her tribulation. They wait. Never do they assail her as on various occasions they attack Aaron, Moses, and God. And their allegiance survives unto her death.[39]

The feminist scholars are right: there is a whole other narrative, a whole other tradition we are not being told here, waiting to be embraced.

THE WATERS OF MERIBAH

Yet it refuses to remain suppressed.

> Three references in Num 20:1—"the people of Israel," "the whole community," and "the people"—emphasize their presence when she dies and is buried in Kadesh. The steadfast devotion of the people to Miriam indicates a story different from the regnant one.[40]

"Patriarchal storytellers," writes Trible, "have done their work well. They have suppressed the women—yet without total success."[41] The seashore was such a moment, and here we have it again. What these references also do is to powerfully underscore Miriam as a prophet of the people, the bond she has with her people, and the power she exercised among them. Miriam's death is mentioned in Num 20:1, and in only seven words. We have to wonder: such a life and only seven words? But the magnitude of the people's devotion to her overrides the measly account.

We are told that the water in the well suddenly dried up. It is never explained why. Verse 2 merely reports that "there was no water for the congregation." But are the dried-up waters of Meribah, before it became yet another, and for Moses, the final place of contestation, a silent cry of mourning for her without whose prophetic leadership the people will now have to face the future, and simultaneously a rallying cry for all those who embrace the prophetic tradition of Miriam and become children of the waters of Meribah? Phyllis Trible's eloquent phrasing and deep insights help us here:

> Nature's response to Miriam's death is immediate and severe. It mourns, and the community suffers. Miriam, protector of her brother at the river's bank and leader in the victory at the

---

39. Trible, "Bringing Miriam Out of the Shadows," 180.
40. Trible, "Bringing Miriam Out of the Shadows," 180.
41. Trible, "Bringing Miriam Out of the Shadows," 169.

sea, symbolized life. How appropriate, then, that waters of life should reverence her death.[42]

Chapter 20 also tells us about the final rebellion that called forth the "sin" of Moses. Miriam dies and there is no water. Once again the people rebel: "Why have you brought us up out of Egypt?" (v. 5) Maarsingh's translation is enlightening: "Why did you deceive us with a promise of a land situated on a higher plane?" Canaan does indeed have a higher elevation, Maarsingh explains, hence the "up" from Egypt.[43] But perhaps this is about more than just geography. Can we read in this expectation of a "higher plane" also the promise of a higher level of leadership than what the people experienced from Pharaoh, his priests, his nobility, and his slave drivers in Egypt? Somewhat like South Africans' expectations of ANC leadership after the immoral morass of apartheid rule: more integrity, more decency, more inclusivity, more love, more truthfulness, and more compassion? A kind of leadership more reflective of the God of the exodus than Moses's God of the "War Song" and the wilderness turned out to be; an elevated leadership of the kind Miriam discerned, tried to exercise, and called for?

These insights carry more relevance than we may have been prepared for. In my 2017 publication, *Pharaohs on Both Sides of the Blood-Red Waters*, I engage the question of global revolutions for justice and freedom captured by imperial forces from within and their surrogates within.[44] In South Africa we are experiencing, on an almost daily basis, the consequences of what economist Sampie Terreblanche calls the "secret elite conspiracy" of 1994 between the wealthy white elite and the black elite within the African National Congress, under the tutelage of the United States and the Bretton Woods Institutions: a fraudulent economic policy that has increased the undeserved wealth of the already white rich; increased the undeserved impoverishment of the already desperately black poor while creating a small, new, unbelievably rich black aristocracy, making South Africa one of the most unequal societies on earth. Our negotiators felt themselves obligated, not to the interests of the people, but to the secret deals made with apartheid South Africa between 1985 and 1994.[45]

42. Trible, "Bringing Miriam Out of the Shadows," 180.
43. Maarsingh, *Numbers*, 71.
44. See Boesak, *Pharaohs*, especially chs. 4, 5, and 6.
45. Perhaps one of the most striking examples of this is President Cyril Ramaphosa's attitude and actions at the time of the Marikana massacre as well as in its aftermath, and in his testimony before the Farlam Commission of Inquiry. The commission treated Ramaphosa (then deputy president of the country and a powerful member of the board), and the company with great deference, and hardly questioned his role or that of the company during the crisis. During a strike action in 2012, 34 miners had been gunned

Because it studiously and quite deliberately avoided social justice, restitution, and the redistribution of power, wealth, and social goods, our reconciliation process, in which black South Africans have invested so much, including the social cohesion it was meant to produce and foster, is under savage strain. In other words, democratic South Africa came into being, in disastrous denial of the revolutionary struggles, sacrifices, aspirations, and hopes of the people, as a triumphalist product of imperialism.

If Black theology had had the insight, wisdom, and courage of the Miriamic tradition, rather than our misplaced allegiance to the Mosaic, patriarchal tradition, and allowed that insight to guide and inspire us during those crucially formative years towards the end of formal apartheid and the beginnings of our democracy, we would have been much more sensitive to the quality of our leadership and much more fiercely protective of the integrity of our liberation. We would have discerned much better the difference between being bamboozled by the expediencies of exile politics and the theater of pre-negotiated negotiations, and being obligated to the sacrifices of our people and the inalienable rights of the poor.

---

down by police in an action that shocked the nation. His subsequent apology five years later, now running for president of the country, has been described as "disingenuous" and "dishonest." In a campaign speech, Ramaphosa apologized for language he used in emails and called it "unfortunate" and "not appropriate." But, argues Peter Alexander of University of Johannesburg's Centre for Social Change, the issue was never language, but "Ramaphosa's actions, and his relationship to the killings." As a powerful member of government and a director of Lonmin, the mining company, "he could have acted to prevent the massacre." But in his two interventions, he was resolutely on the side of strong action by both the minister of mineral resources and the police. In his second intervention, instead of speaking of a "strike action," which it was, Ramaphosa characterized the strike as "a dastardly criminal act," opening the door for the fatal police action that followed. If he had defined the action properly and correctly, Alexander writes, the consequences would have been different. See Alexander, "Cyril Ramaphosa's Marikana Massacre Apology Is Disingenuous and Dishonest." See also Alexander's article in the *Mail & Guardian*, "Why Ramaphosa's Marikana massacre 'apology' was disingenuous and dishonest." The fundamental point here is that Mr. Ramaphosa as wealthy shareholder and director of Lonmin, and as powerful member of the South African Government and the ruling ANC, chose for the interests of wealth, power, and privilege, and against the interests of the poor, the working class, and the powerless. It is a textbook example of what had gone wrong in South Africa's "negotiated settlement" and the subsequent problems created for our burgeoning democracy. Cyril Ramaphosa is now the president of South Africa. In his response to the debate on his first State of the Nation Address, he did mention the tragedy at Marikana, and within the context of "acknowledgement where we have failed," and "healing and atonement." One should hope that Cyril Ramaphosa means what the word "atonement" means in a biblical sense and therefore understands its political consequences. If he does, one might yet have hope that the president will turn his attention to his role in this matter and by setting a personal example, and then through restitution help the country to begin the process of healing.

A Miriamic Black theology and a church in the Miriamic tradition would have known better the difference between being mesmerized by Nelson Mandela and remaining faithful to Jesus of Nazareth. We would perhaps have been bold enough to ask the essential question: "Has the Lord spoken only through Mandela?" Has the Lord spoken only through the celebrated negotiators of the ANC, whose wisdom was extolled as matchless and flawless by the white-controlled media, in South Africa and abroad? Has the Lord not also spoken through us, in the struggles of our people, in the sacrifices made by our youth, in the blood that stained the streets of our townships, in the stubborn, nonviolent militancy of the determined masses; in the revolutionary patience of our elders and in the hopeful resilience of the dreams of the children?

Has the Lord not also spoken through us, in our songs of sorrow and our songs of freedom; in the cries for justice and the outrage against injustice; in our battles against despair and our fierce embrace of hope; in our standing for the truth and in our refusal to submit to the lie? Has the Lord not spoken to us in the bewilderments of our alienation from each other and in our sacrificial reach for genuine reconciliation; in our mourning at the death of those who died too young, and in the celebration of lives given for the sake of others; in our prayers for deliverance and in our joy at the anticipation of freedom? For the struggles that lie ahead, Black liberation theology should drink deep from the waters of Meribah.

The story in Num 20:1–13 reads as if Moses experienced this as a final straw. He does indeed consult God, and God does indeed respond, but this time with genuine concern for the well-being of the people, without any accompanying threat of vengefulness because of their complaints, seemingly surprising Moses totally. Moses shall simply speak to the rock and water shall flow. Moses, however, is angry; his disdain shows in his words and in his deeds. "Listen you rebels!" he says to the people. Now they are no longer God's children whom God must tenderly nurse and nurture (Num 11). That fleeting flicker of femininity has dissipated like slivers of fog in the burning sun of Moses's anger. Now also, there is no distinction between "the people" and "the rabble" who supposedly instigated them to disobedience. Now they are *all* "rebels." Notably, Miriam is no longer there to take the lead in the rebellion and to expose the real character of his leadership and the falseness of his claims upon the God of liberation. But Moses is angered, perhaps because even though Miriam is dead and gone, her subversive memory, her challenge to leadership, and her dangerous ideal of prophetic leadership still linger.

So finally the narrator allows what up to now had seemed impossible: Moses "sins," and that sin is so great that it turns his God against him. Moses "strikes" the rock instead of simply speaking to it, as Yahweh commanded. Scholars have battled extensively as to what is happening here and what precisely Moses's "sin" is.[46] Biblical scholars are agreed that Num 20:2–13 indeed tells us about a rebellion in response to which Moses and Aaron, as Maarsingh puts it, "failed to show [the people] the reflected image of God."[47] Moses's response is "arrogant," claiming that he and Aaron "had the power to provide the water."[48] In the end (Num 20:24; 27:14), the author, with supreme irony, accuses Moses and Aaron of "rebellion."

Rabbi Pinchas Kahn argues for "psychological transference," by which he means that Moses transferred the experience of Rephidim in Exodus 17, where there was a rebellion against Moses, to Meribah, where there was no rebellion.[49] Accordingly, Moses completely misjudges the situation. The people were not complaining or longing for Egypt but were distressed that they were still in the desert rather than in the promised land. "Moses . . . may have misunderstood them, displaying here a transference from the past experience at Rephidim to the present one at Waters of Meribah."[50]

In the process Moses erred on three counts: one, he mistook the people's longing for the promised land for a "rebellion." Two, he misunderstood his own position: at Rephidim, his authority needed to be enhanced. Here at Meribah it was "necessary to diminish" that authority. "That Moses did not understand this necessity was his error, perhaps his sin."[51] Three, Moses and Aaron responded to their own emotional urge, rather than to the needs of the people. All of this comes down to one reality: "they indicated that they were no longer able to be the people's leaders."[52] But Kahn does not explain why there is this sudden "necessity." We have argued that the issue of leadership is not a sudden crisis at all. It has been building up since chapter 11, and that it is about much more than a mistake caused by "emotional transference."

Moses is instructed to "take up his staff" and this too has caused some controversy.[53] Taking up the staff here is reminiscent of his staff at the parting of the Red Sea, but also at the burning bush and before the throne of

---

46. Budd, *Numbers*, 218–19 provides extensive references to these debates.
47. Maarsingh, *Numbers*, 72.
48. Budd, *Numbers*, 218, 219.
49. See Kahn, "Moses at the Waters of Meribah," 85–93.
50. Kahn, "Moses at the Waters of Meribah," 87.
51. Kahn, "Moses at the Waters of Meribah," 89. Actually, Kahn mentions two sins. I added a third.
52. Kahn, "Moses at the Waters of Meribah," 92.
53. Budd, *Numbers*, 218.

Pharaoh and his magician-priests. But it is all clouded in ambivalence. Which staff is it in Moses's hand? At the burning bush, the staff is mentioned along with Moses's reluctance to heed the call of liberation. In front of Pharaoh, the staff is an instrument of futile competition with Pharaoh's magicians. At the Red Sea, the staff is a reminder not of situations focused on Moses's (supposed) power, but where the power of Yahweh is everything. On the other side of the seashore, the staff is not a symbol of Moses's recalcitrance or his inadequate negotiating skills. At the sea, it is not a sign of Moses's power but rather of trust and faith in the unerring love of Yahweh who will secure Israel in justice and peace. Before Pharaoh Moses cannot even speak properly, but at the Red Sea he knows, with seemingly great eloquence, to remind the people of the power of Yahweh: "The LORD shall fight for you." Taking up *this* staff, Moses is at his best. This is probably closer to Moses's real misunderstanding of the situation. He has the staff in hand, but which staff is it? It becomes the turning point.

We may raise other questions: Is Moses so wedded to acts of violence to prove and secure his authority, and so used to the availability of the God who strengthens him in this expectation, that he cannot believe it when he hears God say something else completely? And at this stage, is his confidence in himself, without the violence, so shaky that he willy-nilly clings to what he believes to be the only way that has worked before, the only language the people understand? Maarsingh remarks that the Targum Pseudo-Jonathan "shares the curious information that the first time [when Moses struck the rock] drops of blood appeared."[54] Curious indeed, but perhaps the authors of Targum Pseudo-Jonathan knew better how to metaphorize the hold violence exerts on those who depend on it for strength, respect, and leadership. Can Moses conceive of leadership without fear, intimidation, and the threat of violent suppression? How else would he impress the people and reassert his authority? Deeper perhaps: can Moses conceive of Yahweh only as vain, violent, and vengeful? Whatever happened here, Moses ignores Yahweh's command to let only his words be his power and his authority.

Moses's conundrum is the conundrum of every struggle for freedom and the eternal choice between violence and nonviolence. A revolution without vengeance for the righting of the wrongs, a struggle without the fear-inducing discipline of violence and the gratifying promise of retribution—is that a revolution worthy of the name? If violence, the embrace, the glorification and the romanticization, no, the *worshiping* of it, is the bedrock of our struggle credentials, how shall we claim victory without it? Is the "blood of the martyrs" really the only source that "feeds the tree of

---

54. Maarsingh, *Numbers*, 72.

freedom"? And are those martyrs only the ones willing to take the life of others in the cause of freedom? If liberation is nothing without conquest, the God of the exodus, as in the Mosaic tradition, *must* give way to a god of conquest. If freedom is unthinkable without bloodshed, conquest, and occupation, a compassionate God of love and tenderness is a God too effeminate, too weak for the struggle in Egypt or for survival in the wilderness or for life shared with others in a land of freedom. Moses cannot believe that God does not need the violent act in order to be God. But Moses needs a violent God in order to be Moses. Since he cannot speak to the "rabble," he will not speak to the rock. Since Yahweh refuses to strike the people, Moses strikes the rock.

Is what happens here perhaps a belated realization by this narrator that the God of Israel is after all the God of Miriam, and not the God of Moses? Num 20:2–13 is a narrative critical of Moses and Aaron, says Trible. "In effect, [it] counters the vendetta against her."[55] Trible is right, but at the same time this is not just about Moses and Aaron and the vendetta against Miriam. It is also about Yahweh. The God at the waters of Meribah is not the same as the God of the fire, the feast of death, the swallowing earth, and the plague. Here Moses's God does not come to his aid. Not in anger to smite the rebels, not in vengeful defense of Moses and his leadership, and not in tenderness to comfort Moses. The God that Moses had come to count on now forsakes him. In the end, the voice of Yahweh is heard, not in wrath or retribution or the arrogance of violence, but in the creative, life-affirming word. It is the God that Miriam worshiped in standing her ground on the riverbank, and in song and jubilation at the seashore.

And as the God of Miriam is recalled, the waters of Meribah become a life-giving source. It is the holiness of *this* God that is shown here that verse 13, ending the story, speaks of: not the holiness that has the power to bar Moses from entering the promised land, but the holiness that finally responds to Miriam's prophetic leadership in a rebellion that seeks the future. For the people it is the holiness of mercy, love, and compassionate justice.

OUTSIDE THE CAMP

Trible speaks of "fragments of a pro-Miriamic tradition" that come to the surface despite centuries-long efforts to suppress it. The prophet Micah reclaims her and names her in one breath with Moses and Aaron, making her their equal (Mic 6:4). For Trible, women—from Deborah (Judg 5) to the unnamed woman in Isa 8:3, to Hulda (2 Kgs 22:14–20), and Noadiah (Neh

---

55. Trible, "Bringing Miriam Out of the Shadows," 181.

6:14)—each of them witness "to a heritage rooted in Miriam." Trible concludes, "If Moses be the archetype of the male prophetic tradition, Miriam leads the female."[56]

But I have argued here that humanly speaking,[57] the prophetic tradition in the Bible is the tradition that begins with the midwives in Exod 1. Miriam takes it forward. Miriam is not called a prophet because of any "prophecies" she uttered, of which we find none. She is a prophet because of the *tradition* she represents and preserves. She is a prophet not because she foresees the future, whatever that may mean. She is a prophet because she sees what and as God sees: through the eyes of the oppressed, the despised, the outcasts, the ravaged, the powerless, and those whose imaginations and dreams of justice and peace are transformed by the imagination of God. As such, Miriam opens yet another door. As a strong, faithful, single woman, Miriam stands her ground, sometimes alone, sometimes marginalized, sometimes punished, but always resolute in her prophetic calling. She is a pillar of strength among her people, laying the foundations for the prophetic tradition in Israel.[58]

It is a tradition that calls upon God as the God of slaves, the One who takes the side of the oppressed in their struggles for freedom and justice against the tyranny of oppressors and the domination of empire. This is a God fundamentally different from, and fundamentally in opposition to, the gods of empire, who depend on subjugation, the suppression of all dissent, violence, and the threat of destruction. This God is a God of life-giving hope, whose acts of liberation are acts of radical love, radical inclusivity, radical freedom, and radical resistance. This is the tradition Miriam claims on the riverbank, at the seashore, and in the wilderness. It is the tradition that worships God as the God of the poor and oppressed throughout Israel's history, the tradition in which Jesus of Nazareth plants himself.

This is the tradition rooted in the acts of defiance against empire by Shifhra and Puah; Miriam standing her ground on the riverbank, in prophetic leadership at the seashore and in the wilderness; Hannah and the prophetic power of her Song (1 Samuel 2); Rizpah in her resistance against King David and the palace establishment[59] (2 Sam 21:14-22); Mary in the

---

56. Trible, "Bringing Miriam Out of the Shadows," 181–82.

57. See my argument on the story of the tower of Babel as the story of God as the original voice of dissent against the powers of empire; A. Boesak, *Kairos, Crisis, and Global Apartheid*, 162–67.

58. Rabbinical tradition makes Miriam the wife of Caleb and the mother of Hur, but there is no biblical tradition of Miriam being married. See Marshall et al., *New Bible Dictionary*, 773.

59. See Boesak and DeYoung, *Radical Reconciliation*, ch. 2.

Magnificat; and Jesus of Nazareth. It is the tradition that the "radical Paul," as John Dominic Crossan calls him, will follow in his insistence on the supremacy of the Lordship of Jesus over the claims of Roman imperial theology, and his theology of freedom, justice, and equality as expounded in his letters.[60] The "male, Moses tradition," as we have seen, is seduced by the needs of patriarchy and the desire to imitate the ways of empire in Israel. It is against that tradition that the Miriamic tradition struggles, is faded, but survives.

Trible sees the last reference to Miriam in the book of Micah.[61] But perhaps it is helpful to see Heb 13:13 as a final reference not just to Jesus, but to Miriam. "Let us then go to him outside the camp and bear the abuse he endured." Even though this is a text we are used to reading within the context of a theology of atonement and the "satisfaction theory"—God punishing Jesus for the sake of our sins—this is nonetheless not the point of the text. The text is an invitation, not for us to like Jesus take upon ourselves the sins of the world and seek God's satisfaction through the shedding of blood—after all, who can possibly do that, and more pertinently, does God really want that? The invitation to the disciples of Jesus is to join him in his suffering of shame, rejection, and abuse.

Heb 13:3 is the only place in the New Testament where the words "outside the camp" are used. They echo Numbers 12, where Miriam is punished and condemned to life "outside the camp" until she is cleansed. There, the people refuse to journey on without her as a sign of their solidarity with her and their desire not to move on unless she is restored to their midst.[62] In Hebrews, the Miriam punishment is recalled. The New Testament describes Jesus as the oppressed One who came to liberate and bring justice to the poor, the hungry, the naked, the widows and orphans, the oppressed and the afflicted; those who cannot defend themselves against the powerful. This is how he announces himself (Luke 4:16-18) and this is how he reveals himself in his work on earth and in the experience of oppressed people. So James Cone writes,

> Jesus Christ is not a proposition, not a theological concept which exists merely in our heads. He is an event of liberation, a happening in the lives of oppressed people struggling for political freedom. Therefore, to know him is *to encounter him* in the history of the weak and the helpless. The convergence

---

60. See Crossan, *God and Empire*, 143–90; see also Elliot, "Anti-Imperial Message of the Cross," 167–83.
61. See Trible, "Bringing Miriam Out of the Shadows," 181.
62. Trible, "Bringing Miriam Out of the Shadows," 181.

of Jesus Christ and the black experience is the meaning of the Incarnation.[63]

That encounter takes place in the places of revilement, oppression, and abuse, outside the camp. Jesus is, as Andries van Aarde forcefully and persuasively argues, "fatherless in Galilee" bearing all the rejection, exclusion, and shame such a reality—being both "fatherless" and "from Galilee"—carries with it.[64] He is the oppressed one, bearing the shame and abuse for our sake, in other words, becoming one with the shamed and abused, the despised and rejected, joining their struggles against the powers represented by the temple elites, the palace of Herod with its murderous subservience to Rome, and the Roman Empire itself. It is that identification, solidarity, and resistance that place him "outside the camp." To be "outside the camp" is to be "against the camp" and all it stands for.

Moreover, here in Hebrews, we are not asked to wait until he is cleansed so he can return to the camp. The despised ones were cast outside the gate and outside the camp because the supposition was that inside the camp was the sacred space, where God dwelt, where sanctification was to be found.[65] Their presence defiled that sacred space. Hebrews turns that around: the sacred space is in fact outside the camp, for that is where Jesus is always to be found—among the withered orphans and wailing widows of Yemen, the bewildered refugees from Syria, the despised and targeted LGBTQI+ persons from every community on earth, the oppressed and excluded women who dare to claim the dignity God has given them. It is there outside the camp where they, as Bonhoeffer reminds us, will hear the voice of Jesus:

> You outcasts, you disadvantaged . . . you who are looked down upon . . . Blessed are you Lazaruses of all ages, you broken down and ruined, you lonely and abandoned . . . those who suffer injustice, you who suffer in body and soul; blessed are you for God's joy will come over you and be over [your] head forever. That is the gospel, the good news.[66]

The despised space becomes the sacred space, sanctified by suffering and the liberating presence of Jesus. That is where the good news will be heard, and if, as we have argued, following Franz Fanon and Steve Biko, blackness is not so much a question of skin color but a condition of

---

63. Cone, *God of the Oppressed*, 32–33.
64. van Aarde, *Fatherless*.
65. Lane, *Hebrews*, 543.
66. Bonhoeffer, *Works* 11:446, 447.

oppression, infliction, and resistance, it will be Black liberation theology that is to shout that good news.

We are not asked to wait until he is "restored" by the powers and allowed to continue the journey with us. The invitation is much more radical. We are invited to go to him, knowingly, willingly, and resolutely, not only because it is there that he is to be found, but because that is where we belong. The invitation not just to "bear the cross" with him but to be crucified like him for the sake of those who are crucified daily by the forces of empire— from Palestine to Yemen and South Africa's townships to the blood-streaked streets of America's inner cities and America's sacred Indian lands—is an open one, for as long as God's children are despised, cast off, desecrated, and excluded, thrown out of the camp, trampled upon, and crucified, that is where Jesus will be found.

As I write, the March for Return is unfolding in Gaza week after week as Palestinians march to the Israeli-imposed border as a reminder of their determination to return to the land that was stolen from them. The occupation has, once again, turned into wholesale slaughter, as Israeli Defense Force snipers take careful aim at protesters in wheelchairs and on crutches, youth with stones in their hands, a woman medic as she is kneeling at the side of a wounded person she is trying to help, mothers and children. They cheer as the bullets strike home. Perhaps more than before, the world is professing "shock," and in the United Nations Security Council the ambassador of Bolivia is moved to utter a moving apology to the people of Gaza, and one should be grateful for that one sign of turning. But we should not be surprised by the Israeli actions; neither should we think that the present slaughter is a random act of brutality. It is the inevitable consequences of the theology of conquest in the Mosaic tradition against which Miriam so courageously raised her voice. It is also part of an overall plan the Israelis are ruthlessly executing, and it is becoming the gruesome reality for Palestinians.

"The bleeding edge among Israeli politicians," writes Israeli writer Amitai Ben-Abba, a native of West Jerusalem, "M. K. Smotrich, Minister of Education, Jerusalem Mayor Barkat and their ilk—are nowadays advocating the move into the so-called 'decisive stage' of the Israeli-Palestinian conflict. To transgress from the status quo into *a durable peace* . . . a Final Solution for the Palestinian Question."[67] Ben-Abba goes on to explain where the idea originated. "That vision, á la Smotrich, is taken from the Book of Joshua,

---

67. See Ben-Abba, "Israel's New Ideology of Genocide."

where the invading Israelites enact a genocide on the native Canaanites until *not a single soul is left to breathe,* to paraphrase Rabbi Maimonides."[68]

The shocking and truly frightening words "Final Solution," dripping as they did from Nazi lips, and deliberately employed here by a young, courageous Israeli journalist, should already alert us to the deplorable and lethal intent that lies behind this move. It is a thoroughly evil intent that tragically identifies Israel ever closer with the great evil the Jews have suffered and will not, and correctly so, allow the world to forget. Smotrich, however, Ben-Abba says—and the Bible assures us—is not making this up. At the command of Joshua, in turn commanded by the God of Moses, Israel "devoted to destruction by the edge of the sword all in the city, both men and women, young and old, oxen, sheep, and donkeys" (Josh 6:21). And again, as if the gleeful writer cannot get enough: "They burned down the city, and everything in it, only the silver and gold, and the vessels of bronze and iron, they put into the treasury of the house of the LORD . . ." (v. 24). This is how the tradition of Yahweh as *conquistador,* as the destroyer of peoples and the robber of land, dignity, and hope, works. Now, Zionists "great and small, young and old" rejoice in the slaughter and are apparently ready for more, fears Ben-Abba as he observes the split-screen scenes of smug celebration at the opening of the US embassy in Jerusalem and contrasts these with the wounded or dead children of Gaza carried in the arms of their loved ones: "From the foot soldiers to the big brass, from the flag-waving street folk to the height of academia, Israel is ideologically prepared to enact a Palestinian Shoah."[69]

Taking their stand and placing themselves outside the Zionist camp, opening themselves to revilement, repulsion, and rejection, Amitai Ben-Abba, Ilan Pappe, Norman Finkenstein—and the many, many, other anti-Zionist, righteous Jews such as those in the Peace and Justice for Palestinian movements in Israel, the US and elsewhere—fear correctly that *this* is how Jews will be remembered. Is the Lord only speaking through the voices of the zealots, extremists, and the betrayers of the prophetic tradition started by the women, or is the Lord also speaking through them?

This is the reality within which the questions about the exodus and the Moses/Joshua tradition of conquest and extermination are being asked

---

68. Ben-Abba, "Israel's New Ideology of Genocide." According to the Midrash, Ben-Abba explains, there were three stages to that operation. "First, Joshua sent the Canaanites a letter advising them to run away. Then, those who stayed could accept inferior citizenship and slavery. Finally, if they resisted, they would be annihilated. Smotrich has now presented this plan *publicly* as the shift to the 'decisive stage' of the conflict." Original emphasis.

69. Ben-Abba, "Israel's New Ideology of Genocide."

by Native Americans, Palestinians, and Africans. Miriam's question should become the new quest for Black liberation theology: "Has the Lord only spoken to Moses?" Has the Lord not also spoken through Miriam, through the protesting people of Gaza, and through the secular prophets like Amitai Ben-Abba? This is the context in which Miriam's questions now arise, in which her resistance takes on new, urgent meaning. That is where the good news will be heard, and if, as we have argued, following Franz Fanon and Steve Biko, blackness is not so much a question of skin color, but a condition of oppression, infliction, and resistance, it will be Black liberation theology that is to shout that good news. Miriam and Hannah, Vashti and Martha and Junia, in Mary of Galilee in her magnificent Magnificat and her son Jesus in his life and death and resurrection, in their power and resilience, in their strength and faithfulness, are all children of the waters of Meribah. And we, the children of the waters of Meribah, cannot but stand by the side of the children of Gaza. That is where Black liberation theology finds its meaning, in the company of Miriam and Jesus, taking their stand with the wretched of the earth.

Chapter Five

JESUS, A WOMAN, AND BIKO'S GHOST

Black Theology, Empire, and the Liberation of the Colonized Mind

EMPIRE AND THE COLONIZED MIND

IN CHAPTER 1, DEALING with what we have called "the reality of empire," we described empire as a calculated coalescing of global forces pooling their economic, political, military, ideological, and cultural resources (i.e., powers) together in unprecedented and frightening ways. Apart from the issues raised there we should here highlight yet another way in which empire works. It is, we argued, "the colonization of consciousness, values, and notions of human life by the imperial logic."[1]

This is the colonization of our mind that not only makes us susceptible to the logic of empire, we wrote, quoting Hebrew Bible scholar Walter Brueggemann, it robs us of our "prophetic imagination"; that is, in relentless, continuous acts of dispossession it deprives us of our prophetic discernment and our prophetic critique, which spring from an alternative consciousness, one that serves to dismantle that very imperial consciousness that seeks to colonize our minds and our way of life. In resisting that

---

1. See A. Boesak et al., *Dreaming a Different World*, 2. See also A. Boesak, *Dare We Speak of Hope?*, 59–60.

imperial consciousness, we nurture, nourish, and evoke a consciousness and perception alternative to the consciousness and perception of the dominant culture around us.² In the most ordinary, but simultaneously most deadly, ways, it makes us believe the empire, its propaganda, and its claims. In our growing inability to discern mendacity from truth, we begin to believe that those myths that are the lifeblood of imperial dominance are also the myths that give meaning to our lives. It is, in the language of Black Consciousness, a process of complete self-alienation. Theologically speaking, like ancient Israel, we have "exchanged the glory of God for the image of an ox that eats grass" (Ps 106:2).

We have previously, in our discussion on the midwives of Exod 1, quoted Steve Biko's dictum, "The best ally of the oppressor is the mind of the oppressed." In that discussion we connected it to John Calvin's observation that the goal of tyranny is to oppress the people in such harsh ways that they become "hardened," that is, resigned to their own oppression, experiencing it as the "normal" way of life, "callous to their own bondage." They "renounce all hope" in the possibility of freedom and in God's love for freedom and justice, we hear Calvin say. It is this resignation, the giving up of all hope, that smothers any thoughts of dignity and any longing for freedom as if this longing is unnatural, hopeless, or "not meant for us." This is what allows oppression to flourish and makes the mind of the oppressed the oppressor's "best ally."

So in our own struggle, certainly for my generation, wresting our minds away from the apartheid mindset, the (unconscious, and unthinking) acceptance of its racist propaganda, bowing before its ideological power, embracing its predatory belief systems of white superiority and black inferiority and the determinative value of its ethnic hierarchies, divisive pigmentocracy, and destructive self-perceptions—all of which set the boundaries for our humanity and our resistance against our dehumanization—became a prerequisite for authentic participation in the struggle. This redeemed consciousness, or as the Apostle Paul calls it, the "renewal of the mind" (Rom 12:2) first preceded and then necessitated the physical struggle against the myriad manifestations of colonialist apartheid in South Africa's political, social, and economic life.

This unmissable insight is not new in black struggles for liberation from imperial oppression. African-American Presbyterian minister Henry Highland Garnet argued more than 170 years ago that slavery was a grave sin, resting on the souls of white slave owners, "an evil" and a "tremendous

---

2. See Brueggemann, *Prophetic Imagination*, 3; also A. Boesak, *Dare We Speak of Hope?*, 59.

wickedness."³ Especially expressive of that sin, he argued, echoing John Calvin, was the slave owners' "aim" to make the slave "contented with slavery." As offensive to God and humanity as that was, however, yet another sin was greater, this time placing its heavy burden on the souls of black slaves themselves: the slave's acceptance of that mindset. "TO SUCH DEGRADATION" he wrote in capitals, marking the significance of this sentence in his address, and how important it was to him for his audience to grasp this, "IT IS SINFUL IN THE EXTREME FOR YOU TO MAKE VOLUNTARY SUBMISSION."

But for Garnet, and this is the point I want to make here, it begins with the state of mind. "God will not receive [in exchange] slavery nor ignorance, *nor any state of mind*, for love or obedience to him." And again, as he exhorts slaves to hold on to and assert their fundamental God-given dignity and equality with all human beings: "The humblest peasant is as full in the sight of God as the proudest monarch who ever swayed a sceptre." And yet again, as he reminds them that freedom is God's gift every child of God should embrace and own: "Liberty is a spirit sent from God, and like its Author, no respecter of persons."⁴ The oppressed are heirs to that spirit of freedom, bequeathed to them by God. That is what should capture their mind. Without it, there is no understanding the enormity of the evil of slavery and oppression, nor the truth that no one has the right to subject them to it. Without it there is no understanding of their right, nay, as Garnet himself repeatedly put it, their *obligation* to fight it.⁵ Without it there is no inspiration for revolt against oppression. If they ignore it, lose it, or abandon it, they seal their own fate.⁶ While the enemy without is slavery's oppressive, dehumanizing power, the enemy within is the enslaved, submissive mind.

3. See Garnet, "An Address to the Slaves in The United States," 115–21. In a previous publication, *Pharaohs on Both Sides of the Blood-red Waters* (2017), I referred to this address by Garnet, but the point I made there from this rich piece was entirely different. Capitals in the quote are in the original.

4. Garnet, "An Address to the Slaves in The United States," 115–21. My emphasis.

5. Garnet makes the point with great emphasis: "The forlorn condition in which you are placed, does not destroy your moral obligation to God." This radical freedom of the mind overcomes every spiritual and physical condition. This reasoning leads him to a radical conclusion: "Your condition does not absolve you from your moral obligation. The diabolical injustice by which your liberties are cloven down, NEITHER GOD, NOR ANGELS, OR JUST MEN, COMMAND YOU TO SUFFER FOR A SINGLE MOMENT. THEREFORE IT IS YOUR SOLEMN AND IMPERATIVE DUTY TO USE EVERY MEANS, BOTH MORAL, INTELLECTUAL, AND PHYSICAL THAT PROMISES SUCCESS." Capitals in the original.

6. Again the echo of Calvin can be heard here. "This longing [for freedom and justice]" Calvin writes, "is it not implanted in us by the Lord? It is then as if God hears [Godself] when the oppressed cry 'how long'?" See Calvin, *Commentaries*, Hab 2:11–12.

Steve Biko, matchless prophet of the Black Consciousness Movement in South Africa—in the mould of revolutionary thinkers such as Martinique's Frantz Fanon and Aimé Cesairé and America's James Baldwin—grasped this superbly, and helped generations of freedom fighters to understand the significance of the quest for the freedom of the mind in struggles for liberation. No resistance movement and no process of fundamental change can be sustained if not initiated and nourished by the liberated mind. We shall have cause to return to these insights as this discussion develops, and as, in the following two chapters, we engage the views of one of Africa's most well-known theologians of the younger generation, Musa W. Dube, African feminist and anti-imperial interpreter of the Bible, especially in her analysis of one of the most disturbing but nonetheless intriguing and, for me, most stunning stories in the Gospels: the story of Jesus and the Canaanite woman (Matt 15:21–28). It is in these encounters, first with the Gospel in general, and then with the woman in particular, that it seems we are haunted by Biko's ghost. His wisdom will not let us go, and his insights chide us still.

Musa Dube's best-known, most challenging, and most engaging study is her groundbreaking work on biblical interpretation from an African feminist point of view.[7] She writes as an African concerned about imperialism and colonialism as the framework of Western Christian mission in Africa and the consequences for the people, their culture, their way of life, their land, and their human dignity. Armed with strong intellectual argument, she writes with the righteous anger of "a reader of Sub-Saharan origin,"[8] born into this unholy marriage of imperialism and Christian mission. "The historical experience of sub-Saharan African people," she writes, "finds an intimate relationship between empire and mission." But more than that: African thinkers find and emphasize "an ideological connection between biblical mission passages and imperialism."[9] History more than adequately proves her point. As chapter 1 has shown, I believe she is absolutely correct, and the African consensus runs both deep and wide, among scholars as well as among communities.[10]

---

7. See Dube, *Postcolonial Feminist Interpretation*.
8. Dube, *Postcolonial Feminist Interpretation*, 128.
9. Dube, *Postcolonial Feminist Interpretation*, 128.
10. Few sayings from Africa are as widely known outside the continent as the one ascribed to Kenyan freedom fighter and first president of independent Kenya, Jomo Kenyatta. When the white man came, the story goes, we had the land and they had the Bible. They asked us to pray. We closed our eyes. When we opened our eyes, we had the Bible and they had the land. The issue is not so much the ubiquitous nature of the saying as the emphatic way a new generation of African scholars have embraced it. The question of land, its original ownership and restitution has become one of the most contentious issues in Africa, and especially in South Africa, in the aftermath of the

Dube explores the Gospel of Matthew, seeking to establish the narrative's view toward imperialism by examining two aspects: its historical and ideological perspectives. The historical perspective seeks to establish whether "the Matthean text is rejecting the imperialism of its time or seeking its favor." The ideological view, on the other hand, "seeks to establish whether the Matthean intertextual is geared toward rejecting or accommodating imperialism."[11] She thus reads Matthew's Gospel as a "missionary" text that "presupposes the Hebrew foundation myth of the promised land" which, in turn, embodies imperialistic values.[12] In other words, in the exodus story and the conquest of Canaan as these follow the Mosaic, patriarchal tradition, the Hebrews present themselves as the imperialist interlopers, transgressing into the land of peoples considered inferior, less worthy, less deserving, and completely disposable because they are in Israel's way, or better: they are in the way of God's plans with Israel. They are the sacrifice upon the altar of God's promises to Israel. Hence the conquest and justified annihilation of people, their cultures, and their religions. These are the components and the justification for the Western missionary ventures that came to Africa under the protection of and as precursors of colonialism. This is also why, in the three previous chapters, I have insisted on a different reading of the exodus story by Black theologians, forsaking the Mosaic tradition for the Miriamic tradition.

"If one defines imperialism as an imposition of economic, political, and cultural institutions of dominant nations over foreign ones, then it becomes important to examine mission strategies for extending the biblical religions to foreign nations." For Dube, missions to foreign lands should be examined to "determine whether its strategies advocate power relations that resonate with the model of liberating interdependence or embrace a model that is consistent with imperialistic impositions."[13] It seems to me that Dube, despite her resolute negative assessment of Western missions to Africa, and indeed of "mission" in the Bible in general, here does leave the door open for the possibility that "mission" may resonate with "a model of

---

negotiated settlement and the Truth and Reconciliation Commission, both of which gave no impetus to restitution and the question of the return of the land. It is, as we write, without question one of the most important issues on South Africa's political agenda and will remain so for the foreseeable future. Among the younger generation of scholars, as indicated in chapter 1, this matter is being revisited. It is not an exaggeration to say that it is central in African theologians' reflection on matters like the Bible, colonialism, postcolonialism, and imperialism. Dube's work under discussion is a strong case in point.

11. Dube, *Postcolonial Feminist Interpretation*, 128.
12. Dube, *Postcolonial Feminist Interpretation*, 128.
13. Dube, *Postcolonial Feminist Interpretation*, 128.

liberating interdependence." But for her, as far as Western missions are concerned, even if the possibility might exist, the improbability predominates or negates the possibility.[14]

The judgment on the Bible as a whole as imperialistic is fairly clear: "Historical evidence of modern imperialism" she writes, "thus categorizes the biblical texts as imperializing texts: texts that authorize the imposition of foreign institutions of one nation by another."[15] On that basis, Dube proceeds to examine the Gospel of Matthew to determine whether the text is imperializing. She applies the test in four questions:[16]

1. Does the Matthean text have a clear stance against the imperialism of its time?

2. Does the Matthean text encourage travel to distant and inhabited lands and how does it justify itself?

3. How does the Matthean text construct difference: Is there a dialogue and liberating interdependence, or is there condemnation and replacement of all that is foreign?

4. Does the Matthean text employ gender and divine representations to construct relationships of subordination and domination?

Dube's reading of Matthew uncovers a Gospel written under Roman rule, but without question accommodating empire. A fifth question, as

---

14. See Dube's strongly and convincingly argued chapter 1. Again, as far as Western missions are concerned, she is right. I know only of a few missionaries of the London Missionary Society, specifically Johannes van der Kemp, who came to South Africa in the late eighteenth century and actively took the side of the indigenous peoples in their struggle for human rights against the colonialists. Dube leans heavily on Rene Maunier in her chapter 1 and here quotes him with approval, "The salvation of the conquered became the inspiration which underlay colonization. Expansion was carried out in order to convert" (Dube, *Postcolonial Feminist Interpretation*, 129). Perhaps it is possible for mission, not intertwined with colonialism, to be a model of liberating interdependence. But in this work Christian "mission" itself, since it derives its inspiration from the Bible, cannot be redeemed, since "biblical texts propound values that are compatible with imperialistic tendencies" (*Postcolonial Feminist Interpretation*, 129).

15. Dube, *Postcolonial Feminist Interpretation*, 129. It will be clear from my argument in chapter 1 that on this point I disagree. "Biblical texts," unqualified, have not been exposed as "imperializing texts." In fact, as we have pointed out above in chapter 1, we have come to understand that the Bible as a collection of books was written and compiled under continuous imperial rule. They reflect the struggle against empire as well as empire's appropriation of Scripture for its own ends. See Horsley, *In The Shadow of Empire*, Introduction. A sweeping statement such as this in the service of a preassumed notion about the Bible as a collection of imperialistic texts diminishes an otherwise noteworthy and valuable argument.

16. Dube, *Postcolonial Feminist Interpretation*, 129.

important but raised later in a following paragraph, asks, "Do Matthean perspectives revive and reiterate ideologies of the Hebrew Bible to assert Israel's right to be an autonomous nation or to be an empire as well, or do they reinterpret them to collaborate with contemporary empire?"[17] In a sense this question lies at the heart of the argument. If the issue is about mission as imperial enterprise, and mission as equal to transgression into foreign lands, subjugation, and domination, even annihilation, then it is perfectly legitimate to raise the question with regard to the Mosaic tradition—in contrast with what I consider to be the Miriamic tradition—of the exodus and the conquest of Palestine. Except that one then would have to ask whether the "mission" of the Israelites with and after the conquest was indeed to "win the other nations over to their God." I would say not. Without doubt, however, their mission was to overrun those nations and claim the land, promised to them by their God, as their own which Dube seems to regard as the paradigmatic framework of mission in Matthew and as a consequence, reiterated in Western missionary projects.

The more serious issues arise when Dube reads these questions into not only Matthew's narrative as a narrative of mission to convert the gentiles, but Jesus as the most prominent representative of that mission, seen no more clearly than in the passage dealing with the Canaanite woman. Jesus is an Israelite whose mission falls within the paradigm of "the foundational Hebrew myth" of invasion, conquest, subjugation, and domination. Understood in terms of modern, Western mission, Jesus equally transgresses into foreign territory, as he transgresses into the Canaanite woman's life, seeing her as "needy" and "desperate," and in true patriarchal fashion exploits that need, subjects the woman to humiliation, and dispossesses her (of dignity and self-worth, if not land). Finally pacifying her with crumbs from the master's table (praising her faith and persistence; healing her daughter), Jesus walks away in triumph. Yet another mission completed.[18]

Thus Jesus himself emerges as a privileged Jew, in fact not just accommodating empire but actively collaborating with empire, "pronouncing imperialism as holy and acceptable."[19] Dube deduces this from other incidents in the Gospel as well: the centurion (8:8–12); the tribute (22:15–22); the trial before Pilate (27:1–26); and the temple tax (17:24–27). He has imperial privileges since he can travel freely and traverse into foreign lands, and his patriarchy is undeniable as one observes his attitude towards and exchanges with the woman. Dube might not directly call Jesus an unrepentant racist,

---

17. Dube, *Postcolonial Feminist Interpretation*, 129.
18. See Dube, *Postcolonial Feminist Interpretation*, 117; 129; 144–55.
19. Dube, *Postcolonial Feminist Interpretation*, 132.

hiding behind the Hebrew foundational myth of "chosenness," but certainly, in her view, Jesus sees this gentile woman as deeply unequal:

> That the Canaanite woman is portrayed as accepting the "dog" social category assigned to her and that her request is granted on these conditions, however, has frightening implications for a narrative that foreshadows the mission. The non-Christian followers, who must be sought and taught everything, are not integrated as equals who have something to offer. Instead they are welcomed as "dogs" who have come to follow, beg, and depend on their masters. With the healing of the child granted, the mysterious short story of Jesus' journey to Tyre and Sidon comes to an abrupt end. Jesus departs to Galilee, back to his own people and land (v. 28).[20]

As our argument develops, we shall return to two of the examples Dube claims establish Matthew and Jesus as imperial agents before we turn our attention fully to the Canaanite woman. One cannot argue with the fact that all the characteristics mentioned by Dube with regard to modern Western missionary activity and imperialism and colonialism are true. The extraordinary value of the reading of these texts not just as anti-imperialist, but as an *African feminist* is indisputable and necessary, as her reading of the Rahab story shows.[21] So is her African feminist engagement with postcolonial readings of Western, Eurocentric interpreters.[22]

Without these anti-imperial, anti-colonialist, anti-patriarchal insights and the way she reveals the workings of empire today, a Black theology of liberation would be deeply impoverished. The question is, do we find these critical elements in Jesus, and more specifically in her chosen example, Jesus and the encounter with the Canaanite woman? The deeper question, in line with our exploration throughout this work, must then be: Does Dube's postcolonial, African feminist reading of this text offer a way to help Black liberation theology understand better the life and mission of Jesus of Nazareth? Does it bring us closer to the truth of the Black Messiah, or in the quest for the secret of the Human Child, so vital in the lives of oppressed Christians, their communities, and their struggles for justice and liberation?[23]

20. Dube, *Postcolonial Feminist Interpretation*, 151.

21. See Dube, *Postcolonial Feminist Interpretation*, 76–80; 121–24.

22. It is remarkable, and telling, though perhaps not altogether surprising, that in the important work of New Testament scholars working with the N. T. writings within the framework of the Roman Empire since the publication of Dube's book, her work is hardly mentioned, let alone seriously engaged. See, e.g., the volume of quite valuable essays in Riches and Sim, *Gospel of Matthew in its Roman Imperial Context*.

23. I have posed and discussed this question in my engagement with the work of

JESUS ACCOMMODATING EMPIRE?

As we have noted, Dube's examination of Matthew's Gospel brings her to the conclusion that the implied author writes as subject of the Roman Empire but as one who seeks the approval of empire, exonerating the empire at every turn, in fact "presents the imperial rule and agents as holy and acceptable." Mathew's Gospel is concerned with "mission" to the nations, embracing, reiterating, and confirming "imperialistic values and strategies . . . upholding the superiority of some races . . ." The positive presentation of the empire and the decision to take the word to the nations is born within and as a result of stiff competition for power over the crowds (i.e., Israel) as well as the favor of the empire.[24]

South African New Testament scholar Andries van Aarde harbors no doubts that Matthew's Jesus—which is the perspective we will most, in keeping with Musa Dube's argument, keep in view in this discussion—as well as the evangelist himself, are in conflict with the Pax Romana.[25] Importantly, van Aarde points out that Matthew's conflict is one on two fronts, namely the empire *and* the post-70 CE Pharisees in collaboration with empire. So in his confrontation with these Jerusalem elites, which are prominent in Matthew, we will keep in mind that it is simultaneously a confrontation with the empire. That makes the argument against an empire-compliant Matthew and Matthean Jesus even stronger.[26]

Warren Carter, whose special field of interest is Matthew's Gospel, also comes to an entirely different conclusion. Carter, like Richard Horsley and a growing school of New Testament scholars, have opened new, extremely valuable, and utterly convincing ways of reading and interpreting the New Testament by understanding just how important it is to read these writings and see the work of Jesus of Nazareth within the context of the Roman Empire, its global military power, its occupation of foreign lands, and its economic exploitation and political oppression of peoples under its rule. Their reading of these texts is a strong departure from traditional New Testament

---

South African New Testament scholar Andries van Aarde, who clearly exercises his scholarship from postcolonial, even feminist perspectives as he does in his important work, *Fatherless in Galilee*. See A. Boesak, *Pharaohs*, ch. 3, "The Divine Favor of the Unworthy," in which the central issue discussed is the question "What happens when the fatherless Jesus meets the Black Messiah?"

24. Dube, *Postcolonial Feminist Interpretation*, 154–55.

25. Even though I find it necessary for the historical Jesus, as he is pictured by the synoptic Gospels, to engage our attention as this argument develops and to help us keep the wholeness of that picture in mind, it is the Matthean Jesus that will concern us mostly here.

26. See van Aarde, "Love for the Poor Neighbour," 150–75.

studies and opens insights into the world of the New Testament under Roman rule completely ignored thus far. Carter's major, groundbreaking work[27] has been followed by a school of scholarship that, concentrating on the Gospel of Matthew, has identified the areas of their enquiry, as John Riches summarizes it:

> First, into the nature of empire and colonialism, how such political realities are structured and controlled and how the subject peoples attempt to resist the powerful; second, into the ways in which other groups and individuals responded during this period to the power of Rome; and third, into the ways in which Matthew's gospel itself reflects his and his community's attitudes and beliefs about secular power and authority in general and Rome in particular.[28]

Carter's valuable work, placing Matthew's Gospel in Syria under Roman occupation and control, uncovers the harsh rule typical of Rome, and shows how Roman imperialism was the dominant reality in the lives of those living in the empire, even more so if Matthew was written in Antioch on the Orontes, the capital of the Roman province of Syria.[29] Carter also argues persuasively "that resistance plays a prominent role in this narrative," and the gospel portrays contrasting visions of society and Jesus's legitimacy and authority." Matthew's "audience," the community for whom he writes this Gospel, is from the "margins" of Roman society: not in the center, with power, privilege, or status. Throughout, Jesus, the central figure, is in constant conflict with the religious elite in Jerusalem who, "because of their birth, wealth, training, gender, and social position have the power."[30]

They are the ruling classes who keep and enhance their positions of wealth and power because of their collaboration with Rome. Living in the margins means powerlessness, and Matthew's community needs to find ways to navigate the challenges the vagaries and capriciousness of power present to powerless people constantly under pressure, for example in the matter of having to pay tribute and taxes. Their ability to navigate does not always mean open resistance or even defiance, but always "subversion," that is, actions through which they find the wisdom to understand that the battle is not just with Rome or its surrogates in Jerusalem, but reflects a cosmic

---

27. See Carter, *Matthew and the Margins*, and *Matthew and Empire*. See also van Aarde, who argues that the locality of Matthew's "first readers" was southern Syria, on the border of northern Galilee. See his "A Silver Coin in the Mouth of a Fish," 1–25.
28. See Riches and Sim, *Gospel of Matthew*, 6.
29. See Carter, *Matthew and the Margins*, 37–46.
30. See Carter, *Matthew and the Margins*, 2.

struggle between God and Satan. In these ways they also find the courage to endure until Jesus's return.[31]

In his second major work, Carter goes somewhat further. In contradiction to Dube's reading, Carter argues that Matthew's Gospel "contests and resists" the Roman Empire's claims to sovereignty over the world. The Gospel, he writes, "poses a *social challenge* in offering a vastly different vision and experience of human community, and a *theological challenge* in asserting that the world belongs to God, not Rome, and that God's purposes run through Jesus, not Rome."[32] Carter's reading also illustrates

> the Gospel's interaction with and critique of significant aspects of the Roman Empire: the domination structure of the imperial system, imperial theology, economic exploitation, military might, social hierarchy, dreadful urban and rural poverty and misery, illusions of power, taxation, provincial government and governor's justice.[33]

Carter speaks of a social and theological challenge to Rome and its collaborators in Jerusalem. So, in Matthew's Gospel, this challenge, or subversion, even resistance, would be found in the usage of imperial terms and language but in the service of Jesus's activities on behalf of the reign of God: *basileia* ("kingdom" or "empire") and *basileus* ("emperor" or "king") are pertinent examples.[34] It may very well be that what Carter reads as "subversion," not outright resistance, Dube, from her African perspective, sees as "collaboration" with empire, even "pronouncing empire holy."

We pause here to note two important issues: one, Carter does not speak of a *political* challenge. Richard Horsley, however, speaks of the way in which the gospel narratives, including important aspects such as the Roman Empire itself and Galilee as Roman occupied territory, and subsequently Jesus, have been "domesticated" and "depoliticized."[35] He argues strongly

---

31. Carter, *Matthew and the Margins*, 2, 3; *Matthew and Empire*, Introduction.

32. Carter, *Matthew and the Margins*, 1, emphasis original. Carter will work with these assertions throughout both his works and illustrate them as well in the crucial passages Dube has chosen to prove the opposite.

33. Carter, *Matthew and Empire*, 2.

34. See also among the growing literature, Horsley, *Jesus and the Spiral of Violence* and *Jesus and Empire*; Crossan, *God and Empire*; and, on Paul and imperial/anti-imperial language, Horsley, *Paul and Empire*. See also A. Boesak, *Pharaohs*, 40–41. I follow Horsley and others in reading the usage of this terminology as consistent and not so subtle resistance against Rome and as undermining Rome's and the Caesar's authority. Such reversal of language is essential expression of the freedom of mind necessary for revolutionary action.

35. See Horsley, *Jesus and Empire*, 6–12.

against this tendency. There was, he argues, a "judgmental side" to Jesus's ministry that had a counterpart of deliverance, empowerment, and renewal for the people. In Horsley's view, Jesus, in the judgmental side of the kingdom of God,

> was proclaiming that God was in the process of effecting the "political revolution" that would overthrow the Roman imperial order in Palestine. Then, on the constructive side, in the confidence that God was taking care of the dominant political order, Jesus and his movement were carrying out the "social revolution" that God was making possible and empowering in Galilean village communities.[36]

Thus Horsley does not shy away from the revolutionary nature of Jesus's work as it emerges from a reading of the Gospels as a whole. Andries van Aarde too argues that Jesus was much more than an itinerant teacher and miracle worker. He has made a powerful and, in my view, persuasive case for a historical Jesus who was, as the title of his book announces, "fatherless"; and not just fatherless, but fatherless "in Galilee."[37] This means—and this is our second point here—that Jesus was not just of humble birth but "fatherless," reducing him to one of yet lower status, of the unacceptable classes. On top of all that Jesus was a Galilean, subject to further abuse, humiliation, and prejudice, apart from being subject to oppression by both Rome and the temple elites.

"Fatherlessness" put Jesus in a specific social class, a matter of grave consequence as explained by van Aarde and much earlier confirmed by Joachim Jeremias's magisterial study in which he addresses this very issue. Part IV of his work deals with the "maintenance of racial purity" in ancient Israel. The hierarchy goes as follows: "Israelites of pure ancestry; despised trades and Jewish slaves; Illegitimate Israelites; Israelites with 'slight blemish', (proselytes, freed gentile slaves); Israelites with 'grave blemish'—bastards, Temple slaves, fatherless foundlings, eunuchs, (this whole category described as 'the excrement of the community'); Gentile slaves; Samaritans."[38] But it also explains Jesus's revolutionary stance on issues essential to the maintenance of oppressive hierarchical structures of his time, as van Aarde's exhaustive research concludes:

---

36. Horsley, *Jesus and Empire*, 103.

37. See van Aarde, *Fatherless*. For the political and social significance of Galilee, see especially Horsley, *Jesus and the Spiral of Violence*, and Horsley, *Galilee: History, Politics, People*; see also Hendricks, *Politics of Jesus*.

38. Jeremias, *Jerusalem in the Times of Jesus*, 337.

> Jesus' fatherlessness is probably a historical fact that should be taken into account when one considers his social identity, his non-patriarchal ethos, his behavior toward women and children, and especially his trust in God as his Father.[39]

To put it another way, neatly and succinctly put by Howard Thurman, "If a Roman soldier pushed Jesus into a ditch, he could not appeal to Caesar; he would be just another Jew in the ditch."[40] This historic reality on its own creates considerable difficulties for Dube as she insists that Jesus's "class, race, and gender" made of him a privileged, powerful, patriarchal male forcing his superior status upon the Canaanite woman. Van Aarde is clear: Jesus was "the peasant boy who *probably* became a carpenter and then, *definitely*, a revolutionary teacher and compassionate healer."[41]

Black liberation theologian and New Testament scholar Obery Hendricks takes one step further and explains what this means:

> To say that Jesus was a political revolutionary is to say that the message he proclaimed not only called for change in individual hearts but also demanded sweeping and comprehensive change in political, social, and economic structures in his setting in life: colonized Israel. It means that if Jesus had his way, the Roman Empire and the ruling elites among his own people either would no longer have held their positions of power, or if they did, would have had to conduct themselves very, very differently. It means that his ministry was to radically change the distribution of authority, power, goods and resources, so all people—particularly the little people, or "the least of these," as Jesus called

---

39. Van Aarde, *Fatherless*, 15. This point alerts us to something Horsley points out as typically a problem with Western scholarship's "apolitical" interpretation of Jesus, but with Dube becomes a "politicized" reading: where "a modern Western essentialism of ethnicity, nationality, and culture determines identity . . . All 'Jews' are conceived according to the same essentialized culture, viewpoint, and practices. Thus Herod the Great, Caiaphas the high priest, Gamaliel the Pharisee, and Jesus the Galilean are all conceived of as 'Jews', their primary identity as 'Jewish'. Political differences disappear. Ironically this depoliticization of Jesus' social context results is generalizations that are highly charged in later historical circumstances, such as that 'the Jews' arrested, tried and clamored for the crucifixion of Jesus." See Horsley, *Jesus and Empire*, 9, 10. In her characterization of Jesus as a Jewish, privileged, powerful patriarch, Dube similarly makes no difference between Jesus the Galilean and the powerful, privileged, wealthy elites in Jerusalem he so seriously contends with and who collaborate with Rome in the oppression of the very people Jesus represents as well as in Jesus's death. See Horsley, *Jesus and Empire*, 9, 10. For Dube, it is Jesus's power as a Jewish male that allows him to cross physical as well as personal boundaries vis-a-vis the woman.

40. See Thurman, *Jesus and the Disinherited*, 13.

41. Van Aarde, *Fatherless*, 73, my emphasis.

them—might have lives free of political oppression, enforced hunger and poverty, and undue insecurity.[42]

David C. Sim adds yet another important dimension to this view. Like Carter, he sees in the Gospel a "cosmic battle between the forces of good and the forces of evil." But whereas Carter's eschatological view mostly places the oppressed community of Matthew's Gospel in a situation of "living within two worlds," waiting for the fulfillment of God's judgment on empire when Jesus returns, Sim understands this to have a much more immediate impact. This cosmic battle, he writes, is "similar to what we find in the Book of Revelation." In Jesus's ministry the lines are drawn and radically so. "Humans are inevitably caught up in this conflict. Individuals can choose either to side with God (Jesus) or to side with Satan and his fallen angels; there is no middle ground . . . Matthew inextricably connects Satan and the Roman Empire."[43] This has immediate political implications that underscore Jesus's mission not just as a social and theological challenge, but a decidedly *political* one, a struggle against imperial forces against which Jesus's followers cannot remain neutral—they must take sides.

And again, all of Jesus's ministry is to be understood within the context of Roman occupation, the utter brutality of Roman rule, the popular resistance movements, unrest, protests, and outright revolt against the imperial order that had been imposed by Rome. The crucifixion of two thousand men in 4 BCE in Galilee around the time Jesus was born, the systematic slaughter, the mass enslavement of thirty thousand people of Magadala on the Sea of Galilee fifty years before by Cassius in revenge for a rebellion, the scorched-earth policy of Rome in Galilea—all of it would have made a lasting and terrifying impression on the people in Galilee and caused massive trauma in their wake.[44] It would be completely illogical for Jesus not to have been aware of this as the occupation and oppression by Rome continued, and it is illogical to think that the framing of his mission in the way he did it in Nazareth (Luke 4:16–18) would have been purely incidental. It is no wonder that Jesus knew, by the third time he prophesied his death (=Matt 20:19) that he would not just be "killed," but "mocked and flogged *and crucified*," a form of execution Rome reserved for runaway slaves, bandits, and rebel leaders, a form of terror that was meant to serve also as deterrent for the people to control and destroy their desires for freedom.

42. Hendricks, *Politics of Jesus*, 5.
43. Sim, "Rome in Matthew's Eschatology," 93.
44. See Horsley, *Jesus and Empire*, 14ff.

On this point, I find Hendricks, Horsley, van Aarde, and Sim, more convincing than either Dube or Carter.[45]

AND IN HIS NAME THE GENTILES WILL HOPE

Perhaps before we enter into the more detailed discussion of Dube's perspective on Jesus we should pay some attention to what she herself indicates as the framework within which Jesus is to be understood, namely the Gospel of Matthew, serving empire through its dedication to Jesus's imperialist mission to other nations. Here we should keep in mind the questions she applies to the Gospel, and her conclusion that it "revives and reiterates ideologies of the Hebrew Bible to assert Israel's right to be an autonomous nation or to be an empire as well" and that the mission narratives here "reinterpret them to collaborate with the contemporary empire." This culminates in the so-called Great Commission, where Jesus commissions his disciples to teach the nations all he had commanded them. This is an imperialist model of "subjugation, of conquest, of students, of authoritative teachers, and of travelers."[46]

All the Gospels make clear that Jesus is indeed engaged in a mission. But is it a mission of subjugation, conquest and humiliation, furthering the aims of Rome, an ethnic-religious mission with a Jewish, exclusivist agenda, or is it a mission of resistance, liberation, and inclusion, proclaiming the coming of the reign of God? Taking its cue from Jesus's first publicly recorded words according to Luke 4:16-19, Black liberation theology has chosen for the latter. The growing consensus—even from the circles outside of Black liberation theology—is that this mission is undertaken *within* the Roman Empire, as a mission of resistance to and liberation *from* the empire. The question is of course whether Black liberation theology can offer an adequate response to Musa Dube. This is what I will attempt in the following chapters. It is not necessary here to reiterate the absolute significance of this passage for Black theology both in teaching and preaching and in the life experience of black people in their struggles for liberation and justice, except for a few remarks.

First, the declaration of Jesus's manifesto in the synagogue in Nazareth takes place immediately after the temptation scene in the wilderness. James Cone had correctly observed that "the heart of the matter is Jesus' rejection of any role that would separate him from the poor."[47] But as I argued elsewhere, all the temptations offered Jesus here by Satan are the things

---

45. See A. Boesak, *Pharaohs*, ch. 3.
46. Dube, *Postcolonial Feminist Interpretation*, 148.
47. See Cone, *God of the Oppressed*, 68, 69.

the emperor boastfully claims: miracle provider for the masses (bread); the arrogance of power (over the temple and over the availability of saving powers—angels); limitless imperial power (the kingdoms of the world that are in his hand to give); and through it all a claim on the availability of God based on his own power and divinity.[48] In the resolute, authoritative rejection of Satan's power, protection, security, and worldly glory—"Away with you!"—Jesus rejects all imperial pretense and all things identified with imperial power and establishes the power of God over Satan and the dominions he controls, including the temple on whose roof he possessively plants himself.[49]

Perhaps yet another point should be made. All the temptations Satan offers are singularized. Rewards are offered to Jesus as individual benefits. He, and *he alone*, would be safeguarded by angels; *he* would have food security; *he* alone would receive power over the kingdoms of the world. One after the other, the temptations are shamelessly self-gratifying, self-glorifying, self-securing. Satan is urging Jesus to adopt a "Jesus First" policy. But Jesus had come to save his people. But not only that. In his name *the nations* would place their hope. He had come to bring good news to the poor and release to the captives, liberate the oppressed; to announce the year of the Lord's favor to *all of them*, in all its power and radical inclusivity. It seems to me that the darkest heart of Satan's intentions was that the universality of God's liberating power, saving grace, and compassionate justice should become an individualized, self-absorbed, me-centered reduction. Then, with the plight, the struggles, and the freedom of the people wiped off the table, there would be no radical Messiah with the power to liberate; just one more narcissistic messianic pretender given permission to imitate the messianic cult in Rome, beholden and accountable to Rome. What would then be the difference between Jesus and Caesar, Jesus and Herod, or Jesus and Donald Trump? Or indeed, between Jesus and Satan?

Second, in Luke 4, Jesus quotes from Isa 58:6 and 61:1–2(a). He combines the two, which enhances the message of the two passages and brings both under the power of the first sentence—"Is *this* not the fast that I choose?"—and the force of the rhythmic cadences of justice that follow. In the citation from Isaiah 61, Jesus leaves out the "day of vengeance of our God." Jesus is more interested in liberation, justice, and inclusion than in vengeance. Those who expected reiteration of this beloved theme would have been sorely disappointed. Then he goes much further than Isaiah.

---

48. See A. Boesak, *Pharaoh*s, 108.

49. See Carter, *Matthew and Empire*, 62–63; also Sim, "Rome in Matthew's Eschatology," 93.

Where Isaiah goes on to proclaim the victory over the nations, their humiliation, their plunder, and their slave status to a victorious Israel, Jesus stops and "rolls up the scroll," ending the reading. An imperialistic Israel, imitating the "other nations" is not part of his vision.

Then he speaks the words that alienate the whole audience, even those who were "amazed" and "spoke well of him." The breaking point is the radical inclusivity of his message that follows his "But the truth is. . ." (v. 25) making clear that his mission—the challenge and resistance to the empire through the belief in the reign of God—will not be confined to Israel alone. His mission breaks down barriers, overcomes age-old animosities and hostilities, intentionally does not pamper dearly held prejudices. Calling upon Elijah and Elisha as prophetic witnesses of impeccable integrity, Jesus lifts up "the widow in Sidon" and Naaman "the Syrian," not as objects of mission, but as subjects of God's inclusive, compassionate justice and restoration. The oppressed, the captives, the poor, the sick, the outcasts, and the defenseless under the yoke of Rome everywhere will come to know the power of the one upon whom the Spirit of the Lord rests. The "year of the Lord's favor" shall be radically inclusive, and radically universal. Not just the privileged in Israel, but the hoarders of wealth and power everywhere, are now put on notice.

It should not go unnoticed how quickly the mood seems to have changed in the synagogue that day: from jubilation and praise to murderous intent. It should also not go unnoticed that the poor, presumably unlike the rich who heard him that day, at first rejoiced in Jesus's reading of Isaiah, but then became as one with the rich in their shock and rejection of his radicalization of Isaiah: "All in the synagogue were filled with rage" (v. 28). Challenging the power of Rome is one thing. Challenging precious myths of uniqueness, supremacy, exceptionalism, and chosenness is quite another. Here are the signs of things to come, and in this sense Dube is correct in raising this issue. The alluring and deadly power of this myth endured through the ages: from Puritan invaders of the American lands to Calvinist white Afrikaners in South Africa to contemporary Israelis in their occupation of Palestine and genocidal wars against the Palestinian people. Then as now, these myths, interlaced with racist, ethnocentric, hetero-patriarchal, homophobic ideologies to various extents, provide bonds of solidarity that overcome political, social, and sometimes cultural, and in its recent manifestations, even racial divisions. Then as now, it is the justification of terror, dispossession, and annihilation. The fact that the people of Galilee were all subjugated to Rome, oppressed and humiliated by Rome, or that the ruling classes in Jerusalem were complicit in the oppression of the poor in Israel, was completely submerged in the deluge of fear of openness to and equality with the dreaded Other.

Jesus is not preaching the exclusion of Israel from God's plan of liberation. Rather Jesus is including gentiles in God's plan. In this respect too, Jesus mirrors Miriam at the seashore whose celebration of God's liberation included *all* who left Egypt's bondage. The struggle is not against Israel; it is against oppression and for all the oppressed under Rome's, and its collaborators', brutal rule. Riches writes about Matthew 28, "What was until now a purely Jewish affair suddenly becomes something with unlimited territorial pretensions. The mission becomes universal,"[50] is not so "sudden" after all. With Luke it begins this early, and the specific reference to Sidon, and a woman, and Syria, is recalled as Jesus faces the Canaanite woman.

Not only Luke, but Matthew as well, prepares us for this, as he tells us early on that Jesus's fame "spread throughout Syria" (4:24). First, note how Matthew is careful to begin with what sounds like a general category: "the sick, those who were inflicted with various diseases and pains." Then, in a distinction that is laden with significance, he becomes specific in mentioning diseases that scholars have come to recognize as the result of colonialist oppression, economic deprivation, poverty, social alienation, and trauma. "Demoniacs, epileptic diseases, and paralytics."[51] Jesus's mission is not to pacify or manage the demons, just as he has not come to "manage" life under Rome or to pacify the oppressed. He has come to "vanquish" the demonic forces that threaten human life.[52]

---

50. Riches, "Matthew's Missionary Strategy," 128–42. That Jesus's presence "will no longer be located in the cult in Jerusalem but wherever his disciples at are work. . ." is clear not just at the end of Matthew's Gospel. Apart from Luke 4, Jesus himself makes it clear early in the Gospel of John as well, in his encounter with the Samaritan woman, where Jesus himself is at work, announcing that neither "this mountain" nor "Jerusalem" will matter, but wherever "true worshippers" will worship God "in spirit and in truth" (John 4:21–23).

51. See Carter, *Matthew and the Margins*, 126–27. He cites those scholars: "Illnesses mentioned here like demon possession are related to circumstances of oppression and colonialism, 'social tensions. . . class antagonisms rooted in economic exploitation, conflicts between traditions . . ., colonial domination, and revolution.'" See nn. 35 and 36 on 575.

52. Horsley makes a strong argument for this; see his *Jesus and Empire*, 99–103: the word usually translated as "cast out" (*epitiman* in Greek and *ga'ar* in Aramaic and Hebrew), was used in reference to Yahweh coming in judgment against foreign imperial regimes who have subjected Israel, or God vanquishing Satan. The word refers to the decisive action by which God or God's representative "brings demonic powers into submission, and establishes the rule/kingdom of God and the deliverance of Israel" (see 100).

Second, like in Luke, Jesus is not confined to Galilee. The message of God's liberating power in contention with the oppressive power of Rome should be heard everywhere. Thus, this early in his Gospel, Matthew is clear about at least two things: a), the battle against empire in all its manifestations is on, and b), Jesus is not working within the boundaries set by the theological traditions of Israel. And again, following Luke, deliberate mention of Syria prepares us for the Canaanite woman with her "demon possessed" daughter. Wherever Rome rules, its oppression shall be challenged.

It is against this broad synoptic background that I think the reference to the prophet Isaiah in Matt 12:15–21 should be understood. Among numerous citations from Isaiah throughout the Gospel, here two things are important to note. First, in Isaiah's original prophecy (Isa 42:1–9), the emphasis falls quite deliberately on the liberating work of the Servant of Yahweh, whom Matthew identifies as Jesus of Nazareth. The purpose, the mission of this servant, is "to bring justice."[53] Three times in four verses Isaiah emphasizes:

- he will bring forth justice;
- he will *faithfully* bring forth justice;
- he will *establish* justice.

Not only that, he will establish justice *in the earth*. Not just in Jerusalem, Judea, or Galilee, but in all the earth. That is what the reign of God is all about, and that is what God has in mind for "all the earth." Isaiah, and hence Matthew, are eager for us to understand: this is not some other-worldly promise. "In the earth" means now, in this life. It is a quite astonishing claim. That is why Matthew, this most Jewish of all Gospel writers, takes the liberty to change Isaiah's "the coastlands will await his teaching" to "in his name the gentiles will hope."

Here, keeping Dube's critique in mind, this does not call to mind "students" or mere passive recipients waiting to be transgressed upon. It calls to mind oppressed people, their agency awakened and embraced, eagerly joining the movement toward freedom, their hopes grounded in the One who will "bring justice to the nations." And in that struggle he will not "grow faint," nor will he, and they together with him, "be crushed." His "faithfulness" is his trustworthiness, his determination to fulfill this task. Despite the endless efforts by the powers to "crush" him he will endure and prevail. "Waiting" has a passive quality to it. "Hoping" on the other hand is drenched

---

53. See my reflections on these two texts in A. Boesak, *Dare We Speak of Hope?*, 175–82.

with an urgency "that strains toward active engagement with the future"[54] in order to bend that future toward justice. And here perhaps is what Dube seeks: a mission that is "a model of liberating interdependence."[55]

It is not logical that the nations, already suffering under severe oppression, should hope for more oppression, more exploitation, more dehumanization. Their hope is for liberation, peace, justice, and dignity of life.

SEE, YOUR KING. . .

There are four instances Dube analyzes to prove her hypothesis of Matthew's, and therefore Jesus', willing complicity with Roman rule: the episode in which Jesus heals the centurion's slave, the question of the tribute, Jesus's entry in to Jerusalem, and the trial before Pilate.[56] In the interests of brevity, we will reflect on two: Jesus's entry into Jerusalem (where Dube sees a "politically harmless Jesus") and Jesus's trial before Pilate (where Jesus is surrounded by all the important parties: the crowds, the religious leaders, and the Roman colonial officials—that is, the colonized, the collaborators, and the colonizers). I choose these two instances not because the other two are less important,[57] but because they involve Jesus and his relationship to the people, the "crowds."

---

54. See A. Boesak, *Dare We Speak of Hope?*, 178.

55. This is a very helpful way of understanding Jesus's mission and in chapter 7 below I will return to this phrase.

56. Dube, *Postcolonial Feminist Interpretation*, 139–40.

57. The other two incidents are in fact hugely important and the controversy around the tribute has played a determinative role in the burning issues of the relationship between church and state, or in Dube's words, "the partnership between Christianity and imperialism." Dube finds evidence of Jesus's complicity with empire in these incidents. Carter thinks that in this instance Jesus chooses against both "outright revolt" and "accommodation" but instead for "nonviolent subversion to Rome." That is to say, Jesus teaches us to "pay the emperor while recognizing [in your heart?] God's greater demand of loyalty." In this way of thinking, payment of taxes falls "within the context of God's far greater gifts and authority." "Disciples who live in God's world and in Rome's world are challenged to live faithfully to God in both worlds until Jesus returns to establish God's empire over all." See Carter, *Matthew and the Margins*, 440. In *Matthew and Empire* (130–44), Carter seeks to build an even stronger argument by reading the tribute question in Matt 22:15–22 within the framework of Matt 17:24–27. There the money found in the mouth of the fish is the sign of God's provision of the means to enable the disciples to live in "Caesar's world." God has power and authority even over the animals of the ocean, and since Rome demands the tax to "assert its supremacy to subjugate, humiliate and punish," God's provision through the fish "shows the tax to God's power and sovereignty." Subsequently, since the means to pay the taxes is provided by God, "the audience knows that God's supremacy is supreme." Paying taxes then becomes "an act of subversion." In this matter, Richard Horsley and Obery Hendricks

As Jesus enters Jerusalem (21:1–11) he is met by a large crowd. He is greeted with the messianic title "Son of David" and this is "the only time the Davidic royal sonship of Jesus is publicly recognized by a 'very large crowd' rather than by individuals." The whole city is "shaken by his arrival." Jesus then goes straight to the temple and overturns the tables of money changers. However, these "seemingly politically subversive tones are given a twist by Matthew." Matthew, Dube argues, softens Jesus's form of kingship from "triumphant and victorious" to place all emphasis on Jesus as the humble king, "someone who is meek and lowly." In doing this, Matthew "constructs an apolitical, rather than a political, subversive son of David . . ."[58]

First of all, I do find it somewhat remarkable how, in these instances, Dube prefers the interpretations of conventional readings. A "meek, humble and apolitical Jesus" is exactly the Jesus of the pietistic, other-worldly preachings from white missionaries I remember from my childhood and the classes in seminary taught by white, pro-apartheid teachers. It is exactly the Jesus that suits the empire to a "T," because this Jesus is domesticated, de-justicized, de-conscienticized, and completely manageable. It is the revolutionary, radical Jesus that disturbs empire, to the extent that they do not simply imprison, or flog, exile, or decapitate him, which for the empire would have been the more "humane" punishment, reserved, in extreme cases, for the upper classes;[59] they had to crucify him, an execution, an entirely political, terrorizing act, with *political* designs.

Second, we should point out that with Jesus his meekness and humbleness are not signs of apolitical apathy and weakness, but the gospel's way of stating his absolute solidarity with those who were humbled by their oppressed condition, kept meek through intimidation, one *with*, and one *of* the "scum" that could "only be restrained by terror."[60] He is the righteous

---

offer the more convincing argument. Horsley's analysis places the tribute confrontation within the framework of a) the irreducible demand to every Israelite to "have no other gods before me," i.e., the absolute loyalty to Yahweh as Israel's only king, defying the claims of Rome and Caesar as king, overlord, and master; b) the very Pharisees who set the "trap" for Jesus have as one of their central teachings precisely that, and have followed it at great cost. They knew, as Jesus did, that to pay this tribute would have been "unlawful." Horsley concludes, "If God is the exclusive Lord and Master, if the people of Israel live under the exclusive kingship of God, the implications for Caesar being fairly obvious, Jesus is clearly and simply reasserting the Israelite principle that Caesar, or any other imperial ruler, has no claim on the Israelite people, since God is their actual king and master." See *Jesus and Empire*, 98–99. I am further persuaded by van Aarde, "Understanding Jesus' Healings," 223–36.

58. Dube, *Postcolonial Feminist Interpretation*, 140–41.

59. See Elliot, "Anti-Imperial Message," 168.

60. Elliot quotes from Tacitus's *Annals* (14, 42–45) the Roman lawyer Gaius Cassius, who argued fiercely in court for the crucifixion of four hundred slaves after their

one who resists the arrogance of power through might and terror. And because he is one of them, he knows their oppression, their suffering, and knows intimately their desire for freedom. He is Emmanuel, the one with them in their condition of oppression, and the one with them in their desire for freedom. It is this authenticity that the poor recognize in him, and it is with this integrity that he joins their struggles for liberation and justice.

Third, he is "humble and meek" because his reign is the exact opposite of the rule of the tyrants the people have been experiencing for so long. That is why he is riding on a donkey, and not a horse, an animal of war. He has warned his disciples against those who live to "lord it over" others. He knows that that "lording it over" is possible only through intimidation, suppression, and violence. Their rule is a rule of fear, and based on calculated callousness, self-absorbed paranoia, and insatiable self-aggrandizement. His "let it not be so among you" is superbly demonstrated here, at the moment of glory, when public recognition and the freedom frenzy of the large crowd could have turned his head; when the temptation to display his power would have been great. But as with Satan in the wilderness, he saves his power for when it really matters, as with his healing of people, his feeding of the multitude, his vanquishing of demons—all actions where he uses his power to overcome the empire and its pernicious devastations of the people. And he will do so again, in the temple, at the heart of the Jerusalem elite's sinful and destructive rule in collaboration with the people's oppression. Where it matters.

Fourth, Jesus's entry into Jerusalem is, in fact, a counter-demonstration. "Entrances, like triumphs, expressed the imperial mindset," writes Warren Carter.[61] Citing Chad Myers, he concurs, "They reveal a deep tendency in human nature to conceive of human greatness in terms of power, acquired by military or political victory over actual or potential enemies and to demand public recognition of such greatness."[62] It is a spectacle repeated endlessly by governments across the world. Jesus's entry is a public protest against such hubris, invoking God's victorious reign "even as it replaces one imperial reign over another."

Marcus Borg and John Dominic Crossan also argue that there were in fact two demonstrative processions into Jerusalem that day. As Jesus was entering the city from the east, a military cavalry led by the Roman governor Pilate arrived in the city from the west, bringing troops to the

---

master, the prefect of Rome, was murdered by one of them ("Anti-Imperial Message," 168). See also Carter, *Matthew and the Margins*, 259–60 and 416.

61. Carter, *Matthew and the Margins*, 414.
62. Carter, *Matthew and the Margins*, 600, n9.

city to quell any over-zealous Jews who, in the fervor of this week of the festival, might be calling for freedom from the Roman Empire. Hence such a counter-demonstration is not innocent: it is a public protest. "One was a peasant procession" with Jesus and his followers of peasants, and the other was "an imperial procession," write Borg and Crossan.[63] Pilate, the governor of Idumea, Judea, and Samaria, entered the city at the head of a column of imperial cavalry and soldiers, proclaiming the imperial power of Rome. Jesus's procession proclaimed the kingdom of God. The two processions "embody the central conflict of the week that led to Jesus's crucifixion."[64]

Borg and Crossan write, quite vividly,

> Imagine the imperial procession's arrival in the city. A visual panoply of imperial power: cavalry on horses, foot soldiers, leather armor, helmets, weapons, banners, golden eagles mounted on poles, sun glinting on metal and gold. Sounds: the marching of feet, the clinking of bridles, the beating of drums. The swirling of dust. The eyes of the silent onlookers, some curious, some awed, some resentful.[65]

Jesus's procession is "a prearranged 'counter-procession.' Jesus planned it in advance."[66] I take that to mean *political intent*, calculated to challenge the power, authority, and legitimacy of Rome's imperial presence.

Jesus is putting imperial arrogance and entitlement to shame. This time, he is not silencing the crowd, trying to calm them down, or "soften" the meaning of the exclamations of his kingly rule and their messianic expectations. At the gate, and in going to the temple, Jesus embraces the messianic challenge. Matthew's reference to the prophet Zachariah (9:9–10) is explicit. This king, riding on a donkey in deliberate contrast to Rome's emperor, will banish war from the land—no more chariots, war-horses, or bows. Commanding peace to the nations he will be a king of peace, exposing the fake peace of the Pax Romana for what it was: violent pacification. This is no surrendering to the power of empire. "Jesus's procession deliberately countered what was happening on the other side of the city."[67] It is for all these reasons that Matthew tells us not only that the crowds were ecstatic, but that "the city was in turmoil." What it means is that for the temple elites, things were getting out of control. Carter observes that the word Matthew

---

63. See Borg and Crossan, *Last Week*, 3–5.
64. Borg and Crossan, *Last Week*, 2.
65. Borg and Crossan, *Last Week*, 3.
66. Borg and Crossan, *Last Week*, 4.
67. Borg and Crossan, *Last Week*, 4.

uses, "turmoil," is the same verb used for the earthquake that accompanies Jesus's death and splits the temple curtain.[68]

The "earthquake" comes to the temple as Jesus makes his second entry that day. Jesus's actions in the temple are far from "politically harmless." Jesus goes to a place of opposition, not to sacrifice but to disrupt. He goes to confront and his confrontation is in the overturning of the tables and in the healing of those who have previously been banned from the temple.[69] Even though some read the overturning of the tables as an "outburst of emotion,"[70] Obery Hendricks is persuasive in arguing that it is an act of resistance, a rejection of the suppositions of power underlying the political life and power of ancient Israel. "This is not a temper tantrum," he writes,

> No, this was no spontaneous eruption of emotion. . . The Temple was the center of Israel's economy, its central bank and treasury, the depository of immense wealth. Indeed so much of the activity of the Jerusalem Temple hinged upon buying and selling and various modes of exchange that it is no exaggeration to say that in a real sense the Temple was fundamentally an economic institution.[71]

It might not have been the most direct reason for his execution as van Aarde posits, but it certainly contributed to the anger and lust for revenge against him that led to the actions of the temple elite and his crucifixion by Rome. It was, *as an attack on Israel's center of power*, Hendricks argues further, a very political act. Mark's Gospel tells us not only that Jesus attacked the money changers and dove sellers, but that he and his followers also seized the temple grounds and temporarily halted commercial operations.[72] Jesus's acts of disruption in the temple continue as the marginalized, despised, and discarded invade the temple to lay claim upon the power and mercy of God: the lame and the blind find the courage and "came to him"—suddenly empowered by his acts of defiance of the exclusivist control of the temple elite who kept them outside, away from God's presence and the impartation of God's grace. Much to the chagrin of the powerful, even the children can see what the powerful cannot allow themselves to see and the children's shouts of joy fill the temple: he *is* "the Son of David." In the creative, tension-filled disruption that true inclusivity always brings, the voices of the crowd at the gate are joined by the voices of the lame and the blind and the shouts of the

---

68. Carter, *Matthew and the Margins*, 417.
69. Carter, *Matthew and the Margins*, 418.
70. So for instance van Aarde, *Fatherless*, 78.
71. See Hendricks, *Politics of Jesus*, 113, 114.
72. Hendricks, *Politics of Jesus*, 114, 115.

children in the temple. It must have been havoc inside that holy place that day. The "anger" of the temple elites (v. 15) is not "ridiculous" as Carter suggests.[73] It is, rather, complete, fear-filled political comprehension.

It is again van Aarde who makes a crucial point. He shows how Matthew's Gospel deliberately juxtaposes Jesus and Herod. He speaks of "Matthew's tale of two kings."[74] The birth narrative discloses Matthew's strategy to portray Herod, the "king of the Jews" appointed by Rome as enemy of the true "king of the Jews," Jesus. Instead of leading God's people, Herod kills children. That is the truth about Herod Matthew points to right at the start. Jesus, on the other hand, is characterized completely differently, from a human perspective: he is the (adopted) child of Joseph, and from a divine perspective: the Son of God. So already early on, the confrontation with Rome and its representatives and collaborators is set. This king will be entirely different, in opposition to the kingship that despises, oppresses, and kills.

Matthew emphasizes Jesus's messianic role by situating the beginning (Matt 3:15) and the end of Jesus's public performances within the context of Jesus's relationship with children. Jesus gives a central place to children when he ascribes wisdom and insight to "infants" that has escaped the "wisdom" of the "wise and intelligent" (Matt 11:25–26). In total contrast to the way children were being treated in Jesus's day, he blesses them (Matt 19:13–15). Van Aarde stresses that these are not the children of wealthy and privileged parents—they were "street urchins."[75] When the children flood the temple, unique to Matthew, taken together with the references to Jesus's relationship to children, Matthew ascribes "honor" to them in ways that completely contrasts the treatment of children in Roman society. The presence of the children was a subversive presence, emphasizing the subversive actions of the Jesus to whom they sing hallelujahs.

The position that Matthew offers us an empire-compliant, apolitical Jesus as he enters the city and the temple, is, in my view, not sustainable.

NOW IT WAS THE GOVERNOR'S CUSTOM . . .

Finally, Jesus before Pilate. Dube's reasoning concludes that Matthew goes out of his way to deflect blame from the empire and to put it on the "Israelite intellectuals and the ruling class," and on the people, "the crowd" who chose Barabbas instead of Jesus, while the Romans, Pilate (and his wife) are the innocents in this drama. Pilate, having "failed to persuade the insistent

---

73. See Carter, *Matthew and the Margins*, 420.
74. See van Aarde, "Jesus' Affection Towards Children," 127–47.
75. See Van Aarde, "Jesus' Affection Towards Children," 127–47.

rulers to release Jesus," succumbs to the pressure. To Dube, it is clear that Matthew "seeks the favor of the Roman Empire by presenting the empire as righteous, and holier than the Israelites."[76] When Pilate questions Jesus about his kingship of the Jews, Jesus simply says, "You say it." The expected affirmation of a leader of the resistance does not come. In the end, Jesus is crucified "because of the insistence of the very people he has come to save," and ends up a "meek and lowly Jesus dying silently on a cross."[77] Dube raises the political stakes significantly: the "crowd," "the very people" who clamor for Jesus's death, calling curses upon themselves, are "the colonized."[78] The colonized oppressed abandon the leader who promised them liberation, but as such he is a total failure. The triumph of the empire could not be more emphatic.

Dube will find more than enough proof in traditional readings of this text, followed even by feminist theologian Dorothy Jean Weaver, who describes Pilate as "the powerful governor [who] shows himself to be effectively and ironically powerless not only in relation to the Jewish leaders, but also as far as his soldiers are concerned."[79] For Weaver, it is in the "contrast to the moral courage shown by his wife that Pilate's powerlessness comes into focus most prominently,"[80] but the point, nonetheless, is Pilate's "powerlessness." Again Dube, and again surprisingly uncritically, follows this traditional reading, though her conclusion is starkly different. For her, this episode declares Pilate, Pilate's wife, and Rome innocent, but puts the blame on the "people," the colonized.

The conventional reading is so broadly accepted that Carter finds it necessary to return to this episode in both his major works on Matthew.[81]

76. Dube, *Postcolonial Feminist Interpretation*, 133, 34.

77. Dube, *Postcolonial Feminist Interpretation*, 140.

78. Dube, *Postcolonial Feminist Interpretation*, 140.

79. See Weaver, "Thus You Will Know Them by Their Fruits," 107–27. The quotation is on 117.

80. Weaver, "Thus You Will Know Them by Their Fruits," 118.

81. See Carter, *Matthew and the Margins*, 523–29, and *Matthew and Empire*, 145–68, but especially 157–68. Carter is meticulous in the way he structures his analysis and takes on the arguments one by one. He first deals with the general discussions around Pilate found in NT scholarship: the "Conventional, de-Pilatized, Depoliticized reading" followed by "Priests and political Power" to discuss the relationship between the temple elite and Roman governors, and then "Rome's strategy for control" in its alliance with local elites and Rome's legal bias. Then turning specifically to Pilate and Jesus, he discusses "Pilate among the governors" and "Pilate or Jesus" in a rather interesting contrast with "Jesus or Barabbas." Finally, Carter turns to the question of Pilate's powerlessness in two exhaustive sections where he deals with the question whether Pilate was a mere "powerless puppet" and whether Pilate had after all "limitless power," to which the answer is no, because "Pilate's power enacts death, but it is not the final word, even though

I will summarize the crucial points. Carter begins, quite appropriately and quite rightly, with Rome's claim on "justice," which is what is supposed to happen here. The Roman ruling classes, we learn from Seneca, depicted Rome's justice as "justice enthroned above all injustice." Truly reflective of the mendacity without which empires cannot live, as I have argued in chapter 1, Rome's justice served only the interests of the powerful. "The term trial flatters the proceedings."[82] There is a lack of investigation, serious questioning, oaths, witnesses, and a defense. Pilate, "influenced by the religious elite and worried about the crowd, oversees a process and verdict worthy only of the name 'injustice'." He "abuses his power" to join the religious leaders "in executing a king who threatens their very existence and future..." Note that Carter recognizes the "influence" of the religious elites but that does not make Pilate "powerless"; instead it causes him simply to "abuse his power."[83] Note also that it is clear, irrespective of Pilate's pretense that he does not know, that the one to be crucified is crucified because the fear is that he is indeed a "king"—the title here means "leader of the resistance." That Pilate uses this title so deliberately means he knows that the proceedings, although tolerant of the crowd and the Jerusalem elites as "useful idiots" in a larger political game, are quite beyond their control.

Pilate's questions to Jesus and his quick "referendum" on the choice between Jesus and Barabbas is the usual pretense of justice, the veneer of "civility" that oppressed peoples know only too well. It is the "rule of law" anti-apartheid activists have found in South Africa's apartheid courts; it is the same mockery of justice Palestinian resisters find in Israel's apartheid courts, and it is the same travesty of justice people of color who are the victims of police brutality, including murder on an almost daily basis, can expect to find in the courts of the United States. The justice preserved for the colonizers, the powerful and the privileged, is entirely different from the "justice" experienced by the poor and powerless. The same principle undergirds the empire's need, in its collusion with Western Christianity, for a "theology for the privileged" against a "theology for savages" over whom they rule. It is not the desire for justice that drives the proceedings here; it is ruthless self-interest and pure abuse of power. So, "far from exonerating

---

so often it seems to be. Ironically, the death that Pilate brings about will be the death of him and his imperial system. The risen Jesus who shares 'all authority in heaven and on earth' not with Rome but with God, will return and Rome's empire will end as God's empire is established in full" (see 167). I am persuaded that Carter is quite correct on this issue. I leave the also contested role of Pilate's wife out of this discussion.

82. Carter, *Matthew and the Margins*, 524.
83. Carter, *Matthew and the Margins*, 524.

Rome, 'christianizing' or minimizing Pilate's role, these verses offer a terse and scathing indictment of Roman justice *from below*."[84]

In even greater depth, Carter sets out his arguments in *Matthew and Empire*. Pilate is not "powerless," let alone "innocent," but his power is not limitless, since he and the empire he represents are ultimately vanquished by Jesus and the reign of God. In all other ways, Pilate's (temporary) power is undisputed:[85]

- Pilate is introduced as "governor," the *hegemon*, ruler over this province and representative of the global and irrefutable power of Rome.
- Throughout, Pilate is the center of the action.
- His power may be disguised as "benign patronage" but is in fact enhanced by the interaction with the subservient, dependent, and pleading crowd. He has the power to imprison or release a prisoner. He invites the crowd not to decide but to beg for someone "I can release for you." The sole decision-making power lies with him.
- He has power to determine life or death.
- By contrast both Jesus and Barabbas are "non-actors" in the scene, "dependent on Pilate;" both are "being done to, rather than doing."
- Pilate is not tentative in any of this. In fact, he is "very sure of his power."

We recall that Pilate's question, "Are you the king of the Jews?" and Jesus's response, "You say so," is another reason for Musa Dube to see here a politically humble and humiliated Jesus. But as I see it, understood within the context of the questions by Pilate and the "accusations" on the same charge by the chief priests and the elders when Jesus "refuses to answer," this issue takes on a different hue.[86] Instead of giving any legitimacy to this travesty of justice, and despite the insistent pressure, Jesus ignores them all. His silence is an unbearable public insult; it is not submission, it is resistance. He shall not, by answering their charges, dignify or legitimize this "trial,"

---

84. Carter, *Matthew and the Margins*, 524; my emphasis.

85. Carter, *Matthew and the Margins*, 163–64.

86. In an open letter from 1979, at the start of years of intense and intensifying conflict between the apartheid state and the prophetic church in South Africa, and in defense of the right of Christians to engage in acts of civil disobedience in the struggle against apartheid, I referred to this text and Jesus's defiant silence before Herod, the chief priest, and Pilate as scriptural proof of the stance many Christians were then taking and which I had encouraged them to take. The letter has been widely published, but see here A. Boesak, *Walking on Thorns*, 58–65; also A. Boesak, *Black and Reformed*, 32–41.

nor acknowledge that they have any authority over him. He says as much to Pilate in the trial scene from the Gospel of John. The three words, "You say so," are not an admission of "guilt"; neither are they an evasion in admission of Rome's acceptability. If there is any admission or acknowledgment to be made here, it shall come from the empire. So, in my view, here Jesus's three words mean, "You have heard their accusations, you have heard about me and my work, you know I am who I am, and in front of all these people you will acknowledge it: *you* say it." For the rest, Jesus does not deign to further engage him.

Pilate is a savvy man of power who knows precisely how power works, and he has the required ruthlessness to *make* it work.[87] Jewish philosopher Philo's description of Pilate speaks volumes. Philo sees Pilate as "naturally inflexible, a blend of self-will and relentlessness . . . [guilty of] briberies, insults, robberies, outrages and wanton injuries, executions without trial constantly repeated, ceaseless and supremely grievous cruelty."[88] One must not make the mistake of thinking he does not understand the dynamics of power here. For one so used to wielding that power with brutal constancy, and so anxious to have this crowd acknowledge that power, knowing this was a crucial political moment and that the way he handles this might have far-reaching consequences, the *gall* of this prisoner must have been astonishing.

Carter's remark that Jesus is pictured before Pilate as "totally dependent" on Pilate must not be misunderstood. Carter means to emphasize Pilate's power over Jesus at that moment: he can hold or release him, "hand him over," decide to let him live or die. However, that situation does not nullify, but rather enhances Jesus's power as the "power of the powerless." Jesus, *in the face of all that power*, nonetheless decides to defy him, embarrassing, if not totally shaming him, in public. What, after all, does it mean that the man who holds the *fasces,* the symbols of his office which "also carried the potential of violent repression and execution . . . that is, they secured the perception of the life and death power embodied in and executed by Rome's justice"[89] is ignored, made to look ridiculous, humiliated, and powerless

---

87. See the section "Pilate Among the Governors" in Carter, *Matthew and Empire,* 151–57.

88. In his *Embassy to Gaius,* 301–2, cited in Elliot, "Anti-Imperial Message," 174–75. Even though Philo takes care to put the blame for Pilate's misdeeds on himself alone, not on Rome or the Caesar, Pilate is not "innocent" or "powerless" in any shape or form.

89. The *fasces,* an axe and bundle of six rods, are often ceremoniously paraded to represent the administration of Roman justice. They constituted "a portable kit for flogging and decapitation," and were "brutally functional" (Carter, *Matthew and Empire,* 152–53).

in front of the very people—his colonized subjects, his underlings, his soldiers—he needs to impress as decisive, authoritative, and above all willing to use his power over life and death.

Watching the 2016 presidential race in the United States, it became clear to me as an astonishing fact: all modern candidates for the presidency in the United States understand that if they are not relentlessly ruthless, or willing to publicly express a desire to become a war criminal if elected, or when president unless they are willing to make war on a spectacular scale, they will not be called "presidential."[90] Similarly, Pilate the consummate politician knows how to navigate the politics of the empire and he knows the political and economic value of human sacrifice on the altar of imperial gratification and personal pride. To those under threat from the empire it is bizarre, insane, and lethal, but for the imperial mindset it makes perfect sense. It is as natural as breathing. No wonder Matthew tells us that the governor was "greatly amazed."

It is also the moment Pilate knew: this man is indeed a king, a challenge and threat to Rome. He must deal with him in the only way Rome knows how: he must die—be *crucified*, so that everyone should know for all time that this is the way Rome deals with those who threaten its power. The rest—the meaningless questions, "Then what should I do?" (asks the one who knows exactly what he will do); "What evil has he done?"(asks he who is the personification of evil, as is the empire he represents); and the dramatic washing of the hands (while Matthew and his community know those hands never were clean and never shall be washed clean of the blood of the innocents Rome has killed)—is mere political theater. Matthew describes it all in detail, not to offer proof of "innocence" but to expose the absolute absurdity of imperial politics. For the Matthean community, the inscription at the top of the cross is not for information—they already know. Nor is it for justification, as in, Rome "had no choice." For them, it is

---

90. In order to overcome his "wimp" image problem, "in December George H. W. Bush invaded Panama, ostensibly to capture former American client/human rights monster Manuel Noriega. The *New York Times* cheered Bush for going through the 'rite of passage' of the presidency, which involves 'a need to demonstrate willingness to shed blood.'" See Taibbi, "A Brief History of Everything That Happened." Mr. Obama is of course the outstanding exception here. He ran so explicitly on an anti-war platform that it remains shocking, to this day, how quick and thorough his complete about-turn was once in office, and how thoroughly a "war president" he became, outdoing his predecessor. See Ali, *Obama Syndrome*. In this regard, Ali writes, "Obama is little more than the Empire's most inventive apparition of itself . . . to talk of betrayal is foolish, for nothing has been betrayed but one's own illusions" (33); A. Boesak, *Dare We Speak of Hope?*, ch. 5.

Rome's admission of defeat, and Matthew spells it out in triumphant detail (27:62–66; 28:1–15).

DECOLONIZATION, AFRICANITY, AND CRITIQUE OF EMPIRE

Whereas the crowd present at the trial that day are sometimes described as "the Jews" clamoring for Jesus's death, a generalized depiction we do not share, most, as Carter does, see them as "manipulated" by the religious elite and consequently used by Pontius Pilate "to accomplish [their] own ends."[91] Dube's description of the crowd as the "colonized," however, adds another important dimension. From a colonized person's view, that means that the people, who should be in the struggle against Rome with Jesus, are now betraying both Jesus and their own liberation. In this sense they are no different from Rahab, who "takes sides with the enemy. She misleads her own people in order to hide and save the enemy . . . one who totally wants the rule of the colonizer over her own people and land . . ."[92] Is this what happens here?

I agree with the view that in this scene we have a crowd that falls prey to political expedience and manipulation. It may not be as strange as it sounds. They are indeed the "colonized." But what does that mean? This issue raised by Musa Dube gains importance if we consider the raging debates in South Africa on decolonization, Africanity, and Africanization. One of its most vocal and eloquent advocates is African theologian Rothney Tshaka. In an enlightening essay, and agreeing with African philosopher B. M. Ramose, Tshaka writes that authentic Africanity is informed by two exigencies. One, "that the colonised peoples' conception of reality, knowledge, and truth should be released from slavery and dominance under the European epistemological paradigm." Second, "the evolving common universe of discourse must take into account the rational demands of justice to the colonised arising from the unjust wars of colonization that resulted in conquest as the basis for the disseizing of territory as well as the enslavement of the colonised."[93]

I am in complete agreement. This shows how much the new struggles for authentic Africanity are rooted within the struggles inspired by Black Consciousness, and how relevant our insights formed during those

---

91. Carter, *Matthew and the Margins*, 527.

92. Dube, *Postcolonial Feminist Interpretation*, 77–78ff. From an African, colonized point of view, this is indeed what Rahab does, and I cannot fault Dube's analysis here.

93. See Tshaka, "Advocacy of Africanity," 5.

struggles still are today. Tshaka confirms this when he writes, "Colonialism had as one of its objectives the goal of conquering Africa and relegating her people to the status of being sub-humans."[94] As Black Consciousness knew, postulated, and advocated, it was not only about our territory and its resources, it was also about our humanity. I will continue to plead for two major things here: one, that these struggles be seen as struggles against empire and continuing imperial dominance in Africa by empire. Not only must the colonial and apartheid baggage be engaged, these must be engaged as the result of projects inextricable from the imperialist venture that even today has still not ended. This is the irrevocable context for these endeavors today. That also means that Africanity "refers to the spatiality, specificity, temporality, and particularity of the African conquered in the unjust wars of colonization,"[95] while it also emphasizes, as relentlessly as it can, African agency in the ongoing, determined struggles of Africans to embrace their full humanity, gain their entire liberation, dignity, and the power to self-realization and self-determination, free from the shackles of imperialist imposition.

The second matter is as important. This new struggle must, from the beginning, include women as equal partners, recognize women's agency, and accept women's leadership and unique contribution. If this is not the case, our Africanity cannot be authentic, our Africanness can never be whole, and our processes of Africanization will remain flat and static. Like a sun that sits on the horizon but never rises, it will promise a new, brighter day, but remain chained to the darker impulses of a night that never really let go.

So keeping this context in mind, we should again ponder Musa Dube's valuable remarks. This is not exhaustive by all means, but let us consider the following observations:

1. We should be reminded of Black Consciousness and Biko's insight of "the mind of the oppressed." This taught us a number of lessons. First, as I have indicated, the importance of understanding that the struggle for liberation and justice begins with *understanding*. Second, just as we should be wary of white people's, especially white liberals', tendencies to minimize and even trivialize our oppression, we should be alert to our own tendencies to romanticize the oppressed. Not all oppressed people believed that apartheid was evil, that there was something to fight, suffer, and die for. The desire for freedom through various understandings may have been shared by all, but the necessity for struggle to gain that freedom was not embraced by all. They

---

94. Tshaka, "Advocacy of Africanity," 1.
95. Tshaka, "Advocacy of Africanity," 4.

are, in the incomparable words of Frederick Douglass, like those who "favor freedom and yet deprecate agitation"; they want "crops without plowing up the ground; they want rain without thunder and lightning. They want the ocean without the awful roar of its many waters."[96] It may very well be that the crowd gathered before the governor that day, not *all* oppressed people in Judea and Galilee, may have reflected the colonized mind, the mind that made them allies of the oppressor. That is certainly true for the religious and political elites of Israel. Their collaboration with Rome was deliberate, for the sake of their own security, wealth, and privilege.

2. No project of colonization is ever successful, or could last as long as did South Africa's (almost 300 years of colonization and slavery, and over 50 years of official apartheid), unless the colonizer secures the cooperation of (enough of) the colonized. This was and still is the pattern everywhere. Black South Africans' struggle has been not just against white people who believed in apartheid; it has also been against black people who considered the rich rewards of cooperation with evil more fulfilling than resistance against their own oppression; black people who knew better but for the sake of the benefits of empire justified themselves by arguing that "fighting the system from within" was better than outright struggle. Hence the later distinction between "parliamentary" and "extra-parliamentary" opposition. By the first, we did not mean white people fighting on our behalf in the white parliament. We referred to those black people ("coloreds" and "Indians") who willingly cooperated with apartheid in its last days during the 1980s in joining the "Tri-cameral parliament" in South Africa and the "independent governments" in the Bantustans created by South Africa. Their collaboration gave apartheid a longer lease on life and helped white South Africa gain some form of "legitimacy" in the eyes of the international community, making our task infinitely harder. Our struggle was "extra parliamentary" because we did not believe that "the system" of apartheid could be redeemed, but instead should be irrevocably eradicated. We saw no benefit in pretending that apartheid could be "reformed" from within. It had to be destroyed from without—in the streets of protest and sacrifice.

3. One should not forget those who, out of greed or necessity, worked directly for apartheid's oppressive system: civil servants, police, the army. And, of course, those who sold information to the security police. It is not too surprising that the violent wrath of activists was especially

96. See Douglass, "If There Is No Struggle."

visited upon those persons, sometimes their families, as well as their places of work which have become symbols of the oppressor's presence in and control over our lives. Many of these were shunned and never trusted. During the period that "the necklace" became a favored tool of execution, not a single white person was subjected to this horrific form of death.

4. It is true that submission is easier when livelihood and personal progress are at stake, or when imperial patronage is threatened by revolutionary elements determined to upend finely balanced structures of negotiated subjugation. Oppressed people are human and subject to the temptations of empire. In the South African police, police[men] of color, for instance, could not be promoted beyond the rank of "sergeant" unless they were willing to join the ranks of the security police, effectively making a career decision to sell out their people, at least redefining their dreams of freedom, if they had any. The issue here is not how many gave in to the temptation; the issue is how many, taking into account the enormity of the temptation, resisted.

5. On the other hand, I have had teachers in high school who, forced to teach the curriculum apartheid's ethnocratic education systems demanded, made sure that we heard other and correct interpretations in lessons after school. That was a subversion of the system that opened our eyes to much more than one was supposed to learn at school. Not everyone's mind was immediately liberated, but it was at least *prepared*.

6. Even though we are used to referring to the role of "the church" in the struggle, especially in the late 1970s, the 1980s, and the early 1990s, it is not correct to think of "the church" as a simplistic whole. Not even the Black church in South Africa was always wholeheartedly and undividedly in the struggle.[97]

7. We have, with much pain and through bitter disillusionment after 1994, learned the lesson that putting a black face in office does not make much difference to the lives of the oppressed without the

---

97. Chief Albert Luthuli had some scathing words for those in the Black church who helped cause, in his words, "the wreck of Christian witness" and "the slow drift into nationalist state religion" (see Luthuli, *Let My People Go!*, 132). My own experiences in my denomination (then the Dutch Reformed Mission Church), during those times and now post-1994 as a united church with the part of Dutch Reformed Church in Africa and known as the Uniting Reformed Church in Southern Africa, have taught me unforgettable lessons in this regard. There are reasons why, for example, during my solitary confinement in 1985, two of our colleagues on the executive leadership refused to heed a call for prayer from some congregations for me and my family.

commitment to justice, the embrace of freedom defined by the oppressed themselves, and respect for the sacrifices of the people in the struggle for liberation. We should not be surprised when we discover, after what we thought was liberation, a new Pharaoh that looks like us.[98] Biko's liberated mind continues to both haunt and teach us.

8. Oppression, like Blackness, was a *condition* one had to understand and confront with conscious decisions. It is the mind captured by sacrificial love and the expectation of freedom that is the mind not captured by fear, short-sighted self-interest, and instant gratification at the expense of freedom.

During the civil rights struggle in the United States, Martin Luther King Jr. would make the same point.

> There are Negroes will who never fight for freedom. There are Negroes who will seek profit for themselves alone from the struggle. There are even some Negroes who will cooperate with their oppressors. These facts should distress no one . . . Every people has its share of opportunists, profiteers, freeloaders and escapists. The hammer blows of discrimination, poverty and segregation must warp and corrupt some. No one can pretend that because a people may be oppressed, every individual member is virtuous and worthy. The real issue is whether in the great mass the dominant characteristics are decency, honor, and courage.[99]

In this regard, South Africans' experiences during the last phases of the struggle and especially post-1994, within the context of the battles for decolonization and Africanization, help us to understand how it is that the colonized can be manipulated by their leadership.[100] This may be what Matthew wanted to convey, talking perhaps of the majority of those present, or even a vociferous minority, rather than telling us that "the very people

---

98. See A. Boesak, *Dare We Speak of Hope?*, and A. Boesak, *Pharaohs*.

99. See King, *Why We Can't Wait*, 36–37. King makes a similar point when he recounts the efforts he and his staff had to go to, speaking on successive days, following "a hectic schedule," to "a cross section of our people" to convince them of the necessity of the Birmingham campaign. He raised with them almost all the points he would raise in his "Letter From a Birmingham Jail" intended for white clergy who opposed him. "In most cases, the atmosphere when I entered was tense and chilly, and I was aware that there was a great deal of work to be done." It was not easy: "Somehow God gave me the power to transform the resentments, the suspicions, the fears and the misunderstandings I found that week into faith and enthusiasm" (64–66).

100. See Bond, *Elite Transition*; Calland, *Anatomy of South Africa*; Van der Westhuizen, *White Power*; Terreblanche, *Lost in Transformation*; and A. Boesak, *Pharaohs*.

Jesus came to save" were now not only embracing their own oppression, but were declaring the empire "acceptable and holy." Who knows how much, and for how many among the crowd that day, the high priest Caiaphas's Realpolitik[101] ("It is better that one man die than for the whole nation to be destroyed"; cf. John 12:50) had become accepted wisdom? In Philo's elegant phrasing, "The wise person knows how mightily blow the winds of necessity, fortune, opportunity, force, violence, and princedom" and will therefore take precaution as "an inseparable safeguard to prevent any grave disaster."[102] Clearly, the trial before Pilate was not about Barabbas; it was about Jesus. For that moment, the danger for the people, as Caiaphas saw it, was not Barabbas, but Jesus of Nazareth. And for Rome, whatever Barabbas represented, and however "notorious" he might have been, was not close to the threat Jesus posed. For Pilate, therefore, the swap was an easy one.

And there is more than just the manipulation by the powerful empire and its elite surrogates in Jerusalem at play here. It is possible for oppressed people to weary of the struggle against an overpowering, merciless enemy. It is possible that from time to time, they turn against themselves and their own dreams for freedom, when they, as Calvin warned, "become inured to their oppression" and denounce all hope in God's justice and in their own ability to fight for freedom. But it can also be that very longing for freedom that drives us to decisions that prove, if not always futile, then at least not fruitful. The flame of the desire for freedom may not die, but it sometimes certainly only flickers. Moreover, if Carter is right in proposing that Jesus and Barabbas contrasted "two forms of opposition to the elite's control—violent opposition and nonviolent resistance,"[103] it is possible that in the face of the ruthlessness and brutality of the oppressor the people might well choose the resistance of violence represented by the "bandit" Barabbas that day.

---

101. The fierce debates about the most expeditious way to respond to the oppression of empires were time-honored ones, always causing great tensions among Jewish people who struggled with the most practical ways to survive for the best possible reasons, and those who were convinced that their devotion to the one of God of Israel left them no option but to engage in vociferous and sometime violent struggle against empire. Philo, for instance, thought one should, always depending on the circumstances, choose wisely between accommodation and defiance or between "boldness of speech" (criticizing the ways of empire) and "untimely frankness," which can take the form of "reckless defiance" by which some Jews put their entire community into mortal jeopardy. *De Somniis*, 2.83–84, cited in Elliot, "Romans 13:1–7 in the Context of Imperial Propaganda," 199.

102. *De Somniis*, 2.89, cited in Elliot, "Romans 13:1–7" 199–200.

103. Carter, *Matthew and the Margins*, 525.

Sometimes choosing for violence may seem to those to be the better, more courageous, more respectable, and for some the only way of resistance. Recalling how difficult it became for me during those State-of-Emergency years of relentless violent onslaughts to hold up Jesus's nonviolent example against the blinding light of the impeccable, muscular credentials of the iconic Che Guevara, I think I understand the feeling that the way of Barabbas may have seemed the only way to "prove" their love for freedom. The glorification of the power of violence is as much a fatal temptation as is the deification of the power of the oppressor.

For a people too long oppressed, a Jesus "dying silently on a cross" might not offer the inspiration they might find in Barabbas who, even though he too said nothing that day, nonetheless represented a long tradition of violent resistance held up as a holy war in God's name. On that day, not all of them—not even the male disciples, even though the women battled to make them understand—saw in the cross the nullification of death and its power, embodied in the power of Rome. Paul's "Death where is your sting?," always caught between the hopefulness of faith and the cynicism of politics, was a far-off cry that day. Not all of them would, like the women, understand the resurrection of Jesus as God's *apanastasia*, God's *rebellion* against all evil, including the evil that was Rome, and that the open grave is an open invitation to join God in this revolution in the world to challenge and topple the Caesars, whoever and wherever they may be.[104] Thinking realistically about these matters is not the same as submitting to the empire, much less pronouncing it "acceptable and holy."

In the quest Steve Biko has bequeathed Black people—the quest for true humanity toward bestowing on South Africa (and the world) that "greatest gift possible, a more human face"—it is essential that Black liberation theology, as a prophetic, people's theology, reclaim the Jesus that is, as James Cone holds, "not a proposition, not a theological concept which exists merely in our heads."[105] Neither is he a willing enabler of imperialist realties that continue to destroy the lives of his people—the "least of these." For us, he is the living, breathing Christ, the One amongst the people, the "Crucified among the cross-bearers,"[106] the "event of liberation," the revolutionary, Risen One who calls us, in the face of empire, not just to survive, but to arise.

---

104. see Boesak, *Dare We Speak of Hope?*, 141–45.
105. See Cone, *God of the Oppressed*, 32, 33.
106. See Mofokeng, *Crucified Among the Cross-bearers*.

Chapter Six

THE SECRET OF THE HUMAN CHILD
Black Theology, the Canaanite Woman, and the Walls of Internalized, Imperialist Patriarchy

SOMETHING THERE IS THAT DOES NOT LOVE A WALL

IN ROBERT FROST'S FAMOUS, intriguingly ambivalent poem, "Mending Wall,"[1] the owner of an apple orchard reminds his neighbor, a planter of pine trees, that it is time to mend the wall between the two properties. The speaker in the poem takes the initiative, yet he has grave reservations. It is the conflict within himself that intensifies the ambiguity of the poem.

The poem begins with the gripping line, "Something there is that does not love a wall." As they rebuild, the speaker muses, "we keep the wall between us as we go," emphasizing the sense of separation and expressing his unease with the growing reality of it. Though it is not necessary—"there are no cows here," he muses—conventional wisdom, soaked in fear and prejudice, offers a safety of sorts: "Good fences make good neighbors." The speaker's discomfort now becomes more acute: he wonders "what he was walling in or walling out," then even more so, and more personal, more human: "To whom I was to give offense." Deep down he knows that building walls means that one fears the other who will "give offense," or that one fears of being the one who gives offense, though one might never know the reason why or if anything could be done about it.

1. See https://www.poetryfoundation.org/poems/44266/mending-wall.

Then the first line is repeated, but now with words added, and there is no ambiguity, but clarity, even forcefulness: "Something there is that doesn't love a wall, / *That wants it down.*" The internal, robust resistance continues: there is something hostile, anti-communal; something threatening, even barbaric in that wall. The neighbor carries a stone in each hand "like an old-stone savage armed;" he walks in darkness, "not of woods only and the shade of trees." It is a darkened, savage mind that conceives of walls.

But in the end, while the ambiguity seems to disappear, the hostility is not overcome. The wisdom of questioning the wall, of giving way to the conviction to "want it down," is swallowed up by the relentless pressure of old prejudices, self-induced fears, and false self-preservation: "Good fences make good neighbors," is the line that ends the poem. The wall prevails.

It is no jump of genius to make the connections between this poem and the literal walls of stone and concrete built by the Israeli state on stolen Palestinian land or Donald Trump's wall on the border with Mexico. The concretized repulsiveness of such walls is clear for all to see. Neither is it difficult to read Robert Frost into the symbolic walls of racial supremacy, white chosenness, and manifest destiny the South African apartheid regime wanted to build and maintain between white and black, even as these policies were sanctified by the apartheid theology as God-ordained in their twisted preaching on such texts as Isa 60:18: "And you shall call your walls Salvation." They are all apartheid walls of supremacy and separation. Similarly widely accepted are the walls of separation between rich and poor, or the walls of patriarchal power and privilege that concretize gender inequality, or keeping out LGBTQI+ persons from the fiercely protected compounds of sacralised heteronormativity.

In the fascinating and sometimes bewildering encounter between Jesus and the Canaanite woman in the Gospel of Matthew, it is Jesus's attitudes, words, and actions that call forth our shock and disbelief. The woman, with her unshakably confident engagement of Jesus, calls forth our admiration. The question we need to ask is this: Is Jesus—keeping Robert Frost in mind—using religion, myth, ethnocentrism, patriarchy, and all the power associated with these to build a wall between himself and the woman, and as she attempts to break it down, is he mending it, withholding humanity, compassion, and justice, hiding behind empty but hostile clichés: "Good fences make good neighbors?" What does that do to the centrality of Jesus as liberator and Black liberation theology's Black Messiah, as Latin American liberation theology's revolutionary compañero, or the comrade, our "quintessential ancestor," as African feminist theologians call him?[2]

---

2. See Oduyoye and Amoah, "Christ for African Women," 38.

"YESU, THE GREAT BUSH WITH COOLING SHADES"

In their discussion on the meaning of Jesus for African women today, Mercy Oduyoye and Elizabeth Amoah reflect on the ways male African theologians have portrayed their understanding of Jesus.[3] For John Mbiti, Christ is God caring for the spiritual and physical welfare of people. Emmanuel Milingo employs what he calls a "Christ-Victor theology": Christ is victorious over Satan and all his works in our society today. It is a muscular, triumphalist theology that produces a muscular, triumphalist Christ. But Christ is also our (male) ancestor, the one who mediates between God and our human community. Kwesi Dickson proposes a Christology where sacrifice is central, one in which Christ's sacrifice is sufficient for us and enables us to make the sacrifices life requires from us. But no matter how much their Christologies differ, without exception, for all these theologians, God is indisputably male and the social reality in our context is an unquestioned, male-dominated one, proving Rosemary Edet's point:

> European colonization has further entrenched women's exclusion from positions of authority in the church. Women's views are not taken into account in the church's theological and political discussions . . .[4]

For their part, because African feminist theology is "the theology of the people,"[5] Oduyoye and Amoah begin by drawing on the words of popular prophetess/poetess/Pentecostal Christian Afua Kuma of Ghana:

> Yesu
> [You are] the rock

---

3. Oduyoye and Amoah, "Christ for African Women," 43ff.

4. Edet, "Christianity and African Women's Rituals," 37–38.

5. "[In Africa] the Christ of the theology of the people is the Christ who breaks the power of evil and empowers us in our life's journey" (Oduyoye and Amoah, "Christ for African Women," 38). Similarly the *Kairos Document* of 1985, in its devastating critique of the apartheid system in all its manifestations and its ideological justifications, as well as in its unequivocal stance with the oppressed in their struggle against apartheid, presents itself as South Africa's example of a "people's theology," which is a prophetic theology, distinct from the "state theology" of the apartheid state and the "church theology" of the churches aligned with the powerful. Such a Christ is not with us in a spiritual life's journey divorced from our journey on earth, and the "empowerment" is not a spiritualized moment. It is an empowerment that comes from Christ's standing in solidarity with the poor and oppressed in their struggles for justice. The Belhar Confession of my denomination calls the church to stand where Christ stands: with the poor, the downtrodden, and the meek, "and with *all* people, in any form of suffering and need"; and again, "that the church, *as the possession of God*, must stand where the Lord stands, namely against injustice and with the wronged . . ." (see Art. 10.7; my emphasis).

> We hide under you,
> The great bush with cooling shades,
> The giant tree who enables the climbers to see the heavens . . .

Jesus is all this and more, the revolutionary comrade who empowered women, gave them voice and agency, who has made women see that

> the practices of making women become silent "beasts" of societies' burdens, bent double under racism, poverty, and lack of appreciation of what fullness of womanhood should be, has been annulled and countered by Christ. Christ transcends and transforms and has liberated us to do the same.[6]

Nor are these the views of Africans alone. From Asia, Virginia Fabella testifies that Jesus must be a priest of *han* for the *minjung* women, as healer and comforter.

> Jesus Christ as priest of *han* will not only be healer, exorciser, consoler, friend; he will also be transformer. For he who expelled demons and cured the sick of their infirmities also denounced hypocritical practices and reversed customs and tradition. The feeling of resignation may be misconstrued as defeat, but indignation as such is what underlies the tenacity of will for life, which allows powerless people to survive . . . Jesus Christ can transform the *minjung* women's *han* into an energizing force for social change.[7]

From India, Aruna Gnanadason explains that women's oppression is a "systemic sin" that needs to be exposed, combatted, and overcome. In a patriarchal, sexist, male-dominated, heteronormative society and church, it is a challenging task.[8] No less than a "rediscovery of their biblical heritage" is necessary, and that rediscovery has led them to

> Draw strength from the Jesus community, which was an egalitarian, non-hierarchical community. Sinners, prostitutes, beggars, tax collectors, the ritually polluted, the crippled, and the impoverished—in short, the scum of Palestinian society—constituted the majority of Jesus' followers. These are the last who have become the first, the starving who have been satisfied, the uninvited who have been invited.[9]

---

6. Oduyoye and Amoah, "Christ for African Women," 43.
7. Fabella, "A Common Methodology," 108–17.
8. See Gnanadason, "Women's Oppression," 73–74.
9. Gnanadason, "Women's Oppression," 74.

In Gnanadason's view, Jesus "does not waste his time" trying to upgrade the feminine role by giving new dignity to the old task. On the contrary, "he creates an alternative."[10] That means he does not try to reform old, unworkable, oppressive systems; he overthrows them, and gives women a freedom not derived from revamped patriarchal ideologies that remain unchallenged and unchanged at the core, pretending change but in reality continuing to define women's freedom within the borders of acceptability for men, in which women continue to be "happy slaves."[11] A woman's freedom in Christ, she argues,

> Therefore includes, at the core, her freedom from the system of dominance that diminishes her personhood by imprisoning her womanhood. The Christian feminist viewpoint automatically leads to a critique of historico-cultural traditions that have given women a distorted image of their bodies, their abilities, their roles, their responsibilities, their dignity, and their destiny.[12]

So our question returns: Is this the Jesus we find building and maintaining the very walls these women, like the Canaanite woman, are trying to break down? With these statements and reflections in mind, let us now turn to the passage itself.

BEHOLD, A WOMAN

This is such a well-visited story that we should perhaps begin by stating what is generally agreed upon:

- The story is shocking, seemingly stripped of any pretense, and paints vivid pictures of the Canaanite woman and of Jesus.
- She is a woman, a gentile, from Syria, old enemy territory for ancient Israel, powerless and without any rights a man is bound to respect, with everything those connotations meant in the first-century world in which she lived. In the Gospel of Mark she is called Syro-Phoenician. For Matthew, she is the Canaanite woman, sharpening the framework of hostility.
- She has a demon-possessed daughter. This is no "ordinary" illness. As we have seen above, demon possession brings into play socio-economic, political conditions of oppression, deprivation, poverty, and trauma

---

10. Gnanadason, "Women's Oppression," 74.
11. Gnanadason, "Women's Oppression," 74.
12. Gnanadason, "Women's Oppression," 74.

as a result of colonial occupation and oppression. She comes not from the city, but from "the region," in other words, the rural areas, where poverty was even more acute.

- The fact that she engages Jesus on her own probably means that there is no male in her life to speak on her behalf. She might be a widow, or divorced, or a single mother, abandoned and dependent on her own skills and abilities. Peter's mother-in-law was also a woman, but one with connections to the insider's track: Peter spoke for her. This woman had none of that.

- Unlike the centurion, an oppressor in the service of the Roman Empire who built the village synagogue—proof that he "loves our people," (Luke 7:1-10)—she does not have the means to buy favors from the community, and cannot count on their intervention on her behalf. She is simply an enemy, not a powerful enemy with money, so she is not "worthy." How much easier it is for a rich oppressor who knows enough to exploit a need, even if it is what Paulo Freire calls "false generosity."[13]

- Jesus treats her with unvarnished, religious certainly, perhaps even racist, hostility. The fact that Jesus calls her a "dog" is perhaps the height of the disdain with which he treats her. The insult cannot be explained away by arguing that Jesus is actually speaking of "little dogs," puppies. First, the Aramaic has no diminutive for "dog." Jesus, speaking Aramaic, not Greek, would have known exactly what he said to her. Second, some have argued that this woman perhaps represents a normal, poor Palestinian household where dogs lived in the house. The words would therefore not be taken as an insult. To my ears that sounds unbearably racist: since she knows she is regarded as a dog anyway, she does (should) not take offense, more or less the same as suggesting black people should be used to being called "monkeys." But T. A. Burkill's judgment stands: "Calling a woman a 'little bitch' is no less abusive than to call her a 'bitch' without qualification."[14]

- Jesus is recalcitrant, offensive, and hard-hearted. The shock is so great, not because of his divinity—a god can do whatever he or she pleases, without accountability to anyone—but because this is completely out of character, incommensurate with his humanity, totally in contrast with how we have come to know him in the Gospels. He is not recognizable here.

13. See Freire, *Pedagogy of the Oppressed*, 55.
14. See Burkill, "Story of the Syrophoenician Woman," 173.

- For most, the one characteristic that makes her memorable is her "persistence." For some it shows her humility, for others her faith in Jesus as a miracle worker even though this faith is sorely "tested" by Jesus. Others, even Warren Carter, praise her "submissive posture."[15] It is this humble persistence that is rewarded: her daughter is healed.

In a remarkable analysis, Mitzi J. Smith, reading Mark's version of this story, speaks of this encounter in terms of race, gender, and the "politics of sass."[16] "Sass," she writes, "is an Americanism, a slang created in the context of a patriarchal, gendered, and racialized society," a context within which women who talk back, in other words, claim their right to speak for themselves in defense of themselves, are "sassy." Smith reads the story of the Syro-Phoenician woman "through a womanist hermeneutical lens of sass," and interprets the story "as a black woman who embodies sass." She reads it, intentionally, in solidarity with other Black women conscious of the costs of resistance: "We might, at any time, resist our oppressor, our oppression as sassy black women, but we might not survive."[17]

It is a fascinating piece and deserves singular attention, and not just because of her conclusion: "But oppressions, like sexism, racism, and classism, transcend place and transgress borders because defiled, fallible human beings are carriers of oppression, and Jesus is no exception."[18] Smith reads Mark, but it is with Dube's reading from Matthew that this chapter will mostly concern itself.

For Leticia Guardiola-Sáenz, writing as a Mexican who suffered invasion and dispossession from the people of the United States, convinced, like "the children of Israel" of their chosenness and driven by a God-given "manifest destiny," this is the story of "conviction and struggle in which a displaced woman reclaims her place at the table."[19] The "table" here is the place of equality where the woman stakes her claim for restitution. Hers is a voice not of submissiveness but of protest, and Jesus, as representative of the oppressor/invader, is the target of this protest:

15. Carter, *Matthew and the Margins*, 322.

16. Smith, "Race, Gender, and the Politics of Sass," 95–112, framing her approach to the story within the death of Sandra Bland in detention in Texas after being pulled over by a police officer for not signaling, and taken to jail. But it was not so much the failure to signal when changing lanes, but the fact that Sandra Bland apparently had the audacity to talk back at the officer. She "sassed" him, and that was her great sin that day on that Texas road. Three days after her imprisonment she was found dead in her cell. Authorities claimed that she hanged herself.

17. Smith, "Race, Gender, and the Politics of Sass," 99.

18. Smith, "Race, Gender, and the Politics of Sass," 100.

19. See Guardiola-Sáenz, "Borderless Women and Borderless Texts," 73.

She is fighting back against the oppressor by disrupting and invading the geographical space from which she has been displaced. She is coming to get compensation for what has been taken away from her.[20]

Her "cry for mercy is a cry for restitution" and she "uses the language of the system" to "ironically flatter" Jesus when she calls him "Son of David." Yet Guardiola-Sáenz calls this cry "a confession of faith." I would argue that it is extremely uncharacteristic for oppressed people to cry for mercy to the oppressor in their struggles for justice, and even more rare to "confess" any faith in them or their ability to respond with justice. At most what could be elicited here is the false generosity Paulo Freire has cautioned us not to confuse with the reciprocity of the justice that brings equity and dignity.

This is perhaps a good example for taking cultural and socio-political situatedness into consideration. As a black South African, I should be careful not to confuse "compensation" with "restitution." Compensation is a once-off act, paying a sum of money to the one who has been wronged in one way or another. The same can be said of reparations. Restitution, however, is returning what has been unlawfully taken, stolen, or appropriated: it is to "make good" for the wrong that has been done. It is what the Germans call *Wiedergutmachung*. It is an act within the broader framework of the ongoing "undoing of injustice and the doing of justice," the process of the restoration of justice, rights, and dignity. In the current debate about land restitution, not simply "land reform" in South Africa, these would be important distinctions to keep in mind.[21]

I do not have in mind the kind of "restitution" the out-going administration of F. W. De Klerk tried to foist on the country in what might be called a preemptive strike against genuine restitution of land. The De Klerk government in 1990, after abolishing some key land segregation statutes, adopted the White Paper on Land Reform that prescribed a policy of "restitution" whereby only state-owned land could be restored to its previous owners. This means that all the land in private possession, stolen by whites from the beginning of colonization, would be left untouched while the apartheid government would, in a transparent effort at "reform," claim a program of "land restitution" even before the democratic dispensation. That would not only allow the apartheid regime to claim credit and respectability, but it clearly hoped to forestall genuine restitution through the proper

---

20. Guardiola-Sáenz, "Borderless Women and Borderless Texts," 76.
21. See Boesak, *Pharaohs*, 12–16; and ch. 4, especially 136–39.

redistribution of all land forcibly taken through legalized land theft or by violent means.[22]

It will become clear in the development of these issues that whereas I share the view of the Canaanite woman as an oppressed, subjugated, but nonetheless courageous, determined, and essentially liberated person, "going toe to toe with Jesus,"[23] my reading of Jesus as her counterpart in the story will be markedly different.

If for Leticia Guardiola-Sáenz it is a story of a woman who crosses the border into Jesus's territory to reclaim what is hers, for Musa Dube, the story presents "a land-possession-type scene" full of imperializing characters—Jesus and the disciples, and the victim, the woman. Jesus is the "traveler" whose "divinity, class, race, and gender endow him with privilege and authority."[24] He can leave his geographical boundaries, travel to another country, and return at his own will. As for the woman, "she must parrot the superiority of her subjugators and betray her own people and land in order to survive," and she can survive only "as a colonized mind, a subjugated and domesticated subject."[25] She is a Canaanite, the people whose land had been conquered and occupied by Jesus's people. In his interactions with this woman, Jesus "reiterates" and reaffirms the Israelite myth of supremacy and divine right of occupation. If this is true, then Jesus cannot be but an arrogant Jew imposing his mission upon this Canaanite woman, who has to submit to his transgression in order to survive. "Undoubtedly, the relationship is one of unequals."[26] The fact that her daughter is "severely possessed" indicates a foreign people, the woman and her daughter, "not only as womanlike, but also as intensely evil and dangerous."[27]

Yet Matthew's rather dramatic beginning of the story, "Behold, a woman!" indicates that something extraordinary is at hand. The extraordinariness, I think, is not just about the shocking behavior of Jesus; neither is it because, as Warren Carter suggests, she "recalls Jewish women who benefit from Jesus' actions of healing," demanding the "same blessed treatment."[28] Such reasoning leads precisely to the imperialist/colonialist Jesus giving in to the annoying persistence of a needy heathen, as Dube argues. It is also rather anticlimactic: why would Matthew so emphatically dramatize her

---

22. See Moyo, "Mimicry, Transitional Justice, and the Land Question," 11–12.
23. Smith, "Race, Gender, and the Politics of Sass," 105.
24. Dube, *Postcolonial Feminist Interpretation*, 146.
25. Dube, *Postcolonial Feminist Interpretation*, 147.
26. Dube, *Postcolonial Feminist Interpretation*, 148.
27. Dube, *Postcolonial Feminist Interpretation*, 148.
28. Carter, *Matthew and the Margins*, 322.

entry into the story if she were the same as just another Jewish woman in need? Such a reading agitates completely with the character that emerges here. So in keeping with Matthew's intentions, we will consider our arguments above concerning Jesus's Jewishness, his status as an oppressed person under Roman occupation, as adequate response to Dube's and Smith's (and Guardiola-Sáenz's implied) contention that Jesus was an imperialist, male, patriarchal missionary with power to encroach, transgress, and subjugate this woman. If we look closely, I believe a different picture emerges.

She is the first woman in the Gospel to approach Jesus and speak to him directly. There is a boldness in her actions that belies any suggestion of submissiveness and harmful humility. She strikes me not so much as "uppity" as Sharon Ringe describes her,[29] but as boldly confident, assured of her worth as a human being, and determined not to be shaken in that confidence. Such women, Ringe writes, "are co-opted, ridiculed, ignored, condemned, one way or the other gotten out of the way of the important business of the church and of theology."[30] True, but clearly that does not happen to this woman. Or better put, she does not allow that to happen to her. Sharon Ringe tells us that the woman refuses "to accept the low esteem in which her society held her and her daughter, or its restrictions upon her own behavior."[31] She is correct, but to be sure: this is not "uppity-ness." This woman may be a politically colonized subject, but she refuses and resists the colonization of her mind. She considers herself anybody's equal.

She is not intimidated by the men surrounding Jesus who expect her to accept their authority as males and as gatekeepers, deciding just who might have access to Jesus. The disciples are, as Guardiola-Sáenz describes them, "frightened by the cry of justice raised by the rebellious woman."[32] She makes her way steadily and determinedly, and not quietly, through the mass of people surrounding Jesus, breaking down the walls of hostility as she goes. Then finally confronting Jesus, she speaks to Jesus as if she knows more about him than he does about himself. She counters every argument, even every insult, without any hesitation, with irony, amusement, and above all with robust confidence. That does not strike me as a relationship of inequality. Every suggestion of inequality Jesus makes she rejects with disdain and moves on—not away from, but deeper into the argument—as if she is leading Jesus both back to basics and up to a higher level.

29. See Ringe, "A Gentile Woman's Story," 65. It will be clear that Ringe's "uppity-ness" is not the same as Smith's "sass."
30. Ringe, "A Gentile Woman's Story," 65.
31. Ringe, "A Gentile Woman's Story," 70–71.
32. Ringe, "A Gentile Woman's Story," 77.

Though Dube is certain that Jesus, in accordance with his power and privilege, "transgresses" her territory, the text itself is more ambivalent.[33] Jesus goes to the region, that is, the district controlled by Tyre and Sidon, but she also "comes out." They meet at an unspecified place between the borders, "the interface of Jewish and gentile territory . . . a place of tension and prejudice."[34] If Jesus is crossing borders, she is doing so too, intentionally and purposefully. The two are coming toward each other, and in this place of hostility, ethnic conflict, competing religious claims (especially the trump card—Israel as chosen people), economic needs, and age-old prejudices, Matthew prepares the reader for a confrontational encounter. This is the place where animosities, prejudices, ideologies, historical wrongs and counter-claims to life will clash. She is consciously deliberate in seeking Jesus out, fighting her way through the crowd, as well as the conspicuous patriarchal obstructionism of the male disciples. Not simply ignoring or carefully evading, but confronting and defying every tradition, custom, rule, and law about women's behavior in public, she raises her voice, "crying out" above the men's own insistent shouting at her. In embarrassed admission of their failure to stop her, they have to appeal to Jesus since they cannot control her.

JESUS "WITHDREW"

Vincent Taylor, in trying to understand Jesus's strange behavior, thought we should look for "tensions in Jesus' mind over the scope of his ministry. He is speaking to himself as well as to the woman."[35] Sharon Ringe calls this "wishful,"[36] and in a way she is right, but Carter too, suggests that the

33. Hence Guardiola–Sáenz's insistence that it is the woman who takes the initiative by coming out to meet Jesus.

34. Carter, *Matthew and the Margins*, 321. See also Hagner, *Matthew 14–28*, 441, even though Hagner sees the meeting place as "still Jewish territory." That reading means that she, in crossing the border into Jewish territory is even bolder, stronger, and much less "submissive" than these readings will allow. Even Dube has to acknowledge the ambiguity, though it does not seem to influence her opinion: "Her coming out indirectly implies that Jesus may not have entered the district at all; rather it was the woman who came seeking him," but the ambiguity serves to emphasize her "need" (149). As we have pointed out, Guardiola-Sáenz argues for the woman leaving her territory and entering that of Jesus, to perform her act of challenge and press her claims for restitution. Hence it is not Jesus who is the aggressive imperialist transgressing borders. It is the woman who asserts her agency, and crosses borders to claim her rights.

35. Taylor, *Gospel According to St. Mark*, 347.

36. Ringe, "A Gentile Woman's Story," 69.

woman "challenges Jesus' very identity and mission."[37] It might be worthwhile to take a closer look at this.

"Jesus left that place and withdrew" (15:21). For the sixth time in this Gospel, Jesus feels compelled to withdraw and "put distance between him and the Pharisees."[38] Here, as elsewhere, Matthew is deliberate in his choice of words. Jesus is in danger. Commenting on Matt 14:13, Carter writes,

> To withdraw is to refuse to play in the tyrant's world and by the tyrant's rules. It is to make space for a different reign, God's empire, marked by life-giving structures and compassionate practices such as healing and feeding.[39]

It is withdrawal in response to aggression from imperial power. This is an important observation, for while the element of danger is clearly present in chapter 15, the rest of Carter's point is sharply contradicted by Jesus's encounter with the Canaanite woman. She does not allow him the space for the rest he seeks, nor does she allow any distance, physical or otherwise, between herself and him. She pushes hard against the walls. Jesus, in his turn, is severely reluctant to show any "life-giving" signs of the reign of God: healing, compassion, and feeding. Moreover, Jesus is seeking distance from much more than the Pharisees "after condemning their tradition." The dangers are multiple, the pressures are grave and relentless.

Perhaps we should take a step or two back. The encounter with the Canaanite woman follows a long and exhausting argument between Jesus and the Pharisees about "the tradition of the elders." At the heart of the matter, though, is the question: Who speaks with authority? Is it those who have studied the law, know every reading and interpretation, and pronounce them with the power of their privileged positions, or is it this itinerant, radical prophet from Galilee with his following of peasants, workers, sinners, tax collectors and women, who so easily turns the head of the *am ha'aretz*, the little people, the ignorant masses, endangering societal structures of power built up over centuries and so necessary for control of the masses?

Jesus is openly confrontational: "Hypocrites!" he calls them. Isaiah is speaking of you: "This people honors me with their lips, but their hearts are far from me" (15:8). "You"—lawyers and leaders—are teaching "human precepts." Jesus's uncompromising stance—these "leaders" are "the blind leading the blind"—worries his disciples: does he even know how offensive the elites found him? He does not care: "Every plant that my heavenly father

---

37. Carter, *Matthew and the Margins*, 322.
38. Carter, *Matthew and the Margins*, 305, 321.
39. Carter, *Matthew and the Margins*, 305.

has not planted shall be uprooted" (15:13). Those are fighting words. Jesus is irritated, but not only with the Pharisees. His disciples are not spared: "Are you also still without understanding? . . . Do you [still] not see?" (vv. 17, 18). Jesus can hardly conceal his exasperation. Here, it seems to me, Jesus is deliberately confrontational, making space for the strategy of "creative tension" Martin Luther King Jr. called upon in the confrontation with those in power and opposed to the liberating and humanizing aims of the struggle. It is the "nonviolent militancy" Albert Luthuli spoke of, the "extremism" King thought we, in our struggles for justice and freedom, should be proud to be accused of.[40]

Just before that, in Gennesaret—we read backwards in order to better see the rising line of tension and intensity—Jesus is stormed by hordes of people bringing their sick to be healed (14:34-36). Chapter 14 begins with the chilling rumor that Herod the *tretarch*, who has just had John the Baptist murdered, has declared Jesus "John the Baptist risen from the dead." Herod sees the "same powers at work" in Jesus. That is not a conversational observation, an idle remark, or religious superstition. This is power at work, a premeditated, preemptive justification. The danger is clear, and Jesus "withdrew" to "a deserted place" seeking respite from the demanding crowds and perhaps some reflection time for his disturbed soul. It is not for nothing that Matthew describes the circumstances of John's death in such detail. It is to let the audience know what Jesus knows: this is what is planned for him as well. So he withdraws by boat. But even there the crowds "followed him on foot," which must mean that they have gone around the long way—not straight across the water—in their desperation to capture his attention. He finally does get some time to be "by himself" and pray, but at night, only after an exacting and exhausting day.

At Gennesaret the pressure did not let up. Crowds came to be healed, even if only by "touching the hem of his garment." This denotes enormous pressure. We know that when one woman touched the hem of his cloak, Jesus felt that "power went from him." So what happens with whole crowds pressing for the same? Almost casually, Matthew also tells us, "The people of that place recognized him." A throwaway sentence like that tells us at least two things. One, in a time where mass media as we know it did not exist, it is amazing that Jesus was so easily recognized everywhere he went. That means that apart from people following him everywhere, there were others who spread the word about him, creating new crowds with new expectations. They recognized him, *even in that place*. That does not only show

---

40. See King, "Letter From a Birmingham Jail," 127-45. The discussion on this point is on 130-32, 135-37. See also Albert Luthuli on "militant defiance," *Let My People Go!*, 129.

how popular Jesus must have been among the people, it also indicates the relentless pressure exerted on him. It really makes no difference whether they meant well or that their needs were genuine. His love for the people exposed him mercilessly to the demands of the people. Unless one is the most shameless, narcissistic ego-glutton, no one can endure this for long.

But second, it also explains the depth of the hatred towards him by the elites and leaders of the people. The "powers" of John the Baptist Herod recognized and feared in Jesus were the powers of the true prophet of God: the perspicuity to discern, the power to confront, the boldness to expose, the courage to hold accountable, the fearlessness to judge between right and wrong, the obedience to challenge, the faithfulness to hold up the difference so *the people* can see, judge, and make choices.

The news about John's death and the experiences with the crowds follow the equally disturbing incident in the synagogue in Jesus's hometown, that same Nazareth where he revealed his manifesto in Luke 4. Now, after traveling and preaching, healing and doing deeds of liberation and restoration, and being recognized as the Servant of Yahweh who will bring justice to all the earth, Jesus returns home. It would be an unexpected ordeal, and it begins with denigration through familiarization: "Where does this man get this wisdom and deeds of power? Is this not the carpenter's son?" (Matt 13:54, 55). They do not deny his wisdom nor his deeds of power; they deny that one from among the poor and downtrodden, one such as themselves, could have such power and authority. Such is the power of the internalization of inferiority, powerlessness, and worthlessness that oppression imposes upon the oppressed.

Were they expecting a Messiah from among the privileged and powerful, one who could claim "royal blood?" What good is a Messiah who is "from below," like them, politically powerless and without connections, like them? They too recognize him, but as one to be put and kept in his place. Again we hear Biko: the strongest ally of the oppressor is the mind of the oppressed.[41] They illustrate the kind of petty, false consciousness that stifles the revolution in its cradle. In Luke's Gospel they try to kill him. In

---

41. In one particularly disconcerting moment during that first election campaign for the ANC in 1994 in the "coloured" townships, I was confronted by a "coloured" man grabbing my hand, and refusing to let go, he said to me twice in an urgent voice, "You are just a *hotnot,* (a "n. . ."), just as I am. What do you think you can do for me?" He informed me he would "rather" vote for "the white man," meaning F. W. De Klerk, whose power to "do something" for him was more persuasive, even though that "power" was based on an oppressive, racist past. I do not for one moment claim the status of "messiah" for anyone, but that short but intense conversation, revealing as it does the internalization of powerlessness and unworthiness, remains with me as highly illustrative of the wisdom of Biko's observation and of what is happening to Jesus in this text.

Matthew they try to kill his sense of self, of self-awareness. They deny his divine Servanthood, his messianic calling, and his mission. "And he did not do many deeds of power there because of their unbelief," writes Matthew (13:58). Mark is blunt: "And he could do *no* works there, because of their unbelief" (6:5).

This is singularly shocking: the Messiah who could overcome a parent's unbelief and heal his son (Mark 9:14–29) is here helpless before the unbelief of those from whom he evidently expected much. It is a brutal overturning of Jesus's belief that "all things are possible for the one who believes." They refused to believe because the very thought that *he* might be the Messiah leaves them "deeply offended" (Matt 13:57). Jesus now knows for certain that "a prophet is not without honor, except in their home town, and among their own kin" (13:57). Mark adds, "and in their own house" (Mark 6:4). But we should note the narrowing intensification: town, kin, own house. As the description narrows, the disappointment, tension, and sense of rejection deepen.

What exactly Jesus expected we are not told, but at the very least he had hoped to be recognized as a prophet of God, here among his own people who have been waiting for one such as he all their lives. His people—the colonized!—would rather remain slaves to Caesar and be oppressed by his underlings in the temple than believe that one from among them could be their deliverer. No wonder Jesus, in Mark's Gospel, is "amazed" (Mark 6:6). From the powerful and privileged Jesus expected this; they had too much to lose. But from his "own," the oppressed colonized, this could have been too much.

It should not surprise us at all that by the time we reach chapter 15, the radical Jesus in Luke's synagogue had chosen to surrender to the revisionist Jesus before the Canaanite woman. He wanted to withdraw: from the hate-filled vindictiveness and death-lust of the temple elite; from the threats of the powerful that followed him everywhere; from the sick, hypocritical politics of Herod who pretended to be "grieved" but nonetheless all too ready to kill John with the flimsy excuse of his "regard for his oaths and his guests." Jesus had to withdraw from the people he loved because they would not understand his mission or believe in him.

If Dieter Giorgi is right, and *pistis*, "faith," means "loyalty" and "trust,"[42] then what is at stake here is no less than loyalty to the Messiah and to the mission of liberation; trust in and loyalty to the God of liberation he represents, trust in the trustworthiness of God and God's Messiah. In denying him they denied their own need for liberation, justice, and peace. He had

---

42. See Giorgi, "God Turned Upside-Down," 148.

come to save his people. He now has to face the unthinkable, but painfully possible: that his people do not want to be saved. Here "withdraw" does not mean "creating distance from," it means "giving up on." It is, I think, less a question of Jesus struggling with "the scope of his mission" than of Jesus wrestling with the very fact of his mission.

The issue here, it seems to me, is not so much whether Jesus is in some way wary of "transcending" his mission, expanding the scope of it too much. It is whether there is such a mission at all, and if there were, whether it is *his*; whether the bold manifesto in Nazareth was in fact no more than an overambitious, messianic overreach. Doubtless, the exclusivity he expresses here is roundly in contrast with the inclusivity he has announced and rejoiced in at the beginning of his ministry. So, like Elijah, he leaves, and like Elijah, he goes to Sidon, and like Elijah, he meets a woman. Or better, a woman comes to meet him. But unlike Elijah, he does not go to save her, she comes to save *him*.

THE SECRET OF THE HUMAN CHILD

Above I observed that Jesus had "surrendered." I do not mean that he simply surrendered to exhaustion. He surrendered to the pressures so relentlessly exerted over such a long time; to the religious and social prejudices he had resisted from the beginning; to the theological claims of ethnic superiority that come with religious exclusivism that he had tried to resist and that had almost cost him his life. Jesus was not "low on compassion," he had *surrendered* his compassion.

Like all prophets who would not find a "home" among their own (although they long for one), he has discovered that for people there is perhaps no greater sin than being ahead of one's time. And he *was* that: in his desire to break down the walls of hostility, ethnocentricity, and religious supremacy. In his insistence of the inclusivity of God's liberatory intentions and actions; in his inclusion of women as equals and his embrace of those marginalized by the structures of power, the poor, the sick, the destitute, the fatherless children, and the women without patriarchal protection; the "sinners and tax collectors," and those literally and figuratively beyond the borders of acceptability. In his attacks on power and wealth and privilege at the cost of the poor and vulnerable; in his insistence that the first shall be last and the last first; in his example of leadership as servanthood.

Jesus was ahead of his time then, as he is still now: on the question of justice and the inclusion of women on the basis of equality; of violence and war in his name; on the inclusivity of God's embrace for all God's children and God's preference for the lowest of the low. Jesus was far ahead of the Black church, my own denomination included, as we claim God in our struggles against racism but deny God God's right to do justice for LGBTQ+ persons.

Jesus was reaching beyond the borders of their imagination still held captive by the constraints of convention, fear, and short-term self-preservation. At this moment he seems to cave in to the pressures of exclusivism, chosenness, and patriarchal hegemony, and step away from all those expectations articulated by the women from Latin America and Asia in the beginning of this chapter. The call to liberation he articulated so well in the synagogue in Nazareth has now become a burden too heavy to bear.

Guardiola-Sáenz argues that Jesus, "compelled" by his disciples, whose fear, distress, and uncertainties mirror those of the empire whenever it is so boldly challenged by the subjugated, now "reasserts the exclusiveness of his mission."[43] I think it goes further than just a question of "exclusiveness." It might not at all be implausible that at the very least, he should here be wrestling with the question: Would he not be wiser to reconsider this mission, to seek discretion as the better part of valor? Should he wait a while longer, at least until people were more ready to hear his message? Would a public display of that readiness, in this almost God-given opportunity in Syria, to show his willingness to make accommodation for his own people, not also show an openness they thought he did not have, and get some more support for the more important work and more dangerous confrontations that lay ahead? Would it not be wiser to sacrifice this woman, and her daughter, for the sake of the greater cause?

So the Canaanite woman does indeed encounter a Jesus as the very embodiment of all those historically determined attitudes, religious exclusivism, and racial disdain. And almost every word and gesture seem calculated not just to rebuff her, but to impress his audience. It is a Jesus not so much uncertain about the *scope* of his mission, but resisting the very meaning and efficacy of the mission itself. She catches Jesus in a moment of critical, almost fatal hesitation, one that invites a critical decision. Which way will he go? At this moment it is far from clear where he *will* go. Is this moment, for Jesus, a paralyzing or a galvanizing one? She decides to make it the latter.

It is not as if Jesus does not hear her at first. Matthew is clear: "He [quite deliberately] did not answer her at all" (v. 23). Guardiola-Sáentz suggests that the woman's boldness leaves Jesus speechless (as patriarchal male

---

43. See Guardiola-Sáenz,"Borderless Women and Borderless Texts," 77.

not used to women this bold?).⁴⁴ But perhaps it is more a show of open disdain than surprised speechlessness. Then as his disciples urge him to send her away, he speaks over her head to them, ignoring her completely, but knowing she hears him. When he finally has no choice but to acknowledge her it is only to tell her that she is not of the "chosen people." Like the "For Whites Only" signs that used to remind black people of their inferior status, without rights or any claim to humanity or compassion, Jesus hangs a "For Jews Only" sign around his neck. When that theological argument does not impress her, he sinks lower, shamelessly patronizing her and explaining it in words he did not use towards the equally gentile, but powerful and influential Roman centurion, but now hoping that someone like her is sure to understand: "It is not fair to take the children's food and throw it to the dogs" (v. 26). We have already commented on the use of the word "dogs." But note here that extra sneer: "throw it," not even "give it," or "let them have it."

It is then that she makes the comment about bread and crumbs. Guardiola-Sáenz sees her as the dispossessed woman who comes to Jesus in a spirit of protest and reclamation, determined not to beg, but to *take* bread from the table of those who dispossessed her. That means she approaches Jesus not as a subjugated person, but as an equal.⁴⁵ She is right.

Far from showing her "submissiveness," I think this comment reveals two things. First, it is an almost amused retort, as in "really?" or, more seriously perhaps, "Is this, in this situation, your response?" If irony is indeed a driving motif in Matthew's Gospel, as Dorothy Jean Weaver consistently argues, here is perhaps one of the best examples.⁴⁶ But second, she rises above mere irony. She is aiming at something deeper. She seems to be saying: this myth of religious superiority and racial supremacy you, Jesus, seem to be clinging to, may mean something to you in your need to feel better than others, but if there is any truth in what you have been saying and doing all around these areas (so that your fame spread even to where I live), then

---

44. Guardiola-Sáenz,"Borderless Women and Borderless Texts," 77.

45. Guardiola-Sáenz,"Borderless Women and Borderless Texts," 69. "In my sociohistorical condition of dispossessed neighbor, born and bred in the borderlands of the U.S. empire, I am certainly determined to take the bread from the table and not wait until the crumbs fall from it. I am convinced that it is only at the level of the table—as equals—and not under the table—as inferiors—that a constructive dialogue and fair reconstitution of the world can be achieved" (69).

46. See Weaver, *Irony of Power*, especially ch. 2. As she works with three politically powerful figures in Matthew's Gospel, Herod the king, Herod the tetrarch, and Pilate the governor, her emphasis is rightly on political power as she discusses the workings of irony as resistance "from the bottom up." I think her intriguing argument, although she does not include the Canaanite woman vis-à-vis Jesus in Matthew 15, is as applicable. Only here it is the Canaanite woman who employs this irony with regard to Jesus.

you must know that the God you have proclaimed since your first sermon in Nazareth's synagogue, is not this: a racialistic, ethnocentric, misogynistic, patriarchal, exclusivistic sadist who cannot do justice to, nor find compassion for, a tormented, demon-possessed child. To say nothing of relating to an independent-thinking woman on a basis of equality. She considers the theological value of his *deeds* of more importance than the theological value of the *argument* he makes. And she reveals even more, I think.

Importantly, she comes to him with an appeal to his messiahship. Three times in succession, she calls Jesus "Lord," same as his disciples do, in defiance of the lordship of the Caesar under whose oppressive heel she too, lives. That in itself is an act of resistance at two levels: defying the claims of the Roman Empire *vis-à-vis* the status and power of Caesar, and simultaneously reminding Jesus of who he is, and the difference between him and those who claim exceptionality by divine right.

Then she calls him "Son of David." This is not, I think, the cheap political flattery that is supposed to seduce Jesus into doing, however reluctantly, what she wants, since she, unlike his own people in Nazareth, "recognizes" his "royal blood." To me, that sounds too much like the accusation of "feminine wiles" women are suspected of employing in order to get their way. The title "Son of David" refers to the messianic king, the figure from 2 Sam 7:12–16, the one "whose kingdom would have no end." It does not only mean that his kingdom, his reign, and his authority and power would be eternal. It means it would have no end, no borders, could not be stopped by the demarcations drawn by imperial arrogance, political expedience, socio-economic exclusion, ethnocentric illusions, or theological exclusivism.

But, like the women from the Global South, she speaks with the compelling expectation and authority of the oppressed. Her demon-possessed daughter is the victim of colonialist oppression, and the One whose reign will challenge the empire who inflicted this suffering upon them is the one standing before her, even if he does not want to acknowledge that, or her. This story, writes Lamar Williamson, emphasizes the "messianic secret." Jesus withdrew and "tried not to let his presence be known but he could not be hid" (Mark 7:32).[47] It was this woman who "exposed" him. What Jesus wanted to hide was not so much his physical presence, I believe—the woman has already "blown his cover" and it was no longer relevant—but the fact of his messiahship, his mission, his calling, that he has come to challenge and subvert the mightiest power on earth. He tried not only to keep her from making this secret known, he tried to deny it for himself.

---

47. See Williamson, *Mark*, 139.

This woman, however, knows the secret and is determined that Jesus would acknowledge it: he is the Human Child.

Of course one should not deny or try to diminish the fact that she is a mother, driven by her love for her child. Her feelings as a mother and her love for freedom, justice, and dignity are not mutually exclusive. But we should resist the temptation to make this love a sentimental, helpless love. Her love is a revolutionary, combative love, and her bold engagement of Jesus is no less than a love-driven assault on the walls of compassionless exclusivism.

Her insistence tells us something else. Her appeals to him—"Lord, help me!"; "Son of David, my daughter is tormented by a demon"—are not only appeals for mercy, they are appeals *on the basis of the solidarity of the oppressed*. She uses political titles that call upon his messiahship. She is a woman, one of the poorest of the poor from the rural areas of Sidon and Tyre. Like Jesus, she lives under occupation. Like Galilee, her land has been overrun by the Romans, and they exact from her people, like from his people, the same great human cost. They share the same oppression, exploitation, and deprivation, and they share the same desire for and hope of freedom and dignity. For that reason she insists: her child is not just ill, she is demon-possessed. The demon possession you have seen and healed in Galilee, she seems to tell Jesus, is the same here in Syria: the consequence of oppression, violence, humiliation, and hopelessness. You recognized and exorcized those demons in Galilee; I demand that you do the same here.

Jesus, like her, is a child of God, called to freedom, but living under occupation. That is the point she wants to drive home here: our struggle is the same, and in light of these truths and realities your flight into ancient prejudices, imagined racial superiority entangled with religious supremacy and divide-and-rule politics makes no sense. This is not an appeal of the oppressed to the suppressed humanity of the oppressor, as Dube and Guardiola-Sáenz suggest. *This is an appeal to the solidarity of redemptive comradeship.* Her insistence is based on two things: first her confidence that Jesus cannot deny this, or her. Second, this woman knows the secret of the Human Child. The disciples (still) seem to have no clue, and Jesus is resolutely self-defensive, but this woman knows the heart of God and how it beats in Jesus of Nazareth.

It is for this reason also that she pays no heed to the racially loaded banalities Jesus employs in his attempts to get rid of her. Instead of backing down, she crowds him with her words and her presence, she pushes him with her knowledge of the truth and her convictions about him. In an even more superb irony, she employs the strategy Jesus did a few chapters ago with the opposition from the temple: the nonviolent, militant, creative tension that would not let go. In this she foreshadows the Albert Luthulis and Martin Luther Kings, the women of the great women's march to Pretoria and the Union Buildings, the Winnie Mandelas, Albertina Sisulus, and Adelaide Tambos; the Dorothy Days and the Ella Bakers, the Claudette Colvins and the Rosa Parkses; the masses who followed their lead and filled the streets with the redemptive confrontation of nonviolent, militant defiance.

The way she deals with the insults about "dogs" and "crumbs" has nothing to do with humble submissiveness. She probes and pushes until she penetrates the shield of denialist self-defense Jesus is holding up. Are we really talking of crumbs here, she seems to ask. He is Lord and Messiah, Son of David, the bearer of God's justice for all the earth, the hope of the nations and as he testifies of himself, "the bread of life," the abundant provider of bread for the masses, challenging the deliberate politics of hunger and want the empire depends on, and we are speaking of *crumbs*? The irony is unbearable.

It is no wonder the word "bread" plays such an important role in these passages. It is mentioned in the discussion with the Pharisees, the feeding of the multitude is recalled twice, and Jesus and the Canaanite woman both talk of bread and crumbs. Immediately after the encounter with the Canaanite woman, Matthew tells of the feeding of the multitude. But this is the *second* feeding. In these feeding stories Jesus's act "attacks the injustice of the sinful imperial system which ensures that the urban elite are well fed at the expense of the poor. Jesus enacts an alternative system marked by compassion, sufficiency and shared resources."[48] Matthew's intention cannot simply be to show that Jesus has the power to challenge the unjust imperial system and its socio-economic inequalities. He has already done so in 14:13–18. This second telling must have a different intention. It shows, I believe, the absurdity the woman pointed out: that the one who is able to feed thousands with bread, showing "the alternative system marked by compassion, sufficiency and shared resources," in other words, *abundant* justice, is suddenly unable, or unwilling, to share the generosity of God's justice with a Canaanite woman and her child. And she makes Jesus see this too.

But second, Matthew demonstrates the impact of this woman on Jesus and his mission. Matt 15:29–39 is there as a result of Matt 15:21–28. We must read the last in light of the first. The Jesus who just now spoke of "crumbs" is now sharing the bread of God's goodness, and in such abundance that there is bread left untouched—seven baskets full. The point, again, is the abundance of justice. The seven baskets of left-over bread are not a sign of wastefulness. The more bread is left over, the stronger the attack on the

---

48. See Carter, *Matthew and the Margins*, 305.

systems of imperial injustice and exploitation. It is what our Muslim sisters and brothers in South Africa call *barakat*: food to be taken home by the guests after the feast so that the abundance continues to be shared and the celebration does not come to an end. On the borders of confrontation and self-denial, Jesus thought he had nothing to give this woman except crumbs. Now he feeds the crowds and seven baskets full of bread are left. The one who was "low on compassion" for the woman, now finds it again: "I have compassion for the crowd . . ." (15:32). This is no Jesus hiding behind the paucity of grace and the scarcity of inclusion. This is a Jesus rejoicing in the abundance of justice and love.

Here we meet a rejuvenated Jesus; his strength is restored, his cup overflows. Again crowds swamp him and he does wonders among them. Almost gleefully, Matthew counts them on his fingers: "The lame, the maimed, the blind, the mute," and then, as if running out of fingers, "and many others. . ." There is an undeniable joy in this passage, entirely different from the tense joylessness of the previous story. And behind it all is a Canaanite woman. No wonder Matthew introduces her with, "Behold, a woman . . ." This too, shall stand "in memory of her."

Sharon Ringe eloquently describes the Canaanite woman as a "witness to Jesus," one who ministers to him through her faith, "no doctrinal confession, no flattery of miraculous powers . . . rather an act of trust and engagement, enabling Jesus to see the situation in a different way." She calls his bluff, enabling him to act in a way "apparently blocked to him before." But not only that. She, her wit, her sharp retort, is a gift to Jesus, "a gift that enabled his gift of healing in turn . . . not the gift of submission or obedience seen as appropriate for women in her society, but rather the gift of sharp insight—the particular insight of the poor and the outcast who can see through a situation because they have few illusions to defend."[49] She does more, in fact. She relieves Jesus of the illusion that he cannot be what he is called to be: the Messiah, the liberator of the oppressed and the captives, the healer and comrade, the ancestor who embodies our quintessential selves and gifts that to us. She reveals, first to Jesus, and then to us, the secret of the Human Child.

JESUS, CHILD OF AFRICAN WOMEN

When I first wrote about Jesus and the Canaanite woman in 2005, I had titled the chapter in that publication "The Secret of the Human Son."[50]

49. Ringe, "A Gentile Woman's Story," 71–72.
50. See my *Die Vlug van God's Verbeelding*, ch. 4, 87–110.

Reading African and other feminist theologians since then, however, has convinced me that that title was not inclusive enough. My encounter with Mercy Oduyoye's and Elizabeth Amoah's "Jesus, Child of African Women" has convinced me even further.

In Africa, these two theologians write, where physical suffering seems endemic, where hunger and thirst are the continuous experience of millions, a suffering Christ becomes an attractive figure. "However, Jesus of Nazareth is seen more as a comrade who did not accept deprivation as the destiny of humanity, but, rather, demonstrated in his dealings with people that such suffering is not the plan of God."[51] A comrade is one who knows that suffering with us will not suffice; it is joining in the struggle against suffering that ultimately makes the difference.

South African feminist theologian Christina Landman shows that the matter is even more complex. Women who are in need of healing try to find that in the church. But in the urban settings of South Africa they are caught in a double, even triple bind: trapped between religion and culture, and between Western, township, and traditional cultures. Thus in the search for healing and wholeness, they flee one church for another or one culture for another, but the end is often a greater trauma.[52] And as long as our societies, cultures, and religious spaces are dominated by patriarchal hegemonies, it will always be that way. In many ways, these are experiences at a level of complexity men are not always confronted with.

For African women, the African feminists assert, it no longer suffices to confess Christ only as the One who "suffers with us." Jesus is a "comrade" in the struggle against suffering and oppression. He is the liberator from the burden of disease *and* the ostracism of a society "riddled with blood-taboos and theories of inauspiciousness arising out of women's blood."[53] This observation has never struck me so forcefully, no matter how many times I have exegeted this passage and preached on it. This is a Jesus of an intimacy that is beyond us men, a Savior beyond our ken, but one we must absolutely come to know, since we are the ones burdening the women with those theologies and theories of "inauspiciousness" which in the relations of men and women have always led to women's "unworthiness," despite our proud talk of *"ubuntu."*

Rosemary N. Edet makes the same point. It is true that the proclamation of the Christian gospel is good news for men and women. But, she argues, "Christianity legalizes and reinforces the oppression of women and

---

51. Oduyoye and Amoah, "Christ for African Women," 39.
52. See Landman, "Traumatised between Culture and Religion."
53. See Edet, "Christianity and Women's Rituals," 35.

their subjugation to men in all aspects of life . . . Old, harmful practices in African tradition are taken over [uncritically] by the churches and given biblical foundation."[54] In contrast, and despite this patriarchal post-colonial colonization of Scripture, women have discovered in Jesus someone entirely different and opposite:

> Jesus was a revolutionary. He liberated the woman with the issue of blood and restored the son of the widow of Nain. [But] *he never tortured them, nor demanded purification rites*.[55]

That last sentence, again, underscores the necessity of rereading these texts with the eye of a woman, but then quite specifically, the eye of African women. Without them African men would continue to accept, propagate, and enforce rituals, Christianized and sacralized though they be, but nonetheless harmful, humiliating, and dehumanizing, specifically applied to women under the stern, watchful eye of men who think our misconceived masculinity has given us some divine right. So Katie Cannon is correct in pushing the point. How do womanist theologians in the United States employ "essential strategies . . . that will encourage an ethic of resistance?" How do they find, and teach to men, "an analysis that shows how Black women, underneath patriarchal teachings and relations of domination are complex, life-affirming moral agents?"[56]

Jesus, Mercy Oduyoye and Elizabeth Amoah claim, is our "ancestor," not Emmanuel Milingo's muscular, triumphalist male, but rather "the quintessence of a life of faith."[57] But by the end of their essay they offer an even deeper, much more intimate, entirely persuasive insight. And because it is said with such simple and utter beauty and power, I will quote them at length and let it stand:

> Jesus of Nazareth, by the counter-cultural relations he established with women, has become for us the Christ, the anointed one who liberates, the companion, friend, teacher, and the true 'Child of Women'—'Child of Women' truly because in Christ the fullness of all that we know of perfect womanhood is revealed.
>
> [Jesus] is the caring, compassionate nurturer of all. Jesus nurtures not just by parables but by miracles of feeding. With his own hands he cooked that others might eat; he was known

---

54. Edet, "Christianity and Women's Rituals," 35.
55. Edet, "Christianity and Women's Rituals," 37. My emphasis.
56. See Cannon, *Katie's Canon*, 120.
57. Oduyoye and Amoah, "Christ for African Women," 38.

in the breaking of the bread. Jesus is Christ—truly woman [human] yet truly divine, for only God is the truly Compassionate One.

Christ for us is the Jesus of Nazareth, the Servant who washed the disciples' feet . . . meeting the needs of humanity in obedience to the will of God even to the point of dying, that we might be freed from the fear of physical death . . .

The Christ for us is the Jesus of Nazareth who agreed to be God's 'Sacrificial Lamb,' thus teaching that true and living sacrifice is that which is freely and consciously made; and who pointed to the example of the widow who gave all she had in response to God's love. Christ is the Jesus of Nazareth who approved of the costly sacrifice of the woman with the expensive oil, who anointed him (king, priest, and prophet) in preparation for his burial, thereby approving all that is noble, lovely, loving, and motivated by love and gratitude.

Jesus of Nazareth, designated 'the Christ,' is the one who has broken down the barriers we have erected between God and us as well as among us. The Christ is the reconciler, calling us back to our true selves, to one another and to God, thereby saving us from isolation and alienation, which is the lack of community that is the real experience of death . . . It is this Christ who has become for us, for African women and for Africa, the Savior and liberator of the world.[58]

These are new dimensions to the struggle for justice and for promoting God's reign, the women say, "a dimension that is not ours, but given to us both by the voices of our people clamouring for justice and by God, who inspired and convoked us here. Humanity as a whole, not only women, stands to benefit from the whole endeavour."[59] It is in this endeavor that Black theology's Black Messiah must meet the Jesus that African women call "the Child of Women" and it can only happen if we, with the women, push against those walls of internalized patriarchy, and find with every encounter, within ourselves, the liberating power of "something there is that does not love a wall," and finding it, "want to break it down."

---

58. Oduyoye and Amoah, "Christ for African Women," 43–45.

59. From the "Final Document: Intercontinental Women's Conference," in Fabella and Oduyoye, *Passion and Compassion*, 189.

Chapter Seven

A BUCKET, A WELL, AND THE GENDERED POLITICS OF WATER

Black Theology, Jesus, and the Sister from Sychar

THE WORKINGS OF GENTRIFIED PATRIARCHY

IN THE WORLD OF American televangelism conquering the Global South at a bewildering pace over the last three decades or so, Bishop T. D. Jakes, founder of The Potter's House headquartered in Dallas, Texas, has become a world-class celebrity—a preacher, pastor, author, filmmaker, and CEO of a company worth over $400 million.[1] Probably the best-known American preacher in Africa and large parts of the Global South, he has had an influence no Black theologian could match. In South Africa, we became acquainted with Black theology in its early form through the work of Bishop Henry McNeal Turner of the African Methodist Episcopal Church, a preacher in the prophetic tradition of the Black church in America that took Black South Africans by storm in the late nineteenth century. As a prophetic Black theologian, it was said of him, "no one spoke more eloquently, more learnedly, more effectively, and enunciated more profoundly the eternal principles of human rights than did Henry McNeal Turner."[2] Turner's Black theology resonated strongly with us, and not just with the members of the

---

1. See McGee, *Brand° New Theology*, Introduction.
2. See Johnson, *Forgotten Prophet*, 2.

Ethiopian church who formed early alliances with the fiery bishop and the denomination he represented. It laid the foundation for our warm embrace of the modern expressions of Black liberation theology superbly and inimitably represented by James Hal Cone.

That Black church from America, with that kind of prophetic preaching and challenge to oppression, millions of Black South Africans hardly know any more. It is by no means obliterated,[3] but it has been almost overwhelmed by the television mastery, the magnetic oratory, and the theatrical entertainment phenomenon that is T. D. Jakes.[4] This "new Black church" has caught Black theology mostly off-guard.[5] When Barack Obama turned his back on Jeremiah A. Wright the prophetic preacher, throwing him to the ravaging wolves of the American media, and turned to and embraced T. D. Jakes, inviting him to deliver the sermon at his historic inauguration, Black theologians should have understood how fundamentally the tide has turned from the Black church as the guardian of the prophetic tradition to the Black church as the mouthpiece of a deified, neoliberal, capitalist, "post-racial" Christian nationalism. If we had understood better that turning away from Jeremiah Wright was turning away from prophetic faithfulness, prophetic truthfulness, and prophetic wakefulness, our response to the mutations of empire might have been different.

We would then perhaps not have been so quickly deceived by the *optics* of liberation clothed in political sentiment—by a black hand on Martin Luther King Jr.'s Bible, or the rendering of "Amazing Grace" while the *systems* of death continued to thrive, and the destruction of God's children around

---

3. Of course the brilliant legacy of James Cone will continue to be embraced and honored, inspiring a new generation on both sides of the Atlantic, and the prophetic tradition continues to find new life in the church and even in academia. Most important is the work of Dr. Jeremiah A. Wright, unmatched in his prophetic witness in the US today. See also, e.g., the sterling work of the Samuel De Witt Proctor Conference, a conference of theologians, clergy, and laity that is preserving and enacting the prophetic tradition of the Black church in America. See sdpconference.info. See also McMickle, *Where Have all the Prophets Gone?*, the consistent work of Dwight Hopkins, and the growing *ouvre* of womanist theologians in the US and feminist theologians in Africa.

4. See Walton, *Watch This!*; McGee, *Brand® New Theology*; see also Elna Boesak, *Channeling Justice?* As communication specialist and ethicist, Elna Boesak devotes much time to Jakes's style of communication with his audience, his body language, and his oratory to analyze the underlying ideology of his message—a hetero-patriarchal theology harmful to women and issues of gender justice.

5. In the foreword to McGee, *Brand® New Theology*, Lewis V. Baldwin writes that Jakes and preachers like him, have "millions of followers who are repeating and living out the God-talk of those popular preachers. The theologies of the New Black Church are popular *folk* theologies or *lived religion,* and more accessible and malleable than academic theologies." Emphasis original.

the world in the name of the American Empire went on without taking a breath. We would not have been so surprised that Obama took on as his most intimate coworkers the persons from the list supplied to him by Wall Street bankers, and even less surprised that when the time came to punish those same bankers for causing 10 million Americans to lose their homes, his administration would not prosecute a single one of them.[6] James Cone's prophetic insight from more than thirty years ago haunts us still: "We blacks must not be so naïve as to think that merely electing black public officials is going to affect significantly the lives of the black poor."[7] If Henry McNeal Turner preached the "eternal principles of human rights," T. D. Jakes's eternal principles are sacralized neoliberal capitalism, baptized consumerism, and a sanctified ideology of individualism.

For black Christian communities, T. D. Jakes, blessed by Oprah and Obama, comes to us as the foremost religious warrior of a seemingly unstoppable American ideological imperialism that has taken most of us, certainly in South Africa, by surprise. Elsewhere I wrote of the waves of Christian neo-fundamentalism washing over Africa and much of the Global South with its toxic neo-colonialist package deal of scriptural selectivity, presented as "biblical inerrancy," violent homophobia, patriarchal power, and anti-justice agenda. Its justification of war and violence in the name of Jesus, its religious exclusivism coupled with unbridled political ambition in its so-called dominion theology, and its prosperity gospel grounded in the embrace of and enslavement to capitalist consumerist ideology—these are all real and profoundly disturbing. In its neo-colonialist alliances with capitalist power and the global media, it represents an edge, perhaps in the sense of a precipice, and prophetic theology should be much more aware and much better prepared to take on the challenges posed here. It certainly is dragging Africa, its churches and its societies, to the edge of a disaster every bit as devastating as colonialism.[8]

But Bishop T. D. Jakes is not completely like most fundamentalist televangelists. In a time that gender-based violence has become a pandemic, T. D. Jakes is a different sound. He strenuously condemns physical violence against women. It is something to be appreciated, and certainly the women who follow Jakes, do. But we need a keen ear. Jakes talks about women's

---

6. According to an email from Citygroup executive Michael Froman, revealed by Wikileaks. See Dayden, "The Most Important WikiLeaks Revelation." All of the persons suggested by the Wall Street banker ended up in the most powerful positions and the inner circle of Barack Obama's administration. For the lack of prosecutorial commitment vis-à-vis the bankers, see Cassidy, "Why Didn't Eric Holder Go After the Bankers?"

7. Cone, *For My People*, 195.

8. For a fuller treatment of this matter, see A. Boesak, *Pharaohs*, ch. 7.

liberation, but it is a "liberation" not determined by a true liberation paradigm, but rather by what Elna Boesak calls a "hyper spiritualization" which does not only result "in over-simplified and inadequate interpretations of real-life challenges, but contributes to more pressure on those who are already marginalized and vulnerable."[9] Paula McGee holds that despite the phenomenal growth of this "new Black church" in general and the impact of T. D. Jakes in particular, this model of church, because it pretends to but does not fundamentally take women seriously, is not sustainable. She is right, because Jakes emphasizes women's uniqueness and their potential, but he does not offer them true empowerment to combat generational discrimination, stigmatization, exclusion, and marginalization: "Racism, capitalism, class materialism and hetero-patriarchy are never engaged as causes of inequalities and injustices."[10] And these are precisely the issues of systemic oppression that call out for urgent attention and action today, while the "new Black church" and its theologies are still running strong.

So Jakes's teaching and preaching is not true liberation preaching empowering women, even though he claims it is. It is rather what I would call a gentrified patriarchy. He places women on a pedestal, but affirms this position only in submission to men. Women may be on a pedestal, but men are indisputably on the throne. Recall that above we quoted Jakes on the submission of women: Women have to be submissive to men, but, he cautions men, "No woman wants to be submissive to a man who isn't in submission to God."[11] We again call attention to two things here: that about the submissiveness of women as an objective, natural reality and God-given demand, there is no question. But second, in Jakes's view, women, at least *godly* women, *want* to be submissive, *on condition* that their men are in submission to God. Only, submission to a patriarchal God can only bring results that serve patriarchy. That is not liberation, nor is it empowerment. It is active *dis*empowerment. It creates relationships that are not equal and just, nor healing and reconciling, but instead unjust, in fact toxic, strengthening masculinities contaminated by deep insecurities, harmful cultural traditions, and damaging religious conditioning, and thoroughly in need of challenge, correction, and change.

Jakes castigates men who physically abuse women, and rightly so, but seems oblivious to the verbal abuse he subjects them to in his sermons. He is famous for his "Woman Thou Art Loose" conferences in which women are meant to be empowered. But in actual fact he disempowers them, a point

---

9. E. Boesak, *Channeling Justice*, 199.
10. E. Boesak, *Channeling Justice*, 202.
11. See Success Staff Writer, "17 Powerful T. D. Jakes Quotes to Push You Forward."

eloquently made by Paula McGee.[12] It is a deceitful patriarchy, because it professes to take sides with women as long as the hierarchical patterns, which Jakes in subtle and not so subtle ways strenuously maintains throughout his discourses, remain undisturbed. It is deceitful, because it holds up to women the hope of power through "what is within you" without dealing with objective systems of gender oppression, exploitation, and disempowerment in society. Their "destiny" is spiritual, but it is also material success and fulfillment, disconnected from their community and from the struggles for justice and equality raging in their world, while Jakes' real world of imperialism, neoliberal capitalism, and hetero-patriarchal domination is not only never critiqued, but held up as the ideal. In Jakes's teachings, women can reach their "potential" without having strategies how to deal with male micro- and macro-aggression in its many manifestations in society at large, in the workplace, at home, or in the church. But as with all forms of gentrification, despite the pretense of gentility, there is a subtle but unmistakable and unavoidable element of coercion in his patriarchy.[13] His sermon on "The Waiting Jesus" (from John 4:1–42) is an excellent example of this.[14]

Jakes begins by emphasizing how "busy" Jesus was. He had three years to change the world and he had no time to waste on a woman. Jakes says this not to trivialize women, but to show how they were diminished in the societies of Jesus's day. He is indignant about those ancient societies that denigrated women. He recounts how in the Scriptures, even when the stories are about women, the author does not even bother to mention their names. The women know that he is right. He sets himself up as a champion of women: "It was a totally misogynistic society!" (Track 4@ 4:00) But this Jesus is willing to wait "on of all things, a woman." This highlights Jesus's uniqueness in a patriarchal society.

So, having established his gender-justice credentials, Jakes interprets this text in front of 83,000 women, and millions more on television. These credentials prove to be a thin veneer. It is about Jesus and the nameless woman from Sychar, but it is also about the women who are watching and listening. The language about God is consistently exclusive and sexist, and

12. McGee, *Brand® New Theology*, especially ch. 4.

13. One of the truly striking elements in Jakes's preaching to women is the insistent, emotional manipulation throughout the sermon, punctuated by long interludes of musical build-up and emotional outpourings from the audience directed by the preacher. See, for example, the sermon on "The Waiting Jesus," especially toward the end, the calculated build-up, the deliberate count-down, and the smashing of the vase as shattering climax.

14. I was able to access the audio CD version, preached at the WTAL conference in Atlanta, where a record-breaking 83,000 women attended and millions saw the DVD, published by T. D. Jakes Ministries, Dallas TX, 2012.

not just concerning the woman in the story. The women in the audience are targeted even as they are embraced. But this is what sexist preaching does, and what the worshiping of a male, patriarchal god aims to accomplish: it draws women into worship and into the sermon, *including* them in harmful, patriarchal language and imaging, while simultaneously *excluding* them from meaningful, dignified participation, making them not just victims, but complicit in their own exclusion and denigration. It exults in women's potential, but it denies women equality; it raves about women's destiny, as long as that destiny culminates in a place of submissiveness. It glorifies a certain kind of femininity, even while it stifles women's right to dignity and self-assertion. It is a deliberate process of alienation: from God, from the Scriptures, and from themselves. And it is all about power. On a par with the normalization and justification of slavery and apartheid from the Bible, it is the new idolatry that should be mercilessly exposed, just as apartheid was. It is the kind of theological criminality Black theology should join the women in vehemently resisting.[15]

The identification with Jakes's version of the woman at the well with the women in the audience comes quick, just as Jakes's identification of himself with Jesus is a staple throughout. Just as Jesus waits for her, he is waiting for these listening women: "To grow up, to mature, while we played by the wayside, while we went through foolish antics . . . while you were in a bar, in a hotel room with a man or some lesbian lover. . ." (5@003).

In the sermon, the woman from Sychar is an unintelligent, earthy, needy woman, and her needs are tinged with sexuality: "[Jesus] speaks to her at the level of her understanding, giving her what she is accustomed to, a man who needs her" (6@2:17). The sexual innuendo plays right through the sermon. "Here she comes, down to the well again, making another trip, making another trick . . ." (6@4:33). Jakes is intentional: a "trick" is what prostitutes sometimes call their male customers. So this woman is one of such loose morals that she comes to the well hoping that the man who just happens to be sitting there will be another "trick." Her "immorality" determines everything about her. "This is not her first time coming. She's come here over and over again" (6@4:46). She is caught in a cycle: "Another cycle of the same experiences she's had before. Retreading her own steps . . . Same

---

15. At the beginning of the conference, Bishop Jakes welcomes the women in the audience, as well as "my daughters in the rest of America, in Africa, in Asia . . ." So the tone is set: here is the father, welcoming all "his daughters." Despite the title of the conference and the slogans about "women," all these women are not really women, they are all Jakes's "daughters," his "children." He is their father, and he will instruct them on the way to live their lives since they, as children, have no mind of their own. Once the women accept this framework, there is no escape.

thing, different day ... Same thing, different man ..." (7@1:48). The sexual references become more pointed: the woman is in a "cycle within a cycle ... Her life is a cycle ... Every month she goes through the same thing ... (7@1:48, 49). Until "she meets a man who breaks the cycle. That's what pregnancy does. It breaks the cycle" (7@2:46). Then he "brings it home": "The planting of a seed breaks the cycle—I pray that before you leave one of these sperm cells hits your womb and breaks the cycle" (7@3:05).

It is only a man who can break this cycle and "impregnate" her life with meaning. She is not only needy, unreflective, and entirely incapable of independent thinking. She is an empty vessel, "as empty as the water pot she is carrying." She is "a cavern, unfulfilled, a space, a void. She is a space carrying a space ... a void carrying a void ... She is an emptiness carrying an emptiness ... the pot in her hand is a picture of her life ..." (9@0:50, 51).

At this point in the sermon there is a significant shift in the language and the tone. The "busy Jesus" becomes "the wrestling Jesus." "He wrestles with this foolish woman who is filled with falsehoods, and has the audacity to be argumentative, standing in the face of the truth" (9@3:57, 58). On Jesus's request, "Give me something to drink," she answers, "You have nothing to draw with." Jakes comments, "She thinks she is smart" (10@2:18). Jesus's patience has now run out. He is angry. It is no longer a conversation, "This is a fight." The language of the violence of verbal abuse takes over, and the woman is the target. In this scene at Jacob's well, the preacher reminds the audience of the fight Jacob had with the angel. "The fight with the angel was physical" says Jakes, because Jacob was a man, and "when men fight it is physical. But because Jesus is after a woman, he fights her in her language" (10@2:44). Now the border is crossed. It is a fight. However, it is permissible as long as it is verbal, and Jesus himself sets the example. Because Jesus is the *Man*. Jakes explains how "women fight verbally, even when we knock you down." In the context of that point in the sermon, it is meant as a compliment, and the women agree: the shouts abound (10@2:45). The violent confrontation continues, and because Jakes's identification of Jesus with his own person is so explicit, it is not Jakes, but Jesus who becomes the aggressor, giving men permission to be so without compunction, and conditioning women into acceptance of this. The Jesus at the well is one brimming over with an aggressive virility—the kind that "real" men possess. It is far beyond the danger point, but because Jesus sets the example, the aggression is sanctified.

The woman says, "You Jews have no dealings with Samaritans." Jakes remarks, "Her racial ideology is all messed up" (11@00:37). Jakes now turns the woman into a racist. She is "in a state of denial" (11@00:38) even though historical truth is that it is the Jews who were the racial transgressors *vis-à-vis* the Samaritans.[16] *She* was the one more under racialist pressure rather than Jesus the Galilean. *She*, not Jesus, was the one suffering under *gendered* racialized politics. Jakes draws, as he often does, a direct line between him and Jesus, acting out Jesus's imagined actions. "[As a man] I can relate to Jesus . . ." Jesus "gets tired of this" and becomes even more violent. "While she is chewing out her ideas about culture . . . Jesus goes straight for the jugular . . ." (11@2:54). "Going for the jugular" is the question: "Where is your husband?" This pinpoints the constant allusions to her immorality, the real reason why this confrontation is taking place. There is a smugness in the tone now. This is the "killer question." Finally Jesus has shut her up in her escapist talk "about religion." She is in a corner. When she answers, "I have none," Jesus snaps back, "And the one you have now ain't yours" (12@02:00). And this is the crux of the matter. Again she tries to "escape": her reference to Mount Gerizim as place of worship for the Samaritans means she "runs to religion" with her empty, confused, lonely self. "And Jesus is really sick of it now" (12@02:02). And that's why Jesus "goes straight for the jugular . . ."

One can summarize Jakes's characterization of the woman from Sychar as one of ascending abuse, though we have to keep in mind that in Jakes's reenactment of the scene, it becomes not Jakes's but Jesus's judgment. Denigration: (she is unable to think for herself); diminishment: (she is utterly empty-headed, "foolish"); disdain: (she is full of falsehoods); condescension: (she has the "audacity" to argue with Jesus, thinking "she is smart"); revilement: ("She comes down to the well every day . . . same thing, different man . . ."); stigmatization: (she is a woman of low morals, a whore looking for sex anywhere she can find it); victimization: (she is caught in a cycle—"the same thing every month"—as if her menstrual cycles are somehow her fault, or even worse, a flaw in her character); dehumanization: (she is "empty" in mind and in soul.) In T. D. Jakes's reading, this woman is totally unworthy.

Such are the workings of gentrified patriarchy. The sermon is an incredible performance. It is immensely entertaining. It clearly mesmerizes the women because they seem to be on their feet much of the time. Jakes has to urge them to sit down. They believe Bishop Jakes is on their side in their uneven fight against a relentlessly patriarchal world. But it is doubtful

---

16. I find the quote from Joachim Jeremias worth repeating here in which he addresses this very issue. Part IV of his work deals with the "maintenance of racial purity" in ancient Israel. The hierarchy goes as follows: "Israelites of pure ancestry; despised trades and Jewish slaves; Illegitimate Israelites; Israelites with 'slight blemish', (proselytes, freed gentile slaves); Israelites with 'grave blemish'—bastards, Temple slaves, fatherless foundlings, eunuchs, (this whole category described as 'the excrement of the community'); gentile slaves . . ." Last on the list and at the bottom, "[and] *Samaritans.*" Jeremias, *Jerusalem in the Time of Jesus*, 337, emphasis mine.

whether this sermon has done anything to genuinely empower women in their struggle against patriarchy, generational exploitation, and abuse. They are being offered a gentrified patriarchy, an illusion of equality, a simulacra of independence and freedom. Jakes offers a patriarchy which is not just comforting, but *salvific* for women, without which they are incomplete, which proffers that unless they are "impregnated" they will remain "empty" in their heads, as well as in their lives. It is a disturbing example of the imperialist colonization of the mind we spoke of in chapter 5.

It is clear also that that salvation can come only through a man. The sexual language, the allusions to menstrual cycles that can only be broken by pregnancy, and the salvific power of being impregnated through the words spoken by a man, are pointed and calculated transgressions of the boundaries of intimacy. At the end of the sermon, in an astounding moment of high drama that goes on and on, Jakes does a countdown and smashes a vase on the floor, symbolizing the "smashing" of the empty past. But is he "smashing patriarchy," as the slogan of the women's movement goes? I do not see it.

I have spent this much time on Bishop Jakes and this sermon not only because this pericope forms the subject of our reflections in this chapter, but also because this is what millions of women and men, young girls and boys hear when they tune in on one of the 43 religious channels in South Africa alone—I am not even speaking of the rest of Africa—and this is what thousands of pastors aspire to when they emulate Bishop Jakes in their churches at least three times a week and in their week-long "believers conferences." This is what African societies are grappling with when African women demand justice and equality. In South Africa, this is what we face when the "spiritual battle" is waged against "the forces of evil" in the South African Constitution which seeks to protect the rights of women, children, and LGBTQI+ persons. The background of our reflections in this chapter is not the all too abundant physical abuse women suffer, which in the age of Trump and Vladimir Putin seems to be more openly shameless, and more shamelessly protected, than ever before.[17] That struggle too must continue. But our vigilance must begin with the creation of a climate which condones, cultivates, and pampers a normalized patriarchy and makes space for the normalization of physical gender-based violence. That is the struggle against the gentrified patriarchy of someone like Bishop T. D. Jakes and the multitudes of men who follow him.

---

17. See the new law passed by the Duma in Russia regarding domestic violence, "Russia, Decriminalization of Domestic Violence." https://www.loc.gov/law/help/domestic-violence/russia.php.

In the week I am writing this, someone sent me this prayer circulating on social media in South Africa. It is much longer, but this portion speaks for itself:

> Take me back to the old paths
> When Moms were at home
> Dads were at work
> Brothers went to the army
> And sisters got married BEFORE having children
> Moms could cook, Dads would work
> Children would behave
> Husbands were loving, wives were supportive
> Women wore the dresses, men wore the trousers
> Women behaved like ladies and men were gentlemen . . .

This is what a popularized gentrified patriarchy looks like, and on this point, Black theology of liberation is severely challenged.

This chapter is an effort to read and interpret the story of Jesus and the sister of Sichar at the well differently.

"THE ONE WHO COMES FROM ABOVE . . ."

John offers the reader an intriguing opening to this all-important chapter. Jesus hears disturbing rumors of animosity from some Pharisees—they are angry that he is making and baptizing more disciples than John (4:1, 2). In chapter 1, the hostility towards John comes from "priests" and "Levites" representing the temple. The hostility toward Jesus in chapter 4 comes from the Pharisees, part of the intellectual elite. The consolidation of the onslaught from the powerful and privileged establishment in Jerusalem against this new movement has begun. For the moment it is on two fronts, but after the Baptist's death, the focus will be on Jesus alone. Their concerns about Jesus's growing following is not because they are protective of the Baptist and his ministry—"John, of course, had not *yet* been thrown into prison," the author reminds us (3:24), though that is already the plan—but because they are perturbed that the prophetic work John had started seems to be taken over by Jesus and that Jesus's support amongst the "little people" is growing.

Not only was John baptizing and "the people kept coming" (3:23) now Jesus was "making more disciples" than even John. Clearly matters were getting out of hand. The fact that John goes to the trouble to explain that it was in fact not Jesus, but his disciples who were baptizing people (4:2) shows that the powerful were in no mood for technicalities: the plan was in place, it is Jesus they want, and it is Jesus they will get, no matter what. Such a seemingly innocuous aside opens a world of malicious intent. The empire is at work and John is intent on exposing it. As was the case with the Canaanite woman in Matthew, Jesus withdraws from the conflict—the time for that final confrontation was not yet—leaves Judea, and returns to Galilee.[18]

The confrontations with the established order take place very early in John's Gospel. They not only set the scene for what is coming, they open the curtain on the nature of Jesus's ministry. In chapter 1 (vv. 26–34), John the Baptist, in intense argument with the priests and Levites sent from Jerusalem, points to Jesus as the one chosen by God. It does not matter who I am, he says, what matters is who Jesus is. It is not about me, or Elijah—that is all distraction—it is about another one. That one is "among you"—his presence is not hidden, and it will not be suppressed. He is "coming after me"—he will not only continue this work, he will raise it to deeper intensity and greater heights; for "he ranks ahead of me"—his authority, his power, will be greater than mine. I, even though I stir the hearts of the people and cause discomfort and anger in the hearts of the powerful, am "not worthy to untie the thong of his sandal." Whatever I do, what he will do will be greater, more radical, more powerful.

"There is the Lamb of God who takes away the sin of the world." John says this twice, on two separate occasions. For years, following traditional exegesis, I took this in a "spiritual" sense and preached it as if it were a "revival" text. I now think he refers to "the world" John spoke of in 3:16. You, the religious elites with your power of naming and framing, have declared the world—outside of your borders of sanctity, control, and manipulation—unholy, defiled, filled with sinners: the poor and the downtrodden; the oppressed and the weak; the sick, the lame and the blind; the ones made landless, voiceless, and hopeless through your greed and exploitation. You created a world filled with those you detest and look down upon: tax collectors, prostitutes, fatherless and abandoned children, marginalized women without patriarchal protection, married women useful for childbearing and for serving men but unworthy of dignity and respect; that world of Galileans who "lived in darkness" and whence could come nothing good, and Samaritans, "bleeders from birth" whom you despise;[19] the world of

---

18. Bultmann, *Gospel of John*, 176, states that Jesus withdrew to "a place of safety." It is telling that Judea would be considered so hostile that Samaria, where violent clashes between Jews and Samaritans were not unknown, should also be counted as a "place of safety" for Jesus.

19. "The daughters of Samaria are deemed unclean, in perpetual menstrual condition 'from their cradle'" (in Niddah 4:1; see Tolbert, *Reading John*, 112).

deplorables and expendables.[20] *That* world "this One" is coming to save, for he understands the heart of God (3:16), and he is "the Lamb of God." He will "take away" that which you have declared their "sin," making the victims of your exclusivist lust for power and control responsible for the plight you have caused, their stigmatization and their pain, for the guilt they feel because they do not meet your criteria for acceptability. He will be the savior of "whosoever" believes in him. The radical inclusivity of God's embrace reflects the radical inclusivity of God's radical liberation. The echoes of Miriam will not go away.

This is the announcement of a revolution, and all of this will be seen because he "will be revealed to Israel." His purposes will be clear, unequivocal, and revolutionary, and the people will recognize it as such. They will see what God really has in mind for Israel, and it will not be what is on the agenda of the rich, the powerful, and the privileged. Whatever powers you think I have, his will be greater, for he will be baptized by the Holy Spirit who will "descend on him like a dove," and "remain on him," and he himself will baptize "with the Holy Spirit." Twice John says, "I myself did not know him," but be assured that he who is among you already will be known by all—the great and the small, the rich and the poor, the oppressed and their oppressors, for "this is the Son of God." And because this is of God, and Jesus is the Son of God, there is no power on earth that can buy him, deny him, or defy him. What happens here is quite remarkable: in 1:29–35 John the author allows John the Baptist to bring the lofty words of chapter 1:1–18 down to earth, so that ordinary folk can understand. This is what it means when "the Word becomes flesh." John the Baptist "breaks it down" and "makes it real."

Matthew tells the story of Jesus's birth and the killing of the innocents to show the vast contrast between two kings: King Herod, the appointed collaborator of the Romans, and Jesus the true "king of the Jews." The one will be a true shepherd of God's people, the other a murderer of children. It is "a tale of two kings."[21] It is also the contrast between two reigns: a reign of terror, oppression, exclusion, and dehumanization, and a reign of justice, peace, inclusion, joy, and human dignity. Luke's birth narrative, set

---

20. See van Aarde, "Jesus's Affection Toward Children," 135: "From the perspective of the 'politics of holiness' 'unclean' and 'imperfect' people were the 'sinners' who were under the influence of demons. It is with reference to this that Matthew refers to some of the Galileans as those living 'in the land of the shadow of death.'" Van Aarde quotes Saldarini: "They were some of the expendable class—about 5–10%—for whom society had no place or need. They had been forced off the land because of population pressures or they did not fit into society. They tended to be landless and itinerant with no normal family life and a high death rate"(see Saldarini, *Pharisees, Scribes, and Sadducees*, 44).

21. See van Aarde, "Jesus' Affection Toward Children."

deliberately within the context of the reign of the occupying power, shows the difference the coming of Jesus makes to the lives of the "little people": the poor, the downtrodden, and the despised; Mary and the shepherds, Elizabeth and Zachariah, Simeon and Anna in the temple. The world is ruled by the Roman Empire with its wealth, its military might, its Caesar, and his collaborationists everywhere. Jesus, announcing the reign of the God of liberation, justice and peace, is pitted against these powers and principalities and all they represent. The poor and the angels join in joyous celebration of the coming victory.

John, foregoing the birth narratives, makes precisely that same point by placing Jesus in Cana of Galilee at the beginning of his Gospel. This is Galilee. An ordinary couple from the *am ha'aretz*, celebrating their wedding with their friends.[22] Like in many of our African communities today, no one can really be excluded. The "invitation only" is a (sometimes meaningless) bow to Western culturalism. Here, everyone is welcome. The "everyone" from 3:16 is come down to earth: narrowed down to "everyone" in the village.[23] The inclusivity is taken for granted. Unlike the feasts of the rich where the food is always plentiful and the wine always flows, at this wedding, in a community where a wedding is a village affair and one cannot cater for everyone who comes to celebrate with you, the wine ran out.

---

22. This is the "Galilee of the Gentiles, multilingual, inhabited by pagans and Israelites, many of mixed marriage heritages upon whom the Judeans looked down. These were impoverished people who tried to live according to ancestral traditions; peasants who survived on small pieces of land, landless tenant farmers who worked for absentee landlords in the cities, incurring large debts, while some were forced off their land and turned to carpentry." This is the land where bandits, outcasts, and rebels escaped to the mountains and found shelter in caves. This is the land where people "lived in darkness." This is "where Jesus is to be found." See van Aarde, *Fatherless*, 76. See also Horsley, *Galilee*. Some (see among others Thompson, *John*, 60) suggest that because there is talk of "servants" and a "steward" this signifies wealth. Craig S. Keener suggests they were "free caterers or relatives," *Gospel of John*, 515. Moreover, John deliberately uses the word *diakonoi*, which in the New Testament is more closely associated with service to God in the church; the ones caring for the vulnerable: the poor, the sick, those in prison for their faith, the widows and orphans in the community. The connotation is more to voluntary service out of love than serving a master out of obligation, enslavement, and fear. Consequently, friends of the family who offered their services for this special day as a labor of love and friendship taking the role of "servants" in this context would not be unusual at all. The principle of reciprocity would be at work here (see Keener, *Gospel of John*, 499ff.) and taking this into account it would mean that not many of their friends would have been in a position to bring gifts of wine, in any case not enough to prevent the wine from running out.

23. See also Malina and Rohrbaugh, *Social-Science Commentary*, 70: "A wedding would often include a whole village . . . everyone in the village participated." Neighbors would weigh in heavily with help.

There was no cellar with enough reserves for the overflow of guests. Jesus turns water into wine, and the point, in my view, is not only the miracle, (the Gospel hardly spends time on the miracle itself) even though this was a sign of Jesus's "glory."

More to the point is his presence at the feast of the poor, sharing with them his gifts and his power and his blessings. Running out of wine, which is essential to the joy of the festivities, is a disaster, and the groom and bride's honor was at stake. *Them*, he will not disappoint. For *them*, he will turn water into wine, so the feast can go on. Why should a lack of resources despoil their celebration of this very special day? Why should an uninterrupted, joyful, plentiful feast be the exclusive privilege of the rich? At the much-publicized royal wedding as I write, with its $40m budget,[24] there was no danger of Harry and Meghan running out of wine, or food, or worldwide attention. So the turning of water into wine is once again, like the multiplication of bread for the multitudes, as we have seen in the previous chapter, a sign of the abundance of God's reign, and a scathing critique of the skewed socio-economic realities which are reflected even on this level. This Messiah whom Simon and Andrew had found was to be like none other.

This is followed by the "cleansing of the Temple" with an outraged Jesus "making" the whip himself, driving all the animals out; then turning to the people doing business there, "pouring out," scattering, the money of the money changers onto the floor before overturning their tables.[25] This early, John establishes Jesus's solidarity with the poor and downtrodden; this early does he reveal the revolutionary nature of Jesus's mission.

Then, just to make sure his community understands, John, before he introduces Jesus (the one who comes from above), to the sister who comes from Sychar, makes the point plain: "The one who comes from above is above all" (3:31)—that is, above all earthly power or authority, above all principalities and claims to hegemony. "The one who is of the earth"—the Caesar, with his underlings, his minions, and his collaborators in Judea—"belongs to the earth and speaks about earthly things." He boasts about his wealth, his military might, his ability to do anything with impunity, and his capability to bring "fire and fury" to the earth "like no one has ever seen," because he has "power" on earth. That is his "greatness." But, John says, those are all earthly things; they will not last long, and that entitlement is only temporary. "The one who comes from heaven is above all" (3:31). Those who resist him, deny him, defy him, despite their claims to power

---

24. See Duncan, "How Much Did the Royal Wedding Cost?"

25. For a discussion on whether this was merely a "temper tantrum" as some hold, or a genuine act of revolutionary fury, see Boesak, *Pharaohs*, 99–102.

over life and death, "will not see life." Instead, they "must endure the wrath of God" (3:36). They may be in power now, but their fate is sealed. The empire will fall. John makes this point several times (3:35; 5:27; 13:3; 17:2). In Jesus's confrontation with Pilate, most direct representative of the Roman Empire, John drives it home: "You would have no power over me unless it were given you from above" (19:11). The message to the empire is clear.[26] This is the context we should keep in mind when we read the story of the happenings at the well. John tells us that Jesus, after hearing the rumors, left Judea to return to Galilee. Then John adds, "But he had to go through Samaria" (v. 4).

Of course Jesus did not *have* to go through Samaria. The shortest route to Galilee from Judea did go through Samaria, and many did travel that way.[27] But there was no "must" about it. Any faithful Jew who holds holy the apartheid laws, customs, and traditions Jews held against Samaritans would not shun the longer route for the convenience of a shorter trip. This is more than just a travel announcement. New Testament scholar Craig S. Keener speaks of "holy geography": "God was sending him to Samaria to seek some people who worship him in Spirit and in truth."[28]

But what Jesus has in mind is not just a quicker route: Samaria is not just on the way to Galilee, it is on the way to the fulfillment of his mission, the bringing of the message of the reign of God which will challenge the rule of the emperor in Rome, the empire itself, and its minions in the world, including Judea, Galilee, and Samaria. What Jesus has in mind is not a geographical map of Judea, Samaria, and Galilee; but the strategic map of God's ongoing revolution, at the heart of which was *all* the oppressed, for in John's mind the great love of God for "the world" was defined by its inclusiveness. In Matthew we hear Jesus explicitly instruct the disciples to not go to Samaria (Matt 10:5). In Luke, the Samaritans are an incidental reference, a foil to make a subtle point in an effort to teach about gratitude (17:11–19) and neighborliness, generosity, forgiveness, and what I elsewhere called "combative, revolutionary love"[29] (Luke 10:25–37). There, it

---

26. Warren Carter argues that Jesus's utterances in the Gospel of John, such as overcoming the ruler of this world and who would be driven out (12:31), who has no power over Jesus (14:30), and has been condemned (16:11), are actually anti-imperial texts. "Though often interpreted as the devil these references actually foreshadow the appearance of Pilate, agent of Roman power" (Carter, *John and Empire*, 290).

27. Josephus, *Vita* 52. See Bultmann who thinks Jesus went that way because it was the quickest route (*Gospel of John*, 176). Callahan agrees with him (*A Love Supreme*, 62). See also Schnackenburg, *Gospel According to St. John*, 422, but he sees an "urgency" in Jesus's choice for the route through Samaria.

28. Keener, *Gospel of John*, 590.

29. See A. Boesak, *Kairos, Crisis, and Global Apartheid*, ch. 7, 169–97.

is about shaming "the children of Israel" with the exemplary behavior of people they despised. Here there is no such subtlety, no time for a "teaching moment." For this Gospel's author, Samaria was not to be excluded from the program of radical transformation Jesus has set in motion. That Jesus "had" to go through Samaria was not because it was the shortest route. It was also more than "holy geography." It was because Samaria was on God's revolutionary map. It was the "next step" Jesus *had* to take. The revolutionary from Galilee is also the revolutionary in Samaria. The One from the margins will not exclude the marginalized from Samaria.

"YOU HAVE NO BUCKET . . ."

The response from the woman from Sychar to the request of Jesus for a drink of water encapsulates the gendered politics of water playing out at the well of Jacob as we read this story, and the sister from Sychar and Jesus from Galilee wrestle with it until it becomes a story of the politics of the reign of God, a politics of dignity, justice, and liberation.

The disciples have left for town to buy food, a casual announcement that signifies a major break with rules and custom. Jesus is alone with the woman who comes to draw water from the well. Much is made of the fact that she comes alone, and at noon, the hottest and most uncomfortable hour of the day. She does this, is the long traditional understanding, because she was an "immoral person." T. D. Jakes is not by any means alone in this depiction of her. He is following the vast majority of commentators on this point, especially male interpreters.[30] Meye Thompson is right: Even though Jesus

---

30. See, e.g., the recent, very detailed commentary of Craig Keener, *Gospel of John*, who in the first sentence of the section which covers John 4:1–42 introduces her as a "sinful woman" (584). The fact that she came alone "would underline the likelihood that she was not welcome among the other women . . ." Even though Keener concedes that "it is not clear that she had been committing adultery . . . five husbands had found some grounds to divorce her and she was living with a man to whom she was not married" (595). For Keener, it seems that the "findings" of the husbands are proof enough to condemn her. Malina and Rohrbaugh suggest that she was "socially deviant," whatever *that* may mean; see *Social-Science Commentary*, 98. Rudolf Bultmann is terse but vivid in his judgment: "The woman reels from desire to pleasure" (*Gospel of John*, 188). When I first wrote about this story, even though in my reading this woman emerged as a strong, independent, bold woman who engaged Jesus at a level hardly seen in the Gospels, I too made her "sinfulness" my point of departure. See A. Boesak, *Die Vlug van Gods Verbeelding*, 111–34. As will become clear in this chapter, my views on this point have changed radically.

says nothing further about her "marital status," she remarks, "interpreters have rushed in to fill the void."[31]

More subtle than Jakes but just as scathing, Craig Keener writes, "She might have supposed that Jesus, noting that she had come to the well alone hence was probably morally disreputable to begin with, wanted something else."[32] This reading stigmatizes the woman as effectively, since it presupposes that what was on her mind was "sinful," but projected upon Jesus. The possibility that what was on her mind might have been normal hospitality or generosity—there is no sign that she actually refuses Jesus the drink of water—does not even enter the discussion. Others offer a generalized observation:

> The woman is also symbol for women in general. Here she takes on several stereotypical personas: woman as householder (the one who collects water at the well); woman as wife, and fallen woman (she is not even married to the man with whom she lives) . . . Jesus, with the insight of Divine Word, identifies her as a 'fallen woman' yet he does not dwell on that point, relishing her sin.[33]

One might at first think this is an attack on the stereotyping of women. However, the last sentence negates that first impression. Instead of destroying the stereotype, Jesus confirms it. The gentrified patriarchy remains. In my view, however, the conversation reveals something entirely different. This woman may be "unorthodox"[34] but hers is a liberating unorthodoxy, for her and for Jesus. If it is remarkable that Jesus is breaking social, religious, and cultural boundaries, it is even more remarkable that she does it as well. Seeing the pitfalls of the politics of race, gender, and religion in this situation, a more timid person would have withdrawn from the conversation or at the very least ignored the request from the man who is asking her for water, going on her way without running the risks of engagement. But this woman is far from timid. It is a hermeneutical travesty that her boldness is universally interpreted as lustfulness. With keen awareness of the dynamics at play here, she engages Jesus with a directness that is startling.

She does not refuse Jesus the water, but she raises a fundamental question: "How is it that you, a Jew, ask of me, a woman of Samaria?" (v. 9). She stresses all the critical points: "you, a Jew," "me, a woman of Samaria." She calls him a *Judean*. "Nowhere does Jesus so refer to himself," observes Black

---

31. Thompson, *John*, 103.
32. Keener, *Gospel of John*, 598.
33. Smith and Williams, *Storyteller's Companion*, 60.
34. Keener, *Gospel of John*, 584ff.

liberation theologian Allen Dwight Callahan, "and nowhere does anyone so refer to Jesus. Later in the story Judeans in Jerusalem will be emphatic that Jesus is a Galilean and not one of them."[35] Jesus knows that he is not one of them, but the woman does not. For her, every Jew she meets is a "Judean," an imminent danger, and she puts Jesus on notice that she knows the repercussions of that very hostile relationship, and that she knows to be cautious. Her response is not "arrogant" as Francis J. Maloney supposes.[36] She, a *woman*, and a *Samaritan*, cannot afford the luxury of being careless, entering into an encounter filled with risk, and the consequences of which will be far worse for her than for the man sitting at the well. She does not have the luxury to make subtle distinctions between those whose hatred and racial superiority as a group have been at the cost of her history, dignity, and her very existence. If it is a mistake, it is one she makes out of cautious realism. It is a righteous suspicion that guides her. But she and Jesus both know it is a suspicion justified by centuries of discrimination and revilement.[37] She and Jesus both know that he would have been taught the words of Rabbi Eliezer, "He that eats the bread of the Samaritans is like the one who eats the flesh of swine."[38] She and Jesus both know that it was taught that Samaritan women are deemed unclean, as menstruants from their cradle.[39]

The point here is that she does not turn away and abandon the conversation. She leaves it to Jesus to prove her wrong. The burden of proof that he is not a "Judean" consumed with hatred, bigotry, and patriarchy is on him.

35. See Callahan, *A Love Supreme*, 64.

36. See Maloney, *Gospel of John*, 115.

37. The hostility between Jews and Samaritans goes back to the time of the Judges. After the division of Solomon's kingdom, Samaria became the capital of the rebel northern kingdom. Samaria was destroyed by the Assyrians in 722, was repopulated, and became half Israelite and half pagan. Upon their return from exile, the Jews rebuilt the temple but refused to let the Samaritans collaborate in the rebuilding on the score that the Samaritans were a "mongrel race" tainted by pagan blood. The Samaritans' temple, built on Mount Gerizim, was destroyed by the Maccabean king John Hyrcanus. In the course of time the rabbis came to declare all Samaritans as "unclean"—i.e., as people whom Jews could not associate with, come into contact with, or share drinking vessels with, without becoming unclean themselves. See Ellis, *Genius of John*, 69; Callahan, *A Love Supreme*, 62–64, who writes, "The road from Jerusalem in the south to Samaria in the north runs between Mount Ebal to the north and Mount Gerizim to the south. Long history had made of that valley an abysmal chasm . . . History is necessary to understand this passage."

38. In Shebiith 8:10. For a detailed discussion on the history of animosity between Jews and Samaritans see Callahan, *A Love Supreme*, 64ff.; Keener, *Gospel of John*, 598–601 and the references there.

39. In Niddah 4:1. For both references, see Tolbert, *Reading John*, 111. See also Malina and Rohrbaugh, *Social-Science Commentary*, 99: "Everything a menstruating woman lies upon or sits upon is unclean—so is everyone who touches these items."

And Jesus does that, not by defending himself, but by drawing her further into a conversation that establishes without doubt that he engages her as an equal. If he had heard those disparaging characterizations of Samaritans, he has discarded them as worthless. It is a highly improper conversation to have with a woman: about "the gift of God" and true worship of God in "Spirit and in truth"; about "living water" and "eternal life." Jesus proves that by not withdrawing his request for water, not retreating into the safe grounds of age-old prejudices that would reaffirm his superiority—after all, they are alone; what does he have to lose? What did her opinions matter? Clearly, they mattered a lot. Jesus stays, and talks, because for him this woman is not a "foolish, empty-headed vessel." She is a partner in a conversation that will uncover the depths of the meaning of the revolution God is unleashing through the One "who is from above." But that is the one sitting by the well, talking with her. Jesus is unmasking the pettiness, the unworthiness of the traditions of prejudice, superiority, patriarchy, and bigotry by not even responding to explain why they are wrong. That is almost always the moment of painful but truthful revelation. An unconverted racist trying to explain why a patently racist remark or action is not "really" racist. Somewhat like a man defending, or as the women say, "mansplaining," why a clearly sexist act is not really sexist. These are always "jokes," "just" a remark, always "innocent," not really meant to hurt or demean. The burden is always placed on the intended target who either has no sense of humor or is not broadminded enough to participate in well-meaning conversations. Jesus sees no sense in this kind of demeaning obfuscation. There is a sense of urgency to this conversation—perhaps Jesus has to talk to her before the disciples return. He cannot waste time on things that ultimately do not matter.

So Jesus tries to draw her out of that centuries-deep well of mutual distrust and fear: "If you knew the gift of God, and who it is that is saying to you . . ." He is not the "Judean" she thought he was. He is "the gift of God" who is able to give her "living water." This is a huge paradigm shift in the conversation, and Jesus will keep on doing that, drawing her in deeper, raising the level of their engagement, fully expecting her to go there with him. It speaks of Jesus's great respect for her ability to grasp the mysteries he is unfolding. At first, she is hesitant. Her response remains sober and she answers with a statement. "Sir, you have no bucket . . ." Can it be that Jesus is offering her the kind of dignity and companionship she has not yet seen from a "Judean"? And is this unexpected humility to be trusted? The ground is shifting and she has to tread warily. Is this a step toward reconciliation? But as South Africans are discovering at great cost, reconciliation is never easy, never cheap, always costly.⁴⁰ Oppressed people know that only too well, hence the necessity of a "hermeneutic of suspicion." It is as appropriate as it is wise. Is he really serious about sharing the bucket of a Samaritan, understanding the gendered politics of water at play here?

So, far from misunderstanding him as conventional exegesis holds, she understands him only too well, and responds with the seriousness the situation demands. She goes with him into this new language he is teaching her and completes her sentence: "... and the well is deep." She does not mean the act of reaching the water with a bucket, she means *what the well represents*, is deep. She is talking about traditions and a set of beliefs that have deep roots. Against the disdainful attitude of the Jews about her religion—it is pagan, or idolatry, or at the very least gentile—that well of knowledge and belief fed her people, protected them, gave them dignity. Discarded as a people, that precious connection to "our ancestor Jacob" assured her that they were indeed a people.⁴¹ Forever told that her religion is a mongrelized religion, as despicably "half-breed" as she herself is, that well has slaked her thirst for love and acceptance. The Samaritans have never rebuilt the temple on Mount Gerizim after its destruction by the Hasmonean king, John Hyrcanus. The ruins, clearly visible from the well where they are talking, remain the unhealed wound in Samaritan souls. In its place, the well of Jacob became the holder of their faith, the place of succor and hope. That well was their living water. Is she now to give that up, in this one visit with this man? Hence her two questions: "Where do you get that living water?" and, "Are you greater than our ancestor Jacob?"

The two questions serve the same purpose. This well provided water for living as well as the water for living a dignified life. Where do *you* get your living water? The second question takes the issue deeper. Is what you are offering me greater, better, more life-giving than the traditions I have come to love and draw strength and meaning from? Does your living water offer me something I do not now have—the empowerment to face this world as a woman? The ability to not just survive in a hostile world, but to live a liberated life? The right not just to be tolerated as a Samaritan, but to live with the freedom of a child of God? Will it guarantee me the right to justice, peace, and dignity? Will it restore my humanity in the eyes of those who despise me? "Sir, [*kurie*, Lord] give me this water, that I may never be thirsty or have to keep coming here to draw water" (v. 15).

40. See Boesak and DeYoung, *Radical Reconciliation*; and Boesak, *Pharaohs*, chs. 4, 5, 6.

41. See Callahan, *A Love Supreme*, 62: "The ubiquitous Jacob of the patriarchal narratives was the eponymous ancestor of all Israel, as father of the twelve eponymous ancestors of the twelve tribes."

These questions do not display foolishness, empty-headedness, or unwillingness to understand what Jesus is trying to say. I find such a view unbearably paternalistic. These are the questions neo-colonized people, *all* oppressed people, whether they live in the belly or in the shadow of empire, are duty-bound to ask: is what Jesus offers—not the colonizing, ideologized Jesus of Western imperialistic powers bent on subjugation and domination, but the liberating, liberated Jesus at the well—"greater" than the traditions we were told guarantee us life? Here, African feminist scholar Teresa Okura raises an issue critical for this discussion. The woman's reply in vv. 11–12 is, in effect, a defense of ancestral water. As far as she is concerned no water can be better than that of Jacob's well. "This is not just any well, but one that is renowned for its antiquity and whose usage goes back to the founding father himself . . ." Despite the centuries of use, the well has neither dried up nor become exhausted. This, in addition to its revered ancestry has given the well a character which is almost eternal. Okura poses the fundamental question I am trying to raise here: "Can Jesus, then, possibly produce anything better?"[42]

This is exactly the point I am trying to draw attention to. In my first major work, I argued that doing Black theology must mean a search for a totally new social order, "and in this search it will have to drink deep from the well of African tradition, to use what is good and wholesome for contemporary society."[43] I spoke of African values such as "solidarity, respect for life, [and] humanity."[44] But I was not even close to examining those traditions in the effect they had on African women, and how much *our patriarchal power* would determine what is "wholesome" and "good" for women. African women have risen up in rightful protest at the claiming of African traditions without examining whether they are indeed "good" and "wholesome" for women, in order for them to be good and wholesome for all of society.

African women, we have seen in the previous chapter, seem to think that Jesus does indeed have something better to offer. The women do not want to throw every single African tradition out the window. But the women also offer sharp and justified critique on a post-colonial, androcentric Christianity: we, African men, have bastardized what Jesus has offered with patriarchalism, sexism, and the demands of a twisted masculinity and called it "African tradition." We are perpetuating traditions utterly harmful to women, and we have sanctified them. We have turned a precious ethos

---

42. See Okura, *Johanine Approach*, 89, 99, 100 as quoted in Moore, "Are there Impurities in the Living Water?," 78–97.

43. See A. Boesak, *Farewell to Innocence*, 151.

44. A. Boesak, *Farewell to Innocence*, 152.

we call *ubuntu* that is meant to be a source of life-giving humanizing power, so the women tell us, into an exclusivist, patriarchal practice that does not embrace women, LGBTQI+ persons, and other marginalized members of the community.[45] We have turned the living water of the gospel of liberation into the stagnant water of male-centered traditionalism. For women, it is still the "poisoned well" Biko railed against, but one that they have to "keep coming back to." So the question for Black liberation theology remains: does this Jesus, whom we call the black Messiah, offer something altogether different, an alternative to traditions and customs that chain women to "inauspiciousness," "unworthiness," and "submissiveness"? And if he does, is Black theology and the search for "authentic Africanity" a partner on this journey, or are we just in the way?

"GO, CALL YOUR HUSBAND."

"Go, call your husband . . ." For most, this question is really the heart of the matter. This question reveals who she really is, the fallen woman who is trying in vain to "mislead" Jesus.[46] This is how Keener sees it:

> A denial that one was married may not always have been flirtatious, but it constituted an essential prerequisite for any further steps toward even a casual sexual union . . . she may have thus interpreted [Jesus'] remark about her husband as a final test of her availability. Given her interpretation of the situation in natural terms, she may have viewed Jesus as a potential sexual or marital partner.[47]

This male projection onto the woman's mind, which is not at all clear from the text, goes very far. Some, however, have understood the "five

---

45. See the more detailed discussion on *ubuntu* in A. Boesak, *Pharaohs*, ch. 4. *Ubuntu* is well described in the Zulu proverb, *umuntu, ngamuntu ngabantu,* meaning "I am a person through other persons," or sometimes understood as "I am because we are." For African feminists such as Mercy Oduyoye, Dorothy Ramodibe, and Rose Zoe-Obianga, however, these are mere words, more utopian than reality. This philosophy, despite its lofty ideals, "oppresses, marginalizes, and stereotypes women, keeps women in a state of submission, sanctifying oppressive gender stereotyping." It fosters a "deep-seated patriarchy that entrenches gender inequality and disregard for the dignity of African women." See 126–28 and the references there. I have argued that *ubuntu*, as it is understood and practiced now in South Africa at least, is "in need of *ubuntu*"—it needs the radicalization of justice as held up by the Scriptures in order to be as effective as it should and could be in society today, see A. Boesak, *Pharaohs on Both Sides*, ch 4.

46. See Keener, *Gospel of John*, 605.

47. Keener, *Gospel of John*, 606.

husbands" as a reference to five nations settled in Samaria or to the "five gods" of 2 Kgs 17:30–31.[48] Keener is insistent on this point, but is Jesus speaking of "her marriages" though? Gerard S. Sloyan argues:

> The whole story is fraught with symbolism, so much so that we are right to doubt the literal truth of the woman's having had five husbands and not being married to her present partner (v. 18). Aside from the inherent improbability of such a career, there is the fact that the Samaritans were stigmatized as 'Cuthians' (Berakoth 7,1) and so throughout the Mishna, a tribe of the Assyrian Empire in II Kings 17:24, 30. There were one of five idolatrous peoples of the East identified in Second Kings by their gods and consorts (vv. 30, 31). If the woman's five husbands were these peoples, the present liaison of the Samaritans at the stone surface of sacrifice on Gerizim would be the sixth: an idolatrous cult in Jewish eyes.[49]

Feminist theologian Luise Schottroff reads the story against the background of the position of a widow or divorced woman in the patriarchal societies of Jesus's day. She calls the views of male interpreters such as Bultmann, Keener, and Jakes a "gynophobic type of interpretation."[50] The woman, she argues,

> is portrayed in terms of the pagan idolatry of the Samaritan people. In this interpretation misogyny is combined with discrimination of the Samaritan religion, a metaphor of adultery for infidelity to God.[51]

In such an interpretation, the woman, facing multiple levels of discrimination and condemnation, has no chance. But a woman in her position, Schottroff continues to argue elsewhere, taking the matter of her marital status as a given, "had to make sure that she found another patriarchal owner (husband) because social and economic opportunities were very restricted if she remained unmarried . . . The Samaritan woman probably had a thoroughly typical woman's biography behind her."[52] Keener, however,

---

48. So for instance Ellis, *Genius of John*, 70. Keener disputes this, *Gospel of John*, 606.

49. Sloyan, *John*, 55.

50. See Schottroff, "Samaritan Woman," 157–81, 159.

51. Schottroff, "Samaritan Woman," 159–60.

52. See Schottroff, "Important Aspects of the Gospel for the Future," 209. Thompson agrees with her, though she does not offer as vigorous a defense, and merely states, "[The woman] needs the protection and support of a husband, but has settled for what she can get," (*John*, 103). Keener dismisses this view: "Unfortunately, the charitable

argues, "Rightly or wrongly, most ancient readers would have drawn moral connotations from the number of her marriages."[53] Schottroff does provide valuable insights from a feminist point of view, and she is right to remind us about the real-life situation of women in that society. But still wrestling with the proposition that the woman was married as many as five times and was now living with a sixth man, it does not really help us get to the core of the issue here.

Musa Dube, reading through her African feminist lens, points us in the right direction. Dube has written on this story and there her engagement with Jesus and the Samaritan woman is just as fascinating as her work on the Canaanite woman.[54] She sees African women's lived realities, historical and contemporary, in the encounter of Jesus and the woman at the well.

> It touches our hearts for we have had our own Jewish and Samaritan relationships, both internationally and locally . . . We read this story with a keen eye to understanding how racial and ethnic discrimination works . . . But above all we read this story with a keen search for healing, for a revolutionized world, a just world of loving our neighbors as we love ourselves.[55]

The genius of her interpretation here is already in the title of her chapter in *Talitha Cumi!* In her reading here, the well becomes less a place of encounter and conversation than a place of judgment, for the five husbands are the historical confrontations between African women and the realities of their lives. In what she calls a "dramatic retelling" of the encounter, the five husbands are ethnocentrism and racism, colonialism, economic exploitation and dispossession, the liberation struggle, and globalization.[56] All of these have had devastating impact on Africa, and especially on African women. These are the forces that have "lorded" it over Africa and her women. It is a brilliant exposition, in my view, where she rightly understands the political dimensions of this encounter: "the mountain and the Temple are also economic centers. Religious contest is also a competition for economic power."[57] In the final dramatic scene, the woman meets "Justine" a woman, and she leaves us with an intriguing question hanging: is this woman a

---

reading is probably not the first one which would have occurred to John's first audience" (*Gospel of John*, 606).

53. Keener, *Gospel of John*, 607.

54. See Dube, "The Five Husbands at the Well of Living Waters," in Njoroge and Dube, *Talitha Cumi!*, 44–65.

55. Njoroge and Dube, *Talitha Cumi!*, 44.

56. Njoroge and Dube, *Talitha Cumi!*, 45.

57. Njoroge and Dube, *Talitha Cumi!*, 45.

representation of Jesus, Jesus as a woman, or does this figure replace Jesus altogether?[58]

The conversation takes "an abrupt turn" in verse 16, remarks Allen Dwight Callahan. "The surprise is neither Jesus' command nor the woman's response but Jesus' rejoinder that she has had five husbands. It is more double-entendre than a palor trick."[59] Callahan offers a reading, in some ways closer to that of Dube, I find more intriguing, and takes our discussion in a very different, and in my view, much more profitable direction: In ancient Aramaic, Callahan argues, "five husbands" translates as "five lords" (*ba'alim*):

> According to 2 Kings 17:24 people from Babylon, Cuthah, Avra, Hamath, and Sepharvaim became local Samaritan rulers, and Josephus speaks of the five nations that ruled Samaria (Ant. 9.14.3). Second Kings and Josephus agree that the Samaritans have been subject to five foreign regimes, five *ba'alim*. Jesus speaks of the five *ba'alim* of the Samaritans, and the sixth *ba'al* which is not properly a lord but which has nevertheless reduced Samaria to political concubinage under the Roman imperium ruling from Jerusalem.[60]

This is indeed a surprising turn. The conversation shifts again, from theology to politics, and one has to marvel at the respect with which this woman is treated by Jesus. Jesus does not see the need to correct the woman when she calls him a "Judean." He does not tell her that as a Galilean, he was equally discriminated against, looked down upon, by the Judeans who deemed themselves superior. He does not tell her that his own people called him a "Samaritan demon" (John 8:48). That would have lowered the bar in this conversation altogether, unworthy of both of them. It would also have been a distraction. Recognizing racism is important, but spending one's time fighting racial slurs from racial bigots is not fruitful. The woman understands this. She "catches the political double-entendre of Jesus' rejoinder and continues the conversation in a political key."[61]

We should note three things here: first, despite the vast amount of opinion to the contrary, Callahan is right. This is now a political conversation about power, dominion, subjugation, and resistance. As such, Jesus does not allow the conversation to dwell on personal matters. The personal insults from angry, bigoted people should not cloud the important issues

---

58. Njoroge and Dube, *Talitha Cumi!*, 64.
59. Callahan, *A Love Supreme*, 65ff.
60. Callahan, *A Love Supreme*, 66.
61. Callahan, *A Love Supreme*, 65.

Jesus wants to discuss. The situation is far more serious than that. Allowing personal insults and attacks to distract one from one's ultimate goal is not how revolutions are won. Jesus is not concerned with her morality, neither is he concerned with the morality dictated by bigoted traditions. He is concerned with the morality of *politics.* Second, Jesus's respect for this woman's intellect is so deep that he shares with her his own understanding of their common, dire political situation. As the Canaanite woman did with him, Jesus now does with this woman: he appeals to her at the level of their common oppression: he wants her to understand the solidarity of the oppressed. He, from occupied Galilee suffering under the heel of an oppressive, illegitimate "lord," and she, from occupied Samaria, suffering under an equally oppressive lord. But this "lord" is not "her husband." He is illegitimate. She owes him nothing. Third, far from trying to stereotype her into submission, Jesus respects her agency. He is offering her solidarity in the struggle for justice and freedom. This is an invitation to join him in God's revolution against those "who are from the earth" with their earthly oppressive powers, to gain freedom and dignity, not just for her, but for all her people.

Jesus is not seeking to establish and exert patriarchal power through sanctimonious moral judgment, victimizing and disempowering her. He is seeking comradeship, asking her to join him in the struggle against the hierarchies of oppression that seek to rule and control their lives. They are both oppressed people, they are both facing the supremacism of the Judeans, the despotism of patriarchy, and the terror of Roman imperial occupation. So Teresa Okura is right to pose the question, "What do Jesus and the Samaritan woman have in common?" as central to her reflection on this passage in another piece.[62] But one should begin that answer not with the applied commonality in Africa, but with the direct commonality *in the moment of their engagement.* What they have in common is not only the "shared experience of rejection, prejudice, and isolation" from Judeans, but the systemic injustices, the political oppression, the socio-economic exploitation, the daily humiliations, and the never-ending military aggression in the ongoing occupation from Rome.

Now she understands that the "gift of God" is not an "otherworldly" gift. John was serious when he testified to the love of God "for the world." That world is "now" and "here" just as the hour for true worship is "now here" and she is invited to be part of it. Jesus is offering her a new spirituality and it is a spirituality of struggle. Now we understand also how she grows in this conversation in her knowledge and understanding of him. First she calls him a "Jew," then she acknowledges that he is "lord" (*kurie*); now she

---

62. See Okura, "Jesus and the Samaritan Woman in Africa," 401–18.

knows he is a prophet (v. 19). She does not mean a prophet who "sees" everything in her heart and "knows" her deepest "sinful" desires and every intimate, salacious detail of her life, but the prophet sent from God, who sees what God sees, the misery and the pain that oppression and subjugation bring; the God who has "heard" the cry for freedom; and who "knows" the suffering of God's people. The One before her is the One who "has come down to deliver" the people from the hands of those who call themselves "lord" but are not. Before the conversation is over, she will acknowledge him as "Messiah," the One sent by God, the liberator.

In light of this reading, the message she takes to the village is not the imperialist missionary call that Africans such as Musa Dube rightly urge us to reject. It becomes a call to awareness, resistance, and liberation. Hence it is essential that the Samaritans in her village accept Jesus for themselves, upon a personal meeting with him, not simply on her word. Joining a struggle, and accepting its risks, is an intensely personal decision. Those who joined our struggle "because of Mandela" have left the struggle as soon as Mandela was out of prison, opening the gates of compromise towards the promised land of opportunity, enrichment, and instant gratification. Those who joined on the word of Jesus, stayed, even when all expectations were upended. Accepting Jesus means joining God's struggle to save and transform the world into a place of justice, love, peace, and inclusion. It means to bring an end to powers of domination and destruction that seek to claim God's world for themselves. When the Samaritans meet Jesus, they rightly proclaim him, in direct contradiction to, and nullification of the claims of the Roman Caesar, "Savior of the world!" (4:42). Hence we do not share Keener's surprise that Jesus would commission "this sort of woman" to testify about him.[63] He sends her because she understands completely the revolutionary agenda of God revealed in this prophet she has just met.

"I AM HE..."

It is not necessary to repeat here the centrality of the Jerusalem temple in the faith of Israel, nor the intensity of the tensions between Jews and Samaritans on the question of places of worship.[64] It is equally a holy place for Islam and the centuries-old contentions around Jerusalem have been immeasurably worsened by the decision of Donald Trump to move the US embassy to Jerusalem, thereby inflaming the whole Islamic world, not just the Palestinians. But it has served to focus the attention of the whole

---

63. Keener, *Gospel of John*, 608.
64. For detailed discussions, see, among others, Keener, *Gospel of John*, 613–15.

international community on the exclusivity of Jewish claims to Jerusalem and the consequences thereof for world peace, wholly apart from the question of justice for, and freedom of Palestinians.

What is important here is to note that even as the woman poses this issue to Jesus, she knows that the temple on Mount Gerizim has been destroyed and never rebuilt. Her ancestors worshiped there, but her generation certainly did not. As place of worship, it is no longer relevant, and the tensions around it are kept alive for other reasons. So why does she mention the mountain? Does she mean to provoke Jesus? His answer certainly seems to draw something completely unexpected from him. And it is an answer seemingly filled with contradictions.

First, Jesus responds, "the hour is coming when you will worship the Father neither on this mountain nor in Jerusalem" (v. 21). It is an iconoclastic word that smashes all ideas about holy places and rituals and the connection between those. Not Gerizim, and not Jerusalem. The consequences should be shocking. But then Jesus turns almost demeaning: "You worship what you do not know; we worship what we know, for salvation is from the Jews" (v. 22). The words are unbearably supremacist. Is Jesus actually falling back on the religious exclusivism that embraces an exclusive "chosen" people, thereby after all validating the denigration of the Samaritans? Is Jesus, as with the Canaanite woman, embracing the religious apartheid that has no room for others unless it is in a place of subservience? Within the context of this conversation such a switch hardly makes any sense. Neither does it make sense in light of both the preceding and following verse. But once again, it is Callahan who offers a better understanding of what is happening here. He thinks "this purported Judean jingoism" is a result of an incorrect rendering of the text. The verse is more properly rendered, "For it is salvation from the Judeans." One should let that sink in for a while.

> Jesus offers deliverance from centuries of Judean antipathy; he speaks of liberation from the enormous ideological and political pressure that Judea had exerted on the Samaritans for centuries. This is the 'word' (*logos*) that the Samaritans hear for themselves and receive so enthusiastically.[65]

But if we are consistent in our thinking, it is not just liberation from the Judeans Jesus is speaking of, but liberation from, as Callahan also correctly understands, "the political concubinage under *the Roman imperium* ruling from Jerusalem."[66] Jesus's offer of liberation and his invitation to her

---

65. Callahan, *A Love Supreme*, 65.
66. Callahan, *A Love Supreme*, 65.

to join the struggle for that liberation is more comprehensive, and far more radical: it is not just the collaborators of empire, but the empire itself which is in his purview.

Jesus is inviting her to look beyond the narrow boundaries of local struggles and understand the reach of the global empire Rome represented. As all-consuming as the tensions between Jews and Samaritans might have been, in the bigger scheme of things they are not as life-determining as Jews and Samaritans might think. Issues of tradition, racial and religious prejudices, and ethnic strife should not distract from the larger truth, namely that they are both subjugated by Rome, dominated by its ruthless power, threatened by its brutality. That is where their attention should be.

The issue here is truly not "Jerusalem" or "Gerizim," however much the elites on both sides might want to keep the masses occupied with that thought while thriving on their own relationships with the oppressor, undisturbed by the masses too divided among themselves to focus on what really matters. The great idolatry here is the one imposed by Rome: that Jews and Samaritans, both children of the Torah, are commanded by the one God to serve only one God: "You shall have no other gods before me." That is a religious demand with far-reaching and uncompromising political consequences. Yet Rome demands absolute obedience, absolute loyalty, absolute commitment to another god: the Caesar in Rome. *That* is the blasphemy both Jews and Samaritans should combat. Fighting each other on divisive issues created by the elite is a time-honored and well-tested tactic of empire that oppressed people should understand and resist.

In the utterly scandalous ethnic contestations now raging in South Africa as I write—about the disputed "Africanness" of so-called Indians and "Coloreds," South Africans, so far from freedom still, should not be deluded by these spurious debates.[67] While it is true that open, public debates, with full acknowledgement of how these debates reflect the skewed racialized politics of both apartheid and post-apartheid South Africa, are clearly necessary, one should not be unaware of the deeper political and historical issues concealed here. Apart from the fact that these debates are based on "race," not recognizing it as a political and social construct for the purposes of manipulation and control, these constructs, so effectively used by the apartheid regime, have been equally politically employed by the ANC's "black, in particular African" policies, after the ANC had sought to destroy the political legacy of the Black Consciousness Movement by deliberately

---

67. For some attempts at analysis of these very intense and divisive debates, see Pillay, "Being Coloured and Indian"; also Ramalaine, "Infusing religion."

reinstating racial categorization after their return from exile. These are now the chickens come home to roost as some of us had warned years ago.[68]

But neither should they be distracted by the question of how racist this is (even though it surely is), but should rather pay attention to the question: why this debate now, and whose interests does it serve? Who, in this moment of national engagement of the question of decolonization, Africanization, and authentic Africanity, benefits from this useless distraction? What goes unnoticed (for instance the pandemic that gender-based violence has become; the struggle for justice women have still not won and the fight for dignity LGBTQI+ persons are far too much left on their own to fight, while the struggle for the land as embedded injustice in our Constitution has just begun; the growing chasm between rich and poor; or the pervasive mediocrity and paucity of courage of our politics) while we pay so much attention to the utter stupidity of whether people who are part descendants of the First Nations of South Africa and part-descendants of its first slave populations brought from different parts of the world are truly Africans? Why is the historical fact of the creole nature of South African society, beginning with our DNA, of no account? Why is the debate raging among the descendants of indigenous communities while the president speaks at the centenary celebrations of the *Afrikaner Broederbond*, assuring *them* that they have nothing to be concerned about—they *are* Africans?[69] Why is the historic de-Africanization of South Africa's indigenous children, as Patric Tariq Mellet in his brilliant analysis calls it, including over the last twenty-five years, and the confrontation of real historical experiences of *all* Africans, especially slavery, not the proper political discussion? He writes,

> The colonial and Apartheid system had created a common label of "Coloured" for the descendants of a range of indigenous African tribes—the Nama, Korana, Damara, Griqua, San, Cape Khoi as well as those who had some Khoi ancestry as well as substantial African creole ancestry which some of us refer to as Camissa heritage—70% African slave ancestry mixed with 30% Indian and Southeast Asian Slave ancestry; and including African and Asian indentured labour ancestry and some admixture of non-conformist Europeans. Both the Genocide and Ethnocide faced by the indigenous tribes of the Cape and the crime against humanity—Slavery—faced by these people is the well documented worst experience of all Africans during the first two and a half centuries of colonisation in South Africa.[70]

68. See, e.g., A. Boesak, *Running with Horses*, chs. 1 and 14.
69. See Gerber, "Back Land Reform."
70. Mellet, "National Question: Non-racialism or Ethnicism."

So why are *these* issues not the debate? South Africans should learn from Jesus and the Samaritan woman: it is not about Jerusalem, nor is it about Gerizim. While our eyes are transfixed on temples, one in ruins and the other "a den of thieves" (Matt 21:13), something decisively important is happening to us, and we are not even aware of it.

But we must not think that all this has no spiritual implications. The next verse, rather than compounding the contradictions, is not so surprising, coming from the mouth of this revolutionary, iconoclastic Jesus. Jesus challenges both Jewish and Samaritan tradition. Jesus begins with "but," and the words sound even more radical than the previous verse. True worship has nothing to do with, and shall not be determined by "holy places," laws and traditions. True worshipers will worship God "in Spirit and in truth." No longer shall race or nationality, ethnicity or tribal affiliation, class or status or religion determine what true worship is. All the walls are being broken down. This God is "Spirit" and this is the Spirit of power, empowerment, and freedom; the spirit that infused the women in the birthing chamber and in Jochebed's house, on the riverbank and the seashore. This is the Spirit who inspired Hannah to sing about the bows of the mighty that are broken, and Mary to sing about the God who has brought down the powerful from their thrones and lifted up the lowly, filled the hungry with good things and sent the rich away empty.

She is the same Spirit who made the prophets stand before kings, proclaiming justice, denouncing oppression and violence, standing with the poor and defenseless, preparing "the way of the Lord." This is the Spirit now resting upon Jesus and who will abide in him. Paul got it completely right: "There is no longer Jew or Greek, there is no longer slave or free, there is no longer male and female; for all of you are one in Christ Jesus" (Gal 3:28). She is the Spirit who challenges and undermines the holy propaganda around holy places and holy rituals which serve only to secure the power of the powerful and safeguard the privileges of the privileged. This is the Spirit who, like the wind, "blows wherever she chooses" (3:8) for there is no power that can hold her and her inclusive power sweeps all resistance away. In my view, here is the moment, in John's Gospel at least, that Dube speaks of, where Jesus's mission breaks with the imperialistic, exclusivist ideology of "chosenness" and religious supremacism and becomes an inclusivist "model of liberating interdependence."

Verse 25 brings the sister from Sychar to the brink of the ultimate question: in light of this conversation, is Jesus the Messiah? But she does not ask. She states, as if for her, after all they had discussed, it is a logical conclusion, but one she wants Jesus to draw. Is the time ripe to make that revelation? In *this* land, at *this* place, to a *woman*? She sets the standard for the astounding respect John has for women. Peter's confession that Jesus is the Messiah (Matt 16:16) follows a long argument among the disciples about how Jesus is seen by "the people," and a direct question from Jesus. Peter has to be prompted. In contrast, her remark, like the confession of Martha (John 11:27) comes after intense engagement with Jesus, in a conversation of equals, on deep theological matters. It follows, in other words, on the recognition of the integrity of Jesus's witness by the women, on the truth of his words and the authority of his presence. But it happens only with the women. Martha is direct. This woman is much more subtle in how she approaches this all-important issue. It is almost as if she is daring Jesus to admit to what she knows from her own tradition: the Messiah is coming.[71] And he does: "I am he." And then for good measure, he adds, "the one who is speaking to you." Jesus greatly empowers her.

With this, the woman at the well of Jacob scores a significant victory. She does what even her venerated ancestor Jacob could not do. His nocturnal wrestling with God gains him a blessing (Gen 32:22–32) but his wish to know exactly who he was wrestling with, remained unfulfilled. She, in contrast, hears the Name without asking. Better still: while the confession about Jesus's messiahship has to be wrested from the men, she is the one who invites it from Jesus, and he gives it eagerly. Jacob limps away from his encounter with a disjointed hip. The sister from Sychar leaves her water jar and everything it symbolizes behind, as she leaves all disjointedness inflicted upon her as a woman and a Samaritan behind. She fairly sails into the city to testify about the experience that changed her life, and to tell her people that the day of their liberation has dawned. There is no hesitation here, no thought to first go home and think things over—after all, this was news of tremendous importance. No thought of whether, *as a woman,* she has the right to speak to the whole city about these things. All such hesitation is left behind with that water jar. Her stride is of one confident in her faith and in her ability to overcome. Far beyond and above the gentrified patriarchy Bishop T. D. Jakes offers, this is a truly liberated woman, because she is an empowered woman. She might not be "loosed" in Jakes's eyes, but she is empowered.

---

71. See, e.g., Callahan, *A Love Supreme,* 65, Ellis, *Genius of John,* 71. Keener, *Gospel of John,* 619, insists that "she does not understand what she is saying," but it will be clear that I do not agree with that assessment.

A DIFFERENCE LIKE NIGHT AND DAY

It is surely no coincidence that the stories about Nicodemus the Pharisee and the woman from Samaria are placed next to each other in John's Gospel. Nicodemus, the "teacher of Israel," a rabbi, and, on top of it, a "leader of the Jews." The differences in social status, privilege, education, wealth, power, and acceptability could not have been greater. Nicodemus comes to Jesus "by night," she meets Jesus at the height of the day. The conversations, and their consequences, are as different as night and day.

Nicodemus comes in the night—he does not dare the risks of being seen to be associated with Jesus, this rebellious teacher from Galilee. The woman speaks with Jesus, now known to her as a Jewish messiah challenging the Roman Empire, without fear, even though she clearly understood the risks involved. Nowhere during the conversation is there any hint that those risks would make her break off the conversation. She stays, even when the disciples return and their first reaction was astonishment that Jesus was speaking to her. She probably would have stayed longer. Jesus's admission that he is the Messiah is still just hanging there. The reader gets the clear impression that the conversation was interrupted by the untimely return of the men whose consternation causes an awkward silence. The woman leaves and Jesus is left with the men who irritate him with the insistence of mundane matters like food. Jesus's exasperation is evident.

Nicodemus comes with his immense knowledge of the Torah, the certainty of his righteousness, his power, and the evenness of the playing field he shares with Jesus as a man. She comes laden with the burdens of being a woman, uneducated, poor, and a Samaritan, knowing that as a woman she begins this conversation from far behind, going uphill. Unlike him, she is assumed "unclean." Unlike Nicodemus, she cannot assume anything. If she knew what modern-day commentators would project upon her and write about her, she would probably have given up and walked away in despair. That Jesus respectfully treats her as an equal must have been the greatest surprise for her. It is also the heart of this piece of revolutionary writing by John. Because it is there where it all begins: being equal. If there is a lesson to be drawn for reconciliation here, this is it: no reconciliation without radical, unconditional equality.

Nicodemus has another advantage. He knows who Jesus is. He does not have to feel his way in the dark. "Rabbi, we know you are a teacher who has come from God . . ." It is an astonishing admission. Who is the "we" he is referring to? A group of like-minded rabbis, a dissident minority who might have begun to believe that the official line on Jesus was wrong and who now want to know more? Is he their emissary? Is this conversation a trial balloon to see whether a compromise between Jesus and the ruling classes might be possible? Would Nicodemus succeed where the arrogant Satan has failed? That would certainly cut the revolution off before it properly begins. Is he speaking on behalf of the Pharisees, the rabbis, or the rulers? His first words are perhaps an indication that he was not the only one who was thinking about Jesus in a different light. But perhaps he was speaking only of himself and his friend Joseph of Arimathea who would ask Pilate for the body of Jesus to be buried in that "new tomb in which no one had ever been laid" (19:38–42). We do not know, but it remains intriguing.

Nicodemus and his friend(s)—the cream of the patriarchal world with all their power and privilege and wisdom—are somehow convinced by Jesus, but just like "the crowds" everywhere in John, they were convinced by the "signs" Jesus performed. The Samaritan woman sees no signs, but is convinced by the authority of his words and the integrity of the power of his presence. It is the liberating power of his presence, not the coercive power of signs and wonders, that brings her to trust him. Further on (in 4:43–54) we find the story of the healing of the official's son, and here as elsewhere in the Gospel the issue of "seeing" and "believing" is raised. It is difficult not to read some irritation in Jesus's admonition, "Unless you see signs and wonders you will not believe" (4:48).

It seems to be a sin that has a particular masculine character in the Gospels. John himself relates the story of how he and Peter, on that resurrection Sunday morning, refused to believe. They wanted to "see" first, and very carefully at that, because they could not accept the word of the women (20:5–8). There is some embarrassment in John's telling of the story: "Then the other disciple, who reached the tomb first, also went in, and he saw and believed . . ." In other words, *only then*. He offers as an excuse: "For as yet they did not understand the scripture, that he must rise from the dead" (20:9). But meanwhile the women did not understand everything either, *but they believed*, and testified. Or can John mean that while the men were struggling that long to understand, the women already did? At the well in Sychar it was the same: the men did not understand, and it was the men that in their exchange with Jesus, nagging on about food, displayed the kind of "foolish misunderstanding" commentators accuse the woman of. They were so shocked and scandalized that he was talking to a woman, that none of them asked why (v. 27). John writes this with some astonishment. As if he was now thinking, "If we only asked!" Then they would have understood. Not only then, at the well, but that morning at the tomb, and later, in that room where they were hiding out of fear. Then men, throughout the history of the Christian church, would not have worked so hard to silence, suppress, and marginalize women, to push them from out of the center of

Jesus's community of equals into the margins to try and survive there as ecclesiastical serving wenches, instead of honoring them as the leaders these women clearly show themselves to be.

Between the two great world wars, Dutch theologian G. J. Heering wrote a book titled, *The Fall of Christianity*.[72] It was, and still is, an important book, and argues quite persuasively how soon the early Christian church deviated from the ethical teachings of Jesus by allowing itself to become the church of the Roman Empire, embracing the empire's ways. He was especially concerned about violence and the church's attitude to war. It was, so to speak, the church's "original sin." I was immensely impressed by that book and I remain persuaded by Heering's arguments about violence, nonviolence, and war, and the nonviolent ethic of Jesus of Nazareth. I now think, however, that the church's "original sin" was not the question of violence, as important as that may be. It was the question of the equality of women— *that* sin came first, long before the sin of embracing war. But perhaps the last is the inevitable consequence of the first. And while we have begun to understand our sinfulness in the justification of war, we have not significantly shifted in this matter, nor have we converted from our deeply-rooted, systematized patriarchy. But if it was so easy to do with Miriam and the women of the first hour in Torah, and the tradition they left behind, why should it be more difficult with the women of the New Testament, part of the disciples of the first hour?

A Black theology of liberation has much to learn from the sister from Sychar, the woman who, when Jesus finally entrusted and empowered her with the knowledge that he is the Messiah, understood what that meant. A Jewish Messiah, a liberator ready to engage the mightiest power on the face of the earth, challenging its pretenses, its oppression, exploitation, and subjugation, claiming to be a different Lord, in utter opposition to the Caesar who calls himself "lord"? A Messiah ready to start a movement of revolution, to "save the world" from fear, oppression, and captivity to powers of destruction? She walked away from that well, empowered and inspired, proclaiming that very subversive message about the Savior of the world who is here, who the people must "come and see." She knew that a Jewish messiah in a Roman-controlled world would invite revilement, persecution, and death. And yet she stood in solidarity with him despite the risks. In her, I do not see a despicable, empty-headed woman of low morals ready to seduce Jesus in the wink of a lustful eye. I see rather, the extraordinary child of Meribah, standing in the prophetic tradition of Miriam.

---

72. Written in Dutch, the book was titled *De Zondeval van het Christendom, een studie over christendom, staat en oorlog* (Utrecht: Bijleveld [1928], 1981).

For many reasons which hold globally, discussed in this book and much besides, we have come to a crossroads, a *kairos* moment, if you will. Perhaps as never before, the Black church is challenged on the integrity of its prophetic faithfulness, and the authenticity of its presence in the face of empire. What Allen Dwight Callahan writes for African Americans and their prophetic calling is equally true for all of us:

> As Esau sold his birthright for a bowl of stew, African Americans [and all of us] may forego asking the tough questions of our time and instead choose to savor the hand-me-down emoluments of wealth and power acquired at their ancestor's expense. They would close this deal with the Devil as second class citizens of an imperious imperial nation. Such is the present lot of slavery's children in the land of their birth. The electoral process illegally disenfranchises them. Both major political parties regularly neglect them. The criminal justice system unjustly arrests, incarcerates and executes them. The military disproportionately dispatches them to the front in its many and unjust wars. The executive branch of the federal government refuses to hear them, the judiciary branch refuses to protect them, and the legislative branch refuses to represent them. African Americans may choose to sell their birthright to the descendants of a master class that had proven itself as crafty and unscrupulous as the young Jacob. A century and a half after the fall of the slave regime, these heirs to ill-gotten gains still rule the United States as did their forebears—with scripture and injustice. Or, with the collective critical consciousness that is their heritage, slavery's children may call both scripture and injustice into question.[73]

The sister from Sychar, who with her intuitive, critical, subversive ingenuity had sparred with Jesus, engaged with him, and won both his admiration and the admission that he was the Messiah, returns to the city with a confidence grounded in a liberated consciousness, a decolonized mind, and a renewed spirit. Her invitation to the whole city is an invitation to oppressed people engaged in ongoing struggles everywhere, and to Black theology and the Black church in particular: "Come and see a man who knows everything . . ." If we accept her invitation, "slavery's children" will be able to resist being turned into empire's children, instead becoming children of the waters of Meribah.

---

73. Callahan, *Talking Book*, 246.

BIBLIOGRAPHY

Adamo, David Tuesday. "The Bible in Twenty-first Century Africa." In *The Africana Bible, Reading Israel's Scriptures from Africa and the African Diaspora*, edited by Hugh R. Page et al., 25–32. Minneapolis: Fortress, 2010.
Adler, Margo. "Before Rosa Parks, There Was Claudette Colvin." *NPR*, March 15, 2009. https://www.npr.org/2009/03/15/101719889/before-rosa-parks-there-was-claudette-colvin.
Al Jazeera News. "African Migrants Traded in Libya's 'Slave Markets.'" *Al Jazeera*, April 11, 2017. http://readersupportednews.org/news-section2/318–66/42986-african-migrants-traded.
———. "US: Myanmar Attacks on Rohingya 'Ethnic Cleansing.'" *Al Jazeera*, November 22, 2017. https://www.aljazeera.com/news/2017/11/myanmar-attacks-rohingya-ethnic-cleansing-171122143122930.html.
Alexander, Peter. "Cyril Ramaphosa's Marikana Massacre Apology Is Disingenuous and Dishonest." *The Conversation*, May 11, 2017. http://theconversation.com/cyril-ramaphosas-marikana-massacre-apology-is-disingenuous-and-dishonest-77485.
———. "Why Ramaphosa's Marikana massacre 'apology' was disingenuous and dishonest." *Mail and Guardian*, May 15, 2017. https://mg.co.za/article/2017-05-15-why-ramaphosas-marikana-massacre-apology-was-disingenuous-and-dishonest.
Ali, Tariq. *The Obama Syndrome—Surrender at Home, War Abroad*. London: Verso, 2010.
Allen, John L., Jr. "Africa: Christianity's greatest growth, and greatest threat." *Crux*, December 30, 2015. https://cruxnow.com/faith/2015/12/30/africa-christianitys-greatest-growth-and-greatest-threat/.
Alsaafin, Linah. "The Role of Palestinian Women in Resistance." *Open Democracy*, April 17, 2014. https://www.opendemocracy.net/north-africa-west-asia/linah-alsaafin/role-of-palestinian-women-in-resistance.
"Amnesty International calls on Myanmar to end Rohingya 'apartheid.'" *SBS News*, November 21, 2017. https://www.sbs.com.au/news/amnesty-international-calls-on-myanmar-to-end-rohingya-apartheid.
Ateek, Naim. *Justice and Only Justice: A Palestinian Theology of Liberation*. Maryknoll, NY: Orbis, 1989.
Bay, Mia. *To Tell the Truth Freely: The Life of Ida B. Wells*. New York: Hill and Wang, 2009.

Ben-Abba, Amitai. "Israel's New Ideology of Genocide." *Counterpunch*, May 21, 2018. https://www.counterpunch.org/2018/05/21/israels-new-ideology-of-genocide/.

Biko, Stephen Bantu. *I Write What I Like: A Selections of His Writings*. Edited by Aeldrid Stubbs. San Francisco: Harper and Row, 1986.

Boardman, William. "Obama is Pathetic on Human Rights in North Dakota." *Reader Supported News*, November 4, 2016. http://readersupportednews.org/opinion2/277-75/40082-obama-is-pathetic-on-human-rights.

Boesak, Allan Aubrey. *Black and Reformed: Apartheid, Liberation, and the Calvinist Tradition*. Eugene, OR: Wipf & Stock, 2015.

———. *Dare We Speak of Hope? Searching for a Language of Life in Faith and Politics*. Grand Rapids, MI: Eerdmans, 2014.

———. *Die Vlug van Gods Verbeelding: Bybelverhale van die Onderkant*. Stellenbosch: Sun, 2005.

———. *Farewell to Innocence: A Socio-ethical Study of Black Theology and Black Power*. Eugene, OR: Wipf & Stock, 2015.

———. *If This is Treason, I am Guilty*. Grand Rapids, MI: Eerdmans, 1987.

———. *Kairos, Crisis, and Global Apartheid: The Challenge of Prophetic Resistance*. New York: Palgrave Macmillan, 2015.

———. *Pharoahs on Both Sides of the Blood-red Waters: Prophetic Critique on Empire—Resistance, Justice, and the Power of the Hopeful Sizwe—A Transatlantic Conversation*. Eugene, OR: Cascade, 2017.

———. *Running with Horses: Reflections of an Accidental Politician*. Cape Town: JoHo!, 2009.

———. *The Tenderness of Conscience: African Renaissance and the Spirituality of Politics*. Stellenbosch: Sun, 2005.

———. *Walking on Thorns: the Call to Christian Obedience*. Grand Rapids, MI: Eerdmans, 1984.

Boesak, Allan Aubrey, and Curtiss Paul DeYoung. *Radical Reconciliation, Beyond Political Pietism and Christian Quietism*. Maryknoll, NY: Orbis, 2012.

Boesak, Allan Aubrey, and Len Hansen, eds. *Globalisation I: The Politics of Empire, Justice, and the Life of the Church*. Stellenbosch: Sun, 2009.

Boesak, Allan Aubrey, et al., eds. *Dreaming a Different World, Globalisation and Justice for Humanity and the Earth, The Challenge of the Accra Confession for the Churches*. Stellenbosch: The Globalisation Project, 2011.

Boesak, Elna. *Channeling Justice? A Feminist Exploration of North American Televangelism in the South African Constitutional Democracy*. PhD diss., University of KwaZulu-Natal, 2016. https://researchspace.ukzn.ac.za/xlmui/bitstream/handle/10413/14466/Boesak_Elna_2016.pdf?sequence=1&isAllowed=y.

Bond, Patrick. *Elite Transition: From Apartheid to Neoliberalism in South Africa*. Pietermaritzburg: University of KwaZulu-Natal Press, 2005.

Bonhoeffer, Dietrich. *Dietrich Bonhoeffer Works 11*, Minneapolis: Fortress, 2012.

Borg, Marcus J., and John Dominic Crossan. *The Last Week: What the Gospels Really Teach About Jesus's Final Days in Jerusalem*. New York: Harper Collins, 2006.

Brenner, Athalya, ed. *A Feminist Companion to Exodus to Deuteronomy*. Sheffield: Sheffield Academic, 2000.

Brenner, Athlaya, and Carol Fontaine, eds. *Reading the Bible, a Feminist Companion: Approaches, Methods, and Strategies*. Sheffield: Sheffield Academic, 1997.

Broad, William, and David E. Sanger. "As U.S. Modernizes Nuclear Weapons, 'Smaller' Leaves Some Uneasy." *The New York Times*, January 11, 2016. https://www.nytimes.com/2016/01/12/science/as-us-modernizes-nuclear-weapons-smaller-leaves-some-uneasy.html.
Brueggeman, Walter. *The Prophetic Imagination*. Minneapolis, Fortress, 2001.
Budd, Philip, J. *Numbers*. Word Biblical Commentary. Waco, TX: Word, 1984.
Bultmann, Rudolf. *The Gospel of John: A Commentary*. Philadelphia: Westminster, 1971.
Burkill, T. A. "The History of The Story of the Syro-Phoenician Woman (Mark VII: 24–31)." *Novum Testamentum* 9 (July 1967) 161–77.
Burns, Rita, J. *Has the Lord Indeed Spoken Only to Moses? A Study of the Biblical Portrait of Miriam*. Atlanta: Scholars, 1987.
Byron, Gay L. and Vanessa Lovelace, eds. *Womanist Interpretations of the Bible—Expanding its Discourse*. Semeia Studies 85. Atlanta: SBL, 2016.
Callahan, Dwight Allen. *A Love Supreme: A History of the Johannine Tradition*. Minneapolis: Augsburg Fortress, 2005.
———. *The Talking Book: African Americans and the Bible*. New Haven: Yale University Press, 2006.
Calland, Richard. *Anatomy of South Africa: Who Holds the Power?* Cape Town: Zebra, 2006.
Calvin, John. *Commentaries*, 22 vols. Translated and edited by John King et al. Grand Rapids, MI: Baker, 1981.
Cannon, Katie. *Katie's Canon: Womanism and the Soul of the Black Community*. New York: Continuum, 1998.
Cape Times. "Editorial: Our rape crisis." *IOL*, February 11, 2013. https://www.iol.co.za/capetimes/editorial-our-rape-crisis-1468063.
Carter, Warren. *John and Empire: Initial Explorations*. New York: T. & T. Clarke, 2008.
———. *Matthew and Empire: Initial Explorations*. Harrisburg, PA: Trinity International, 2001.
———. *Matthew and the Margins: A Sociopolitical and Religious Reading*. Maryknoll, NY: Orbis, 2000.
Cassidy, John. "Why Didn't Eric Holder Go After the Bankers?" *The New Yorker*, September 26, 2014. https://www.newyorker.com/news/john-cassidy/didnt-eric-holder-go-bankers.
Cohn, Marjorie. "Israel's Collective Punishment of Gaza." *Huffington Post*, February 6, 2009. https://www.huffingtonpost.com/marjorie-cohn/israels-collective-punish_b_155700.html.
———. "Israel Inflicts Illegal Collective Punishment on Gaza." *Truthout*, July 14, 2014. truthout.org/articles/Israel-inflicts-illegal-collective-punishment-on-gaza.
Cone, James H. *Black Theology and Black Power*. Maryknoll, NY: Orbis, 2001.
———. *A Black Theology of Liberation*, Maryknoll, NY: Orbis, 1986.
———. *The Cross and the Lynching Tree*. Maryknoll, NY: Orbis, 2015.
———. *For My People: Black Theology and the Black Church, Where We Have Been and Where Are We Going?* Maryknoll, NY: Orbis, 1984.
———. *God of the Oppressed*. Maryknoll, NY: Orbis, 1997.
———. *My Soul Looks Back*. Nashville: Abingdon, 1982.
———. *The Spirituals and the Blues*. Maryknoll, NY: Orbis, 1992.
Cone, James H., and Gayraud S. Wilmore. *Black Theology: A Documentary History, Volume 2*. Maryknoll, NY: Orbis, 1993.
Crossan, John Dominic. *God and Empire*. San Francisco: HarperOne, 2007.

———. "Roman Imperial Theology." In *In the Shadow of Empire: Reclaiming the Bible as a History of Faithful Resistance to Empire,* edited by Richard A. Horsley, 59–74. Louisville, KY: Westminster John Knox, 2001.

Cumming-Bruce, Nick. "Rohingya Crisis in Myanmar Is 'Ethnic Cleansing,' U.N. Rights Chief Says." *The New York Times,* September 11, 2017. https://www.nytimes.com/2017/09/11/world/asia/myanmar-rohingya-ethnic-cleansing.html.

Dawkins, Richard. *The God Delusion.* New York: Houghton Mifflin, 2008.

Dayden, David. "The Most Important WikiLeaks Revelation Isn't About Hilary Clinton." *The Independent,* October 14, 2016. https://newrepublic.com/article/137798/important-wikileaks-revelation-isnt-hillary-clinton.

De Gruchy, John, and Charles Villa-Vicencio, eds. *Apartheid is a Heresy.* Cape Town: David Philip, 1982.

Dey, Kathleen. "Rape Victims' Care Centres Funding Drying Up." *Cape Argus.* December 1, 2017. https://omny.fm/shows/afternoons-with-pippa-hudson/rape-victims-care-centres-face-funding-drying-up.

Douglass, Frederick. "If There Is No Struggle, There Is No Progress." https://www.blackpast.org/african-american-history/1857-frederick-douglass-if-there-no-struggle-there-no-progress/.

———. "My Bondage and My Freedom." http://etc.uf/edu/let2go/my-bondage-and-my-freedom1507/receptionspeech.

Dube, Musa. "Fifty Years of Bleeding: A Storytelling Feminist Reading of Mark 5:24–43." In *Other Ways of Reading: African Women and the Bible,* edited Musa Dube, 50–60. Atlanta: SBL, 2001.

———. *Postcolonial Feminist Biblical Interpretation.* St. Louis: Chalice, 2008.

Dube, Musa, ed. *Other Ways of Reading: African Women and the Bible.* Atlanta: SBL, 2001.

Duncan, Amy. "How Much Did the Royal Wedding Cost and Who Paid for It?" *Metro News,* May 22, 2018. https://metro.co.uk/2018/05/22/much-royal-wedding-cost-paid-7567772/.

Durham, John I. *Exodus.* Word Biblical Commentary. Waco, TX: Word, 1987.

Edet, Rosemary. "Christianity and African Women's Rituals." In *The Will to Arise: Women, Tradition, and the Church,* edited by Mercy Odoyoye and Musimbi R. A. Kanyoro, 25–39. Eugene, OR: Wipf & Stock, 2005.

Elliot, Neill. "The Anti-Imperial Message of the Cross." In *Paul and Empire: Religion and Power in Roman Imperial Society,* edited by Richard A. Horsley, 167–83. Harrisburg, PA: Trinity International, 1997.

———. "Romans 13:1–7 in the Context of Imperial Propaganda." In *Paul and Empire: Religion and Power in Roman Imperial Society,* edited by Richard Horsley, 184–204. Harrisburg: Trinity International, 1997.

Ellis, Peter. *The Genius of John: A Composition-Critical Commentary on the Fourth Gospel.* Collegeville, MN: Liturgical, 1984.

Exum, J. Cheryl. "Second Thoughts About Secondary Characters: Women in Exodus 1:8–2:10." In *A Feminist Companion to Exodus to Deuteronomy,* edited by Athalya Brenner, 75–87. Sheffield: Sheffield Academic, 2001.

———. "You Shall Let Every Daughter Live: A Study of Ex.1:8–2:10." In *A Feminist Companion to Exodus to Deuteronomy,* edited by Athalya Brenner, 37–61. Sheffield: Sheffield Academic, 2001.

Eynikel, Erik, et al., eds. *Internationaal Commentaar op de Bijbel*. Band I. Kampen: Kok/Averbode, 2001.

Fabella, Virginia. "A Common Methodology for Diverse Christologies?" In *With Passion and Compassion: Third World Women Doing Theology*, edited by Mercy Oduyoye and Virginia Fabella, 109–17. Maryknoll, NY: Orbis, 1989.

Fabella, Virginia, and Mercy Amba Oduyoye, eds. *With Passion and Compassion: Third World Women Doing Theology*. Maryknoll, NY: Orbis, 1989.

"Facing the Second Day of the TRC Hearings." *Sunday Times Heritage Project*. http://sthp.saha.org.za/memorial/articles/facing_the_second_day_of_the_trc_hearings.htm.

Felder, Cain Hope. *Race, Racism, and the Biblical Narratives*. Minneapolis: Fortress, 2002.

———. *Troubling Biblical Waters, Race, Class, and Family*. Maryknoll, NY: Orbis, 1992.

Fewell, Donna Nolan, and David M. Gunn. *Gender, Power and Promise: the Subject of the Bible's First Story*. Nashville: Abingdon, 1993.

Foner, Philip S. *Selections from the Writings of Frederick Douglass*. Chicago: Lawrence Hill, 1999.

Freire, Paulo. *Pedagogy of the Oppressed*. New York: Penguin, 1972.

Fretheim, Terence E. *Exodus: Interpretation: a Commentary for Teaching and Preaching*. Louisville, KY: Westminster John Knox, 2010.

Friedman, Richard Elliot. *The Bible With Sources Revealed: A New View Into the Five Books of Moses*. New York: HarperCollins, 2003.

———. *The Exodus*. New York: HarperCollins, 2017.

Frost, Robert. "Mending Wall." *Poetry Foundation*. https://www.poetryfoundation.org/poems/44266/mending-wall.

Garnet, Henry Highland. "An Address to the Slaves of the United States." In *Crossing the Danger Water: Three Hundred Years of African-American Writing*, edited by Dierdre Mullane, 115–21. New York: Anchor, 1993.

Genovese, Eugene, D. "Marxism, Christianity, and Bias in the Study of Southern Slave Society." In *Religious Advocacy and American History*, edited by Bruce Kuklick and D. G. Hart, 83–95. Grand Rapids, MI: Eerdmans, 1997.

———. *Roll, Jordan, Roll: The World the Slaves Made*. New York: Pantheon, 1974.

Gerber, Jan. "Back Land Reform, Ramaphosa Tells Broederbond." *News24*, June 6, 2018. https://www.news24.com/SouthAfrica/News/back-land-reform-ramaphosa-tells-afrikanerbond-20180607.

Gilbert, Kenyatta R. *Exodus Preaching: Crafting Sermons About Justice and Hope*. Nashville: Abingdon, 2018.

Giorgi, Dieter. "God Turned Upside-Down." In *Paul and Empire: Religion and Power in Roman Imperial Society*, edited by Richard A. Horsley, 148–57. Harrisburg, PA: Trinity International, 1997.

Giroux, Henry A. *America at War with Itself*. San Francisco: City Light, 2016.

Gnanadason, Aruna. "Women's Oppression: A Sinful Situation." In *With Passion and Compassion: Third World Women Doing Theology*, edited by Mercy Oduyoye and Virginia Fabella, 69–76. Maryknoll, NY: Orbis, 1989.

Gollwitzer, Helmut. *Die Kapitalistische Revolution*. Munich: Kaiser, 1974.

———. *The Way to Life: Sermons in a Time of World Crisis*. London: T. &. T Clarke, 1981.

———. "Why Black Theology?" In *Black Theology: A Documentary History, 1966–1979*, edited by Gayraud Wilmore and James H. Cone, 152–73. Maryknoll, NY: Orbis 1993.

———. "Zur Schwarze Theologie." *Evangelische Theologie* 34 (1974) 41–69.

Gordon, Rebecca. "Trump's Recycling Program, War Crimes and War Comrades, Old and (Potentially) New." *Reader Supported News*, March 29, 2018. https://readersupportednews.org/opinion2/277-75/49226-focus-trump-recycling-program-war-crimes-and-war-criminals-old-and-potentially-new.

Gostoli, Ylenia. "'Bad Palestinians' under Israel's Collective Punishment." *Al Jazeera*, October 15, 2016. https://www.aljazeera.com/news/2016/09/palestinians-israel-collective-punishment-160929083644838.html.

Gottwald, Norman. *The Tribes of Yahweh: A Sociology of the Religion of Liberated Israel 1250–1050 BCE*. Maryknoll, NY: Orbis, 1979.

Graetz, Naomi. "Did Miriam Talk too Much?" In *A Feminist Companion to Exodus to Deuteronomy*, edited by Athalya Brenner, 231–42. Sheffield: Sheffield Academic, 2001.

Graybill, Lyn S. *Truth and Reconciliation in South Africa: Miracle or Model?* Boulder, CO: Lynne Rienner, 2002.

Griffen, Wendell. "Racial Justice, Public Theologians, and the Challenge of Sacralized Evil." Unpublished paper, Inaugural Racial Justice and Public Theology Collaborative Summer Conference, June 8, 2018. Vander Bilt University Divinity School, Nashville, TN.

Guardiola-Saentz, Leticia. "Borderless Women and Borderless Texts: A Cultural Reading of Matthew 15:21–28." *Semeia* 78: *Reading the Bible as Women* (1997) 69–82.

Hagner, Donald A. *Matthew 14–28*. Word Biblical Commentary 33B. Dallas: Word, 1995.

Harding, Vincent. "Black Power and the American Christ." In *The Black Power Revolt: A Collection of Essays*, edited by Floyd Barbour, 94–105. Boston: Sargent, 1968.

———. *There is a River: the Black Struggle for Freedom in America*. Orlando, FL: Harcourt Brace, 1981.

Heering, G. J. *De zondeval van het christendom: een studie over christendom, staat, en oorlog*. Utrecht: Bijleveld, 1981.

Hendricks, Obery M. *The Politics of Jesus: Rediscovering the Revolutionary Nature of Jesus' Teachings and How They have Been Corrupted*. New York: Doubleday, 2006.

Hopkins, Dwight. *Shoes That Fit Our Feet: Sources for a Constructive Black Theology*. Maryknoll, NY: Orbis, 1993.

Horsley, Richard A. *Archaeology, History, and Society in Galilee: The Social Context of Jesus and the Rabbis*. Harrisburg, PA: Trinity International, 1996.

———. *Bandits, Prophets, and Messiahs: Popular Movements at the Time of Jesus*. Harrisburg, PA: Trinity International, 1999.

———. *Galilee: History, Politics, People*. Harrisburg, PA: Trinity International, 1995.

———. *Jesus and Empire: The Kingdom of God and the New World Disorder*. Minneapolis: Fortress, 2003.

———. *Jesus and the Spiral of Violence: Popular Jewish Resistance in Roman Palestine*. Minneapolis: Fortress, 1993.

———. *Religion and Empire: People, Power, and the Life of the Spirit*. Minneapolis: Fortress, 2003.

Horsley, Richard A., ed. *In the Shadow of Empire: Reclaiming the Bible as a History of Faithful Witness Against Empire*. Louisville, KY: Westminster John Knox, 2008.

———. *Paul and Empire: Religion and Power in Roman Imperial Society*. Harrisburg, PA: Trinity International, 1997.

Hose, Phillip. *Claudette Colvin: Twice Toward Justice*. New York: Square Fish, 2011.

Huie, William Bradford. "The Shocking Story of Approved Killing in Mississippi." *Look Magazine*, January 1956. Reprinted at *PBS.org*, American Experience. "The Murder of Emmett Till: Killers' Confession." http://www.pbs.org/wgbh/americanexperience/features/till-killers-confession/.

Jacob, Benno. *The Second Book of the Bible: Exodus*. Hoboken, NJ: Ktav, 1992.

Jakes, T. D. "Woman, Thou Art Loosed!" Atlanta conference, DVD/CD audio recording. T. D. Jakes Ministries, Dallas, TX, 2012.

Jansen, Gerald J. "Song of Moses, Song of Miriam, Who Seconded Whom?" In *A Feminist Companion to Exodus to Deuteronomy*, edited by Athalya Brenner, 187–99. Sheffield: Sheffield Academic, 2001.

Jenkins, Philip. *The New Faces of Christianity: Believing the Bible in the Global South*. New York: Oxford University Press, 2006.

Jeremias, Joachim. *Jerusalem in the Time of Jesus: An Investigation into the Economic and Social Conditions during the New Testament Period*. Philadelphia: Fortress, 1969.

Johnson, Andre E. *The Forgotten Prophet: Bishop Henry McNeal Turner and the African American Prophetic Tradition*. Lanham, MD: Lexington, 2012.

Kahn, Pinchas. "Moses at the Waters of Meribah—A Case of Transference." *Jewish Bible Quarterly* 35 (2007) 85–93.

Keener, Craig S. *The Gospel of John, Volume 1*. Peabody, MA: Hendrickson, 2003.

Keil, C. F., and Delitzsch, F. *Biblical Commentary on the Old Testament, Volume 1*. Peabody, MA: Hendrickson, 2006.

King, Martin Luther, Jr. "Letter from a Birmingham Jail." In *The Radical King*, edited by Cornel West, 127–46. Boston: Beacon, 2015.

———. *The Radical King*. Edited and introduced by Cornel West. Boston: Beacon, 2015.

———. *The Strength to Love*. New York: Harper & Row, 1964.

———. *The Trumpet of Conscience: The summing-up of his creed, and his final testament*. New York: Harper & Row, 1967.

———. *Where Do We Go from Here? Chaos or Community?* New York: Harper & Row, 1967.

———. *Why We Can't Wait*. New York: New Library, 1964.

Kirk-Duggan, Cheryl A. "Divine Puppeteer: Yahweh of Exodus." In *A Feminist Companion to Exodus to Deuteronomy*, edited by Athalya Brenner, 75–102. Sheffield: Sheffield Academic, 2001.

———. "How Liberating is the Exodus, and for Whom? Deconstructing Exodus Motifs in Scripture, Literature, and Life." https://www.uva.nl/binaries/contents/personalpages/br/a.../en/asset?.

Kolkata Symposium on "Dalit Theology in the Twenty-first Century" (2008: Bishop's College). *Dalit Theology in the Twenty-first Century: Discordant Voices, Discerning Pathways*. New Delhi: Oxford University Press, 2011.

Kramer, Phyllis Silverman. "Miriam." In *A Feminist Companion to Exodus to Deuteronomy*, edited by Athalya Brenner, 104–33. Sheffield: Sheffield Academic, 2001.

Krog, Antjie. "Facing the Second Day of the TRC Hearings." SAHA/Sunday Times Heritage Project. http://sthp.saha.org.za/memorial/articles/facing_the_second_day_of_the_trc_hearings.htm.

La Monica, Paul. "Tomahawk maker Raytheon Stocks Rise." https://readersupportednews.org/news-section/2/318-66/429.

Landman, Christina. "Traumatised between Culture and Religion: Women's Stories." *HTS, Teologiese Studies/ Theological Studies* 68 (2012). https://hts.org.za/index.php/hts/article/view/1147/2290.

Lane, William. *Hebrews*. Word Biblical Commentary 47B. Grand Rapids, MI: Zondervan, 1991.

Lapsley, Jacqueline, E. *Whispering the Word: Hearing Women's Stories in the Old Testament*. Louisville, KY: Westminster John Knox, 2005.

Lind, Millard. *Yahweh Is a Warrior: The Theology of Warfare in Ancient Israel*. Scottdale, PA: Herald, 1980.

Lodge, Tom. *Black Politics in South Africa, 1945–1990*. Johannesburg: Ravan, 1992.

Luthuli, Albert. *Let My People Go! Autobiography of Albert Luthuli*. Cape Town: Tafelberg, 2006.

Maarsingh, B. *Numbers: A Practical Commentary*. Text and Interpretation. Grand Rapids, MI: Eerdmans, 1987.

Malina, Bruce J., and Richard L. Rohrbaugh. *Social-Science Commentary on the Gospel of John*. Minneapolis: Fortress, 1998.

Maloney, Francis J., *The Gospel of John*. Sacra Pagina. Collegeville, MN: Liturgical, 2005.

Maluleke, Tinyiko S. "African Ruths, Ruthless Africas: Reflections of an African Mordicai." In *Other Ways of Reading: African Women and the Bible*, edited by Musa Dube, 237–50. Atlanta: SBL, 2001.

———. "Black and African Theologies in the New World Order: A Time to Drink from our own Wells" *JTSA* 96 (1996) 3–29.

———. "The Rediscovery of the Agency of Africans: An Emerging Paradigm of Post-Cold War and Post-Apartheid Black and African Theologies." *Journal of Theology of South Africa* 108 (November 2000) 19–37.

Mamdani, Mahmoud. "Amnesty or Impunity? A Preliminary Critique of the Truth and Reconciliation Commission of South Africa." *Diatrics* 32 (Fall-Winter 2002) 33–59.

Marshall, I. H., et al., eds. *New Bible Dictionary*. Downer's Grove, IL: Intervarsity, 2003.

Masenya, Madipoane. "Women, Africana reality and the Bible." In *The Africana Bible*, edited by Randall C. Bailey, et al., 33–38. Minneapolis: Fortress, 2010.

Mazrui, Ali. *Cultural Forces in World Politics*. London: James Curry, 1990.

McGee, Paula. *Brand® New Theology: The Walmartization of T. D. Jakes and the New Black Church*. Maryknoll, NY: Orbis, 2016.

McMickle, Marvin. *Where Have All the Prophets Gone? Reclaiming Prophetic Preaching in America*. Cleveland: Pilgrim, 2006.

Mellet, Patric Tariq. "The National Question: Non-racialism or Etnicism—Poised on a Threshold: A Reflection on the 58th Freedom Charter Day." June 26, 2013, posted on his Facebook page.

Mofokeng, Takatso. *The Crucified Among the Cross-bearers: Towards a Black Christology*. Kampen: Kok, 1983.

Moore, Jack. "The Full Details of Trump's Botched Yemen raid that Killed Nine Children." *Newsweek*, February 10, 2017. http://readersupportednews.org/news-section2/318-66/41888.

Moore, Stephen D. "Are There Impurities in the Living Water?" In *A Feminist Companion to John, Volume 1*, edited by Amy-Jill Levine, with Marianne Blickenstaff, 78–97. Sheffield: Sheffield Academic, 2003.

Mosala, Itumeleng. *Biblical Hermeneutics and Black Theology in South Africa*. Grand Rapids, MI: Eerdmans, 1989.

Moyo, Khanyizela. "Mimicry, Transitional Justice, and the Land Question in Racially Divided Former Settler Colonies." *International Journal of Transitional Justice* (2014) 1–20.

Mullane, Deidre, ed. *Crossing the Danger Water: Three Hundred years of African-American Writing*. New York: Anchor, 1993.

Newsom, Carol A., and Sharon H. Ringe, eds. *Women's Bible Commentary*. Louisville, KY: Westminster John Knox, 1998.

Njoroge, Nyambura, J. "The Bible and African Christianity—a Curse or a Blessing?" In *Other Ways of Reading: African Women and the Bible*, edited by Musa Dube, 207–36. Atlanta: SBL, 2001.

Njoroge, Nyambura, J., and Musa W. Dube, eds. *Talitha Cumi! Theologies of African Women*. Pietermaritzburg: Cluster, 2001.

Nodjimbadem, Katie. "Emmett Till's Open Casket Funeral Reignited Civil Rights Struggle." *Smithsonian.com*, September 2, 2015. https://www.smithsonianmag.com/smithsonian-institution/emmett-tills-open-casket-funeral-reignited-the-civil-rights-movement-180956483/.

Noth, Martin. *Exodus: A Commentary*. London: SCM, 1962.

Oduyoye, Mercy Amba. *Daughters of Anowa: African Women & Patriarchy*. Maryknoll, NY: Orbis, 1995.

Oduyoye, Mercy Amba, and Elizabeth Amoah. "The Christ for African Women." In *With Passion and Compassion: Third World Women Doing Theology*, edited by Virginia Fabella, and Mercy Amba Oduyoye, 35–46. Maryknoll, NY: Orbis, 1989.

Oduyoye, Mercy Amba, and Musimbi R.A. Kanyoro, eds. *The Will to Arise: Women, Tradition, and the Church in Africa*. Eugene, OR: Wipf & Stock, 2005.

Okura, Teresa. "Jesus and the Samaritan Woman in Africa." *Theological Studies* 70 (2009) 401–18.

———. *The Johannine Approach to Mission: A Contextual Study of John 1:1–12*. WUNT 2/32. Tübingen: Mohr, 1988.

Oliver, Guy. "For Nomondo Calata, the Truth is Not Enough." *Mail & Guardian*, October 30, 1998. https://mg.co.za/article/1998-10-30-for-nomonde-calata-the-truth-is-not.

Olsen, Dennis T. *Numbers*. Interpretation: A Bible Commentary for Teaching and Preaching. Louisville, KY: John Knox, 1996.

Painter, Neill Irvin. *Sojourner Truth: A Life, A Symbol*. New York: Norton, 1997.

Pew Foundation. "Tolerance and Tension: Islam and Christianity in Sub-Saharan Africa." *Pew Forum on Religion & Public Life*, April 2010, Washington, DC.

Pillay, Suren. "Being Coloured and Indian in South Africa after Apartheid." *Africa is a Country*, June 2018. https://africasacountry.com/2018/06/being-coloured-and-indian-in-south-africa-after-apartheid.

Pollack, Norman. "Price Tag for International Villainy." *Counterpunch*, February 4, 2015. https://www.counterpunch.org/2015/02/04/price-tag-for-international-villainy/.

Potgieter, Cheryl, and Sarojini Nadar. "Living it Out: Liberated Through Submission?" *Journal of Feminist Studies in Religion* 26 (Fall 2010) 141–51.

Powery, Emerson B., and Rodney S. Sadler Jr. *The Genesis of Liberation: Biblical Interpretation in the Antebellum Narratives of the Enslaved*. Louisville, KY: Westminster John Knox, 2016.

Raboteau, Albert J. *Slave Religion: The Invisible Institution in the Antebellum South*. New York: Oxford University Press, 1978.

Ramalaine, Clyde N. "Infusing religion into the Indian racism debate is problematic." *Africa News 24/7*, June 26, 2018. https://www.africanews24-7.co.za/index.php/voices/infusing-religioun-indian-racism-debate-problematic/.

"Rape victims' care centres face funding drying up." *IOL*, November 3, 2017. https://www.iol.co.za/capeargus/opinion/rape-victims-care-centres-face-funding-drying-up-11845771?.

Rashkow, Ilona. "Oedipus Wrecks: Moses and God's Rod." In *A Feminist Companion to Exodus to Deuteronomy*, edited by Athalya Brenner, 59–74. Sheffield: Sheffield Academic, 2000.

Redfield, Robert. *The Little Community and Peasant Society and Culture*. Chicago: Chicago University Press, 1960.

Riches, John. "Matthew's Missionary Strategy." In *The Gospel of Matthew in its Roman Imperial Context*, edited by John Riches and David C. Sim, 128–42. New York: T. & T. Clarke, 2005.

Riches, John, and David C. Sim. *The Gospel of Matthew in its Roman Imperial Context*. New York: T. & T. Clarke, 2005.

Rieger, Joerg. *Christ & Empire, From Paul to Postcolonial Times*. Minneapolis: Fortress, 2007.

Ringe, Sharon H. "A Gentile Woman's Story." In *Feminist Interpretation of the Bible*, edited by Letty M. Russell, 65–72. Louisville, KY: Westminster John Knox, 1985.

Rooks, Charles Shelby. "Toward the Promised Land: An Analysis of the Religious Experience of Black America." *The Black Church* 2 (September 1973) 1–48.

Rosen, Armin. "Trump on nuclear weapons: 'The power, the devastation is very important to me.'" *Business Insider*, December 16, 2015. https://www.businessinsider.com.au/donald-trump-nuclear-weapons-cnn-debate-2015-12.

Rubenstein, Nechama. "The Untold Story of the Hebrew Midwives and the Exodus." *TheJewishWoman.org*. https://www.chabad.org/theJewishWoman/article_cdo/aid/1465248/.

Ruether, Rosemary Radford. *America, Amerikkka, Elect Nation and Imperial Violence*. Oakville, CT: Equinox, 2007.

Russell, Letty M., ed. *Feminist Interpretation of the Bible*. Louisville, KY: Westminster John Knox, 1985.

Saldarini, Anthony J. *Pharisees, Scribes, and Sadducees in Palestinian Society*. Grand Rapids, MI: Eerdmans, 2001.

Schnackenburg, Rudolf. *The Gospel According to St. John*. New York: Herder and Herder, 1968.

Schottroff, Luise. "Important Aspects of the Gospel for the Future." In *What is John? Volume 1*, edited by Fernando Segovia, 205–10. Atlanta: Scholars, 1996.

———. "The Samaritan Woman and the Notion of Sexuality in the Fourth Gospel." In *What is John? Volume 1*, edited by Fernando Segovia, 157–81. Atlanta: Scholars, 1996.
Segovia, Fernando, ed. *What is John? Readers and Readings in the Fourth Gospel*. Atlanta: Scholars, 1996.
Setel, Drorah O'Donnel. "Exodus." In *The Women's Bible Commentary*, edited by Carol A. Newsom, and Sharon H. Ringe. Louisville, KY: Westminster John Knox, 1998.
Siebert-Hommes, Jopie. "But if She Be a Daughter . . . She May Live." In *A Feminist Companion to Exodus to Deuteronomy*, edited by Athalya Brenner, 62–74. Sheffield: Sheffield Academic, 2001.
Sim, David C. "Rome in Matthew's Eschatology." In *The Gospel of Matthew*, edited by John Riches and David C. Sim, 93. New York: T. & T. Clarke, 2005.
Sloyan, Gerard S. *John*. Atlanta: John Knox, 1988.
Small, Adam. "Blackness versus Nihilism: Black Racism Rejected." In *Black Theology, the South African Voice*, edited by Basil Moore, 11–17. London: C. Hurst, 1973.
Smith, Dennis E., and Michael E. Williams, eds. *Storyteller's Companion to the Bible, Volume 10: John*. Nashville: Abingdon, 1996.
Smith, Mitzi J. "Race, Gender, and the Politics of 'Sass': Reading Mark 7:24–30 through a Womanist Lens of Intersectionality and Inter(con)textuality." In *Womanist Interpretations of the Bible—Expanding its Discourse*, edited by Gay Byron and Vanessa Lovelace, 95–112. Semeia Studies 85. Atlanta: SBC, 2016.
Success Staff Writer. "17 Powerful T. D. Jakes Quotes to Push You Forward." *Success.com*, June 13, 2017. https://www.success.com/17-powerful-td-jakes-quotes-to-push-you-forward/.
Taibbi, Matt. "A Brief History of Everything That Happened Because of George H.W. Bush's Insecurity." *Rolling Stone*, December 10, 2018. https://readersupportednews.org/opinion2/277-75/53829-a-brief-history-of-everything-that-happened-because-of-george-hw-bushs-insecurity.
Taylor, Vincent. *The Gospel According to St. Mark, According to the Greek Text*. New York: MacMillan, 1973.
Terreblanche, Sampie. *Lost in Transformation: South Africa's Search for a New Future*. Johannesburg: KMM Review, 2012.
Thompson, Marianne Meye. *John: A Commentary*. New Testament Library. Louisville, KY: Westminster John Knox, 2015.
Thurman, Howard. *Jesus and the Disinherited*. Boston: Beacon, 1996.
Tolbert, Charles H. *Reading John: A Literary and Theological Commentary on the Fourth Gospel and the Johannine Epistles*. New York: Crossroads, 1992.
Trible, Phyllis. "Bringing Miriam Out of the Shadows." In *A Feminist Companion to Exodus to Deuteronomy*, edited by Athalya Brenner, 166–86. Sheffield: Sheffield Academic, 2001.
Tshaka, Rothney. "The Advocacy of Africanity as Justice against Epistemicide." Unpublished paper, 2018.
———. "How Can a Conquered People Sing Praises of their History and Culture? Africanization as the Integration of Inculturation and Liberation." *Black Theology: An International Journal* 14 (2016) 91–106.
UN Chronicles. "Women and the Arab Spring." *UN Chronicle* 53.4 (December 2016). https://unchronicle.un.org/article/women-and-the-arab-spring.
van Aarde, Andries. *Fatherless in Galilee: Jesus as Child of God*. Harrisburg, PA: Trinity International, 2001.

———. "Jesus and the Son of Man—A Shift from the 'Little Tradition' to the 'Great Tradition.'" *Ephemeredes Theologicae Lovanienses* (December 2004) 423–38.

———. "Jesus' Affection Toward Children and Matthew's Tale of Two Kings." *Acta Theologica* 24 (2004) 127–37.

———. "The Love for the Poor Neighbour: In Memory of Her, (Matthew 26:6–13)." *Acta Theologica* 23 (2016) 150–75.

———. "Perspektiewe op die interpretasie van die Evangelie van Mattheus." *In die Skriflig/In Luce Verbi* 51 (2017). https://www.researchgate.net/publication/313803759_Perspektiewe_op_die_interpretasie_van_die_Evangelie_van_Matteus.

———. "Reading the Areopagus Speech in Acts 17 from the Perspective of Slave Manumission in Ancient Greece." *Theology Bulletin* 47 (2016) 177–85.

———. "A Silver Coin in the Mouth of a Fish, (Matthew 17:24–27): A Miracle of Nature, Ecology, and Economy and the Politics of Holiness." *Neotestamentica* 27 (1993) 1–25.

———. "Understanding Jesus' Healings." *Scriptura* 74 (2000) 223–36.

van der Westhuizen, Christi. *White Power and the Rise and Fall of the National Party*. Cape Town: Zebra, 2008.

Vellem, Vuyani. "Hermeneutical Embers from the 'Zone of Non-Being.'" Unpublished paper, presented at the Council on World Mission DARE conference. Bangkok, Thailand, May, 2017.

Villa-Vicencio, Charles. "An All-Pervading Heresy." In *Apartheid is a Heresy*, edited by John De Gruchy and Charles Villa-Vicencio, 59–74. Cape Town: D. Phillip, 1983.

Walton, Jonathan. *Watch This! The Ethics and Aesthetics of Black Televangelism*. New York: New York University Press, 2009.

Warrior, Robert. "Canaanites, Cowboys, and Indians." *Christianity and Crisis* 49 (1989) 261–65.

Weaver, Dorothy Jean. *The Irony of Power: the Politics of God Within Matthew's Narrative*. Eugene, OR: Pickwick, 2017.

———. "Thus You Will Know Them By Their Fruits." In *The Gospel of Matthew in its Roman Imperial Context*, edited by John Riches and David C. Sim, 107–27. New York: T. & T. Clarke, 2005.

Weems, Renita. *Just a Sister Away: A Womanist Vision of Women's Relationships in the Bible*. Philadelphia: Innisfree, 1988.

Wells, Ida B. *Southern Horrors and Other Writings: The Anti-Lynching Campaign of Ida B. Wells, 1892–1900*. Edited with an introduction by Jaqueline Jones Royster. Boston: Bedford, 1997.

West, Cornel, ed. *The Radical King*. Boston: Beacon, 2015.

West, Gerald. *The Stolen Bible: From Imperial Tool to African Icon*. Leiden: Brill, 2017.

Williams, Dolores. *Sisters in the Wilderness: The Challenge of Womanist God-talk*. Maryknoll, NY: Orbis, 1993.

Williamson, Lamar, Jr. *Mark*. Interpretation: A Commentary for Teaching and Preaching. Louisville, KY: Westminster John Knox, 2009.

Willimon, William H. "Preacher-Prophet Obama." In *The Audacity of Faith, Christian Leaders Reflect on the Election of Barack Obama*, edited by Marvin McMickle, 81–86. Valley Forge: Judson, 2009.

Wilmore, Gayraud S. *Black Religion and Black Radicalism: An Interpretation of the Religious History of African Americans*. Maryknoll, NY: Orbis, 1998.

Wilmore, Gayraud S., and James Cone. *Black Theology: A Documentary History*. Maryknoll, NY: Orbis, 1979.
Wilson, Nigel. "Israel's collective punishment follows Jerusalem attack." *Al Jazeera*, January 10, 2017. https://www.aljazeera.com/indepth/features/2017/01/israel-collective-punishment-jerusalem-attack-170110084017716.htm.l
Wimbush, Vincent L., ed. *African Americans and the Bible: Sacred Texts and Social Texture*. Eugene, OR: Wipf & Stock, 2000.
"Women Are 'Backbone' of Native Actions Against Dakota Pipeline." *Telesur*, January 16, 2017. https://www.telesurenglish.net/news/Women-Are-Backbone-of-Native-Actions-Against-Dakota-Pipeline-20170116-0028.html.
Zuurmond, Rochus. *Het Bijbelse Verhaal: Verteller en Vertaler*. Mededelingen van de Van der Leeuw Stichting 41. Amsterdam: Private Edition, 1970.

INDEX

#BlackLivesMatter, 57, 62n7
#FeesMustFall, 57
#Menaretrash, xix
#MeToo, 57
#ThisMustEnd, 57

Abd al-Rahim al Nashin, 78
ABRECSA Charter, xvii
Abu Zubaydah, 78
Adamo, David Tuesday, 13
Adler, Margo, 61n5
African National Congress (ANC), 47, 52, 57, 64, 74, 77, 83, 110, 111, 112, 172n41, 212
African theology, xvii,
Al Jazeera News, 78n36
Alexander, Peter, 111n45
Ali, Tariq, 151n90
Allen, John J., 12
Alsaafin, Linah, 60n3
Amoah, Elizabeth, 160n2, 161, 162n6, 181n51, 182n57, 183nn58–59
Arab Spring, 60n3

Baker, Ella, 61, 179
Bay, Mia, 61n4
Belhar Confession, the, xvii, 83, 161
Ben-Abba, Amitai, 119, 120, 121
Biko, Stephen Bantu, xxiii, 22, 23, 25, 42, 118, 121, 125, 158, 172, 205
Black church, xix, xxi, xxiii, xxiv, 24, 28, 36, 79, 83n48, 87, 155,175, 184, 185, 187, 219
Black Consciousness, xxii, xxiii, 10, 85, 123, 125, 152, 153, 179, 212

Black gospel, the, xiv, xix
Black liberation theology, xiv, xv, xvi, xvii, xix, xx, xxi, 14, 24, 25, 29, 30, 33, 38, 82, 87n56, 88, 90, 112, 119, 121, 129, 136, 158, 160,185, 205
Black Messiah, the, 3, 129, 130n23, 160, 183, 205
Black theology, xiii, xiv, xvi, xvii, xix, xx, xxi, xxii, xxiii, xxiv, 2, 5, 9, 10, 11, 13, 20n51, 21, 129, 136, 24, 31, 32, 33, 34, 35, 38, 40, 44, 52n61, 57, 100n31, 111, 112, 129, 136, 183, 184, 185, 189, 193, 204, 205, 218, 219
Boardman, William, 54, 55,
Boesak, Allan Aubrey, xiiin3, xvin7, xvin8, xxiiin14, 2n3, 3n8, 8n19, 15n37, 25n67, 26n69–70, 28n73, 30n76, 42n41, 48n51, 48n52, 52n61, 60n3, 62n7, 62n9, 63n11, 66n13, 80n42, 82n47, 110n44, 116n57, 116n59, 122n1, 123n2, 130n23, 132n34, 136n45, 137n48, 140n53, 141n54, 149n86, 151n90, 156n98, 156n100, 158n104, 166n21, 186n8, 197n25, 198n29, 199n30, 203n40, 204n43, 204n44, 205n45, 213n68
Boesak, Elna, 8n17, 76, 77n34, 78n37, 185n4, 187
Bond, Patrick, 48n51, 156n100,
Bonhoeffer, Dietrich, 29, 118,
Borg, Marcus J., 143, 144,

Index

Botha, P. W., 47
Brenner, Athalya, 34n9, 38n24, 40n31, 80n41
Broad, William, 49n55
Brueggemann, Walter, x, 25, 105, 122, 123n2
Budd, Philip, J., 91, 94, 95, 113n46, 113n48, 113n53
Bultmann, Rudolf, 194n18, 198n27, 199n30, 206
Burkill, T. A, 164n14
Burns, Rita, J., 59n2
Bush, George, 48, 78

Calata, Nomonde, 62–64, 67
Callahan, Dwight Allen, xxi, 17, 18nn44–45, 198n27, 201, 203n41, 208, 211, 215n71, 219
Calland, Richard, 48n51, 156n100
Calvin, John, 40, 41, 42, 43, 49, 50, 57, 73, 123, 124, 157
Canaanite woman, the, ix, xxii, 101n31, 125, 128, 129, 134, 139, 140, 160, 163, 167, 170, 173, 175, 176n46, 179, 180, 194, 207, 209, 211
Cannon, Katie, v, xi, xxi, xxiv, 20, 37, 182
Cape Times, 79n39
Carter, Warren, 130, 131, 132, 135, 136, 137n49, 139n51, 141n57, 143, 144, 145nn68–69, 146–49, 150, 152, 157, 165, 167, 169, 170, 179n48, 198n26
Cassidy, John, 186n6
Central Intelligence Agency (CIA), the, 78
Centre for Social Change, University of Johannesburg, 111n45
Clinton, Bill, 48
Clinton, Hilary, 77
Cohn, Marjorie, 94n13
Colvin, Claudette, 61, 67, 179
Cone, James H., v, xi, xxi, xxiii, xxiv, 2, 3, 4, 5n12, 8, 19, 20, 31n16, 35–36, 38, 100n31, 117, 118n63, 136, 158, 185, 186n7

Council on World Mission's DARE conference, ix
Crossan, John Dominic, 16n38–39, 24n61, 27, 117, 132n34, 143, 144
Cumming-Bruce, Nick, 78n36

David, Son of, 142, 145, 166, 177–79
Dawkins, Richard, 101,
Day, Dorothy, 179
Dayden, David, 186n6
Deborah, 73, 74, 79, 81, 115
Defiance Campaign, the, 60
de Klerk, F. W., 7, 47, 166, 172n41
Delitzsch, F., 41
Dey, Kathleen, 78
DeYoung, Curtiss Paul, xvin8, 25n67, 116n59, 203n40
Douglass, Frederick, 21, 23, 29, 154
Dube, Musa, xxi, xxii, 9, 26, 125, 126–30, 132, 134, 136, 138, 140–42, 146–47, 149, 151–53, 165, 167–169, 178, 207–8, 210, 214
Duncan, Amy, 197n24
Durham, John I., 52, 74

Edet, Rosemary, 161n4, 181, 182nn54–55,
Eldad and Medad, 92–93
Elizabeth and Zachariah, 196
Elliot, Neill, 74, 117n60, 142nn59–60, 150n88, 157nn101–2
Ellis, Peter, 201n37, 206n48, 215n71
Exum, J. Cheryl, xxii, 38, 40, 41nn34–37, 43, 44, 46, 53, 95, 98
Eynikel, Erik, 90n3

Fabella, Virginia, xvnn5–6, xxi, 162, 183n59
Felder, Cain Hope, 5, 96n22
Fewell, Donna Nolan, 39, 43, 44, 52n62
Freire, Paulo, 164, 166
Fretheim, Terence E., 44, 45, 46, 52, 71, 74n23,
Friedman, Richard Elliot, 74
Frost, Robert, 159, 160

Garnet, Henry Highland, 123, 124

Index   237

Genovese, Eugene D., 17
Gerber, Jan, 213n69
Gilbert, Kenyatta R., 31n1
Giorgi, Dieter, 173
Giroux, Henry A., 51n59
Gnanadason, Aruna, xxi, 162, 163
Gollwitzer, Helmut, 1, 2, 4, 7, 27, 86
Gordon, Rebecca, 78
Gostoli, Ylenia, 94n13
Gottwald, Norman, 93
Graetz, Naomi, 90, 91, 93, 96, 97, 98n27, 99, 100n30, 102, 103nn34–35, 104
Graybill, Lyn S., 65n13
Griffen, Wendell, 6, 7
Guardiola-Saentz, Leticia, 165, 166, 167, 169n33, 175, 176,178,
Gunn, David M., 39, 43, 44, 52n62

Hagar, 35, 38
Hagner, Donald A., 169n34
Hannah, 19, 40, 44, 57, 66, 82, 83, 87, 101, 116, 121, 214
Hansen, Len, 26n69
Harding, Vincent, xiii, xiv, xv, xix
Haspel, Gina, 78
Heering, G. J., 218
Hendricks, Obery M., 24n62, 133n37, 134, 135n42, 136, 141n57, 145
Horsley, Richard A., 16, 22n56, 23n60, 24n61–62, 24n65, 127, 130, 132, 133, 134n39, 135n44, 136, 139n52, 141n57, 142n57, 196n22

International Monetary Fund, the, 7

Jacob, Benno, 41, 46, 56, 73, 81, 83, 84
Jacob (later called Israel), 190, 199, 203, 215
Jakes, T. D., 24, 77, 184, 185, 186, 187, 188, 189, 190, 191, 192, 199, 200, 206, 215
Jansen, Gerald J., 74n23
Jenkins, Philip, 12nn30–31
Jeremias, Joachim, 86, 133, 191n16,
Jochebed, 35, 40, 59, 60, 61, 62, 67, 68, 69, 70, 72, 83, 214

Johnson, Andre E., 184n2
Josephus, 198n27, 208
Joshua, 75, 83, 90n4, 92, 93, 119, 120
Junia, 121

Kahn, Pinchas, 113
Kairos Document, the, xvii, xx, 161n5
Keener, Craig S., 196n22, 198, 199n30, 200, 201n38, 205, 206, 207n53, 210nn63–64, 215n71
Keil, C. F., 41
King David, 116
King, Martin Luther, Jr., 28, 32, 33, 48, 62n7, 81, 82, 156, 171, 179, 185, 195
Kirk-Duggan, Cheryl A., 33, 34, 38
Kolkata Symposium on Dalit Theology in the Twenty-first Century, xiv*n*3
Kramer, Phyllis Silverman, 96n20
Krog, Antjie, 62, 63

Landman, Christina, x, 181
Lane, William, 118n65
Lapsley, Jacqueline, E., 34
Lind, Millard C., 73n19, 74, 75, 76n32
Lodge, Tom, 60n3
Lonmin, the mining company, 111n45
Look Magazine, 62n8
Luthuli, Albert, 82, 155n97, 171, 179

Maarsingh, B., 91, 92n11,98, 110, 113, 114
Mahambehlala, Lelethu, (PoeticSoul) South African Spoken Word poet, ix, xvii
Malina, Bruce J., 196n23, 199, 201n39
Malcolm X, xiii
Maloney, Francis J., 201
Maluleke, Tinyiko S., 5n12, 11, 18
Mama Africa, 26n68
Mamdani, Mahmoud, 63n11
Mandela, Nelson, 47, 112
Mandela, Winnie, 67, 179
Manuel, Trevor, 28
Marikana (massacre), 57, 77, 110–11n45
Marshall, I. H., 142n58

Index

Martha, 19, 101, 121, 215
Mary Magdalene, 83
Mary, mother of Jesus, 19, 40, 82, 83, 87, 88, 101, 116, 121, 196, 214,
Masenya, Madipoane, 14
Mazrui, Ali, 9n21
Mbeki, Thabo, 28, 47
McGee, Paula, 7n17, 24n63, 87, 88n57, 184n1, 185nn4–5, 187, 188
McMickle, Marvin, 24n63, 88n57, 185n3
Mellet, Patric Tariq, 213
Meribah, waters of, xxiv, xxv, 109, 112, 113, 115, 121, 219
Miriam, xxii, xxiv, xxv, 16, 18, 19, 35, 40, 58–60, 67, 69–75, 79–87, 89–91, 93–112, 115–17, 119, 121, 126, 128, 139, 195, 218
Miriamic Tradition, 58, 61, 62, 111, 112, 115, 117, 126, 128
Mofokeng, Takatso, 158n106
Moore, Jack, 204n42
Moore, Stephen D., 28n74
Mosala, Itumeleng, xx, 9, 24n62
Moses, xxii–xxv, 34–35, 39–40, 43–47, 56, 58–59, 68, 70–75, 81–86, 88, 90–107, 109–10, 112–17, 120–21
Moyo, Khanyizela, 167n22

NAACP, 61n5
Nadar, Sarojini, 76, 77n34
National Party, 48n52
Newsom, Carol A., 39n29
Njoroge, Nyambura, J., 13, 14n35, 207nn54–57, 208n58
Nodjimbadem, Katie, 61n6
Noth, Martin, 52

Obama, Barack, 28, 48, 49, 77, 185, 186n6
Oduyoye, Mercy Amba, xvnn5–6, xxi, 160n2, 161, 162n6, 181n51, 182n57, 183n58–59, 205n45
Okura, Teresa, 204, 209
Oliver, Guy, 64n12
Olsen, Dennis T., 86, 91

Painter, Neill Irvin, 60n4
Palestine/Palestinian, 32, 33, 51, 60, 94, 119, 120, 121, 138, 148, 160, 162, 164, 210
Parks, Rosa, 61, 179
Paul, 16, 20, 83, 117, 123, 132n34, 158, 214
Pew Foundation, 12n32
Pillay, Suren, 212n67
Pollack, Norman, 50, 51n59
Potgieter, Cheryl, 76, 77n34
Powery, Emerson B., 17, 23, 32n2

Raboteau, Albert J., 31, 32n2
Ramalaine, Clyde N., 212n67
Ramaphosa, Cyril, 28, 47, 110–11n45
Rashkow, Ilona, 35n15
Reagan, Ronald, 48
Redfield, Robert, 15n38
Riches, John, 131, 139
Riches, John, 129n22, 131n28
Rieger, Joerg, 3,
Ringe, Sharon H., 39n29, 168, 169, 180
Rizpah, xn1, 116
Rohrbaugh, Richard L., 196n23, 199, 201n39
Rosen, Armin, 49n56
Rubenstein, Nechama, 38n22, 46
Ruether, Rosemary Radford, 87n56

Sadler, Rodney S., Jr., 17, 23, 32n2
Saldarini, Anthony J., 195n20
Samson, 83
Samuel De Witt Proctor Conference, 185n3
Sanger, David E., 49n55
Schnackenburg, Rudolf, 198n27
Schottroff, Luise, 206, 207
Setel, Drorah O'Donnel, 39, 74, 75, 76, 79
Shifrah and Puah, 19, 41–42, 44–46, 52, 56, 76n31, 84
Siebert-Hommes, Jopie, 69, 70
Sim, David C., 129n22, 131n28, 135, 136, 137n49
Simeon and Anna, 196
Sisulu, Albertina, 179

Sloyan, Gerard S., 206
Small, Adam, 52
Smith, Dennis E., 200n33
Smith, Mitzi J., 165, 167n23
Strijdom, Hans, 47
Success Staff Writer, 187n11

Tambo, Adelaide, 179
Taibbi, Matt, 151n90
Taylor, Vincent, 169
Terreblanche, Sampie, 48n51, 110, 156n100
Theological Rationale for the Prayer for the Downfall of Apartheid, the, xvii
Thompson, Marianne Meye, 196n22, 199, 200n31, 206n52
Thurman, Howard, 16n40, 134
Till-Mobley, Mamie, 60–62, 67
Tolbert, Charles H., 194n19, 201n39
Treurnicht, Andries, 47
Trible, Phyllis, 94, 109
Trump, Donald, 10n26, 28, 48, 49, 57, 78, 137, 160, 210
Truth and Reconciliation Commission, the (TRC), 6, 63, 126n10
Truth, Sojourner, 60
Tshaka, Rothney, xvi, xvii, 152, 153
Tutu, Desmond, xvii, 62

UN Chronicles, 60n3
United Democratic Front (UDF), 48n52, 62
United Nations(UN), 77, 78, 119

United States (US), xiii-xix, xxi, 2, 5, 54, 60, 87n56, 102, 110, 124, 148, 151, 156, 165, 182, 219

van Aarde, Andries, x, 15n38, 118, 130, 131n27, 133, 136, 142n57, 145, 146, 195nn20–21, 196n22
van der Westhuizen, Christi, 156n100
Vellem, Vuyani, xix, 9, 10, 11
Verwoerd, Hendrik, 47
Villa-Vicencio, Charles, 8n18
Vorster, John, 47

Walton, Jonathan, 7n17, 185n4
Warrior, Robert, 33
Weaver, Dorothy Jean, 147, 176
Weems, Renita, 96, 97, 103
Wells, Ida B., 60, 61n4
West, Gerald, x, 29
Williams, Dolores, 35, 38, 44
Williams, Michael E., 200n33
Williamson, Lamar, Jr., 177
Willimon, William H., 55, 56n65
Wilmore, Gayraud S., xi, 2, 5n12, 8, 19n48, 31n1, 35n16, 36nn17–18
Wilson, Nigel, 94n13
Wimbush, Vincent L., 18
World Bank, the, 7
World Communion of Reformed Churches (WCRC), xivn3

Zuma, Jacob, 28, 47, 57, 82
Zuurmond, Rochus, 69, 70, 72

www.ingramcontent.com/pod-product-compliance
Lightning Source LLC
Chambersburg PA
CBHW030823230426
43667CB00008B/1353